Diametrical Nationalisms

Rulers, Rebels, and Masses in Manipur

DIAMETRICAL NATIONALISMS

Rulers, Rebels, and Masses in Manipur

Malem Ningthouja

Diametrical Nationalisms: Rulers, Rebels, and Masses in Manipur
Malem Ningthouja

First Published, 2015

ISBN 978-93-5002-271-9 (Pb)

Published by
AAKAR BOOKS
28 E Pocket IV, Mayur Vihar Phase I, Delhi 110 091
Phone : 011 2279 5505 Telefax : 011 2279 5641
aakarbooks@gmail.com; www.aakarbooks.com

Printed at
Sapra Brothers, Delhi 110 092

I dedicate this book to

my younger brother, late Khunthoknganba Ningthouja
(17 December 1980 to 4 September 2013)

He was a victim of the unrestrainted chemical war perpetrated by Indian drug dealers under the overall capitalist pogrom inherent in the privatization of the medical sector and commodification of medicine.

He was
a labourer by profession; a sympathizer to the Campaign for Peace & Democracy (Manipur), a member of the Labour Research and Organisation Foundation (Manipur); and the General Secretary of Lei-Ingkhol Youth Development Organisation (Manipur).

He passed away quite young and all of a sudden while the final touches to the book were being given, leaving to other behind the social responsibilities and the political commitment to fight for development, peace, and unity.

Contents

Acknowledgements

I express my heartiest thanks and gratitude to Professor Dilip M. Menon for his selfless supervision of my research. I also wish to express my gratitude to the following persons who have encouraged me: my father, N. Manihar; my mother, N. Nganbi; my brothers (late) Khunthoknganba, Ningthoinganba and Lanngamba; Ms Salam (o) Radharani, Salam Arunkumar, Dr Tripta Wahi, Vijay Singh, Mrs Lara Jacob, L. Sushila, R.K. Mobi, Khangembam Somorendro and his wife Indira, and all my friends.

I would also like to thank the following funding institution and individuals for their financial support: the Indian Council of Historical Research for granting me JRF for certain period of time; Khangenbam Somorendro and Khangembam Indira.

I acknowledge the teachers who taught me history: Mr Chungmang (Model Higher Secondary School, Saikul, Manipur, 1992); Miss Picardo (AKI's Poona College of Arts, Pune, 1993); Dr Tripta Wahi, Dr D.N. Gupta, Dr Suchitra Gupta, Tarika Oberoi, Vipul Singh, Ruchitra and Mrs. Leshma (Hindu College, Delhi); late Prof P.S. Gupta, Prof Kumkum Roy, Prof Monika Juneja, Prof Sumit Sarkar, Prof Suhash Chakravarty, Prof Sahid Amin, Dr Rana, Dr Archana Verma, Dr Nazaf Haider, Dr Arup Benerjee, Dr Sunil, Prof B.P. Sahu, Dr Radhika Singha and Dr Dilip Menon (History Department, University of Delhi).

I would like to thank the following persons who had supported me in getting access to source materials: late Padmashree N. Khelchandra; Dr W. Sushila, (Director Manipur State Archive); Mr Indramani, Mr Lukhoi, Mr Kalam and Mrs Ibeyaima and other staff of Manipur State

Archive; Staff of the National Archives, New Delhi; Sanjeev Thingnam; Miss Victoria Potsangbam; M. Anil and G. Nilachandra (JAC against the Eviction of Lei-Ingkhol); Chongtham Surjit and Homeshwor (Committee on Human Rights, Manipur); Hareshwor Goswami (Retd. MCS); Jagat Thoudam and Tompok (All Manipur United Club Organization); Kh. Nandini (MACHA LEIMA); Jibon (All Manipur Ethnic Socio Cultural Organization); Sapamcha Jadumani, Gourshyam, and Y. Dilip (United Committee of Manipur); L. Jadumani (United People's Front); Ibotombi Khuman (International Peace and Social Advancement); S. Bheigo (Superintendent, Manipur State Archaeology Department); Labanggo Mangang (Kangla Pao); H. Bhubol (National Research Centre, Manipur); Y. Mohendro (Manipur Historical Society); L. Iboyaima (Janata Party); Sanasam Mani (Former instructor of the Red Guard under comrade Irabot); office bearers of Democratic Students' Alliance of Manipur; office bearers of All Manipur Women's Volunteer Association; Staff of Manipur University Library; Achou Singh Ningombam (Geographical Society, Manipur); Yangoi Piba (Yaibilen); Oinam Jugindro (Directorate of Census Department, Manipur); Mr Churamani (Ethno Heritage Council of Manipur); Nongmairen (United Meetei Mayek Academy, Imphal); Aslam Makacham (Threatened Indigenous People's Society, Manipur); Yumna Jiten (Citizens' Concern for Dam & Development); Prof Amit Bhattacharyya (History Department, Jadavpur University); all those who had offered themselves voluntarily for interview; and many others whom I could not recollect.

I wish to express many thanks to my colleagues, volunteers and members of Manipur Students' Association Delhi, Campaign for Peace & Democracy (Manipur) and other friends in civil societies for their encouragements and support. I thank my publisher Mr K.K. Saxena of Aakar Books, Delhi for his cooperation and encouragement.

I wish to convey to my son Wakhalloi (Ideologue), that he should grow up fast to fulfill my dream to read, understand, and contribute to the fight for a democratic world free from subjugation, exploitation, and oppression.

7 September 2014
New Delhi

Malem Ningthouja

Abbreviation

AFSPA	: Armed Forces Special Powers Act, 1958
AGSOP	: Agreement for Suspension of Operations
AMADA	: All Manipur Anti Drug & Alcoholism
AMAWOVA	: All Manipur Women's Voluntary Association
AMESCO	: All Manipur Ethnical-Socio-Cultural Organisation
AMKIL	: All Manipur Kanba Ima Lup
AMSCOC	: All Manipur Students Coordinating Committee
AMSU	: All Manipur Students' Union
AMUCO	: All Manipur United Clubs Organisation
ANSAM	: All Naga Students' Association Manipur
AOC	: Assam Oil Corporation
APSF-TUCS	: All Private School Forum of Tamenglong, Ukhrul, Chandel and Senapati
ASEAN	: Association for South East Asian Nations
BDR	: Bangladesh Rifles
BNLF	: Bru National Liberation Front
BPL	: Below Poverty Line
BSEM	: Board of Secondary Education Manipur
BSF	: Border Security Force
CADA	: Committee Against Drug and Alcoholism
CCDD	: Citizen's Concern for Dams and Development
CD	: Compact Disc
CID	: Criminal Investigation Department
CLAHRO	: Civil Liberties and Human Rights Organization
CLK	: Chanura Lamjingkon Kangleipak
CM	: Chief Minister
COFPAI	: Committee for Peace and Integrity
COHR	: Committee on Human Rights

CORE	: Centre for Organisation and Research Education
CP	: Capital / Capitol Project
CPI (M)	: Communist Party of India – Marxists,
CPI	: Communist Party of India
CPMP	: Centre for Progress of Manipuri People
CRPF	: Central Reserved Police Force
DESAM	: Democratic Students' Alliance of Manipur
DONER	: Ministry of Development of Northeastern Region
EIA	: Environment Impact Assessment
EMP	: Environment Management Plan
FEZ	: Fortified Elite Zone
FM	: Foreigner's Mauzadar
FREINDS	: Federation of Regional Indigenous Societies
FWPLK	: Fourth World People's League of Kangleipak
GOI	: Government of India
HERICOUN	: Ethno Heritage Council
HPC	: Hmar People's Convention
HPC-D	: Hmar People's Convention – Democracy
HRA	: Human Rights Alert
HRD	: Human Resource Development
ICCPR	: International Covenant on Civil and Political Rights
INA	: Indian National Army
IPPU	: Integrated People's Progressive Union
IPSA	: International Peace and Social Advancement
IRB	: Indian Reserved Battalion
ISKCON	: International Society for Krishna Consciousness
JAC	: Joint Action Committee
JBWG	: Joint Boundary Working Groups
KCP	: Kangleipak Communist Party
KLA	: Kuki Liberation Army
KNA	: Kuki National Army
KNA	: Kuki National Assembly
KNF	: Kuki National Front
KNO	: Kuki National Organisation
KRA	: Kuki Revolutionary Army
KRPA	: Komrem People's Army
KYKL-MDF	: KYKL (Military Defence Force)
KYKL	: Kanglei Yawol Kanna Lup
LAC	: Line of Actual Control
LEWS	: Leprosy Patients' Welfare Society

LIKLA	: Lei-Ingkhol Khunsem Leimarol Apunba
LYDO	: Lei-Ingkhol Youth Development Organisation
MAFYF	: Manipur Forward Youth Front
MAO	: Manipur Administration Order
MAPALUP	: Manipur Pari Apunba Lup
MAPI Council	: Manipur Peace and Integrity Council
MCP	: Manipur Communist Party
MEELAL	: Meetei Erol Eyek Loinasillol Apunba Lup
MLA	: Member of Legislative Assembly
MEPWAK	: Meira Paibee Women's Association of Kangleipak
MIC	: Mizo Integration Council
MNF	: Meetei National Front
MNF	: Mizo National Front
MNRF	: Manipur Naga Revolutionary Front
MoU	: Memorandum of Understanding
MP	: Member of Parliament
MPCB	: Manipur Pollution Control Board
MPLF	: Manipur People's Liberation Front
MPNOC	: Meira Paibee Numit Observation Committee
MSC	: Manipur State Congress
MSF	: Manipur Students' Federation
MSLA	: Manipur State Legislative Assembly
MSRTC	: Manipur State Road Transport Corporation
NBSE	: Nagaland Board School Education
NEDFI	: North Eastern Development Finance Corporation Limited
NEEPCO	: North Eastern Electric Power Corporation Limited
NFA	: Naga Federal Army
NFG	: Naga Federal Government
NGO	: Non Government Organisations
NH	: National Highway
NHTA	: Naga Hills - Tuensang Area
NIC	: Naga Integration Committee
NIPCO	: National Identity Protection Committee
NNC	: Naga National Council
NOC	: No Objection Certificate
NPC	: Naga Peoples Convention
NPMHR	: Naga People's Movement for Human Rights
NSA	: National Security Act
NSCN–IM	: National Socialist Council of Nagaland -Isaac and Muivah faction

NSCN–K	: National Socialist Council of Nagaland -Khaplang faction
NSCN	: National Socialist Council of Nagaland
NSF	: Naga Students' Federation
NWUM	: Naga Women Union Manipur
PANMYL	: Pan Manipuri Youth League
PDM	: People's Democratic Movement
PLA	: People's Liberation Army
PM	: Prime Minister
Poirei	: Poirei Leimarol Apuba Meira Paibee Lup
POTA	: Prevention of Terrorism Activities Act
PREPAK	: People's Revolutionary Party of Kangleipak
PSMA	: Prevention of Seditious Meetings Act
PSS	: Praja Shanti Sobha
PWD	: Public Works Department
RAP	: Restricted Area Permit
RJC	: Revolutionary Joint Committee
RNP	: Revolutionary Nationalist Party
RPF	: Revolutionary People's Front
SoS	: Suspension of Operation
SPO	: Special Police Officers
TIPS	: Threatened Indigenous People's Societies
UAPA	: Unlawful Activities Prevention Act, 1967
UCM	: United Committee Manipur
UCO	: United Club Organisation
UKLF	: United Kuki Liberation Front
ULFA	: United Liberation Front of Assam
UNGA	: United Nations General Assembly
UN	: United Nations
UNC	: United Naga Council
UNLF	: United National Liberation Front
UNPC	: United Naga People's Council
UPF	: United People's Front
UPLA	: United People's Liberation Army
UPPK	: United People's Party of Kangleipak
VDF	: Village Defence Forces
ZORO	: Zo Re-unification Organisation
ZRA	: Zomi Revolutionary Army
ZRO	: Zomi Reunification Organisation

Glossary

AFSPA: The Armed Forces Special Powers Act 1947, which replicates the Armed Forces Special Powers Ordinance 1942 imposed by the British to suppress quit India movement, became an act in 1948. It was repealed in 1957. However on 22 May 1958, the Government of India promulgated the Armed Forces (Assam and Manipur) Special Powers Ordinance to suppress liberation movement spearheaded by Naga National Council in the Naga Hills areas of Assam, parts of the then North Eastern Frontier Agency and Manipur. The Ordinance became an Act on 11 September 1958. In 1972 the title of the Act and certain clauses were amended in order to encapsulate newly demarcated administrative regions in the Northeast. In 1983 a version of the Act entitled the Armed Forces (Punjab and Chandigarh) Special Powers Act 1983 was enacted to suppress Khalistan movement in Punjab. In 1990 the Armed Forces (Jammu & Kashmir) Special Powers Act, Act No. 21 of 1990, was enacted to deal with the Kashmir question.

Apokpa Marup: Formed at Jaribon village in present day Assam in 1930; a pioneering Meetei revivalist organisation.

Cheiraoba: Meetei new-year day at the end of the month *Lamda* i.e. middle of the month April.

Cheitharol Kumbaba: Royal chronicle in Manipur that record events beginning from 33 A.D; first published in 1967.

Colonial monarchy: A system of government characterized by collusion of the British Colonial authority and Manipur monarchy.

Cosmetic solidarity: Solidarity extended for name's sake.

Decolonisation: The process of establishing freedom from colonial rule; e.g., independence by the various Western colonies and protectorates in Asia and Africa after World War II.

Desanskritisation: Desanskritisation is a reverse process of doing away from the presumed Hindu connection, e.g. changing names and terms, assertion of 'indigenous' language and script, reclaiming of the *Kangla fort* and reviving traditional cultural practices.

Developmental aggression: Arbitrary imposition of projects that are considered to be destructive, through militarization and repression.

Eemaleipak: My motherland.

Eereipak: My blood-land.

Forward policy: Territorial expansion through deployment of troops in the name of national security.

Hao: Meetei term used for those listed in the Scheduled Tribes list.

Kabow Valley: A highland valley in northern Burma (Myanmar), western Sagaing division. It had been a contentious region between Meetei king and Burmese king for several centuries. The British transferred the right to occupy it to Burma in 1834 in lieu of annual compensation. Many considered that Kabow Valley was arbitrary transferred to Myanmar without the consent of Manipur by Jawaharlal Nehru in 1953. The nostalgia to reclaim Kabow Valley is persistent to certain section of the population in Manipur.

Kangla Sha: A mythical animal, symbolically representing Meetei power and achievement; it reminds their victory over the 'Chinese' who erected the statue of it.

Kangla Fort: The capital of the Manipuri kingdom founded by the first historical king Nongda Lairen Pakhaba, who came to power in 33 A.D.

Lei–Ingkhol: A suburban village located at Village No 8 Mantripukhri, Sheet No 2, Tahsil Imphal Eat II, in Manipur; founded in late 1940s by socially ostracized migrant tuberculosis and leprosy patients.

Locale: Village or locality level organisation.

Maibas and Maibees: Priests and priestesses among the Meeteis.

Manipur: Manipur lies in the latitude range of 23°83" and 25°68"(North) and in the longitude range of 93°03" to 94°78" (East). It became part of India following the imposition of the Manipur Administration Order on 15th October 1949 as per the provisions of a secret and controversial Shillong Accord signed between King Bodhachandra of Manipur and the representatives of the then Dominion of India on 21st September 1949 at Shillong. Manipur attained statehood on 21st January 1972. Manipur in 2012 was composed of officially recognized indigenous peoples viz., Aimol, Anal, Angami, Any Kuki tribe, Any Mizo (Lushai) tribe, Chiru, Chothe, Gangte, Hmar, Kabui, Kacha Naga, Kharam, Koirao, Koireng, Kom, Lamgang, Liangmei, Mao, Maram, Maring, Meetei / Meitei, Meetei Panggal, Monsang, Moyon, Paite, Poumai, Purum, Ralte, Rongmei, Sema, Simte, Suhte, Tangkhul, Tarao, Thadou, Thangal, Vaiphei, Zemei and Zou. Others are being perceived as outsiders.

Mayang: Meetei term for all the non-mongoloid Indians except those who are being perceived as the aboriginals of the Northeastern states.

McMohan Line: Named after Sir Henry McMahon, foreign secretary for BritishIndia and the chief British negotiator of the convention, it was a borderline agreed to by British India and Tibet as part of Shimla Accord, which was a treaty signed in 1914. Although the Chinese government refused to accept the Accord, during the postcolonial period the line was regarded by India as the legal border between India and China.

Meetei revivalism: A socio-religio-cultural movement aimed at asserting a Meetei identity that is considered to be culturally dissociated from the identity of the Mayangs.

Meetei: One of the co-existing communities in Manipur; about 60% of the total population of Manipur; also settled in certain parts of Assam and Tripura states and in certain areas in Myanmar and Bangladesh.

Meira Paibees: Literarily meirapaibee means woman torchbearer; the origin is traced in 1980 when women bgan organizing voluntary human rights groups to defend human rights.

Mera Houchongba: A one day festival in October marked by the gathering of the delegates of communities at the royal compound at Kangla. In the nineteenth century it was a festive gathering of the delegates of communities at the royal compound in Kangla.

Nagalim: Spatial expression of Naga nationalism.

Ningol Chakkouba: Meetei festival of married women to feast and present of gifts by relatives at the parental home.

Nupi Lan: Generally referred to as women's war, it was agitation spearheaded by the women during the British colonial period; the first agitation in 1904 was against forced labour and taxation by the British and the second was in 1939 against the export of rice leading to famine.

Official nationalism: Nationalism that is officially created, articulated, propagated or diffused amongst the people.

Panggal: Manipuri Muslim

Pareihanba: A reconversion ritual from Hinduism to Meetei religion.

Pogrom: The word pogrom (Russian: погром) came from the verb громить, Russian pronunciation: (groˈmʲitʲ); "to destroy, to wreak havoc, to demolish violently". Uri Avnery describes classical pogroms as "riots by an armed mob intoxicated with hatred against helpless people, while the police and the army look on".

Poknapham Lamdam: My birth-land.

Puyas: Puyas are Meetei sacred texts on various subjects dealing with cosmology, rituals, genealogy, hymns, culture and so on.

Rasa Dance: King Bhagyachandra invented the Manipuri Rasa Dance in the 18th century; based on the theme of romance between Radha and Krishna of the epic Mahabharata.

Sagol Kangjei: It is hockey on pony-back or polo. Many trace the origin of polo in Manipur, which was exported by the British to other parts of the globe in the 19th century. The Prince of England is the patron of the Manipur Polo.

Shillong Accord: An accord signed between King of Manipur and the representatives of the then dominion of India on 21st September 1949.

Siroy Lily: (*lilium mackliniae sealy*); the only flower of its kind naturally grown in the Shirui Hills in Ukhrul District. The plant hunter Kingdom Ward exhibited it in London and won a merit award from the Royal Horticulture Society in 1948.

Sustainable development: A developmental process that is proven harmonious with people, environment, resource and progress.

Village Defence Force: Underpaid, irregular, less trained auxiliary armed personnel recruited on the contract basis by the government to assist in the functioning of policing and intelligence.

Zale'n-gam: Spatial expression of Kuki nationalism.

Introduction

Manipur in Northeast India bordering Myanmar, has been known for its geo-strategic importance. The British invaded Manipur in 1891 and occupied it till 1947 because it was the best position from where they could defend British India from Burmese influence. During the Second World War, Manipur was a battle front for the Axis and Allied forces. During the war INA/Azad Hind Fauz claimed territorial occupation in Manipur by unfurling its flag on 14 April 1944 at Moirang. In the 1940s, British and Indian rulers made some attempts to merge Manipur with other 'tribal' regions to form new administrative regions. Manipur was annexed by the Indian State in 1949. Since then, people have been entrapped by vexed terror syndromes of armed resistance/insurgency and counter-insurgency. Violation of human rights and suspension of peaceful democratic livelihood have been order of the day.

On 19 May 2009, the Manipur State Cabinet decided to induct 1600 more Manipur Police Commandos (MPC), in addition to pre-existing 1600 MPC, to suppress insurgency. The Cabinet also agreed to recruit, 678 riflemen in order to add one company each to the existing six Manipur Rifle Battalions, 2400 police constables, and gave a nod to the proposed recruitment of 500 Village Defence Forces (VDF) in addition to the pre-existing 2537 VDFs. A few days after the 19 May Cabinet decision, Manipur-based Kuki and Naga civil societies opposed government policy to the deploy Indian Reserved Battalion (IRB) and MPCs in the hill districts on the ground, saying that it was extension of State terrorism.

In principle, human rights activists and other civil societies were expected to collectively oppose State terrorism. However, there was communal colouring of the issue. Most Imphal Valley-based civil societies had maintained a strict silence on the issue. Some of us who hailed from Imphal suggested some Naga, Kuki and Hmar organizations to jointly organize protests in Delhi. We were applauded by some circles but most community centred organizations failed to attend when protest demonstrations was organized. We could not organize a more inclusive demonstration as late as 10 September 2009.

Weeks before the September demonstration, on 23 July 2009, a gruesome killing spree was unleashed by police at Imphal.[1] Chief Minister (CM) Okram Ibobi shielded the perpetrators and held insurgents responsible for the killing. Not a single MLA in the Assembly sought for an enquiry, but accepted the version of the CM. Those eyewitnesses who protested the killing were arrested. The crime was exposed by New Delhi-based *Tehelka Weekly* on 31 July 2009.[2] It ignited a month-long agitation demanding justice. The CM resorted to suppressive tactics and justice was delayed.[3]

The protest in Manipur was mostly confined to Imphal Valley except courteously released solidarity statements by few hill-based civil societies. The protest did not deter the CM from strengthening his aggressive policy. On 17 August, he 'submitted proposal to the Ministry of Home Affairs for support to strengthen and upgrade the State Intelligence Wing ... to provide dedicated security and additional police manpower for effective administration in the State....'[4] But civil societies remained divided along different 'national' inclinations.

The media overviews of State militarization, fake encounters repressive tactics, civil society disunity, partisan and sectarian approaches, human rights violations and demand for justice are together a journalistic prologue of larger political questions. They raise some interrelated questions: what is the political economy of State terrorism? What discouraged valley-based civil societies from protesting induction of MPC/IRB in hill districts? Why were hill-based civil societies hesitant to mobilize and coordinate with valley-based civil societies against State terrorism? To properly address these questions, one needs a thorough understanding of larger dialectics of diametrical nationalisms that contributed to the vexed cycle of assertions and counter-assertions. These may be thematically analysed.

Firstly, the State and different insurgent parties, broadly grouped into Indian, Kangleipak (Manipur), Nagalim, and Zale'ngam nationalist camps in making different nations, were enemy to one another and have commonality in waging war against enemy. They perpetuated diametrical nationalisms, which are intricately officially manifested in orchestrated populism. State terrorism was an integral course of counter-insurgency and suppression of civil society's democratic assertions.

Secondly, the Manipur ruling class, comprising of landlords, contractors and bureaucrats primarily accumulated wealth through misappropriation of public funds, extraction of commission from projects, corruption, and exploitation of resources and labour. They relied on repressive forces and terror activities to retain power and to fulfil vested material interest. On the other hand, police, mostly middle-class upstarts who had paid huge bribe money to get into the job and lacked modest discipline, indulged in corruption and criminal activities to recover the bribed money and for wealth, award and promotion.

Thirdly, Imphal Valley is predominantly inhabited by those who are adamant in defending Manipur's *status quo* and are opposed to the Nagalim, Zale'n-gam, or Zogam propositions. They considered deployment of MPC/IRB in the hill districts, thinking it would neutralize 'dissenting' forces. On the other hand, Nagalim and Zale'n-gam or Zogam protagonists, who had strong bases in hill districts, preferred to work along exclusivist and sectarian lines in order to interweave human rights issues with communal propaganda against the Kangleipak agenda.

All these proposed a predominant role for the Indian State as a contending force. Perhaps, Indian nationalism entered a new phase from 15 August 1947 onwards. British colonialism came to an end and Indian big bourgeoisie began to hasten in bringing under its control the territory that we today call India. On 26 January 1950 the Indian Republic was formally declared. Henceforth, India would be defined by a totalizing term, that is, 'nation'. Pre-existing diametrical nationalisms are being overshadowed by derogative official jargons such as 'disturbance', 'secessionism', and 'terrorism'. The fiction of an inviolable Indian nationhood became deep-rooted among many who were blindly misinformed by the State and its version of nationalism. I attempt to analyse beyond this premise.

The book has four chapters with sections and sub-sections.

The first chapter is about 'Nation-state and Nationalism.' It argues that nations are neither primordial nor fixed as claimed by the protagonists. Many 'nation-states' are products of historical invention and their *status quo* is subjected to changes over time. It analyses the role of the Indian big bourgeoisie in making India, their economic and geo-strategic interest in the Northeast, the policy of militarization to suppress insurgency, and the formulation of discourses of terrorism and backwardness to cover up colonial expansionist characters. It concludes that constraints under oppressive capitalist path, instead of winning hearts, perpetuated diametrical nationalisms.

The second chapter on 'Diametrical Nationalisms vis-à-vis Dominant Nationalism' argues that state formation cannot be universally identified with nationhood. The modern state comes first and establishes a 'political community' but does not necessarily uproot pre-existing nationalisms. It discusses the paradoxes of the State's 'national security' policy and commitment to democracy, and dialectics of civil society assertions and anti-colonial discourse. The chapter has a section on women and nationalism with a focus on Meira Paibee movement.

The third chapter on 'Coordination and Conflict among Nationalisms' argues that India or Bharat or Hindustan, Manipur or Kangleipak, Nagalim, and Zale'n-gam or Zogam or Zoram were predominant nationalisms engaged in comparative quagmire of *status quo*. A section on the timeline of diametrical nationalisms provides with chronologically arranged data of tactical coordination and conflict among nationalist forces in twentieth century. The chapter discusses paradox of nationhood inherent in respectively articulated one-nation theories and questions the very idea of orchestrated populism in the process of construing nationhood.

The fourth chapter on 'People's Democratic Aspiration' argues that conflicts in Manipur are modelled and perpetuated under an overarching neoliberal political economy. It concentrates on the micro analysis of contradiction between policies and democratic aspirations of the people at the receiving end. The manner in which communal conflicts are being engineered in the name of 'nation' is also being cited. It discusses problems of democratic struggles due to diametrical nationalisms, communalism, sectarianism, and opportunism. It suggests that civil societies end up in creating 'camp follower' masses that were loosely organized pressure groups and were neither revolutionary nor radical reformists.

To sum up, writing the history of politically sensitive contemporary issues has been unsatisfactory for want of large volumes of information that were being classified by both the State and insurgents for security reasons. A scholar is also a potential suspect in the eyes of diametrical forces. This invokes the question of historical objectivity in a historical domain hegemonised by the story of the State and its enemies or among enemies. On the other hand, research becomes a test of a scholar's ability to access or 'spy' on expanding information networks. This book, however, is an attempt to contribute to an understanding of the Manipur question.

NOTES

1. (a) Ms Thokchom (Ongbi) Rabina and a medical attendant Chongkham Sanjit were killed.
   (b) Wankheirakpam Gitarani (40) of Tengdongyang, Ningthoujam Kishorani (43) of Narakonjin, Golmei Mangal (58) of Maha Kabui Namching, New Keithelmanbi, Pangambam Lukhoi (30) of Heingang Makha Leikai and Kangabam Subhachandra (40) of Kha-Potsangbam were injured.
2. 'Murder in Plain Sight', Delhi, *Tehelka* Vol. 6, Issue 31, August 2009.
3. On 28 August Manipur government appointed Justice (Retd) P.G. Agarwal to head an investigation.
4. CM demand for strengthening of State Intelligence Wing; Imphal, Hueiyen Lanpao, 18 August 2009.

1

Nation-state and Nationalism

I. INDIAN NATIONHOOD: A CONCEPT

India, a political concept embodying in it an expanding geographical expression, is a UN recognized nation-state and plays important roles in the South Asian geo politics. Generalized political terms such as 'nation' or 'nation-state' accorded to India in the international statute and India's effort in registering its concern for decolonization, and 'national security', and series of diplomatic and military engagements in 'counter-insurgency' are collectively bent on the adoption of pre-existing political terms.[1] As terms represent concepts that are reinforcing in framing and justifying policies, the term 'nation' accorded to India had far-reaching varying political implications to different sections of peoples. Understanding the functionality of certain terms adopted by the Indian State requires critical reading.

To begin with, it has been widely upheld that a nation exists and its existence is perceived or expressed in material forms, that is, population, territory, economy, culture, social relationship, and political set up. National cause is the guiding principle of economic planning, political decision, social schemes, and foreign policies. Even if the revolutionary slogan of world socialism, capitalist globalization or liberalization, and the two World Wars had transgressed national boundaries, what is significant is that all of this had occurred within national boundaries. The League of Nations and United Nations Organizations were formed to defend the national interest of the member States. The vocabulary of terms like Transnational Company, International Monetary Fund and Amnesty International give due recognition to a nation as a viable unit of global politics. The significance of nation is continuously upheld.

Many questions can be raised. Does the Indian nation exist? If it exists, then what is the material form of existence and how do we describe it? There is only a *yes* or *no* answer to the first question and many of us will disagree over the second answer. Why? The answer is simple. We perceive India through either of two opposing versions: the national hegemonic version of State and the anti-colonial discourse of insurgents. Both agree with the existence of an entity called India. But terminology accorded to it so far and descriptions about it remain contentious. The two versions are diametrical and differed in orientation. The difference is reflected in armed conflict.

The argument is that India exists, but it had not developed into a nation. For the purpose of analysis, I have used the Marxist definition of nation as the yardstick of measurement.[2] Pakistan and India were created as peoples were not forged into one nation. Multinational compositions under an undemocratic system and controversial occupation in Kashmir and the Northeast had particularly provided preconditions of rendering the hasty big bourgeoisie attempt to build a nation into a debacle. Not surprisingly, recalcitrant Manipur was 'arbitrarily' annexed on 15 October 1949. Formal annexation had been continued as late as 1975 in the case of Sikkim. It is an illusion to forge people belonging to different social, cultural, racial, linguistic, and psychological expressions into a nation mechanically within a short span of time, at gunpoint, by the neoliberal regime that rested on the extraction of surplus value from the oppressed masses by keeping them disunited along conservative and sectarian blocks. The big bourgeoisie course in this context is not heading towards a nation. It is exploiting and oppressing in the name of 'nation'. What is wrong if the people of newly occupied territories are dissatisfied with an oppressive regime? What is wrong if the oppressed peoples wish to enjoy freedom? Where does nation exist if people are oppressed and massacred in the name of 'national security' to serve the interest of the few who exploit peoples?

The Indian rulers and corporatized media are juggling with deviating concepts to divert attention from the unresolved national questions in India. Class aspects of national subjugation and the oppressive character of bourgeoisie democracy had been out of focus. Sponsorship for bourgeoisie sociology, promotion of NGO sectors to invest in tribal and ethnic studies, widespread circulation of derogatory terms such as 'terrorism', 'disturbed areas', and 'national security', are primarily carried out within the ideological framework of nationhood to propagate reformism within an oppressive system. It promote uncritical consumption of the State articulated notions about an Indian nationhood. It leads to loss of intellection precision and amnesia, as the focus of attention is deviated from the core national questions. It has created prolonged deception of many.

The public consent, thus manufactured against this backdrop under the big bourgeoisie initiatives, construe legitimacy of certain 'national' policies and indulge in undemocratic military options. In short, most 'mainstream' Indians who subscribe to a fixed notion of Indian nationhood, to defend a misconceived 'Mother India', are relatively ignorant about the geography, multinational composition of India, and validity of the right to self-determination of nations. Their moral, political, physical, and logistic support to suppress insurgency had cost lives and destroyed properties. They remain ignorant that, under an oppressive regime, they cannot erase inequality or national differences. Nor can there be psychological unity towards common goal. The nationhood concept, therefore, embodies material perspectives, that is, economic viability, military power, successful administration, and successful management of media and diplomacy of the rulers. How long will it be possible to govern them through deceptions and military options?

Historically, the shape and size of India had been fluctuating depending on the power and prowess of the Indian big bourgeoisie. Chandernagore was ceded to India on a *de facto* basis on 14 August 1949 and *de jure* on 2 May 1950. On 1 November 1954, *de facto* control over Yanam, Mahe, Pondicherry, and Karaikal was transferred to India, and in May 1962, *de jure* control of the enclaves was transferred. On 18 December 1961, the Indian army entered Goa,

Daman, and Diu which were under the possession of Portugal. Portugal surrendered its possessions to India on 19 December. On 10 April 1975, the Sikkim Assembly passed a resolution calling for full integration into India. This resolution was endorsed by 97 per cent of the vote in a referendum held on 14 April 1975. Following it, the Indian State amended the Constitution to admit Sikkim as the 22nd state. The Indian State entered into a treaty with Bhutan in 1949. Since then, the external affairs of Bhutan has been abiding to the terms and conditions of the Indian big bourgeoisie. What is then apparent is an ever expanding territorial base of the Indian big bourgeoisie.

The course of expansionism and the military policies being exercised are being covered up by adopting generalized terms that are relevant elsewhere in different historical contexts. They borrowed the term 'nation' and construed the one-nation theory for India. They formulated Indian nationhood as a linear historical course, and an invincible entity. It is worth reminding that the Communist Party of India had acknowledged multinational composition for India and espoused the right of secession of nations till 1951,[3] when it changed the line towards national chauvinism of the Indian big bourgeoisie. In the meanwhile, the Indian State promulgated the phrase *unity in diversity* to act as surrogate in depicting India as a nation.

Concurrent to the concept of nationhood, there exist reformulated concepts such as colonialism and decolonization. Colonialism or imperialism suggested foreign domination and justified anti-colonial or the decolonization movement. The Indian State had acceded to the Charter of the United Nations 1945, Universal Declaration of Human Rights 1948, International Covenant on Civil and Political Rights 1966, and several other declarations such as the Declaration on Granting Independence to Colonial Countries and Peoples 1960, International Decades for the Eradication of Colonialism 1990, and so on. In the 1950s they had 'ceaselessly seeks to establish itself in a firm position as the leader of the anti-colonial movement everywhere'.[4] It had supported Burmese independence in 1948, Vietnam's independence from France and the US, and Bangladeshi resistance against Pakistan in

1971. It recognized the independence of East Timor in 2002 and sympathized Tibetan movement for self-determination. However, it refuses to apply the terms colonialism and decolonization with regard to the national question in Kashmir and the Northeast.

A new term, 'postcolonial India', has been under circulation to encapsulate Kashmir and the Northeast under the rubric of a concocted term 'domestic' or 'internal'. Universally, the 'domestic' constitutes an exclusive domain of an established State. It is expected to be immune from international intervention. Manipur, which was under the purview of the Department of Foreign Affairs under British rule, was relegated to the lower hierarchy of the 'domestic' with Part C status and under central rule till 1972. It is to govern the 'domestic' that the most controversial Armed Forces Special Powers Act was enacted in 1958 for Assam and Manipur. Foreigners' visit to Manipur, other than immigrants from Bangladesh, Nepal, Burma (who were encouraged by the Indian bourgeoisie for political reasons) and Bhutan, were restricted for several decades under the Protected Area Permit 1958 and Restricted Area Permit 1963(RAP). In other words, 'a foreigner is not normally allowed to visit a protected/restricted area unless the Government is satisfied that there are exceptional reasons to justify it.'[5] The 'exceptional reasons' mentioned in the RAP, the exceptional reasons for declaring Manipur a 'disturbed area', the exceptional reasons for imposing AFSPA, the exceptional reasons for governing, were indications of a permanent state of siege that Agamben had termed as 'State of Exception'.[6] The PAP, however, has been temporarily lifted from 2011 in order to facilitate the Indian big bourgeoisies' commercial interest in Southeast Asia.

The Indian State had won internationally in officially invalidating 'decolonization' in the context of India. It continues to defend the position that the 'domestic' has been disturbed by anti-national terrorists. The terrorists and those who sympathize with them had to be suppressed or physically eliminated. Nehru, who had theoretically 'never challenged the right of my country to defend itself; it has to. We will defend ourselves with whatever arms and strength we have, and if we have no arms we will defend ourselves without arms',[7] however, had taken a militant path with respect to the Northeast (Manipur inclusive). Nehru's 'pro-communist' and Sardar Patel's 'pro-mongoloid prejudice' communities in the 1950s, had to be suppressed. New terms such as national security and terrorism were denominated as justification jargons.

Despite the State and its hegemony, resistance movement in Kashmir and the Northeast has drawn the attention of critics who subsequently have explored different versions of history that challenges the State and its hegemonic versions. These constitute an anti-colonial discourse that offers a different perspective of re-interpreting the State and its 'national' history. It also offers to rethink a particular context where manipulated terms such as colonization, decolonization, neo-colonialism, national liberation movement, national security, democracy, had terrorism had far reaching policy orientations and different impacts on different sections of the population.

Stankiewicz's understanding that the concept of nation could have preceded formation of states could be loosely applied in the formative stage of India and the continued efforts to overrule the domestics.[8] If some semblances of 'banal nationalism'[9] in the form of 'mainstream' populist slogans such as *hamara bharat, jai hind* and *bharat mata ki jai*[10], encompassing Kashmir and the Northeast are conjured up by those who subscribe to Indian nationalism; applying Noam Chomsky's analysis of relationships between institutionalized propaganda and the governed public mind[11] would suggest that those are the combined product of deception and manipulated media. It may reflect a particular character of nationalism or chauvinist psychological expression of the misinformed 'mainstreams' but does not make a perfect description about the character of the State and the multinational composition of India.

To sum up, a centralized geopolitics in the name of a quasi federal state superstructure, created primarily to promote exploitative capitalist expansionism, have had important bearings on perpetuating pre-existing nationalisms in the newly occupied territories, where there is combination of military oppression and some degree of constitutional tolerance to civic assertions[12] of democratic rights. Diametrical nationalisms flourish despite repressive laws, installation of puppet regimes, cosmetic economic packages, and military occupation.

II. THE AMBIVALENT RITUAL OF 1947

> Long years ago we made a tryst with destiny, and now the time comes when we shall redeem our pledge, not wholly or in full measure, but very substantially. At the stroke of the midnight ... (a) moment comes, which comes but rarely in history, when we step out from the old to the new, when an age ends, and when the soul of a nation, long suppressed, finds utterance...
>
> An excerpt from speech delivered by Jawaharlal Nehru, Prime Minister of the Dominion Government of India on the occasion of the first Independence Day on 15 August 1947.

Panoramic Jubilation

Nehru jubilated millions of Indian patriots with his famous political speech, *Tryst with Destiny*, on 15 August 1947. The political rhetoric of an Indian nationhood that was embodied in the speech and the ecstatic panorama of the Independence Day ritual raised the epitome of an imagined India among millions of consumers who were inclined to Nehru's national agenda. Perhaps, on the eve of the 'independence' there was widespread imagining, '...there has arisen in Indian, an Indian nation, an Indian nation with an Indian culture and an Indian civilization'...[13]

Perhaps the making of India entered a new phase from 15 August 1947 onwards. Symbolically, British colonialism was replaced by the agenda of the Indian big bourgeoisie to inherit British colonial territorial assets and installation of a regime control over the territories that subsequently became to be known under a geo-administrative rubric called India. On 26 January 1950, the Indian Republic was formally ritualized with a spectacular effect so as to have resonance of a mechanised perception called *unity in diversity*. Henceforth, India has been officially defined by an institutionalized totalizing meaning, that is, 'nation'. All these exemplify the State's construction of a trope, that is, the sacrosanct *territorial de obsession*[14] of the Indian big bourgeoisie.

The spectacular semblance of the first ritualized Independence Day, the rhetorical speech, the Constitution, the ecstatic Republic

Day celebration and the totalizing political term such as 'nation' applied for India constituted effective visual and audio ingredients for the promotion of the Indian nationalist trope. These effects could find resonance among a large bulk of the consumers who upheld Nehru's agenda. However, there were defiant, resilient, and rebellious others. Insurgency and counter-insurgency continued. Insurgency produced history that interpreted the *Tryst with Destiny* as deceptive.

Covering Chauvinism

Nehru had used deceptive terms to cover up his expansionist course and the racial and cultural prejudice towards the Northeast. In the words of Guido Zernatto, a term denotes 'a more comprehensive or a more restricted concept'.[15] In politics, terms have political value and are policy oriented. There are instances of terms pitting against terms to fit into policies; 'president rule' against 'emergency' and 'military action' against 'terrorism', and so on. Pretext or context of a particular situation can be represented by a term. Terms are readymade narratives that embodied descriptions. Terms are procured and distributed to twist and mould knowledge to form opinion or to draw attention. A term become deceptive when used anachronistically to serve a vested purpose. In Manipur, thousands of lives have been lost, properties worth millions of rupees have been destroyed and thousands of people have been oppressed in the name of 'law and order' and 'counter-terrorism' to defend 'national security'. Deceptive terms misrepresent, de-contextualize and negatively influence the subjective consciousness of many.

Deceptions are evident in the post 1947 Indian nationalist historiography writing about Manipur. In all such works, pre-independent India is identified with a nation and Manipur is located in it. Two examples can be cited.

Firstly, there are historians who construe primordial Hindu religio-cultural connection between India and Manipur. They trace the cosmology of Manipur to the pristine vedantic rituals and the *Mahabharata* epic, that is, Hinduism. They argue that the Hindu god Shiva, using the *trishul,* had drained out Manipur from an ocean. There is no doubt that large-scale sanskritization of Meeteis began around the middle of the eighteenth century. However, the above history suffers from holistic determinism of identifying India and Manipur with Hinduism, that is, ignoring the multi religion-cultural composition of both Manipur and India. It also misrepresents cultural boundary with geo-political boundary.

Secondly, there are modernist historians who stress on cultural commonality, that is, 'unity in diversity', to bind people into Indian nationhood. They trace it in the forces of integration under the British colonial rule. British colonialism had outlived 'Asiatic' conditions of subjective and objective isolation of peoples, and as a result, consolidated changes. Integration became inevitable and the only viable option for modernity, that is, nationhood, citizenship, rights and duties, security, peace and progress. According to Nehru, 'the future of Manipur State obviously lies with the Union of India. ... (Manipur's) business of defence must be shouldered by the Union. In other ways too... the Union would, no doubt, help Manipur State to develop itself in many ways.'[16]

The chauvinist trend was also the ideological underpinning of expansionist policy. The then architect of Indian 'integration' Sardar Patel, had articulated that the Northeast with the Himalayas had been a frontier throughout the history of India.[17] Subsequent Indian leaders had selectively referred to the Hindu *Upanishads*, the *Mahabharata*, the *Ramayana* and several other literatures to argue that 'the striving of the Indian spirit was directed towards these Himalayan fastnesses.'[18] The concept of *Bharatavarsha,* an imagined landscape extending from the Himalayas to the seas, was identified with a constructed jargon 'Mother India'. Cosmology for Assam and Manipur that had established Hindu connexion between these regions and other parts of India from time immemorial were circulated.[19] The Anglo-Manipur war of 1891 has been shown as influenced by the Indian Sepoy Mutiny of 1857. Any form of pre-1947 anti-colonial resistance in Manipur has been shown as an integral part of Indian tribal resistance. Any form of post-1949 resistance against the Indian State is duped as atavism incarnated in the form of 'modern' terrorism. They drew a terrorist caricature for Manipur liberation movement and justified military intervention.

Different Discourse

There are counterpoising histories vis-a-vis the history crafted by the rulers. In other words, different histories coexist. The predominance of a particular version of history representing a vested interest can be long lasting only when no different histories exist. For instance, the history of peaceful Indian integration into nationhood merely reflects the success story construed by the Indian rulers. The Indian rulers try to suppress any counter history by others. A section of chauvinists had labelled those who raised counter histories as 'Gang of separatists: A grave threat to internal security'[20] and sought for punitive action under the provisions of National Security Act, 1980 (NSA) and Prevention of Seditious Meetings Act, 1911. In the early 1950s, those who fought for responsible government[21] or expressed political dissent were arrested and booked under repressive laws.[22]

But counter histories cannot be completely erased. Dyakov's work on the national question in India in the late 1940s[23] and the Memorandum of the Communist Party of India submitted to the British Cabinet Mission in 1946[24] are few sources that argue for a multinational composition of India. The CPI had, till 1951, acknowledged multinational composition for India. Insurgency in Kashmir and the Northeast continue to produce counter histories. The existence of counter histories has proven that the semantics of successful integration articulated by the Indian national protagonists is a cover up laying beneath it several weaknesses. It cannot be erased from history that Manipur in 1947 was yet to become part of the Indian union. If Indian nationhood had been founded on voluntary federation, the Manipur national question would not have become a serious concern for the Indian leaders in 2004, who after 57 years of the jubilant Independence Day ritual have taken the pain of vowing to the Indian Constitution and condemn for '... on 14 of August (2004), as you all know, Sir, they have celebrated their independence. They unfurled their own flag. It is a question of seceding from the Union of India and the anti-Indian feelings are precipitating in Manipur ... This is all about Manipur.'[25]

Racist Course: Conceptually, if Anderson's *horizontal comradeship* or Stalin's *common psychological makeup* was a necessary qualification for nationhood, insurgency illustrates the missing psychological cohesion towards one nation. Mere encapsulation of the Manipur policy within an Indian national paradigm does not create a nation. There has been a wide gap between what is being represented as nationhood and the military pogrom in the name of national security. A fraternal common psychological footing might have developed had the Indian rulers reverted imperial objectives and extended fraternalism. The fraternity is still missing. Not surprisingly, the Indian rulers till date conceive racial perceptions in dealing with Manipur (the Northeast inclusive).

The Indian national protagonists of the 1940s had gazed upon Northeast with an exotic imagination. For them, the Northeast was an unexplored resource, a strategic frontier, an anthropological cultural showpiece, a wild space of different racial inhabitants that must be tamed by the Indian civilizing hands, and of course, an inheritable British colonial asset. The Report of the Sub-Committee on North-East Frontier (Assam) Tribal and Excluded Areas, submitted to the Constituent Assembly of India on 28 July 1947 substantiates my argument. It is an irony that, while the Indian leaders, who talked about Indian nationhood encompassing the Northeast on the eve of Independence, were still ignorant about the Northeast and that they had to rely on the information that was available to them only as of July 1947. How many of them had time to read the report in detail is doubtful, as most of them were intensively preoccupied with issues on communalism, the caste question, and anti-communism. Their concern for the Northeast was imperial hangover for territorial control over what Sardar Patel had termed 'weak spots'.

Nehru's constant fear for the Northeast inclination towards what he perceived Chinese communism[26] and the constant effort of carrying out a 'forward policy'[27] in his *Jewel of India*,[28] Sardar Patel's racial prejudice and subsequent speeches and statements of several Indian political stalwarts are self-explanatory with respect to the indifferent attitudes towards the Northeast. Nehru had a deep rooted fear for potential rebellion by the people of the Northeast. For an Indian leader like Sardar Patel, the *Iron Man of India* who had taken the pains of fulfilling an extensive 'territorial vision', Indian racial affiliation and cultural characteristics seemed to him all forms of racial and cultural features but minus what he believed as characteristically Tibetan and Mongoloid.[29] Logically, only those who would possess Indo-Aryan physical features were the first-class citizens, trustworthy; the rest were suspects. They had, therefore, adopted a forward policy to keep the Northeast under military control.

Enduring Distance: Persons have changed but the character of the ruler is retained. The pace of psychological distance has been continued even after 50 years of 'rule.' If Shivarj Patil's 'brothers, men and officers of the Armed Forces, are living thousands of miles away from their homes and from their places and exposing themselves to all kinds of dangers that are involved in countering insurgency...,'[30] he had not only drawn a distance between Manipur and India (reciprocally representing distant land and home) but had also derecognized from Indian-ness those Manipuris who were serving in the Indian army and deployed in Manipur. According to Mr P.R. Kyndiah, a Member of Parliament from Meghalaya, there had been 'a very wrong perception about the Northeast. The analysis was over simplistic'. In fact, Kyndiah had raised in the Indian Parliament on 8 March 2001 that:

> 'When there was some police firing or militants' firing in Shillong, seven businessmen were killed and in one of the newspapers they said, 'Five Indian businessmen have been killed', as if Shillong was not in India. Is this the media perception too? This is wrong. When there was a change of Government in Manipur and the Samata party took over power, they said: 'Kohima calling'. They did not know that the capital of Manipur was Imphal. This is how we look at the North-East. How can we solve the problems of the North-East if we do not know even the state capitals and if we do not know that Shillong is a part of India? ...When I was the Head of the state in Mizoram, I received a letter from the Ministry of Defence addressed to: 'P.R. Kyndiah, Governor, Mizoram, Agartala'. Agartala is the capital of Tripura. This is the kind of ignorance that is there about the North-East. This is unthinkable.'[31]

Not surprisingly, L.K. Advani made a speech on 13 August 2008.[32]

He traced the genesis of Manipur in pre-1947 India. On the other hand, he located India somewhere outside Manipur. His emotional invocation that Manipur could be far away but would never be far away from 'our heart,' was rhetoric fitting an exotic land into a landscape that was his own imagining.

There are several other instances that suggest institutionalized racism. The Regional Passport Office in Delhi would not issue Indian passports to someone who was born in the Northeast unless the Ministry of Home Affairs issued a clearance. This would imply that one who is born in the 'disturbed area' is a suspect or criminal or guilty unless proven innocent. The National Archive in Delhi classifies most of the files related to the Northeast from 1913 onwards, thereby barring an ordinary person or scholar from getting access to the material. In June 2005, the Vice Principal of Kirori Mal College in Delhi prescribed salwar kameez to be the dress code for the Northeast women students on the ground of pre-emptive measures to prevent sexual harassment. In June 2007, the Delhi Police widely circulated a booklet entitled *Security Tips for Northeast Students/Visitors in Delhi,* which laid down the norms of decency, food habit, dress code, traffic rules, etcetera, to be observed by the people from the Northeast. It was protested. There are several instances when police refused to register FIRs submitted by Northeast peoples residing in Delhi. Intimidation, forced vacation of tenants by landlord, financial difficulty, time constraints, and lack of local support make the people of the Northeast handicaped in any prolonged legal fight for justice against the mainstream residents. These explain social discrimination, harassment, and alienation.

The parliamentary debate, dated 4 May 2012, on the issues arising out of the widespread protest against the mysterious death of two students from the Northeast in May 2012,[33] had emphasized more on the improvement in roadways and railways in the Northeast to ensure psychological integration.[34] The discussion upheld bourgeoisie initiatives to keep the Northeast within India. But it did not focus on rooting out the exploitative neoliberal regime that is responsible for forced emigration of students and workers[35] from the Northeast to the Indian metropolitan cities only to become laughing stocks and objects of racial discrimination and harassment in institutions, residential areas, and public places. In an interaction on this issue on 10 May 2012, the Prime Minister Dr Manmohan Singh had denied racism in India. Coincidentally, the same day, an official advisory was released by the lower officials of the Ministry of Home Affairs.[36] It appears from the advisory that the MHA had more or less clubbed the entire people from the Northeast in the category of SC/STs, while trying to refute racism in India. Such homogenous depiction into an official category to befittingly describe a people by certain pre-existing jargon is deliberate and insulting. The statement of the Prime Minister was also proven wrong as: (a) racism is a relative term and reciprocally expressed by many from the Northeast vis-à-vis the 'mainland' Indians as well, and (b) there was targeting of Northeast migrant workers and students in Pune, Bangalore, and other metropolitan cities, leading to mass exodus in August of the same year.

On the whole Indian rulers are trying to cover up racism in order to articulate the one-nation theory for India. However, the discovery of a wide gap between depiction of Indian nationhood and the hegemonic attitude of the Indian rulers had rendered Nehru's *Tryst with Destiny* paradoxical.

Recapitulation

Since its formative stage, the Indian big bourgeoisie had adopted capitalist path, which is based on exploitation under military back-up. The initial phase, till 1958, had revealed a mixed up phenomenon of jingoism and racial arrogance towards the Northeast. In fact, in India, the caste system had been a socio-culturally manifest class order. The *raisons d'êtres* of the then contemporaneous Dalit and Dravidian movements, revivalism in Manipur, and biblical exilic worldview among Christianized tribes in the Northeast were response to the economic, political and cultural hegemony of the rulers who happened to be from the upper castes. Logically, Nehru's bourgeoisie expansionism (AFSPA inclusive) had actually conformed to upper caste chauvinism (*sic* varna class order) and militant statecraft enshrined in *Manusmriti*, *Arthasatra*, and the Machiavellian *Prince*. In 1931 he was expelled from the League against Imperialism and for

National Independence on the charge of deceiving 'the revolutionary youth and the working masses' and a traitor to the cause of independence and an agent of imperialism.[37] Nehru's combination of racial mistrust and neo-colonial expansionism was persistent and it has been continued till date.

The deceptions, if not delusive representations, are widely articulated by the 'mainstream' media to confuse many. Resistance, however, asserts anti-colonial discourse and keeps alive counter history. In other words, the *carrot and iron policy* adopted to integrate Manipur into the projected Indian nationhood[38] has not been fulfilled till the end of twentieth century. Nehru's *Tryst with Destiny* can be interpreted as a ploy integral to bourgeoisie geo-politico-economic agenda. The Independence Day ritual of 1947 remains ambivalent and paradoxical from what it tried to convey among the Indian population.

III. DIALECTICS OF DOMESTICITY AND INTERNATIONALITY

> Now, it is a question of fact whether this village or that village or this little strip of territory is on their side or on our side. Normally, wherever there are relatively petty disputes, well, it does seem rather absurd for two great countries...immediately to rush at each other's throats to decide whether the two miles of territory are on this side or on that side, and especially two miles of territory in the high mountains, where nobody lives. But where national prestige and dignity is involved, it is not the two miles of territory, it is the nation's dignity and self-respect that becomes involved. And therefore this happens.
>
> An excerpt of the statement by Jawaharlal Nehru,
> Lok Sabha, 4 September 1959[39]

Nehru's articulation was an intricate power expression and he rightfully emphasized correlation between power and territorial limit.[40] The kingdoms and republics of ancient India, the Mughals of medieval India, the British Indian Empire, the Ningthouja kingdom in Manipur and the Indian State after 1947 had created territories. Each size and shape of territorial possession has been determined by the limit of power.[41]

The absolute authority to govern a territory is presumed to be rested in the State either by *de jure* or by *de facto* or a combination of both. According to Leach, 'in the ideology of modern international politics all states are sovereign and every piece of the Earth's surface must, by logical necessity, be the rightful legal possession of one and only one such state.'[42] And there could be no permanent territorial overlapping of two adjacent States. In other words, territory cannot be extended beyond the limit of power vis-à-vis competing powers, that is, external invasion or internal rebellion.

Nehru argued that the tests of sovereignty, that is, power, autonomy and territorial possession, were the capacity for international relations and the capacity for declaring war.[43] He considered power, sovereignty, and territorial independence as synonymous. 'The future of Manipur obviously lies with the Union of India... Manipur can hardly be expected to defend itself unaided in case of troubles on the frontier. This business of defence must be shouldered by the Union.'[44] Those who cannot win the tests of sovereignty waged by the Indian State must become part of India. Herein lies a crucial paradigm: power sets the limit of territory.

But power or territorial size is not necessarily permanently rooted. In other words, if modern States are expected to derive power from the 'collective' or 'sovereign' will of the citizens, then, the power is relatively weak in those areas that are forcibly occupied in order to build a country but where the people remain dissenting. In this context, potential disintegration of territory remains perpetual. What becomes apparent is a cycle of diametrical nation building in which insurgency and counter-insurgency are the order of the day. Consistent attempt to invent an Indian nationhood substantiates the understanding.

The idea of a historically evolved and primordial Indian nationhood is a fiction. In 1940s protagonists of the two nations theory for Hindu and Muslim, Mohammed Ali Jinnah had propounded that 'talk of Indian unity as one central constitutional government of this vast sub-continent is simply a myth.'[45] Peter

Robb argues for India that '(British) colonialism was important, not just as a stimulus, foil and opponent for Indians, but in its constructions of the state (and an identity).'[46] According to V.P. Menon, the arch-manoeuvrer of Indian expansionism,[47] 'throughout her long and chequered history (India had) never achieved political homogeneity. ... not even in the palmist days of the Hindu and Moghul empires did the entire country come under one political umbrella.'[48] He eulogizes successful building of India by 1950, and thus, acknowledges recent invention.

Invention was a corollary of the growth of the Indian big bourgeoisies. Perhaps, in 1947 political power of British India was transferred to the monopolistic capitalist groups of Tata, Birla, Dalmia, Singhania, Bhatt, and comprador section of Bombay bourgeoisie, capitalists from among Gujaratis and Parsis, Marwari moneylenders, Tamil usurers, et cetra.,[49] who were intimately linked to the princes, landlords, and British capital. They adopted a capitalist socio-economic system. Capital, which is both a precondition and outcome of capitalism, requires territorial base to thrive on. Indian big bourgeoisie were eager to compete with the rising Chinese, Burmese, and Pakistani counterparts and to expand control in Asia. Nehru carried forward the ambition to create a super-national state stretching from the Middle East to South-East Asia and to exercise an important influence in the Pacific region; '[Nehru] stands for a South Asia federation of India, Iraq, Iran, Afghanistan and Burma.... in the world of today there are two big powers, Russia and America. In the world of tomorrow, there will be two more, India and China –there will be no fifth.'[50-51] If Nehru had charged Chinese social imperialism as ten times more dangerous than Western imperialism, his green signal to the 'Forward Policy'[52] of militarizing the entire Northeast was equally imperialistic. According to Nehru, 'the danger really is not from military invasion but *from* infiltration of men and ideas'[53] and he had to deal with a strong hand to suppress resistance. If there was Indian apprehension for the Kuomintang infiltration into Burma and potential clamp down by China on the soil of Burma, that may create strategic danger for India, it suggested that the Northeast was already being presumed as the permanent frontier for India. On the other hand, the Indian rulers were not passive spectators to the Chinese interest, if at all, in Burma. They were taking up an aggressive policy towards Burma to hasten up demarcation of a permanent Sino-Burmese borderline on the one hand, and to defend Indian maritime interests in the Burmese sea on the other. Already, in the 1940s K.M. Panikkar had intimated that 'the defence of Burma was in fact the defence of India, and it was India's primary concern no less than Burma's to see that its frontiers remain inviolate.'[54]

The Indian big bourgeoisies continued with British expansionism,[55] and decided to create a 'Curzonic Scientific Frontier'[56] comprising the Himalayan kingdoms of Kashmir, Nepal, Bhutan, Sikkim and Tibet,[57] and the Northeast. Patel had presumed that 'our Northern or Northeastern approaches consist of Nepal, Bhutan, Sikkim, Darjeeling and the tribal areas in Assam.'[58] In Tibet, the British Mission in Lhasa became officially Indian Mission on 15 August 1947.[59] Furthermore, when a Tibetan Trade Mission headed by Tsepon Shakabpa visited Delhi in January 1948, the Indian State refused to talk about trade matters unless the Tibetans had recognized that the Indian State was 'the legal inheritor of the treaties, rights and obligations of British India.'[60] In 1949, India signed a treaty with Bhutan to guide the latter's foreign affairs. In the same year, India seized the opportunity of a local uprising against Sikkim ruler to send in troops and bring the state into closer dependence as a protectorate than it had formally been under the British.[61] 'Nepal, too, according to Nehru, was certainly a part of India.'[62] The Treaties of Peace and Friendship, and Trade and Commerce (1950) subjected Nepal to the extent of compelling Nepal to consult the Indian State before buying war material from any other country.[63] Whether a territory should be annexed at any cost, as in the case of Hyderabad and Manipur, or kept as a subordinated neighbour as in the case of Sikkim (till annexed in 1975), Bhutan, and Nepal or entered into treaty alliance as in the case of Burma, were worked out to serve bourgeoisie interests.

According to Nari Rustomji, it was the advanced economies who, for the purposes of industrial development, strategic necessity or other considerations of self-interest had initiated contacts.[64] Had it not been for the occupational interest in the Northeast, then, the

Indo-China war of 1962 and the ongoing boundary tensions and border skirmishes with bordering countries might have not occurred. Secondly, strategic importance[65] and administrative exigency were capitalist objectives.[66] The Northeast, inhabited by economically backward tribal and peasant communities, apart from strategic calculation[67] had been important for: (a) labour, resources (water, uranium, oil, coal, precious stones, minerals, plantation, flora and fauna, tourism, carbon credits, and forest products), and market, (b) a buffer to counter Chinese social imperialism, and (c) a military stockpile and commodity stocked for commercial expansion in Bangladesh, Bhutan, Burma, Laos, Cambodia, Vietnam, Thailand, Indonesia, et cetra. They annexed Northeast, forced integrated it into inter-territorial division of labour and subjected to the restructured economic order as the primary supplier of labour, raw material, market, and military stockpile for the Indian capitalist expansionism. Thirdly, the 'weak spots' must not go in the hands of potential competitors such as China and erstwhile East Pakistan. 'The state of Sikkim and the District of Darjeeling connect Tibet with the Indian Union, and Assam, the eastern-most frontier of the Indian Union, is linked with the rest of India by a narrow strip of land consisting of portions of Darjeeling district and Jalpaiguri. These areas in view of their strategic importance need to be strengthened and consolidated.'[68]

The polemical assertion of occupation in Northeast was based on claiming legal inheritor of British colonial treaties and Acts. In the words of Menon, 'it was assumed that (integration) could be done by an adaptation of the Government of India Act of 1935 and that there was no necessity for a specific provision in the Indian Independence Bill for the accession of states.'[69] Territorial expansion was arbitrary and militant. 'Any state which did not come into the Constituent Assembly would be treated by the country as a hostile state. Such a state, he added, would have to bear the consequences of being so treated.'[70] The Resolution of the Constituent Assembly, moved by Nehru on 13 December 1946, where representatives of princely states were not present[71] had logically approved expansionism. The Constituent Assembly adopted a special resolution on 21 December 1946 to include Bhutan and

Sikkim within the scope of a Negotiating Committee, obviously, for future expansion, that is, keeping Bhutan under India's Sphere of Influence by the treaty of 1949 and annexation of Sikkim in 1975.[72]

Territorial expansionism was deceptively shown in a radical and hasty federation proposal that had no provision of either voluntary federation or secession. It was resented by Manipur State Durbar in 1939 as 'the durbar has not been given any time to consider the Hydari Report and similar papers (all related to federation proposal). The durbar regrets that, in the very short time at its disposal it has not been able to study the question sufficiently thoroughly to give His Highness the Maharaja any advice as to whether it would be advisable to federation or not.'[73] The hasty and drastic character was the result of fixed agenda to annex 'frontiers groups'[74] by any means. By 1946, some members of the Indian Constituent Assembly were trespassing in Manipur.[75] Manipur was arbitrarily represented in the Indian Constituent Assembly, twice only by India nominated 'outsiders', Himmat Singh, K. Maheshwari, and G.S. Guha, who were neither familiar about Manipur nor mandated by the people. They merely presented credentials and signed the registration respectively on 14 July 1947[76] and on 22 August 1949.[77] Any democratic assertion in Manipur was condemned as 'very harmful to the (Indian) nation and must be prevented.'[78]

The Indian big bourgeoisie were eager to disempower Manipur from taking any protectionist decision. They called for enacting laws that would allow all Indians to freely move in and around Manipur without any restriction.[79] They were worried whether people living in the Naga Hills were 'misguided by certain persons into thinking that, with the withdrawal of British authority, the country would go back to them... The fact that the Naga Hills have always been part of India, have never been anything like a state, has not been pointed out to them.'[80] Assam should at any cost be controlled. Otherwise, if Assam were to go into the hands of somebody who is 'not in favour of the whole of India, if Assam were in the hands of an adverse power, the whole of India would have gone too.'[81] Sardar Patel had to take up 'my bounden duty to work for the consolidation of freedom.'[82] He had no time to seek the voluntary consent of 'small fry',[83] such as Manipur, to either integrate in the Dominion of India or not. He used force in annexing Manipur.[84]

When the Constitution of India was finally adopted in 1950, Part I, Article 1, Clause No. 3 and Sub Clause No. C of the Constitution sanctioned further territorial expansion. It had no provision of the right to secede. The Acquired Territories (Merger) Act, 28 December 1960,[85] the Armed Forces (Assam and Manipur) Special Powers Act, 1958,[86] the Criminal Law Amendment Act, 1961,[87] et cetra were imposed to suppress political dissent. Manipur was downgraded to Part C status, since it happened to be one of the territories that required direct control for administrative reasons and strategic necessity[88] and where one had to construct a network of 'communications for the movement of troops and provisioning of supplies in the event of attack from the north.'[89] It paved the way to subjugation and dissention, insurgency and counter-insurgency. Perhaps 'the present consecration of these British-made lines as heirlooms in the successor state's national heritages is an unexpected and unfortunate turn of History's wheel,'[90] as described by Arnold Toynbee in the context of an India-China border war, can be applied to explain the Indian big bourgeoisies' interest in Northeast.

The bourgeoisie expansive course has not been peaceful but expensive. According to Nehru, 'there are limits beyond which we cannot go, at least 'for some years, and a spreading out *of* our army on distant frontiers would be bad from every military or strategic point of View.'[91] Neville Maxwell argues, '... empires in their expansive phases push out their frontiers until they meet the resistance of a strong neighbour, or reach a physical barrier which makes a natural point of rest or until the driving force is exhausted.'[92] Nehru admitted India's expansive course in 1950 and said, 'India and China are two of the biggest countries of Asia bordering on each other and both with certain expansive tendencies, because of their vitality.'[93] Quarrel or dispute or skirmish or war for security and territorial control arose from the need to translate imagined zones into lines, and from the failure to agree on a method to share or distribute the border. Lord Curzon had emphasized that 'frontier' war was inevitable when states expanded to a point 'at which the interests or ambitions of one state come into sharp and irreconcilable collision with those of another.'[94] In the words of Calvin, 'nations continue to go to war, especially if negotiations yield no compromise, over issues that are strategically important to them.'[95] According to Mark Purcell, 'the struggle is important because actors do not simply imagine national territory, they also struggle to realize that imagined territory in the physical landscape that surrounds them.'[96] Border wars, insurgency, and counter-insurgency are indeed integral to the processes of fixing territorial limits. To realize their goal, the Indian big bourgeoisie had invested huge money in the four conventional border wars[97] and the ongoing fencing and militarization along international borders as well as in counter-insurgency measures.

Functionally, the bourgeoisie expansionist course created two domains: (a) international and (b) domestic.

(a) The International Domain is the domain across established territories recognized by the UN as a nation state. In this domain, India's geopolitics towards immediate neighbours such as Myanmar, Bangladesh, and China has been a cycle of friendly negotiation, exchanges, armed conflict, and fencing borderlines.

In regards to Myanmar, the Indian State had tried to appease Myanmar by ceding away Manipur's coveted Kabow Valley in 1953.[98] However, despite a cultural link, common regional interests on several issues, and economic cooperation, India invested huge money in fencing along the Manipur-Myanmar borderline. The eleventh Indo-Myanmar joint meeting held in October 2005 raised border issues and the two countries agreed to improve border relations.[99] Fencing that was incompleted as of 2003[100] has been resumed. Unfortunately, the ongoing military fencing is being carried out at a 10 kms distance inside Manipur. Protests are looming on this issue.

With regard to China, India-China armed propaganda over the controversial McMohan Line had culminated into an open war in 1962. Though India asserts that, as per the India-China Resolution of 1962, Arunachal Pradesh had been an integral part of India,[101] both the Chinese and Indian authorities continue to have differences on the perception of the Line of Actual Control (LAC). Provision of joint agreements such as Agreement on Maintenance of Peace and Tranquillity along the LAC in the India-China Border Areas

(1993) and the Agreement on Confidence Building Measures in the Military Field along the LAC in the India-China Border Areas (1996) constituted a certain framework for the maintenance of peace and tranquillity in the India-China border areas. Both sides continue with armed patrolling along the LAC.[102] Fear of Chinese intrusion has been reported from time to time.

Regarding Bangladesh, although India had supported the Bangladeshi independence of 1971, there has been a cycle of negotiation, agreement, exchanges and armed propaganda, or skirmishes on the border issue. Perhaps, the Indo-Bangladesh Treaty of 1972 decided to exchange enclaves between India and Bangladesh[103] and it was endorsed by the India-Bangladesh Land Boundary Agreement of 1974.[104] However, the 111 enclaves that India claimed from Bangladesh and the 51 enclaves that Bangladesh claimed from India had not been exchanged as late as 2000.[105] On the other hand, India charged Bangladesh against 'unprovoked and unwarranted intrusion by the Bangladesh Rifles.'[106] India, therefore, deployed primarily the Border Security Force (BSF) along the India-Bangladesh border.[107] Routine flag march, extension of outposts by both sides, and sporadic skirmishes had been reported from time to time.[108] India had approved fencing disputed areas along the borderline.[109] By the end of 2001, a total length of 854 kms was fenced.[110] In the meanwhile, the two governments constituted two Joint Boundary Working Groups in 2001 to resolve all pending issues relating to implementation of the Land Boundary Agreement of 1974, including exchange of enclaves.[111] The first meeting of the JBWG was held in Dhaka from 2 to 4 July 2001.[112] The second meeting of the Joint Boundary Working Groups was held in New Delhi on 26 and 27 March 2002.[113]

(b) The Domestic Domain is directly administered by the Indian State and deemed immune from international intervention. The domestics have no rights to secession and rebellion. In this domain militarization, counter-insurgency, propaganda, cosmetic economic packages, et cetra, are crucial aspects of governance. I shall briefly mention the different courses that the Indian State had taken in dealing with Manipur, Mizo, and Naga insurgencies.

(i) Firstly, Manipur had a constitution and a responsible

government in 1948. It was arbitrarily annexed by the Dominion of India on 15 October 1949 and relegated to the position of Part C State status in 1950. It was upgraded to a 32-member Territorial Council in 1950 and further to Union Territory with a 32-member Legislative Assembly on 16 August 1957. It was upgraded to a 32-member Territorial Legislative Assembly in June 1963 and furthermore to statehood on 21 January 1972. The status change is considered lineal and constitutes the success story of the Indian integration trajectory.

But resistance convey a different history. Many, in late 1940, had opposed integration with any other entities. Initially, King Bodhachandra opposed signing the Shillong Accord. If he was genuinely defending sovereignty or simply bargaining for a Privy Purse, it would have been a different story. However, it is being reported that he was kept under house arrest 'to ensure that all should be well.'[114] In that situation, according to Rustomji, 'the Maharaja was beside himself with emotion, now bursting into tears, now wrapped in sullen melancholy.'[115] According to Bhogendro, '(Sri Prakasa) simply wanted the king to put his signature, by 20 September, on a prepared document ceding full and exclusive authority regarding the governance of Manipur to India.'[116] One Dasgupta, the Superintendent of Police in the Criminal Investigation Department, warned the King that the Indian State had planned to install a new King for Manipur if he refused to sign the Accord.[117]

The Accord was signed on 21 September 1949 and administration was taken over under the Manipur Administration Order on 15 October 1949. Thereafter, suppressions began. Communist armed resistance was suppressed in 1951 and repressive steps were taken up against Revolutionary Nationalist Party in the 1950s. From the early 1960s, counter-insurgency steps were intensified to suppress Meetei State Committee, Revolutionary Government of Manipur, United National Liberation Front (1964), Revolutionary Peoples' Front (1979),[118] Peoples' Revolutionary Party of Kangleipak (1977), Kangleipak Communist Party (1980), Kanglei Yawol Kanna Lup (1994),[119] and the United People's Party of Kangleipak (2008).

(ii) Secondly, in regards to Mizo insurgency, the Indian State had successfully kowtowed the Mizo National Front. To recall, the

British had created Lushai Hills (Mizoram) as a separate district in Assam in 1898. It was declared a 'Backward Tract' and an 'Excluded Areas' under the Government of India Acts 1919 and 1935. The Indian State constituted it into a Union Territory on 21 January 1972 and granted statehood on 20 February 1987. Before statehood, insurgency to integrate the Mizo people and liberate them from India was carried out by the Mizo National Front (MNF) under the leadership of Laldenga. The MNF, formed on 22 October 1961, declared its objective on 21 December 1961, rose in a widespread movement by February 1966, and declared independence on 1 March 1966. The Indian State suppressed it, brutally using aerial bombings. MNF regained and became active particularly from 1975. However, the Indian State succeeded militarily in bringing the MNF to the negotiating table in 1984. According to the Mizo Accord of 30 June 1986, the MNF laid down arms. A similar carrot and stick policy had been carried out in dealing with the parties that were demanding the integration of Mizos under a single administration such as the Hmar People's Convention since 1986, Zomi Reunification Organization since 1993, Hmar People's Convention-Democracy since 1995, Bru National Liberation Front (formed in 1997), and others.

(iii) Thirdly, in regards to the Naga question the British, in 1866, had constituted Naga Hills District in the then Assam province. By 1940s a large section of the Nagas living in the Naga Hills and Tuensang Areas openly rose in asserting Naga identity. About a decade back, in 1929, a Naga Club was formed and it submitted memorandum to the Simon Commission asking for protection of their rights. In 1945, the Naga Hills District Council was formed. It was converted into the Naga National Council (NNC) in 1946. The NNC rejected integration with the Dominion of India. However, in June 1947, an agreement known as Nine Point Agreement was signed between Sir Akbar Hydari, the then Governor of Assam and the NNC.

The agreement envisaged considerable autonomy for Naga people. NNC however was dissatisfied with the outcome and held a referendum in May 1951, in which 99 per cent of the voters had supported independence for Nagaland (present day Makokchung and Tuensang Area). The referendum was not recognized by the Indian State. As a result the NNC continued with the struggle. On 18 September 1954, it declared the sovereign Naga republic.[120] On 22 March 1956, the NNC formed the Naga Federal Government (NFG) and the Naga Federal Army (NFA).

Meanwhile, the Indian State was able influence a moderate section. Accordingly, Naga Peoples Convention (NPC) comprising representatives of various tribes was held in August 1957. In response to the recommendation of the NPC the Indian State created the Naga Hills - Tuensang Area (NHTA) on 1 December 1957. Furthermore, a Sixteen Point Agreement was signed between the NPC and the Indian State in July 1960. Accordingly, the State of Nagaland Act was passed in September 1962 and the Nagaland state was inaugurated on 1 December 1963.

However the NNC remained active. In order to defuse the conflict a Peace Mission was constituted under Shri Jai Prakash Narayan in April 1964. In response to the recommendation of the Peace Mission, an agreement called Agreement for Suspension of Operations (AGSOP) was signed on 6 September 1964. Another agreement known as the Shillong Accord was signed on 11 November 1975. However, those who were dissatisfied with the agreement repudiated Phizo's leadership and formed National Socialist Council of Nagaland (NSCN) in 1980. Differences within NSCN culminated in the formation of NSCN (Isaac and Muivah faction) and NSCN (Khaplang faction) in 1988. The Indian State and NSCN-IM entered into a ceasefire agreement since 1 August 1997. Apart from a separate peace dialogue with the NSCN (Khaplang), the Indian State had to engage diplomatically and militarily with the newly constituted armed parties such as National Socialist Council of Nagaland-Unification (NSCN-U) formed on 23 November 2007, the United Naga People's Council (UNPC) formed on 30 April 2008, Zelianrong Unifed Front (ZUF) formed in February 2011 and others.

Coming back to the point, the Indian big bourgeoisie had mapped Northeast within Indian domestics. Apart from militarization the Indian State had adopted a policy similar to what Anderson had described for 'a systematic, even Machiavellian, instilling of nationalist ideology through the mass media, the education system, administrative regulations, and so forth.'[121] It had institutionalized stereotypes and jargons to cover up intransigence attitude and territorial expansionism. One such stereotype is the continuous anthropomorphic depiction of 'India' as a personified *mother India* that is identified with nation (*Sic.* territorial integrity).

The dignity and integrity of *mother India* is shown threatened by external enemies such as Inter Services Intelligence and its agents in Kashmir and other areas, the People's Liberation Army of China in Arunachal Pradesh, Bangladesh Rifles of Bangladesh in Tripura, Military Intelligence of Myanmar in Manipur and others. They had created terrorist caricature of national democratic struggles in Northeast. The democratic activists were being shown as working with external enemies. *Mother India* had to be defended. War for justice and dignity had to be upheld. According to Nehru, such wars involved self-respect and dignity.

To invoke emotional thrust for an 'imagined' Indian nation and to justify domestic claims treaties and documents were cited. But the citations under the Nehruvian era require critical assessment. According to Maxwell, the Indian State had indulged in cartographic forgery to legitimize claims over the disputed areas. He argues that in the early 1950s, Indian maps were being redrawn under Nehru's indignation and reproduced with internationally disputed areas located within Indian border. According to him, the Indian maps reproduced in 1954 had shown Bhutan and Sikkim, which were independent, within India.[122] Suniti Kumar Ghosh asserts that 'cartographic forgery initiated by Olaf Caroe was completed under Nehru in 1954.'[123] Mapping Manipur within India constituted formalization and ritualization of what Hobsbawm had termed 'inventing tradition.'[124]

Whether there had been cartographic forgery, 'cloak for aggression'[125] and other fair and foul tactics to cover up Indian bourgeoisie expansionism or not is a procedural matter. What is interesting is that the State version of nationhood and discourse of terrorism had found receptive resonance among a bulk of 'mainstream' India 'consumers.'[126] The version has been officially recognized by the UN and other international bodies. Despite continuous effort by the insurgents to wage international propaganda to assert sovereignty, the two decades (1990 to 2010) of proclaimed International Decade for the Eradication of Colonialism remained without meaningful implication.

IV. GOVERNING THE DOMESTIC: DISCOURSE OF TERRORISM

According to Nehru, the tests for sovereignty involved military strength and war. Northeast, being important from Nehru's geographical and strategic points of view,[127] Patel's suspect communities and 'virile people'[128] had to be militarily dealt to suppress insurgency. According to V.P. Menon, 'for administrative reasons or strategic necessity and in view of its position in the border it was decided to take over Manipur as a Chief Commissioner's Province.'[129] Manipur was centrally ruled till 1972 and by puppet regimes thereafter. On the other hand, Manipur was governed militarily under President's Rule from time to time, 16 October 1969 to 20 March 1972, 28 March 1973 to 05 March 1974, 13 May 1977 to 14 January 1980, 28 February 1981 to 19 June 1981, 07 January 1992 to 08 April 1992, and 31 December 1993 to 13 December 1994. The data of increasing militarization and policing between 1949 and 2000s would explain the scale of the two.

To begin with, on 31 March 1893, two years after the British invaded and ruled Manipur, the strength of the State Military Police was 383 including European officers, local officers, non-commission officers, and sepoys. On 15 October 1949, Manipur had only five police stations and seven outposts and the corresponding strength of civil police and Manipur Rifles was 364 and 133, respectively. By 2000, the numerical strength of Manipur police had grown up tremendously. In 2008, the strength of Manipur Police consisting of all ranks was 14,224.[130] As of 1 December 2011 the total sanctioned strength of the State Police department stood at 33,505 while the total posted strength stood at 24,975.[131] According to the media report, the strength was increased to about 28,000 in December 2012.[132] There are other auxiliary forces such Village Defence Forces and Home Guards. By the end of 2008, the

Government of India had sanctioned the budget for recruitment of more than 1,500 Special Police Officers and Village Defence Forces. The exact figure at present is wanting.

Deployment of Indian military and paramilitary forces had also increased tremendously. The total strength of Assam Rifles was increased from two battalions under Indian Ministry of External Affairs in 1949[133] to several thousand by 2002.[134] For security reasons, exact number of Indian troops deployed in Manipur could not be officially obtained. However, in the Northeast, the strength of Assam Rifles had increased from five battalions in 1947 to 17 battalions in 1960, 21 battalions in 1968,[135] 31 battalions in 1987–88[136] and to 46 battalions in 2008.[137] According to the report and map released by the Revolutionary People's Front, apart from 30 thousand Manipur state forces composed of Manipur Police, Manipur Rifles, plain clothes men and agents, there were 111 identified stations manned by Indian Border Security Force, Central Reserved Police Force, Field Regiment, Gurkha Regiment, Indian Reserved Battalion, Jammu and Kashmir Light Infantry, Madras Regiment, Mahar Regiment, Punjab Regiment, Punjab Regiment, Rajputana Rifle, Rashtriya Rifle, Sikh Regiment, Special Services Bureau, and Village Volunteer Force in the strategic areas of Manipur in the period between 1998 and 2002.[138]

According to a report prepared by Committee on Human Rights, 'not less than 50,000 Indian soldiers in addition to several thousands of police, mercenaries, spies etc in a population of 2.4 million are deployed... Out of 1700 sq. kilometers of land in the central Imphal valley of Manipur, a great portion of land is occupied by the Indian armed forces.' For instance

> 'in a distance of hardly 5.5 Kilometers from Sangakpham bazaar and Koirengei Duck Farm in Heingang Constituency the land allocated to security forces was 470 acres: 2 acres at Sangakpham to Assam Rifles; 3 acres at MSRTC complex to CRPF; 80 acres at Tandan Pukhri Maning, Mantripukhri to CRPF; 231.47 acres to Assam Rifles at Lamlongei, Matai, Khabam Lamkhai and Luwangsangbam; 74.20 acres at Koirengei old Air field; 50 acres at Koirengei Bazaar to BSF; two acres at Nilakuthi Vanaspati factory to Assam Rifles and another 2 acres to BSF at Nilakuthi Drug Formulation Centre.'[139]

By 2000, the Indian State had formulated special scheme for modernization of police forces, that is, more provision for vehicles, communication equipments, arms and ammunition and other security related items to be provided in kind. Under the scheme of reimbursement of 'Security Related Expenditure', expenditure incurred by the Manipur government on security is reimbursed by the Central government.[140] The series of other measures that were taken up include, construction of border roads, border fencing, raising of additional battalions of Border Security Force, reduction of gaps between Border Outposts, intensification of patrolling both on the land and the riverine border, increase in the number of outpost towers, provision of surveillance equipments including night vision devices, and so on.[141]

In the overall scenario, a collusion of forces had been operating; (a) the army, paramilitary forces, regional infantries, et cetra (b) the local police, rifles, and underpaid auxiliary forces that were recruited on contract basis (e.g., Village Volunteer Forces, Village Defense Forces), et cetra, (c) armed gangsters groups who operated either from jail or under the command of government forces or in association with undercover secret agents, (d) communal warlords and conservative reactionaries who worked with puppet regimes and indulged in extortion and misappropriation of public funds.

Militarization and suppressive tactics are justified by articulating deceptive jargons such as national security, counter-terrorism, law and order problem, et cetra. The morale of the repressive forces that indulged in crime had to be politically defended[142] by creating a 'state of exception'. Repressive laws such as the Armed Forces (Special Powers) Act, 1958, Unlawful Activities Prevention Act, 1967 (UAPA), the National Security Act, 1980 (NSA), Prevention of Terrorism Activities Act, 2002,[143] Prevention of Seditious Meetings Act, 1911, and Unlawful Activities Prevention Act were imposed at various instances.

The Armed Forces Special Powers Act had been the most controversial. Firstly, section III of the Act empowers the government to declare any area to be a disturbed area. Secondly, section IV of the Act permits any commissioned officer, warrant officer, non-commissioned officer or any other person of the equivalent rank in the armed forces in a disturbed area to carry out a 'reign of terror' even to the extent of killing anyone on suspicion. Under this provision, the armed forces can arrest anyone without warrant or torture them in the custody without any definite time framework, that is, the ambiguous 'least possible delay'. Thirdly, section VI practically provides impunity to any armed personal who had committed crime in the disturbed area. It says 'no prosecution, suit or legal proceeding shall be instituted, except with the previous sanction of the Central Government against any person in respect of anything done or purported to be done in exercise of the powers conferred by this Act'.

What is the inference? Loyalty had been imposed and the essence of democracy, freedom, and fraternity had been undermined. The Supreme Court of India in 1997 defended AFSPA on the ground of constitutionality.[144] Insurgency was addressed from the perspective of a legal paradigm. This is paradoxical. The legal operates as a means of managing order by the Indian bourgeoisie in their interest. AFSPA cannot be separated from the politics of the rulers and their larger economic interest to govern. The Supreme Court order was issued after 15 years of legal struggle against the Act. While defending the Act the Apex court had recommended a set of ambiguous do's and don'ts for the armed forces to protect human rights. But the recommendation failed to root out the draconian character of the Act. Human rights violations had been continued.

Militarization exemplifies the paradox of nationhood and democracy. Interference by the armed forces in the civil administration, politics, and judiciary were repeatedly reported. I shall not reproduce a complete list of human rights violations. But to cite a few instances, the Indian troops operating in Manipur upheld that 'the norms of decency followed by us here are different from those in Delhi'. It was a response from a major of the Assam Rifles to a member of the Planning Commission from Delhi that had gone to Ukhrul in 1988. The major had barged into the room where the team was meeting and demanded explanations for their presence.[145] Elected representatives (including Chief Minister) could be debarred from moving beyond lines drawn by the armed forces. They were supposed to aid civil administration but they carried out operations without either request from or involvement of the state government.[146]

They interfered in the legal and political affairs. In 1987, when the then Chief Minister, Rishang Keshing, submitted a memorandum to the union Home Minister protesting against the atrocities carried out by the Assam Rifles in Oinam village in Senapati district, he was promptly removed from Chief Minister-ship due to the pressure of the armed forces.[147] In 1988, Assam Rifles prevented the Registrar (Judicial) of the Guwahati High Court from interviewing women rape victims. Pressurized by the Assam Rifles, the Home Minister of Manipur, Tombok Singh, went to Oinam village to tell villagers to withdraw the writ petition that they had filed against the Assam Rifles.[148] In 1989, every day at the sessions court in Imphal, the Assam Rifles personnel who were facing a case filed by the Naga People's Movement for Human Rights, carried a table and a pair of chairs to the courtroom on the plea that ordinary benches used by the public in the court were not good enough for them. When the judge ordered that there must be equality before the law and treatment given to the petitioners and respondents must be alike and same, the Assam Rifles had gone to the Guwhati High Court challenging the order.[149] As if a norm, lawyers and democratic rights activist were faced with the bared bangs of the Indian armed forces.[150] Officials of the state government—both magistrates and police officers—could be detained and their offices raided by the armed forces.[151] Several instances of fake encounters, massacres, cold-blooded murder, torture, harassment, detention, forced disappearance, killing as a result of 'mistaken identity,'[152] rape, molestation, sodomy, infliction of 'Post-Traumatic Stress Disorder'[153] and varying forms of oppression and subjection had been continued.

Army, paramilitary forces, regional infantries, et cetra, had been occupying and converting several strategically important hilltops, tourist centres, grazing grounds, communal lands, institutional and religious campuses, et cetra, into barracks (including those in the residential areas). Normally, every installed post was authorized to operate in an extensive operational zone in the adjacent surroundings. Normally, residential areas, villages, forests/jungles, cultivation fields, inland routes, economic zones, social spots, et cetra were forced located in an operational zone. Regular flag marches, frisking, mock war drills, combing operations, detention, harassment, and other aggressive forms often culminating into human rights violations were carried out in the operational zones. The involvement of military officials in drug smuggling was recently exposed.

The presence of aggressive military and police personnel, often targeting civilians because of suspicion and as a form of fun, created fear and terror hysteria among many. Necessarily such terror hysteria in the operational zones had serious repercussions on the social mobility for economic livelihood. Those in the remote and rural areas who were dependant on cultivation, livestock farming, resources in forest/jungle, distant communal land, remote fields, grazing fields, et cetra were badly affected. For fear of being sexually targeted by male chauvinist troops, several women who would otherwise be relying on outdoor cultivation, gathering, and collection were forced to confine themselves to the home and they locked in the development of skills. The situation had the indirect impact of compelling many women to indulge in illicit means of economic survival.

The troops also imposed a typical war economy in the operation zones in the remote rural areas, for example, forced rationing of supplies and Military Civic Action Programmes (MCAP).

(a) Firstly, under forced rationing, the troops counted the heads of a particular village. They speculated the quality and quantity of food, clothing, logistic, or other materials required for each family for a week or month. They imposed a ban on the purchase of certain items beyond the speculated quantity prescribed by them. Granaries were frisked and dismantled. It seriously affected the people as their stocks ran out quickly and they had to frequently walk for several miles to the market to purchase food and goods. In the absence of storage, they suffered a lot during scarcity and price rise in the market.

(b) Secondly, under MCAP, troops provided first aid medical services, organized public excursions, organized periodic distribution of gifts, and intervened in petty civil disputes. But these activities had negative repercussions. It undermined the role of civil administration. On the other hand, MCAP did not bring qualitative improvement of productive forces and relation of production. On the contrary, MCAP went side by side with militarization of destructive projects and suppression of democratic dissentions. MCAP was primarily designed to cover up military excesses, to divert attention by creating a clique of beneficiaries who became unpaid irregular agents.

Coming back to the point, at present, the discourse of terrorism has been articulated by the corporatized Indian 'national' media, which is the propaganda machinery of the Indian big bourgeoisie. It depicts an Indian nationhood and plays an important role in transplanting what Anderson characterized as 'official Nationalism.'[154] The media eulogizes the Indian State as the harbinger of *ahimsa* (non-violence). The 'nation' and *ahimsa* are shown as integral to modernity, progress and humanitarian. While construing *coevalness* in time and space, that is, modernity and territorial limit of the 'nation', India is symbolized with peace and 'integrity.' Insurgency is shown as the characteristic of backwardness and insanity of those who destroy peace. Therefore, it was 'our bounden duty to see that the morale of the armed forces also is not allowed to be attacked.'[155] But this policy is proven to be terrorizing and colonial. A colonial situation did not come from the changing exigencies of oppressed people 'but from the colonial authorities' perception of the structures necessary to govern.'[156] Since colonialism presumes a particular style of managing dissent,[157] the Indian State has been manipulating public consciousness through circulation of what edward Said considered 'labels'[158] and 'essentialised caricatures'[159] about insurgency.

Media bias against Northeast insurgency is a propaganda war to set up a vast complex of political disinformation among 'mainstream' and 'international' consumers, and to create certain 'hate' stereotypes against liberation movement. According to D. Volkogonov, propaganda war, in its spiritual and physical aspects, is based on manipulation of the consciousness of the masses and the planting of carefully selected and directed disinformation in them.[160] The communities of interpretation and management of symbols by the Indian 'national' media have dehumanized the insurgents by reducing them to a few insistently repeated negative phrases, images and concepts. Thus, most of the people outside the 'disturbed areas' are kept in darkness about the colonial situation in Manipur. To them, Manipur meant 'backwardness', 'terrorism', 'drug addiction', 'AIDS infection', 'sexual liberty', and several other prejudicial racial terms. They thus disorient themselves from the national question in India.

The media's power of constant repetition had given the news and pictures delivered by it the status of objective truth in millions of consumers.[161] Constant repetition makes the news a reality perception at receiving ends.[162] The majority of the Indian public consumed insurgency to be nothing different from habitual criminality. As a result, the larger bulk of the Indian 'public' are continually critical about the people of Manipur for their seeming ingratitude to the Indian State. And since a connection is being conceptually built between Manipur and 'terrorism', the criminality of the people of Manipur has been taken as axiomatic; only the measures for controlling them needed to be worked out in a deal. Conversely, the need to police, suppress and control them has had the effect of making terrorists of them. The concept of 'suspect community' becomes a pretext for military actions. It places the targets of attack outside the perimeter of human rights and democratic safeguarding. The people's assertion for human rights is being forfeited. A sepoy can suspect anyone and kill. The discourse of terrorism, therefore, has genocidal impact. It promotes killing and oppression.

In response to the Indian propaganda war, a report on human rights practices that targeted insurgency and 'Maoists' in India was released by the State Department (USA) on 11 March 2008.[163] The selection of target is not surprising. Most Indian big bourgeoisie are connected to and dependent on the American capital. They corroborated in uprooting Indian industrial growth, imperialist liberalization and finance intrusion in Southeast Asia. They had opened up secret joint military exercises in Mizoram and some other areas in the Northeast. Necessarily US had to show favour to the Indian allies. Therefore, the Report was devoid of any gesture of goodwill to the victims of State terrorism in India. While one may not disagree with the State's remark, 'credibility of reports of human rights abuses is often difficult', the Report juggles with stereotypes and pseudo- facts to browbeat opinions into accepting aggressive Indian militaristic actions in suppressing insurgency.

The Report articulates Indian nationhood and expresses liberation movement as 'internal conflict', that is, a domestic affair to be unilaterally resolved by the Indian rulers as per they want. It labelled national liberation movement in the Northeast on a par with reform, communal, regional, Dalit or upper caste, elite and hooligan upsurges within India's domesticity. Such homogenization/ distorting phrase overlooked nationality question and certified bourgeoisie aggression in the name of 'national security.' Deliberate omission and manipulation of facts in the Report, that is, anachronism endemic to the US imperialist protagonists, in order to boost up Indo-US capitalist ties, subvert authentic reporting. There is sheer neologism and adoption of pre-emptive official jargons such as 'Indian nation' and 'disturbed area' while referring to the Indian bourgeoisie' landscape and occupied territories respectively. It uses, 'national security' and 'counter-terrorism' to camouflage capitalist pogrom. It uses deceptive terms such as 'terrorism' and 'insurgency' to misinform liberation movement. The term 'law and order problem' depoliticizes the context. The Report restricts the scope of reporting in a watertight legal discourse independently of politics and economy. It fails to contextualize human rights condition in a broader historical context of the neo-liberal political economy. The Report, therefore, suffers from escapism and reductionism. The essence of the Report, however, lies in the symbolic position it exhibits as an US imperialist artefact to act as surrogate to Indian bourgeoisie propaganda about domesticity.

To sum up, the discourse of terrorism deceives the 'public' through deliberate arrogance and systematic disinformation. It caricatures the imperilled Manipur, dehumanizes the victims of State oppression, glorifies capitalist pogrom, and discourages democratic movement. But subjection, suppression, and exploitation by the Indian troops have been exposed from time to time. On few cases, State instituted commissions and Supreme Court rulings had also admitted certain crimes such as extra judicial killings or fake encounters. Therefore, whatever pacifist and peace-loving pasture the Indian rulers may strike, and whatever such pacifist propaganda camouflages, Indian bourgeoisies' stuffing vis-à-vis Manipur remains militant, aggressive and bellicose. The discourse of terrorism, therefore, is proven unauthentic, biased, vituperative, and exaggeration.

NOTES

1. Concepts such as colonization, decolonization, national liberation movement, national security, terrorism, war against terrorism, etc.
2. A nation is a historically evolved, stable community of language, territory, economic life, and psychological make-up manifested in a community of culture.
3. Naorem Sanajaoba, 'Manipur's Aborted 1950 Revolution, On Afoji Hari alias Jogeshwar alias Irabot'; private circulation, 2008.
4. Irene W. Meister, 'The Bandung conference: an appraisal' in Harry W. Hazard and Robert Strausz-Hupe, eds., *The Idea of Colonialism,* New York, Frederick A. Praeger, 1958, p. 235.
5. http://mdoner.gov.in/writereaddata/sublinkimages/main4808714493.htm, accessed in May 2009.
6. 'A Brief History of the State of Exception' in Giorgio Agamben ed., *State of Exception*, University of Chicago Press, 2004, pp. 11–22.
7. Indian Prime Minister Nehru's speech to the Bandung Conference Political Committee, 1955, reprinted in G.M. Kahin, *The Asian-African Conference*, New York Cornell University Press, 1956, pp. 64–72.
8. W.J. Stankiewicz, 'Nationalism' in *World Encyclopaedia of Peace*, 2nd ed., Vol. III, pp. 345–6.
9. Michael Billig, *Banal Nationalism,* London: Sage Publications, 1995.
10. *Lit.* victory to India or Hindustan and victory to mother India.
11. David Barsamian and Noam Chomsky, *Propaganda and the Public Mind*, Delhi: Madhyam Books, 2001.
12. Greenfield uses the term civic in a loose sense characterised by comparative freedom of individuals; Liah Greenfield, 'Nationalism in Western and Eastern Europe Compared' in Stephen E. Hanson and Willfried Spohn, eds., *Can Europe Work? Germany & the Reconstruction of Postcommunist Societies*, London: University of Washington Press, 1995.
13. Statement of hon'ble Mr Shri Krishna Sinha (Bihar: General) on

Monday, 16 December 1946, *Constituent Assembly Debate*, Vol. I.

14. Steven R. Ratner, 'Drawing a Better Line: Uti Possidetis and the Borders of New States' in *American Journal of International Law*, Vol. 90, Issue 4, 1996.
15. Guido Zernatto, 'Nation: the history of a word' in John Hutchinson and Anthony D. Smith eds., *Nationalism: Critical Concepts in Political Science,* Vol. I, London: Routledge, 2002.
16. Jawaharlal Nehru's letter to the Maharaja of Manipur, dated 22 May 1947; *Selected Works of Jawaharlal Nehru*, Vol. 2, New Delhi: Nehru Memorial Fund, p. 257.
17. Sardar Patel's Letter to Jawaharlal Nehru, dated 7 November, 1950 reproduced in Karunakar Gupta, *Spotlight on Sino-Indian Frontiers*, Calcutta: Friendship Publications, 1983.
18. Neville Maxwell, *India's China War*, Bombay: Jaico Publishing House, 1970, p. 127.
19. Amalendu Guha, 'The Indian National Question: A Conceptual Frame,' in *Economic and Political Weekly*, Vol. 17, No. 31, July 31, 1982, pp. PE2-PE12.
20. *http://www.vijayvaani.com/ArticleDisplay.aspx?aid=1519*.
21. Order, Guwahati High Court, Bench BNC in Ram Manohar Lohia and Ors. vs. V.S. Sundaram on 26 April, 1955, Equivalent citations, 1955 CriLJ 1603.
22. Judgment, Guwahati High Court, Bench BNJC, Sagolsem Indramani Singh and Ors. vs. State of Manipur on 26 May, 1954, Equivalent citations, 1955 CriLJ 184.
23. A.M. Dyakov, 'The National Question in the Indian Union and Pakistan' in *Revolutionary Democracy*, Vol, IX, No. 2, New Delhi, September 2003.
24. G. Adhikari, ed., *Marxist Miscellany*, Vol. 8, Bombay: People's Publishing House, 1946, pp. 120-24.
25. Statement of Shri Manjo Bhattacharya on Law and Order Situation in Manipur; Lok Sabha, Tuesday, 17 August 2004.
26. Prime Minister Nehru's Note on China and Tibet, dated 18 November 1950, reproduced in Gupta, *Spotlight on Sino-Indian Frontiers.*
27. Military intervention and bureaucratic control are pre-emptive measures to defend India's geo-political interest in the Northeast.
28. Indian bureaucrats and officials 'came to Manipur with linear pockets but went home with fatter ones. It was, for them, indeed, a land of jewels', Maloy Krishna Dhar, *Open Secrets: India's Intelligence Unveiled*, Delhi: Manas Publication, 2006, p. 98.

29. 'Sardar Patel's letter to Jawaharlal Nehru', 7 November 1950, reproduced in Gupta, *Spotlight on Sino-Indian Frontiers*.
30. Statement of the Minister of Home Affairs Shivraj V. Patil on Law and Order Situation in Manipur; Lok Sabha, Tuesday, 17 August 2004.
31. Further discussion on the Motion of Thanks on the President's Address initiated by Dr Vijay Kumar Malhotra and seconded by Dr S. Venugopal on 7 March, 2001; Lok Sabha, 8 March 2001.
32. Speech delivered by L.K. Advani, on the occasion of Manipur Patriots Day, 13 August 2008, organized by the Manipur Diaspora Community, Delhi.
33. Mr Richard Loitam (19) from Manipur, a student of B. Arch (1st year) at Acharya's NAV School of Architecture on 17 April was allegedly murdered by hostel mates in his hostel in Bangalore, and Miss Dana Silva M Sangma (21) from Meghalaya committed suicide on 24 April 2012 due to the reported humiliation by exam invigilators at Amity University in Gurgaon.
34. Calling attention to discrimination and racial profiling faced by the students from the North eastern states in some parts of the country; Parliament debate, dated 4 May 2012.
35. This includes job seekers of all types of profession.
36. Office Memorandum under the subject 'Advisory on the discrimination and racial profiling faced by Indian citizens North-eastern states in some parts of the country – Measures needed to curb regarding. F. No. 15011/34/2012 – SC/ST –W, Government of India/Bharat Sarkar, Ministry of Home Affairs/Grih Mantralaya, North Block Delhi/CS Division, New Delhi, 10 May, 2012.
37. Resolutions adopted by the Executive Committee of the League Against Imperialism and for National Independence, Berlin, 2 June 1931.
38. Nari Rustomji, *Enchanted Frontier,* Bombay: Oxford University Press, 1971. p. 107–9.
39. Maxwell, *India's China War.*
40. The terms state, power, and rebellion are interchangeably used.
41. 'The territories of Manipur have fluctuated at various times with the fortunes of their princes'; R.B. Pemberton, *The Eastern Frontier of India*, (first published in 1835), Delhi: Mittal Publications, 2000, p. 20.
42. E.R. Leach, 'The Frontiers of Burma' in *Comparative Studies in Society and History*, Vol. 3, No. 1, October 1960, Cambridge University Press, pp. 49–68.

43. V.P. Menon, *Integration of Indian States*, Madras: Orient Longman, 1985, p. 87.
44. Nehru's Letter to Maharaja of Manipur 1947.
45. M.R.T., *Nationalism in Conflict in India*; Delhi: Discovery Publishing House, 1986.
46. Peter Robb, 'The Colonial State and Constructions of Indian Identity: An Example on the Northeast Frontier in the 1880s' in *Modern Asian Studies*, Vol. 31, No. 2, May 1997, Cambridge University Press, pp. 245–83.
47. Rustomji, *Enchanted Frontier*, p. 107.
48. Menon, *Integration of Indian States*, p. 1–3.
49. Dyakov, 'The National Question in the Indian Union and Pakistan'.
50. Suniti Kumar Ghosh, *India's Nationality: Problem and Ruling Classes*, Calcutta: January 1996, p. 31.
51. Neville Maxwell, *India's China War,* pp. 67–8.
52. Suniti Kumar Ghosh, *The Himalayan Adventure: India-China War of 1962, Causes and Consequences*, Mumbai: Research Unit for Political Economy, 2002.
53. Sardar Patel's Letter to Jawaharlal Nehru, 7 November 1950, Gupta, *Spotlight on Sino-Indian Frontiers.*
54. K.M. Panikkar, *The Future of India and South East Asia*, Bombay: Allied Publishers, 1945, p. 43.
55. '...from 1911, Government of India embarked on a deliberate advance of the northeastern boundary, which looked not only to bringing the tribal territory under 'loose political control' but also to annexing a salient of territory which the British had recognized to be China's ever since they reached Assam nearby ninety years before' Maxwell, *India's China War,* p. 45.
56. Text of the 1907 Romanes Lecture on the subject of Frontier by Lord Curzon of Kedleston, Viceroy of India (1898–1905) and British Foreign Secretary (1919–24) (Henceforth Curzon's Frontier).
57. Ghosh, *The Himalayan Adventure...*
58. Sardar Patel's Letter to Jawaharlal Nehru, 7 November 1950, Gupta, *Spotlight on Sino-Indian Frontiers.*
59. Hugh Richardson, the last British Representative was nominated the first Indian Head of Mission.
60. 'The Evolution of Nehru's Policy on Tibet: 1947–1954,' *Tibetan Bulletin*, Official Journal of the Tibetan Administration, May-June 2000.

61. Maxwell, *India's China War,* pp. 67–8.
62. Ghosh, *The Himalayan Adventure...*
63. V.N. Khanna, *Foreign Policy of India*, 4th edn., New Delhi: Vikas Publishing House, 2001, pp. 141–2.
64. Nari Rustomji, *Imperilled Frontiers*, Delhi: Oxford University Press, 1983, p. 20–1.
65. 'For, if Assam is invaded by her neighbours and reinforcements were not promptly rushed there from the rest of India, she will very soon cease to be a part of India. Can you envisage such a contingency with complaisance?' Statement by members of the Constituent Assembly, Monday, 8 August 1949; *Constituent Assembly Debates*, Vol. IX.
66. Misra argues that there had been systematic exploitation of the rich resources of Assam such as oil, tea, jute and forest products by the Indian state after 1947; Tilottoma Misra, 'Assam: A Colonial Hinterland' in *Economic and Political Weekly*, Vol. 15, No. 32, 9 August 1980, pp. 1357–9, 1361–4.
67. (a) Statement by Shri Ari Bahadur Gurung and Rev J.J.M. Nichols Roy in the Constituent Assembly of India, respectively on Wednesday, 23 November and Saturday, 19 November 1949
68. Statement by Shri Ari Bahadur Gurung on Wednesday, 23 November 1949; Constituent Assembly of India.
69. Menon, *Integration of Indian States*, p. 104.
70. Threat warning to States by Nehru on 18 August 1947, ibid, p. 78
71. Statement of resolution, Friday, 13 Dec. 1946, *Constituent Assembly Debates*, Vol. I.
72. Statement of debate, Wednesday, 22 January, 1947, *Constituent Assembly Debates*, Vol. II.
73. Manipur State Durbar Resolution No. 12, 12 July 1939.
74. Such as Sikkim, Cooch Behar, Cooch Behar, Tripura, Manipur and Khasi States; Annexure A to the Presentation of Credentials and Signing of the Register, Tuesday, 27 January 1948; *Constituent Assembly Debates*, Vol. VI.
75. Manipur State Durbar Resolution No. 10/20-11-1946.
76. Debate of the Constituent Assembly, Monday, 14 July 1947.
77. Ibid., Monday, 22 August 1949.
78. Statement of Shri Kishorimohan Tripathi (C.P. and Berar States) in the Constituent Assembly of India, Tuesday, 9 November, 1948; *Constituent Assembly Debates*, Vol. VII.
79. Statement of Shri Rohini Kumar Chaudhari in the Constituent

Assembly, Thursday, 2 December 1948, ibid.

80. Statement by Mr Jaipal Singh in the Constituent Assembly of India, Wednesday, 30 July 1947; Ibid., Vol. IV.
81. Statement by Rev J.J.M. Nichols Roy in the Constituent Assembly of India, Saturday, 19 November 1949, ibid., Vol. XI.
82. Menon, *Integration of Indian States*, p. 93.
83. Rustomji, *Enchanted Frontier*, p. 107.
84. 'Sardar simply inquired whether we had not a Brigadier in Shillong –and it was clear from the tone of his voice what he meant'; ibid., p. 109.
85. An Act to provide for the merger into the States of Assam, Punjab and West Bengal of certain territories acquired in pursuance of the agreements entered into between the Governments of India and Pakistan and for matters connected therewith.
86. Article 4 (a) of the Act empowers the army to kill anyone on suspicion and Article 6 provided the Indian army with impunity except on the condition sanction by the Central Government; Act No. 28 of 1958, dated 11 September 1958.
87. 'Whoever by words either spoken or written, or by signs, or by visible representation or otherwise, questions the territorial integrity or frontiers of India in a manner which is, or is likely to be, prejudicial to the interests of the safety or security of India, shall be punishable with imprisonment for a term which may extend to three years, or with fine, or with'; Article 2. (1), Criminal Law Amendment Act, 1961, Act No. 23 of 196, 17 May 1961.
88. Menon, *Integration of Indian States*, p. 297.
89. Rustomji, *Imperilled Frontiers,* p. 18.
90. Arnold Toynbee, *Between Oxus and Jumna,* London: Oxford University Press, 1996, p. 190.
91. Jawaharlal Nehru's Note on China and Tibet 1950; Durga Das, ed., *Sardar Patel's Correspondence,* 1945–50, Vol. 10.
92. Maxwell, *India's China War.*
93. Jawaharlal Nehru's Note on China and Tibet 1950. Das, ed., *Sardar Patel's Correspondence,* p. 173.
94. Curzon's Frontier.
95. Calvin James Barnard, *The China-India Border War*, Marine Corps Command and Staff College, 1984.
96. Mark Purcell, 'A place for the copts: imagined territory and spatial conflict in Egypt' in *Cultural Geographies*, DOI: 10.1177/096746089800500403, 1998.

97. Three wars with Pakistan in 1947, 1965 and 1999 over the disputed Kashmir; and one with China in 1962 over the disputed McMahon.
98. No document is available in this regard.
99. Lok Sabha Unstarred Question No. 1076, to be answered on 29 November 2005.
100. Fencing on Myanmar Border, Lok Sabha, Lok Sabha Unstarred Question No. 275, to be answered on 22 July 2003.
101. The Minister of External Affairs' statement on Reported statement made by the Ambassador of China on Arunachal Pradesh, submission by Members; Lok Sabha Synopsis of Debates, (Proceedings other than Questions & Answers) Friday, 24 November 2006.
102. Chinese Intrusion in Arunachal Pradesh; Lok Sabha Unstarred Question No. 840, to be answered on 23 November 2000.
103. Lok Sabha Unstarred Question No. 1680, to be answered on 28 November 2001.
104. Exchange of Enclaves between India and Bangladesh; Lok Sabha Unstarred Question No. 972, to be answered on 1 March 2000.
105. Ibid.
106. Border Clash with Bangladesh; Lok Sabha Unstarred Question No. 1422, to be answered on 31 July 2001.
107. Lok Sabha, Starred Question No. 31, to be answered on 24 July 2001.
108. Border Clash with Bangladesh; Lok Sabha Unstarred Question No. 1422, to be answered on 31 July 2001.
109. Fencing on Tripura Bangladesh Border; Lok Sabha Unstarred Question No. 3490, to be answered on 20 March 2001.
110. Lok Sabha Unstarred Question, No. 4637, to be answered on 19 December 2001.
111. Lok Sabha Starred Question No. 155, to be answered on 30 July 2003.
112. Lok Sabha Unstarred Question No. 4637, to be answered on 19 December 2001.
113. Lok Sabha Unstarred Question, No. 4579, to be answered on 18 December 2002.
114. Rustomji, *Enchanted Frontiers,* p. 109.
115. Ibid.
116. Bhogendro Singh, 'Manipur the Right of Self-determination, a Summary', (n.d.).
117. Anandamohan Singh, *Shillong 1949*, Imphal: M. Akshayakumar Singh,

2005, p. 38

118. Phanjaobam Tarapot, *Bleeding Manipur*, Delhi: Har Anand Publications, 2003, p. 180.
119. Ibid., p. 181.
120. Moamenla Amer, 'Identity and Autonomy Issues in Nagaland' in L. Muhindro Singh, ed., *Conflict Transformation Peace and Ethnic Divide in India's Northeast: The Context of Recent Trends,* Guwahati: Kamakhya Publishing House, 2013, p. 92
121. Benedict Anderson, *Imagined Communities, Reflections on the origin and Spread of Nationalism*; London: Verso, revised ed., 1995, pp. 113–4.
122. Maxwell, *India's China War,* p. 83.
123. Ghosh, *The Himalayan Adventure...*
124. Eric Hobsbawm, 'Introduction: Inventing Traditions', in Eric Hobsbawm and Terence Ranger, eds., *The Invention of Tradition,* Cambridge (reprinted): 1996, p. 4
125. Maxwell, *India's China War,* p. 109.
126. Kosaku Yoshino, ed., *Consuming Ethnicity and Nationalism*; Hawaii: University of Hawaii, 1999.
127. Nehru's letter to the Maharaja of Manipur 1947, pp. 256–8.
128. In a letter to Vallabhbhai Patel, dated 10 May 1949, Debeshwar Sarmah, the President of the Assam Provincial Congress Committee, had warned 'these hills, full of virile people, arms and ammunitions – the latter a legacy of the last war — promise to be a very dangerous breeding ground and springboard for foreign ideologies and interest'. Das, ed., *Sardar Patel's Correspondence 1949-50*; Vol. 8, 1973. pp. 318–9.
129. Menon, *Integration of Indian States*, pp. 297–306.
130. http://www.manipurpolice.org, accessed in December 2008.
131. http://kanglaonline.com/2012/04/police-recruitment-spree-continues/ (accessed on 24 January 2012)
132. http://www.indianexpress.com/news/manipur-to-recruit-2000-male-police-constables/1046965/
133. *Bharatki Loilam Manipur* (Manipur the colony of India); Imphal: Pan Manipuri Youth League, 1993.
134. Prior to 1965 Assam Rifles was under the Ministry of External Affairs, Government of India.
135. Kuldeep Mathur, 'The State and the Use of Coercive Power in India' in *Asian Survey*, Vol. 32, No. 4, April 1992, University of California Press, pp. 337–49.
136. Ibid.
137. http://en.wikipedia.org/wiki/Assam_Rifles as accessed in June 2009.

138. http://www.geocities.com/rpf_manipur/memorandum/map014.html as accessed in January 2008.
139. Submission of Committee on Human Rights (COHR), Manipur on Human Rights Situation in Manipur (India) to OHCHR Concerning the Universal Periodic Review of the Government of India at UN Human Rights Council in April 2008.
140. Law and Order situation in Manipur is a cause of concern; Rajya Sabha Unstarred Question No. 371, to be answered on 25 July 2001.
141. Ministry of Home Affairs, Lok Sabha Unstarred Question No. 6610, to be answered on 9 May 2000.
142. 'The armed forces have gone there in discharge of their responsibility to the unity of India and we cannot, in any fashion, lower their morale (by repealing the AFSPA) or to call into question their relevance in combating insurgency'; Statement of Jaswant Singh on AFSPA 1958; Lok Sabha, 17 August 2004.
143. Repealed on Thursday, 9 December 2004.
144. All India Reporter, 1998; Supreme Court of India, pp. 463–4
145. 'Different Norms' in *Economic and Political Weekly*; Vol. 23, No. 34, Mumbai, 20 August 1988. pp. 1713–4.
146. Gautam Navlakha, 'Growing Indo-US Military' in *Economic and Political Weekly*; Vol. 30, No. 36, Mumbai, 9 September 1995, pp. 2228-9.
147. 'Different Norms...', pp. 1713–4.
148. Ibid.
149. 'Army vs Civil Administration' in *Economic and Political Weekly*; Vol. 24, No. 6, Mumbai, 11 February 1989, pp. 273–4.
150. On Tuesday, 24 January 1989, at 8.30 pm, Assam Rifles raided the Working Women's Hostel in Imphal, searched the chamber of advocate cum human rights activist Nandita Haksar and forcibly took away case files. The Assam Rifles did it arbitrarily without informing the police; Tapan Bose, 'Obstructing Justice' in *Economic and Political Weekly*; Vol. 24, No. 5, Mumbai, 4 February 1989, p. 214.
151. 'Army Rule' in *Economic and Political Weekly,* Vol. 22, No. 40, Mumbai, 3 October 1987, pp. 1670–1.
152. 'Guarding the Guards' in *Economic and Political Weekly*, Vol. 25, No. 23, Mumbai, 9 June 1990, p. 1228.
153. 'Damaged in Body and Mind Source' in *Economic and Political Weekly,* Vol. 25, No. 37, Mumbai, 15 September 1990, p. 2025.
154. Anderson, *The Imagined Communities*, p. 113–4.
155. Statement by the Union Minister of Home Affairs Shivraj V. Patil

in the Lok Sabha, 17 August 2004.

156. Nandini Sundar, *Subaltern and Sovereigns, An Anthropological History of Bastar 1854–1996,* Delhi: Oxford University Press, 1999, p. 4.
157. Ashis Nandy, *The Intimate Enemy, Loss and Recovery of Self Under Colonialism*; New Delhi, Oxford University Press, 2004, p. 3.
158. Edward W. Said, *Covering Islam, How the Media and the Experts Determined, How We See the Rest of the World*; New York: Vintage Books, 1997, p. 10.
159. Ibid., p. 28.
160. D. Volkogonov, *The Psychological War*, Moscow: Progress Publishers, 1986. p. 96.
161. Tanya Reinhart, *Israel/Palestine: How to End the War of 1948*, Delhi: Left World Books, 2003, p. 22.
162. Edward W. Said, *The End of the Peace Process*, New Delhi: Penguin, 2002, p. 147.
163. *Country Reports on Human Rights Practices 2007*, Bureau of Democracy, Human Rights, and Labour, USA, 11 March 2008.

2

Diametrical Nationalisms vis-à-vis Dominant Nationalism

Insurgency for 'sovereignty' is nationalism. It refuted the idea of Indian nationhood. At the same time it would be self-defeating to term Manipur a nation in the light of Nagalim and Zale'ngam assertions. There remains a wide gap between nationhood propaganda and grassroot compositions that are manifested in different psychological expressions. Imposing vertical territorial boundaries along nationalism remains impractical as propaganda maps cannot conform to amalgamated communities having shared material livelihood. Practically, nations had not been formed but that are orchestrated populisms of diametrical nationalisms.

Some of my friends who are waging a protracted war for Manipur sovereignty may refute my proposition. There are reasons for that. Firstly, the idea of a diametric recognizes *status quo* of different nationalisms. But my friends have a different view. For them, there is no legitimate Indian nationalism rooted in Manipur but colonialism. Nagalim and Zale'ngam assertions are not nationalism but internal dissention. There are no diametrical nationalisms but a collusion of colonial rulers and internal dissenter to subjugate and uproot the Manipur nation. Secondly, the idea of modernity of Manipur nationalism is an antithesis to the primordial claim of nationhood in pre 1947 period.

However, I have a different view. Precolonial Asiatic condition was marked by self-sustaining, sparsely inhabited, small tribal dialectical groups and feudal village communities that were not collectively evolved into a stable community. The kingdom was concentrated in the valley which is 1/10th of the present geographical area although fluctuating feudal relations and alliances with tribal chiefs could not be ruled out. Modern means of forging common psychological cohesion such as print, audio, visual media, educational curriculum, centralized administration and economic cohesions were comparatively missing.

In the 1940s there was elite coordination across communities. A constitution was adopted on an experimental basis of five years, federalism was recognized and a responsible government was formed in 1948. However, what was created was a mechanically constituted 'political community' of diverse communities that had not been psychologically forged into a nation. After annexation, the Indian capitalist path did not create the economic foundation necessary for the evolution of peoples into a nation. On the contrary, Manipur elites indulged in sectarianism and communalism in their scramble for political power and wealth. That kept the people divided along different nationalisms. Under similar conditions, both *Nagalim* and *Zale'ngam* remained unfulfilled agenda.

I. SIMULTANEITY IN THE DOMESTICITY

In the post annexation period Manipur nationalism was perpetuated as a result of combined factors. Firstly, there was continuous effort carried out by insurgents to keep alive Manipur nationalism. Secondly, the Indian State's policies towards Manipur were perceived as discriminatory, impoverishing, humiliating and distrusting. Thirdly, the Indian State's commitment to democracy had, in principal terms allowed civil society assertion of democratic rights within the constitutional framework. Initial or prolonged repression and delaying response by the Indian State played off its democratic and peace loving postulations. It created anti-India sentiment and aroused pro-liberation ideology. For want of space, I shall take up only few issues to substantiate the argument. More on ethno-regional assertions has been discussed in my previous book, *Freedom from India.*

(a) Statehood Assertion

On 30 March 1972, the then Governor of Manipur, B.K. Nehru addressed to the Manipur State Assembly that 'this session marks the beginning of a new chapter of full statehood which the people of Manipur have now acquired in full measure of equality with the people of other states in our great country of India.'[1] The phrase 'now acquired in full measure of equality with the people of other states' suggested that Manipur was treated on unequal terms in the preceding decades. There was prolonged injustice. The 'new chapter' was the result of a series of radical and bloody struggles.

Chronologically, Manipur, between 1934 and 1948, had witnessed anti-feudal assertion for responsible government.[2] As the pressure for the adoption of a Manipur constitution and a popular government got intensified the Manipur Durbar gave assent to constitutional reform[3] and King Bodhachandra was compelled to issue orders for the formation of a Constitution Making Committee.[4] The Committee was formed on 20 January 1947 and it was announced on 10 March 1947.[5] After several rounds of meetings on 14, 25, 27, and 29 March 1947, which laid down the principles, the Committee finalized the constitution drafting in July. Manipur Constitution Act was finally adopted on 26 July 1947.[6] In the meanwhile, the Durbar was abolished and administration was entrusted to a newly formed Interim Council, headed by a chief minister and six ministers.[7] However, agitation went on demanding responsible government and the Council was compelled to announce on 23 November that a full responsible government would be established by April 1948. There was some delay but election to the Assembly took place in June-July. The ratio of the MLAs was 30 for the 'valley', 18 for the 'hills', three for the Muslims, one from Commerce and one from Education, thus coming to a total number of 53 MLAs.[8] A non-Congress coalition ministry headed by Praja Shanti Sabha was inaugurated on 18 October 1948. However, the dream and endeavour of the elites to fight elections in order to capture power was threatened by the annexation policy of the Dominion of India.

A dominant section of the elites other than Manipur Congress Party, was against merger with India. The Manipur Socialist Party and Hijam Irabot of the 'Communist Party of Manipur' were against arbitrary annexation by India as they wanted that the people should decide on whether or not to merge.[9] After Irabot went underground in September 1948, he launched armed resistance and a pamphlet called on the people to disobey what he termed 'fascist' government of India.[10] The Praja Shanti Sabha insisted on having a cordial relationship without merging Manipur with India.[11] The memorandum of the PSS, dated 23 March 1949, submitted to the Governor of Assam, argued that Manipur and India were culturally and linguistically different and also pointed out that 'merger' would lead to 'exploitation by the richer states of India.'[12] The hill MLAs, when they met at Imphal on 27 July 1949 under the chairmanship of S. Lunneh[13] strongly protested the policy of MSC to merge with India.[14] A historic public on 3 August 1949 under the joint leadership of Solel Haokip, Habi Mia and Nandalal Sharma opposed the 'merger'. T.C. Tiankham, the then Speaker of Manipur Assembly opposed the 'merger' and pleaded that the Assembly should decide on the issue.[15] A. Daiho was against 'merger' [16] and he sent a telegram to the Governor General of India saying that Mao community in Manipur did not approve merger with India. The protest in North Manipur under the leadership of Daiho was brutally suppressed leading to casualties and killing of a youth by police.[17] The Manipur media covered anti-'merger' voice. The newspaper *Ngashi* (today) consistently argued against the merger and as a result its edition on 13 July was banned by the State.[18] The daily *Bhayabati Patrica* tried to arouse public opinion against merger.[19] An article that appeared in its editorial column on 20 September 1949 reads, '...we are insulting the honour of our forefathers if the consequence of an independent India is going to be the enslavement of Manipur.'[20] An editorial column on 21 September 1949 stated, '...Manipuris do not want to be subservient to another nation, history provides ample proof for that ... What we want to have is...nothing more than self-rule in this land, as we had always since the beginning of history under a king.'[21] There were public protests against the 'merger' "...but an eerie silence prevailed for many months (after 21 September 1949) due to ban imposed against freedom of speech and association (and)... heavy deployment of paramilitary forces.'[22]

There was, however, a section of elites who did not oppose the merger. The Manipur Durbar, as early as 1935, had agreed in principle to demand for at least one full seat in the proposed Council of India[23] In 1939, King Churachand and the Durbar were aware of the proposed formation of the Federation of India. Although indecisive they did not outrightly rejected the federation proposal.[24] By February 1940, it was very clear that the King was willing to join it.[25] On 30 April 1947, the Durbar, accordingly, resolved to 'suggest that a small committee of three (one official, one hill and one valley representatives respectively) should be appointed by the Constitution Making Committee to act as advisors to M.K. Priyobratta Singh who is advisor to the state representatives in the Constitutional Assembly.'[26] As the transfer of power was speeding up, the Durbar felt that it was essential for Manipur to formally join the Constitution Assembly of India without any further delay. According to the Durbar resolution of 4 June 1947, the Durbar did not consider that it was of importance that Manipur should have a Manipur representative. The Durbar advised the King to give consent to the appointment of Mr Guha of Tripura, who was appointed by the Indian leaders to represent Tripura and Manipur in the Constituent Assembly.[27] A few days later, the resolution was passed subsequent to Nehru's letter to the King, dated 22 May 1947[28] rejecting the demand for separate representative in the Constituent Assembly.

What was revealing is that, although the section of elites had chosen federation, the desire to safeguard Manipur's 'regional' identity was paramount. The joint sitting of the Nikhil Manipuri Mahasabha[29] and Manipur Praja Mandal on 5 April 1947 decided, 'Manipur will remain as free Manipur state inside free India.'[30] Consequently, the King signed Standstill Agreement and Instrument of Accession on 2 July and 11 August 1947 respectively. Even if the King and his subordinates were not aware of an 'intrigue' to immediately make him sign the Shillong Accord on 21 September 1949, there can be no denying that they were prepared to merge with India under some favourable conditions. In the meanwhile, a section of elites formed the Manipur State Congress Party on 4 October 1946, and it got affiliated to All India States' Peoples' Conference in 1948.[31]

It worked in close coordination with Indian National Congress and supported the proposed creation of a *Purbanchal* state[32] and the 'merger'.[33] The elitist ambition across parties to enjoy power was turned *topsy-turvy* after the annexation, as Manipur was denied statehood till 1972.

For more than two decades from October 1949 to January 1972 Manipur elites had spearheaded radical assertions for responsible government. They were suppressed. The Manipur Communist Party was phased out after the death of Irabot in 1951; the leaders of Revolutionary Nationalist Party of Manipur were arrested in 1953[34] for articulating 'satyagraha movement and formation of independent buffer state in Manipur under the UN Trusteeship if the demand to establish a responsible government headed by Manipuris was not met within 15 days of the meeting.'[35] Jawaharlal Nehru outrightly rejected the petition by a delegation led by Rishang Keishang in 1953 on the ground that, 'I told them that we did not think any such step (statehood) was desirable at this stage and that probably it would lead to all kinds of difficulties.'[36] On 11 April 1955, the Indian Praja Socialist Party leader Dr Ram Monohar Lohia and six other Manipuri were arrested for organizing a meeting in regards to the demand for statehood.[37]

Denial of democratic rights had developed hatred, mistrust, and radical assertions. A climax of radicalism was occurred when the then Prime Minister Indira Gandhi visited Imphal on 23 September 1969. According to eyewitness, 'There was uproar ... There was pelting of stones, lathi charge and firing... buses went up in flames on 23 September 1969.'[38] Maloy recounts the scene

> '... the truth hit us in the form of stones and assorted non-lethal missiles ... The milling crowd, mostly women and youths, tried to obstruct the VIP cavalcade and a small group surged forward ostensively to submit a memorandum ... R.D. Kapur, a young IAS officer, dispersed the hostile mob with another round of baton charge. Police fired from their muskets and the crowd retaliated by burning the jeep of the IFP and killing a CRPF sepoy. The situation could be controlled only by imposition of curfew and by deploying the Army, which carried out flag march in the capital town and the adjacent localities.'[39]

In the mid-1970s, an Eight Parties Statehood Demand Coordinating Body announced a civil disobedient movement from 17 August. It boycotted Republic Day celebration.[40] Many were injured in police repression and about 160 volunteers were arrested.[41]

Examples are many. Suffice it to say that the demand for statehood 'was the single major issue which agitated the Manipuri mind most. But there was nobody in Delhi sensitive enough to gauge the depth and intensity of their feelings.'[42] In the words of Constantine '(the years) were punctuated by sullen resentment at the loss of her political status.'[43] Many lost faith in the Indian bourgeoisie. The decades were also perplexed by a sense of humiliation and injury caused by central legislations such as the Armed Forces Special Powers Act 1958, the creation of Nagaland State on 1 December 1963,[44] violent suppression of the hunger march in 1965, Manipur integrity issues in the 1960s, economic underdevelopment, corruption of the Indian bureaucrats, et cetra. In the words of Maloy,

> the statehood agitation had entered a crucial stage. The ranks of the All Manipur Students' Union,[45] the All Party Statehood Demand Committee and other organizations[46] were infiltrated by the elements of the Meitei State Committee, Consolidation Committee of Manipur, United National Liberation Front, Revolutionary Government of Manipur, Pan Mongolian Movement, the Pan Mongolian Youth League and all reckonable major and minor political forces.[47]

Therefore, by the time the statehood was granted in 1972, there were many in Manipur who, by the mid-1960s, had joined insurgency. According to UNLF, the statehood was too little and too late for a 'generation of Manipuris (who were) brought up without their parents' wishful thinking about India's freedom struggle but wiser from their own bitter experiences of the Indian rule.'[48]

(b) Xenophobia

There was Manipuri xenophobia manifested in targeting the British and the Mayangs during British colonial period. After the 1949 annexation, the targets were Mayangs in particular and Bangladeshi, Nepalese, and Myanmarese immigrants in general. Conceptually, the use of the term xenophobia may be debateable. Firstly, the term is inappropriate since Mayangs and Manipuris are 'Indians'. Secondly, the notion of 'insider' and 'outsider' operates at community levels in Manipur. The Kuki-Thadou rebellion (1917–19), the Zeliangrong movement (1929–30s), Kuki-Naga Clash (1992–96), et cetra, had illustrated fear for and hatred against perceived outsiders. But these events are being interpreted as having occurred within Manipur—therefore, an internal issue. If these are 'internalized', then Manipuri hatred against the Mayangs must also be internalized within India's domesticity and cannot be termed as xenophobia. Thirdly, Manipuri assertion against perceived foreigners suffers from an inability to detect foreigners who are ethnically assimilated and enjoy safeguards.[49] Therefore, the term xenophobia sounds irrelevant. However, I have used the term Manipuri xenophobia from the perspective of those who termed Mayangs as foreigners.

Xenophobia is primarily conceived on the basis of presumed threat of unrestraint immigration and perceptions about immigrants' control of economy, polity, and cultural hegemony. Xenophobic expressions are manifested in: (a) pre-annexation agitations of targeting Mayangs, (b) post annexation anti foreigners' assertion and demand for Inner Line Permit System, (c) the Meetei religio-cultural revivalist movement, (d) cultural restrictions and physical targeting of outsiders. For the purpose of clarity, it is worth mentioning that Mayang, before British rule, was a generic term used when referring to Bengalis, Cacharis, and a section among Assamese. During British rule, it meant British Indian subjects from 'mainstream' India. In the second half of the twentieth century, the term Mayang covered almost all the Indians except those who were regarded as 'indigenous' of the Northeastern states.

Chronologically, Manipur had foreigners' policy before and after British rule. During British rule, Mayangs were settled in the British Reserves as traders and were subjected to foreigners' tax. They were suspected as colonial agents and were the prime targets of attacks during the Bazaar Boycott in 1920 and the Second Women's War in 1939. During the post-Second World War period, Manipur was the passage of Mayang exodus from Myanmar.[50] During this period, apprehension about Mayang control of economy was also growing among a section of Manipuri entrepreneurs. As a result, the Durbar was 'not prepared to allow (virtual monopoly of trade to the exclusion of state subjects) in future... Manipuris should be given an opportunity of taking up the lease (of the shops in the British reserves if the foreigners had returned to Manipur after the Second World War) if necessary allotting alternative sites in exchange to the previous lessee.'[51] In the meanwhile, in order to check population influx, the Manipur Naturalisation Act in 1947 was enacted to identify 'alien or foreigners means a person who is not a state subject.'[52] The intention of the King and the Manipur State Council to continue with the permit system against the Mayang was emphasized in a correspondence letter sent to British Political Agent on 2 July 1947.[53] Accordingly, the Manipur State Council passed a resolution on 19 September 1947 to retain permit system.[54]

However, the Indian State had enforced an immigration policy to permit unrestraint entry of Mayangs in Manipur. On 25 August 1949, few weeks before the controversial Shillong Accord was signed, P.C. Deb, the then reform officer issued a notice for provisional enrolment of Mayang refugees in the electoral roll of Manipur.[55] Few days before the annexation; Himmat Singh, in his inaugural speech to the Members of the Advisory Council of Manipur at the First Session of the Council on 9 October 1950 ordered that 'people of other parts of India can no longer be treated as "foreigners" and discriminatory treatment against them is neither possible nor wise.'[56] On 18 November 1950, a year after 'annexation', the permit system for entry into and exit from Manipur was abolished.[57] Opinions to retain permit system so that outsiders come in with an account and scrutiny[58] were turned down.

After annexation immigrants began flooding due to the absence of appropriate law to regulate entry of 'outsiders'. The Foreigners (Protected Areas) Order, 1958 which did not restrict the entry of Nepalese had led to unrestraint immigration of Nepalese who subsequently 'firmly settled in colonies in several parts of Manipur.'[59] After the introduction of military regime in Myanmar in 1962-63 and pro-democratic uprising in August 1988 several Myanmar refugees infiltrated through the southern borders in Churachandpur and Chandel Districts.[60] Data analysis of population growth suggests that there had been drastic high in the decadal growth rate after

1951.[61] According to the UCM's report growth of migrants population during the period 1961- 2001 was: 1,96,849 (1961-1971); 1,28,042 (1971-1981); 1,79,566 (1981-1991); and 2,200,031 (1991-2001). The accumulated number of migrants during the period was 5, 38,887 and the total number of birth was estimated at 1,65,601. The total number of migrants was estimated at 7,04,488,[62] thereby, constituting about 31 per cent of the total population of Manipur.[63] This is considered a threat.

The increase in the population growth increased pressure on land. The density of population increased from 13 persons per square kilometre in 1901 to 26 persons in 1951, and 103 in 2001.[64] Although the census report does not present actual size of habitable areas during the corresponding period of the survey, it is quite sure that the five hill districts that comprised 20,089 square kilometres (90 per cent of geographical area of Manipur) were mostly hilly and infertile. According to Sunder 'the limited area of cultivable land, poor quality of soil, rugged topography, forestry and ravine explain the (sparsely habitation) of population in the hilly tracts. In the hill areas, however, there are thick clusters of population in wider valleys, while steep slopes and scarps are practically uninhabitable.'[65] Therefore an increase in the population had enormous pressure on the inhabitable villages, towns and resources. The Imphal Valley (2,238 square kilometres) was the backbone of food production and other economic activities. An increase in the population in the valley reduced areas under economic production. In this situation immigration was considered a threat.

The immigrants include besides Mayangs, others from Myanmar, Mizoram, Nepal and Bangladesh. However, anti-immigration sentiment was being used to conjure up anti-colonial sentiment directed against Mayangs. There are reasons for this. In the context of Assam, the solution to the 'foreigners' issue lies mostly in assimilation' and in the sealing off of the borders.[66] In Manipur it was difficult to identify and deport Myanmerese, Mizo, and a section of Nepalese immigrants, as they were ethnically assimilated with friends and relatives.[67] But Mayang immigrants, including Bangladeshis whose looks were Mayangs, remained unassimilated ethnically and culturally. Rustomji's understanding that 'the influx ...

of even a handful of families of alien culture has an immediate impact, psychological as much as physical, on the indigenous population' is applicable in Manipur.'[68] On the other hand, Mayangs were active in politics, administration, economy, and the military. As a result, anti-Mayang xenophobic expression was motivated by interplaying combinations of (a) political, (b) economic, (c) racial, and (d) cultural perceptions. The political and economic shall be discussed at length in different sections. I shall first analyse anti-Mayang racial and cultural perceptions.

(a) Culturally, in the post-annexation period, there was Meetei revivalist movement to reconvert from religious belief and cultural practises that were deemed Mayang oriented. The revivalist initiatives of Apokpa Marup (in Assam) by Naoriya Phulo since 1930 had a profound impact in Manipur. In 1945, a resolution to 'discard the prevailing religion (Hinduism), which is borrowed religion, and try our best to revive the traditional religion of the Meeteis that is associated with us from time immemorial,'[69] was followed by formation of Manipur State Meetei Marup on 14 May. Thereafter several revivalist organizations were formed to 'revive cultural heritage of Meetei people, to do research in the ancient history and other literature, to revive Meetei script, to worship and chant religious hymns in the mother tongue.'[70] The movement intensifed from the mid-1960s and revivalists played important roles in language assertion and the Kangla Fort restoration agitations. Revivalism provided food for cultural nationalism and added to the prevailing distrust, fear, and hatred against the Mayang.

Coincidentally, the Indian State was adopting a cultural policy that was negatively perceived as imposing Mayang hegemony. New names of streets, buildings, public places connected to the Mayangs such as Gandhi Avenue, INA complex, Indira Park, Nehru Dance Academy, Nehru Hospital, and Luxmi Bazaar were coming up. Bollywood movies and Hindi songs were ousting and undermining the growth of Manipur films and songs. Institutionalized chorus or rhymes in schools and official rituals were Mayang originated 'Jana Gana Mana' or 'Vande Matram'[71] that had no connection with Manipur. These were perceived as humiliating and insult as these were coincidental with the Meetei perception of subversion of 'indigenous' script, language, culture, religion and identity to Mayang cultural hegemony.[72] It coincided with the feeling of deprivation and loss of sovereignty under Mayang rule. Anti-colonial discourse was charging any form of relation with the Mayangs as a colonial relation. Indian 'National Education Programme' was perceived as intellectually impoverishing as the educational curriculum did not include local history, folktales, folklores and moral subjects. Rumours were widespread about the Indian State's pogrom in the name of counter-insurgency[73] to impose Mayang hegemony. All these semblances of Mayang hegemony were contradictory to what Rustomji had thought about for a different context: 'it is only if they can be convinced that their culture and way of life are not in jeopardy and will not be undermined by alien pressures that there is hope for a peaceful and secure frontier'.[74]

(b) Economically, the gap between daily experience of 'underdevelopment', expectation of economic security and progress, and the Indian State's propaganda of welfare state was widened. Agriculture was not improving, and everything ranging from food to other essential commodities was imported. Economic decisions and policies were taken by the Central Government. At the market the Mayangs were enjoying monopoly and in the service sectors all the high posts were occupied by Mayangs. Subsequent growth of competition between Manipuris and Mayangs for control of the economy and political power became serious concern. Day-to-day subordination experiences in the market, bureaucracy, clerical work and the labour market made many to feel insecurity and humiliation under Mayang hegemony.

(c) Politically, there were negative perceptions about community background and relations of power. Political decisions by the Parliament were bent on Mayang interest and the Indian *statute* was derived from Mayang. Decisions and laws were enforced with an attitude of patronizing condescension, with a strong military presence through the Governor, himself a Mayang, who was assisted by a class of bureaucracy numerically dominated by the Mayang. A corresponding figure of Chief Commissioners, Lieutenant Governors, Governors, Director General of Police and Chief Secretaries revealed a predominance of Mayangs. On the other hand, the armies and paramilitary forces dominantly composed of Mayangs had been perpetrating crimes with impunity. The sense of the loss of self-honour, dignity, peace, and livelihood to enemy India, that is, the motherland of Mayangs who belonged to a different cultural identity, was ill-conceived and circulated continuously.

Against this backdrop, Maloy in the late 1960s, noticed that Manipuris were abusing any visible 'mainland' Indian as Mayangs (outsiders) and they were highly suspicious of all outsiders.[75] Constantine, in the late 1970s, says, 'Mayang, however, in current Manipuri parlance speaks more of the injured and exploited feeling of Manipur, real or imagined.'[76] In the 1970s, anti-Mayang propaganda was widespread in print media. The Pan Manipur Youth League, carried in its journal *Lamyanba* series of anti-colonial discourses identifying India with Mayang. Pre-existing allegorical phrase such as *Kari kwakno, Mayang kwakne* (Which crow, Mayang crow) was used to draw attention against Mayang immigration to 'blur our identity and rule over us.'[77] In 1988, Nameirakpam Bisheswar, the founder leader of People's Liberation Army, after retirement, in his booklet entitled *Manipur gi neta anouba Santidas Gosaini* (new politician of Manipur is a Santidas Gosai), drew a similarity between cunning and selfish Mayangs and 'puppet' Manipur politicians. Former member of People's Revolutionary Party of Kangleipak, Paonam Labanggo Mangang drew a linkage between politics and culture and warned that Mayang immigration would speed up Indianisation.[78] Anti-Mayang xenophobic polemics were found in the booklets of United National Liberation Front[79] and the memorandums of the Revolutionary People's Front submitted to the UN in 1996.[80]

Among civil societies, the All Manipur Students' Union[81] and All Manipur Students' Coordinating Committee launched anti-foreigner agitation on 15 February 1980.[82] The State repression led to casualty and killing of agitators on 17 April.[83] Due to strong pressure, the State at two rounds of meetings with agitators on 22 July and 5 August, promised to initiate identification, detection and deportation of foreigners before the end of 1980. The promise was not fulfilled. Repeated assurances made on 9 November 1994 to quell agitation on the same issue in the year, which reads, 'the

Agreement signed between the AMSU and the AMSCOC and the Government of Manipur on 22 July 1980 shall be followed in letter and spirit keeping in view of the provisions of the Foreigners Act 1946 and other relevant laws' was not materialized.

In the early 2000s, ideological underpinning to anti-immigrant campaign, which took the form of demand for implementation of Inner Line Permit System, was provided by United Committee Manipur's compilation entitled *Influx of Migrants into Manipur: A Threat to the Indigenous Ethnic People* (2005) and Sapamcha Jadumani's book entitled *Kangleipakta Inner Line Permit System Amasung Masigi Eehou* (2011). An ILP Demand Committee, to defend a 'homeland' for the people of Manipur by restraining immigration in general and by prohibiting the 'outsiders' from purchasing land in particular, was formed in 2006. ILP became a burning issue during and after the 10th Manipur Assembly General Election. On 5 July 2012 the Committee was superseded by a Joint Committee on Inner Line Permit (ILP) of several organizations.[84] The ILP movement achieved a symbolic landmark on 13 July 2012 when Manipur State Assembly passed a resolution to extend and adopt Bengal Eastern Frontier Regulation 1873 with necessary changes and to urge the Indian State to comply the same. But the resolution had not been complied with.

Insurgents took up xenophobic assertions. In 2000, Revolutionary People's Front imposed a complete ban on screening of Bollywood movies and listening to Hindi songs from 12 September onwards. Xenophobic assertion revealed terrorizing assaults in 2006, 2008, and 2009.

Firstly, on 16 August 2006, a bomb was lobbed into the crowd which were congregating inside the compound of International Society of Krishna Consciousness, Imphal to celebrate the Hindu festival Krishna Janmasthami.[85] At least five persons, including the International Director of ISKCON, Swami Damodara were fatally wounded and several others were injured. No one had claimed responsibility for the bomb attack.

Secondly, on 17 and 18 March 2008 fifteen Mayang labourers were killed in several parts of Manipur.[86] Stickers attached to the bodies read 'go back to your home state.' No one had claimed responsibility for the killing. In response to the killing, RPF moved away slightly from its position as mentioned in the 1996 Memorandum and the 2000 ban, and condemned the killing on the ground that 'our fight is against the Indian Government of India, not Indians.'[87] However, the same year, RPF attempted a policy of encouraging Manipuri business agents so as to do away with the Mayang control of the market. Coming back to the point, Kanglei Yawol Kanna Lup refuted its role in the March killing. However, it said 'though the action of killing the migrant workers is wrong, there is the need to drive back the (Indian or Aryan) migrant workers.'[88]

Thirdly, there was killing of Mayangs in sporadic manner in March 2009. Although no one had claimed the killing, a joint statement of KYKL and UNLF under the banner of Joint Coordination Committee, dated 5 April 2009 reads,

> the mass influx of outsiders today poses a threat to the identity of the people of Manipur (therefore) to save the people from the effects of influx of outsiders as well as Indianisation process and promote co-operation and unity as well as to neutralise the culture of corruption encouraged by India and try to build a new society...(there will be torching of) vehicles bringing in such outsiders, awarding harsh punishments to the drivers transporting them as well as expelling the outsiders.[89]

Fourthly, in 2012, the Coordination Committee of seven (now six) underground organizations asked outsiders to leave Manipur by December 31. In October, it published list of outsiders (particularly Mayangs) living in rents and list of landlords renting rooms to them. It appealed landlords not to rent room to outsiders. The dateline, however, was not effective. On the other hand, cultural policing has been continued. In 2012, a young woman actor, Hijam Bala, was temporarily banned by CorCom from acting in Manipur films became she had acted in a Bollywood movie. In April 2013 RPF summoned the woman singer, Madhuri, and music director, Dina Oinam, to seek clarification on their recording a Hindi album.

In summing up, stereotype was widespread that Manipuris were gradually becoming the pathetic minority in Manipur. Increasing immigration of Mayangs was perceived as a policy of population grafting or a design to dump foreigners in Manipur to fulfil complete Indianization of Manipur and to establish Mayang hegemony.[90] It was interpreted from a racist perspective. Negative remarks about Mayangs became a point of reference for a desperate section of the population looking for an explanation of the cause of poverty and inferiority complexes in various aspects of livelihood. The Mayang was the primary target of attack in the anti-colonial discourse.

II. INTERNATIONALIZING THE DOMESTICITY

An excerpt from the Manipur Administration Order (MAO) 1949 reads;

> Manipur administration order 1949 issued under Notification No. 219-P in the Gazette of India dated the 15th Oct, 1949, incorporates the provision that as from midday of Saturday the 15th Oct, 1949, the Ministers of Manipur State shall cease to function and the legislature will stand dissolved..[91]

After about fifty years, a solidarity statement under the title 'Boycott India's Republic Day', released by insurgent organizations in 2001 reads;

> ... As a symbolic rejection of India's legitimacy to rule the Region through its enforced Constitution and sharing the brunt of brutality of Indian Occupation Forces against its peoples, (it has been decided) to boycott India's Republic Day in the whole region and also to call a general Strike on that day. ... Overthrow Indian Colonial Rule!... 'Forge Unity at All Levels!'

Two years earlier, in 1999, a news report reads;

> Like in the past this year too October 15 was observed by various political groups in Manipur as a protest day. It was in 1949 on this day when Manipur was formally merged with India, now termed as 'annexation' of Manipur by the Indian State by these different groups.[92]

After about a decade, in 2009, insurgents imposed a genral strike on Republic Day. As a result the official celebration was confined in the Kangla Fort. Many State employees did not attend the function, either in support of the strike or because of fear or simply to bunk duty. In retaliation, the State suspended six school principals and a teacher on the charges of failure to participate in the celebration and failing to let their students participate in the Republic Day Parade.[93] The suspension order was widely protested. The boycott, the suspension order, and the protest opened up an unprecedented public debate on the relation between the State, its ritual, and the democratic rights of the people to either attend or not attend the Republic Day celebrations. The question is, should nationalism be spontaneous or people be penalized for not adhering to certain prescribed rituals and norms of orchestrated populism?

What is relevant for the present discussion is that the excerpts cited above informed the vexed cycle of symbolic assertion and resistance amidst diametrical nationalisms to justify action against one another. Insurgency efforts were primarily to articulate anti-colonial discourse, to organize people, and also to promote international propaganda. The core of the anti-colonial discourse comprises; (a) annexation debate and (b) the underdevelopment theory. This shall be discussed at length.

(1) Annexation Debate

The success story of peaceful Indian integration has been counteracted by the anti-colonial discourse. An annexation debate has been raised. The communist armed resistance in 1949–51; insurgency from the 1960s, polemical journals from the 1970s, and civil society pamphlets and campaigns particularly from the 1990s continuously keep alive annexation debate. From the 1970s, Nari Rustomji's memoir *Enchanted Frontier* has been an important source of construing annexation. The annexation debate achieved a milestone in 1993 when a three day 'national' seminar resolved that the '(Indo-Manipuri Shillong Accord) signed by and between the (King) of Manipur and the representative of the Dominion of India on the 21 September, 1949 did not have any legality and constitutional validity.'[94] It paved the way to widespread circulation of forced annexation polemics. The release of a memoir entitled *Shillong 1949* written by Mayengbam Anandamohan in 2005, the only living person from Manipur who in the capacity of ADC to the King had taken part in the Shillong 'debacle', added substantiations to the idea of forced annexation.

The anti-colonial discourse invalidated the Shillong Accord of 21 September 1949. The Manipur Administration Order (MAO) has been interpreted as coercive, illegal, unconstitutional, and undemocratic. The MAO, applicable to a foreign territory only since the order was issued under extra provincial jurisdiction Act 1947 or Foreign Jurisdiction Act 1947,[95] was considered a colonial instrument of subjugation.[96] The Stand Still Agreement (2 July 1947) and the Instrument of Accession (11 August 1947) had been attributed colonial meaning. Firstly, the Standstill Agreement was imposed under extreme threat by Lord Mountbatten[97] and under the premise of the colonial Indian Arbitration Act 1899. It recognized the Indian State as the legitimate successor of the British Crown. Therefore, it was a colonial continuity and undemocratic. Secondly, the Instrument of Accession placed Manipur at the mercy of the Indian big bourgeoisies by acceding currency, external affairs, defence, communication, et cetra. It was signed with pre-independent India that did not have treaty-making power as on 11 August 1947. It was executed under 'limited sovereignty' extended to Manipur under British control and there was absence of free and informed consent of the peoples.[98] It was inapplicable to independent Manipur in 1949 on the ground that 'by a proviso of Section 7(1) (b) and (c) of the Indian Independence Act, 1947, whatever prejudicial relation Manipur had with the British Government before independence had been denounced and repudiated or any obligation arising out of the Instrument of Accession were washed away with the promulgation of the Manipur State Constitution Act, 1947 and the Indian Independence Act, 1947.'[99]

Similarly, the Shillong Accord has been interpreted as signed under coercion and misinformation. The King has been shown as an innocent person quite unprepared for the treacherous plots by an invincible Indian expansionist force.[100] Such picturization of the emasculated King at Shillong has been aimed at defending the King against any theory that would undermine monarchy as an institution responsible for betraying Manipur. Depicting the King as a dupe of Indian authority did not necessarily mean a defense of monarchy but substantiation with facts of the illegality of annexation. Three arguments had been put forward.

Firstly, it has been argued that the Accord is not binding to Manipur since the people or their representatives were not signatories to it. This has been based on the formulation that Manipur, at the time of annexation, was enjoying popular sovereignty. The King did not represent Manipur when he signed the Accord. The King, as per the provisions of the Manipur Constitution 1947, was just a nominal head and had no legal or constitutional power to enter into any treaty with any foreign power in 1949.[101] The King admitted it to the Indian representative. When he signed the Shillong Accord, neither was he a deputed delegate nor had there been any formal approval or ratification of the Accord by the government of Manipur.[102]

Secondly, it has been propounded that Manipur and British India were two different entities and that the lapse of British paramountcy in 1947 had further lapsed all forms of treaty obligation between the two. The popular government formed in 1948 was manifestation of 'sovereign people's republic.'[103] The Indian State had bypassed the Manipur Constitution and had violated international standards such as UNGA Resolution 1514 (XV) of 1960 which states that 'integration' or 'merger' should be the result of the freely expressed wishes of the territory's peoples acting with full knowledge of the change in their status. The MAO has been shown as violating Article 2(4) of the UN Charter, the UN GA Resolution 2625 of 1970[104] and other international norms. The Manipur Assembly had never ratified the Accord but was arbitrarily dissolved. Civil societies called the action imperialistic and colonial.[105]

Thirdly, it has been argued that there had been procedural loopholes that had left scope for revoking the Accord. There had been two loopholes.

(a) The Accord 'which partook of the nature of a treaty between two sovereign states of Manipur and India has got to be ratified, and it can have no binding effect unless it has been ratified.'[106] The failure to ratify it suggests that the right of the Manipur people to self-determination was not exercised in 1949, or thereafter, and that Manipur's right to self-determination had not been extinguished.[107]

(b) The Manipur Constitution Act 1947 had not been amended in order to suit the MAO, nor had it been repealed.[108] The United Committee Manipur reaffirmed to the President of India in 2002 that the Manipur State Constitution Act, 1947 still had legal validity.[109] As action was taken neither by the President for a period of three years nor by the Parliament under Article 239 and Article 245 (1) of the Constitution of India, the Manipur State Constitution Act 1947 cannot be deemed to have been repealed.[110] All laws existing in Manipur before annexation have been considered continuing without repealing or amendment.[111]

To conclude, annexation has been shown as a corollary of subversion of sovereignty, suspension of democracy, loss of territorial rights, and extinction of national identity. Extinction of national identity has been explained by referring to the devaluation of the political status of Manipur to a Part C state,[112] muzzling of the press and banning of all public meetings,[113] deployment of armed forces to suppress communist revolution; imposition of Armed Forces (Special Powers) Act in 1958, militarization and State terrorism; communal divisive policy; misrule of puppet regimes since 1972; and increasing pauperization due to underdevelopment.

2. Underdevelopment Theory

Since the early 1960s, liberation discourse has been articulating the idea of an underdeveloped Manipur. Initially, it was largely oral and lacked systematic formulation. In the late 1970s and early 1980s, the journal *Resistance* and PLA's publication *Dawn* raised the issue of Indian subversive economic policy in Manipur. The formulation gained some momentum in the mid-1990s through the print media. Two of the pioneering documents that advanced the underdevelopment theory in this period were a propaganda booklet entitled *Why Manipuris Fight for Right to National Self-Determination* published by the United National Liberation Front (UNLF) Manipur in 1996 and the memorandum of Revolutionary People's Front submitted to the United Nations Decolonization Committee in 1996. The central arguments of underdevelopment articulated in these two documents were:

According to UNLF,

> "the so-called development activities undertaken by India from the late (1960s) onwards were naturally conditioned by considerations of India's security and territorial integrity ... With its vast untapped natural

> and mineral resources, with its perennial rivers, the Indo-Burma region has the potential to generate huge surplus power and become a well-developed region. But India's colonial rule has ensured that it remained the least developed and the most backward region thereby making it totally dependent on India."[114]

According to RPF,

> the national liberation movement in Manipur has strongly endorsed the view that Manipur has socio-economically and politically been exploited by the Indian colonial regime...The people of Manipur have been deprived of their inalienable birth-right to determine their political and socio-economic status on their own. They have been deprived of their inalienable right to exploit their natural resources as per their self-determination[115]

There were ideas, comments, writings and prints from different circles that were indirectly conforming to or providing data inputs to these two documents. Gradually, the underdevelopment theory interplayed with growing apprehension about capitalist projects that had brought or were likely to bring displacements and destructions. To be more precise, underdevelopment theory argues for constraints of capitalism in Manipur as colonial manifestation. The syndromes of the constraints are being discussed as: (a) correlation between capitalist exploitation and militarization leading to violation of human rights in the name of 'national security', (b) gradual decline in productions and lack of State incentives to improve the means of production and the productive forces, (c) increasing dependence on import, leading to drain of wealth, (d) geometrical rise in the number of poor and growth of criminals and illicit trades leading to social malaise, (e) predominance of corruption and bribery as a means of wealth accumulation leading to further degradation of the moral economy and political consciousness.

Economic crisis contradicts the growth postulated by the State. Observing 1972 as a turning point towards political autonomy and economic development, the then Governor of Manipur, B.K. Nehru, in 1972, stressed, 'in its march for progress and development, Manipur has made strides for the last few years through the Five Year Plans, and a good deal has been achieved towards creating infra-structural facilities.'[116] He argued for a successful State initiative in achieving gradual economic growth after 1949. Uncritical reading of State reports would presume steady economic growth in the second half of the twentieth century. The reports said that, under the Indian Five Years Plans the growth in the number of towns was from one in 1951 to 33 in 2001. Similarly, comparative analysis of the Five Years Plans revealed a rise in the gross estimates of plan outlay, particularly after the fourth Five Years Plan. According to the Planning Commission of India, plan outlay for Manipur was increased from Rs 2 crores, to Rs 6 crores, to Rs 12.9 crores, and finally Rs 30.25 crores in the first four Five Years Plans consecutively.

During the post-1972 period, Manipur benefitted from economic programmes of the North East Council. An increase in fund inflow from the Centre became apparent by 1980, for example Central assistance to Manipur increased from Rs 286.51 crore in the Sixth Plan, to Rs 613.44 crore in the Seventh Plan, to Rs 1,230.03 crores in the Eighth Plan, to Rs 2,493.61 (agreed) in the Ninth Plan and to Rs 2,166.42 (projected) in the Tenth Plan.[117] Plan outlay for Manipur was dramatically increased from Rs 30.25 crores in the Fourth Five Years Plan to Rs 430.00 crores in the Seventh Five Years Plan (1985-1990). It was further increased to Rs 1787.01 crores (Expenditure) in the Ninth Five Years Plan and further to Rs 2804.00 crores (Outlay) in the Tenth Five Years Plan.

Manipur has been enjoying the status of Special Areas, that is, being strategically important and backward it has been funded and managed by various institutions such as North Eastern Development Finance Corporation Limited, established on 9 August 1995, and Ministry of Development of Northeastern Region, established in September 2001. Apart from receiving investment under Border Area Development Programme, funds and grants had been allocated through Non-Lapsable Central Pool of Resources. By the time the Indo-ASEAN Car Rally for promotion of international trade was held in November 2004, Manipur had been an economic focus of India's 'Look East Policy'. The State projected positive growth for Manipur in the North Eastern Region Vision 2020.

Underdevelopment theory, however, contradicted the State version. It interpreted the Shillong Accord of 1949 as the threshold to Indian colonial rule. The interpretation has been centred on three interrelated logics: firstly, loss of political autonomy leading to loss of control over the economy; secondly, loss of self-reliance leading to perpetual subordination under colonial economic system and; thirdly, projection of economic growth in a sovereign nation state. The analysis may be categorized into: (a) perceptions of economic welfare, (b) loss of natural resources, (c) agrarian question (d) industrial decline, (e) marginal peasants and workers, and (f) on class contradiction and revolution

(a) Perception of economic welfare

The overall economic condition has been considered precarious and unfavourable to growth. Firstly, economic welfare is a material condition founded on productive utilization of natural resources and human skills. Productive production is the precondition of creating and supplying effective demands. Secondly, production constitutes the backbone of political economy, and as such, good governance is a precondition to achieve it. These two understandings interrelate polity and economy. Under democracy, people expect the State to maintain good governance and economic welfare of the people. This expectation has not been fulfilled by the Indian bourgeoisie, as their primary interest has been concentration and centralization of capital through subjugation, exploitation, and oppression.

The underdevelopment theory has been generating the golden age myth about precolonial sovereignty and self-reliant economy. Nostalgia about a pristine precolonial period, when people had not been dependent on external funding and imports for subsistence has been circulated. During the British colonial period, per capita income of Manipur was the highest in the Northeast and also above the all India average. The number of small-scale establishment was encouraging. The number of textile establishments was 33,927, while that of non-textile establishments was 608 in 1951. Although geographical isolation was a constraint on development, the prospect of 'high-value-production' rather than 'high-volume-production' could not be ruled out.[118] 'The state had surplus production in agriculture, handloom and handicraft sector were also fairly developed.'[119] However, after 1949, a decline had set in and people had not improved beyond the level of subsistence.[120]

It has been further argued that Manipur would have had tremendous economic growth during Central rule from 1949 to 1972 had it not been for the discrimination and super profit agenda of the Indian bourgeoisies. According to the United Committee Manipur, during this period, various mega industrial establishments costing thousands of crores of rupees to the Consolidated Fund of India were set up in mainland India.[121] However, till the Fifth Five-Year Plan, Manipur got Rs 1.55, 6.25, 12.88, 30.15 crores, respectively, that is, too little for development.[122] And the 'corrupt' Indian bureaucrats did not fully utilize it for any initial stage of development.[123]

According to the report of the Institute for Human Development, New Delhi, Manipur, as late as 2005, continued to be largely underdeveloped and in regressing agrarian condition with a weak industrial sector and inflated services sector. Analysing growth and interstate disparities in India would reveal that Manipur, which had a low-ranking economy in the period beginning with 1960–1 had continued to be in lower rank throughout the period till 1995–6.[124] In developmental and fiscal deficit, 'the share of the state in the All India Net Domestic Product remained stagnant at 0.2 per cent almost throughout the period 1991-2 to 2001–2.'[125] Till 1993, Manipur had a deficit of Rs 158 crore.[126] As a result, Manipur's own resources in the Tenth Five Years Plan was Rs 362.42 crores[127]. Per Capita Income of Manipur in 1980–1 (at 1993-94 Prices) stood at Rs 4,901 against all India income of Rs 5,966; and correspondingly at Rs 5,811 against Rs 8,759 in 1993–4; Rs 8,963 against Rs 12,496 in 2001–2, respectively.

According to the 55th Round of the National Sample Survey Organization's (July 1999 to June 2000), though the poverty ratio had declined, the number of poor had increased from 5.86 lakhs in 1973–4 to 7.19 lakhs in 1999-2000.[128] The NSSO 61st Round survey report showed a drastic decline in the number of poverty to 3.95 lakhs in 2004–5. But the decline estimate was based on new methodology of poverty estimation and didn't calculate actual number of poor persons whose access to basic requirements of subsistence has been fast declining.

'Unemployment' problem among the youth had been increasing

beyond controllable stage.[129] Financial position of Manipur had been considerably weakening and it had resulted in the State treasuries remaining open for a few days only in each month. 'Many have not got their wages for many months'.[130] The Manipur Rifles had attempted a coup in 1999 for delaying their monthly salary for months. In 2002, the State could no longer discharge debt-service burden.[131] In 2005, out of the total number of 356,193 households, 115,600 households were living on the Below Poverty Line.[132]

(b) Loss of natural resources

The underdevelopment theory has argued that the relation of production was designed to serve the interest of the Indian bourgeoisie. It argued that there had been gradual loss of control over the natural resources (including land). Resources had been regularly deregulated and transferred for private use to outsider agencies and corporate bodies for economic exploitation without the consent of the people.[133] Natural resources had no longer been absolutely managed by the people. 'Forests are stripped off, water bodies destroyed by pollution, hydro-electricity generation projects and neglect of maintenance.'[134] At the turn of the twenty-first century, the Indian State began to execute series of controversial construction projects such as dams, office buildings, military camps, institutions, oil exploration and drilling. Many projects were protested for arbitrary enforcement at gunpoint, lack of transparency and public accountability, suppression of public opinion, corruption, mismanagement, and destructive tendencies. Examples cited were the Loktak Hydro Electricity Power Project, the construction of Mapithel Dam, Tipaimukh Dam, Capital Complex, National Institute of Technology, Airport Expansion and Oil Exploration and Drilling.

What is relevant for the present discussion is that at the turn of the century the notion of 'developmental aggression' has been pitted against the notion of 'sustainable development'. It has been construed that 'developmental aggression' represented capitalist material interest imposed through militarization under repressive laws whereas 'sustainable development' stood for public demand to meet the needs of the present without compromising the ability of future generations to meet their own needs. In the unceasing struggle between 'projects' and 'rights', many suffered from casualty, arrest, humiliation, displacement, marginalization, and loss of traditional collective ownership of land and resources.

(c) Agrarian question

Attention given to agricultural development in Manipur from the First to the Fourth Five Years Plan was inadequate for a possible breakthrough into an advanced agriculture. The plan outlays in agriculture from the first to the fourth Five Years Plans were only Rs 6.30; 109.51; 190.97 and 305.66 lakhs respectively. According to Mohendro 'one cannot possibly expect "impressive" turn with this meagre outlay.'[135] A sound planning to strengthen agricultural base in terms of improvement in: land system, irrigation, technology, institutional finance and etc was missing. According to a survey published in 2006, only eight per cent of the total geographical area of Manipur was under agricultural operations, compared to the all India average of 64 per cent. The spread of irrigation was comparatively poor with merely 15.5 per cent of the total area cultivated being under irrigation. The share of agriculture in the state's income had declined from 45.6 per cent in 1980–1 to 24.7 per cent in 2003–4.[136] According to the Manipur Assembly, Manipur had no agricultural policy as late as 2007.[137] On the contrary, two trends that had adverse impact on agricultural had been deliberately carried out by the State. The trends were: (a) destruction of agricultural land to construct institutional infrastructures and (b) proposed import of cheap rice from Southeast Asian countries. The first trend downsized the area under cultivation and the second trend will discourage local investment in agricultural production. It contributed to the wiping out of the local production skill and varieties of crops without any hope of recovery. The two trends had been moved ahead to serve the interest of the elites who had been the major stakeholders in construction works and import benefits.

(d) Industrial decline

Industrial growth has been given less attention. The token outlay of Rs 0.60 lakhs in the First Five Year Plan was marginally increased to Rs 13.06 lakhs and Rs 49.39 lakhs only respectively in the Second and Third Five Year Plans. During the Third Five Year Plan, sericulture received a share of Rs 4.29 lakhs only as plan allocation. No skill inventory was prepared. The Industrial Policy of 1982 had laid primary emphasis on development of large and medium industries. The Industries Policy of 1990 focused mainly on the development of the small-scale sector. However, Manipur had not witnessed desired level of industrial activity.[138] A new State Industrial Policy was announced in 1996.[139] But it was silent on the necessity for an earmarked industrial area. It had not declared any Industrial Area. Industrialization attempts had been on paper only. No substantial investment in constant capital for industrial take off had been initiated.

A High Level Commission Report to the Prime Minister, Government of India in 1997 had stressed that the Northeast (Manipur inclusive) had little or no plan resources but was heavily indebted in spite of high per capita plan outlays and subventions. Huge establishment costs exceeded state revenue collections as government service provided the sole and certainly the principal avenue of employment. In terms of per capita, state domestic product or other standard development indices such as power, road length or hospital beds, the Northeast ranks well below the 'national' average.[140] Between 1993–4 and 2000–1 in Manipur, the share of industry in Net State Domestic Product had risen from 15.73 per cent to 21.75 per cent, that is, an aggregate increase of 38.27 per cent. The increase was due to the high share of the construction sub-sector, for example, dams, office buildings and beautification projects. However, Manipur had the largest decline in the share of manufacturing in Net State Domestic Product from 4.61 per cent in 1980–1 to 3.37 per cent in 1995-6. In 1996-7, the state accounted for the lowest share in the Northeast region.[141]

As late as 1997, Manipur was in possession of only 898 diesel engine pump, 501 electric pump set, 560 agricultural power tillers, 937 wheeled agricultural tractors, 375 disc harrow, one seed-cum-fertiliser drill, 3 mould broad plough, four levellers, 26 power-operated maize seller, et cetra. By 2002, the number of registered factories by class of industry in Manipur, as reported by the Directorate of Commerce and Industry was 1,618 rice mills, 96 oil mills, 208 saw mills, three dal mills, 47 flour mills, five iron works, three printing and 34 others. The situation had not been improved as late as 2005. In 2005, most of the state-owned corporations were closed. About 30.86 per cent of small scale industry units were sick and 90 per cent of micro enterprises were in trouble.[142] The underdevelopment theory, therefore, argued that the productive capacity of Manipur was not built up over a long period of time, and therefore, the resource base could not be effectively moulded into the development process of Manipur.[143]

(e) Marginal peasants and workers

The period from 1950 and 2000 had revealed dramatic rise in population and corresponding rise in the consumption demand. However, slow growth in the productive scale, slow scale improvement in the instruments of production and disproportionate investment could not satisfy demands. In other words, the Indian State had de-invested when economically backward Manipur had required for State investment in the public sectors. As a result, the productive capacity of Manipur had not been built up over a long period of time and development process was delayed.[144] Food grains, pulses, vegetables, fruits, edible oil, milk, and dairy products, medicines, snacks, liquor, poultry products, fish, and almost all varieties of consumer goods were imported. Effective demand for import led to export of currency that was realized from service sector, Central loan and 'grants'. As a result, there was a drain of wealth.

A steady rise in the number of poor was indicated by the steady growth of marginal workers such as drivers, rickshaw pullers, coolies, wage labourers, barbers, workshops, petty shopkeepers, launderers, shoe-menders, sweepers, rag-pickers, destitute children, prostitutes, emigrant labours, and drop-out students and so on. According to the official record, the number of marginal workers had been increasing from 40,469 in 1981, to 66,621 in 1991 and to 285,849 in 2001. During 1991–2001, the growth rate of marginal workers was 329 per cent.

The growth in the number of poor was a corollary of decline in landholding and continuous breaking down of household subsistence economy. According to the report of the Statistics Department, Government of Manipur 2002, the actual area under landholding increased by 16,734 hectares between the years 1975 and 1990. The increase was due to deforestation and claiming of hitherto unclaimed lands. However, total number of holders increase by 281 only. Analysing the breakup of the statistics reveals that actual area of large holding (above 10 hectares) increased by 45 hectares only and the number of holders by 9 only. The corresponding figure was 4,685 hectares and 811 holders in case of medium (between 4 and 9.99 hectares), and 6,082 hectares and 1,392 holders in case of semi-medium (between two and 3.99 hectares) respectively. The statistics reveals a different picture in case of both the small (between one and 1.99) and marginal (below 1 hectare) holdings. In the case of a small holding, the actual area under this category increased by 6,109 hectares but the number of holders was declined by 343 holders. In the case of a marginal holding, both the area under this category and number of holders declined by 187 hectares and 1588 holders respectively. The overall area of holding of marginal class in 1990–1 was 37,820 hectares against the overall area under holding, that is, 174,981.

It is likely that a sizable number of the marginal holders completely parted with land but some new holders emerged all of a sudden taking over those parted lands or pre-existing richer holders bought up the parted land. There appeared to be transfer of holdings without causing much affect in the number of holders in that category. A further fall in the number of the holders of the marginal category was rather prevented due to three reasons. Firstly, big holders above the level of marginal produced both small and marginal holders through fragmentation of inheritance among family members. Secondly, fragmentation by those in the category of marginal produced the category of marginal only. Thirdly, family without any inheritance of holding became better off and started buying up land of that category.

An equally alarming situation was the process of the conversion of cultivation areas into constructions. It created disequilibrium in the household subsistence economy that relied heavily on land for kitchen garden products. Firstly, in the Imphal

Valley areas, the total area declined between 1985 and 2001 under the category of forest, non-agricultural usage area, barren, pasture, or grazing, miscellaneous land, cultureable waste land, fallows was 20,760 hectares. Since the area actually used for showing crops during the corresponding period increased by 15,305 hectares only it is likely that the rest of the 5,454 hectares were used for the purpose of constructing roads, government and private complexes, institutions, and settlement areas. Secondly, there was considerable scale of conversion of household gardens for construction purposes. People could not afford to build multistoreyed buildings and, therefore, they extended their construction horizontally on ground floor. One then had to increasingly depend on the market for everything including those items hitherto available in the respective household gardens. And since the opportunity to earn money was scarce, material interest of the large chunk of poor remained unfulfilled.

(f) On class contradiction and revolution

The Indian big bourgeoisie had imposed a capitalist socioeconomic system where social relations were based on commodity exchange, in particular private ownership of the means of production, and on the exploitation of labour and resources. The number of peoples affected by the system has been on the rise. The system has been perpetuated through suppression, subjective psychological propaganda, and other sectarian and counter-progressive tactics. The Indian big bourgeoisie work with the collusion of local ruling class composed of landlords, usurers, contractors, commission agents, corrupt bureaucrats, et cetra who has been dependent on the former for political and economic powers. This class did not directly create capital through investment in production but relied on accumulation of wealth through corruption and misappropriation of funds. At the market, the Mayang monopolists controlled price and accumulated wealth at exorbitant profits. Their wealth was mostly repatriated to their respective home states. Therefore, whatever cosmetic economic grants allocated for Manipur, in the absence of local production, were under circulation in the market for sometimes and siphoned off outside Manipur. At the receiving end, the larger chunk of peasants and workers remained disinvested and without significant economic opportunities.[145]

The underdevelopment theory has been propagating national and social liberation. Firstly, it caricatured the Indian State and Mayangs as being two sides of the same coin. Secondly, it urged the people to invest in economic self-recovery. In the mid-2008s the RPF encouraged to replace Mayang traders. In December 2008, UNLF announced a National Economic Policy.[146] Subsequently, a Joint Task Force of UNLF and KYKL initiated a mission called 'food self-sufficiency.'[147] Whether these were effective or not is a different issue. Thirdly, it exposed class rule and the role of what they perceived as internal enemies.[148] However, insurgents subscribed to the policy of 'no internal bloodshed' as they considered the Indian State as the primary threat. According to the RPF, political independence of Manipur should be the priority concern of the people of Manipur.[149]

III. FROM THE DOMESTIC PREMISE VIS-À-VIS THE DOMESTICITY

In India's domestic the insurgents were being branded unconstitutional, outlawed and banned. However the Indian State's commitment to democracy, to some extent had allowed civil society democratic assertions. The civil society space has been a contested space between pro-India and pro-liberation groups raising democratic issues in order to organize themselves towards respective sides. It is in this space that democratic assertions, either interplaying with or reinforcing to anti-colonial discourses, have been raised. Insurgents' attempt to expand mass base through investment in civil societies cannot be ruled out. The contact might be tight or loose and varied from organization to organization.

Call it coincidental, growth of civil society became increasingly evident after UNLF was formed in 1964 and the subsequent emergence of other parties. Prior to that, the short lived Communist Party of Manipur (1948–51), Meetei State Committee, and the Revolutionary Government of Manipur in the late 1960s did not have much constituency in civil society fronts. The Revolutionary

Nationalist Party showed no sign of existence other than its activity in 1953. From the mid-1960s, many civil societies came into existence. Some of the pioneering organizations were 'All Manipur Cultural Youth League, Post Graduate Students Union, Manipur People's Convention, Cultural Integration Conference'[150] that focused on statehood and territorial integrity. Meetei revivalist organizations, All Manipur Students' Union,[151] Pan Manipuri Youth League,[152] and Women Development and Reformation Samaj[153] were considered pro-liberation. PREPAK in the late 1970s, had attempted but could not materialize in converting Young Universe Manipur into an over-ground front.

To list some, in the 1980s, there was an emergence of Manipur-centred women human right vigilant groups called *Meira Paibees*, Civil Liberties and Human Rights Organization (1983), and People's Democratic Movement.[154] In the early 1990s, the All Manipur Ethnical-Socio-Cultural Organization (1992),[155] the All Manipur United Clubs Organization (1993),[156] the Committee on Human Rights (1993),[157] and the Committee for Peace and Integrity[158] became active. From the mid-1990s, many civil organizations including those considered as human rights NGOs, emerged. Alphabetically, some of them were; All Manipur Anti Drug & Alcoholism (December 2005), All Manipur Kanba Ima Lup, All Manipur Women's Voluntary Association, Centre for Organization and Research Education,[159] Centre for Progress of Manipuri People,[160] Chanura Lamjingkon Kangleipak, Committee Against Drug and Alcoholism,[161] Democratic Students' Alliance of Manipur (January 2002), Ethno Heritage Council,[162] Fourth World People's League of Kangleipak[163], Federation of Regional Indigenous Societies,[164] Human Rights Alert, Integrated People's Progressive Union,[165] International Peace and Social Advancement, Kangla Mei, Manipur Forward Youth Front, Manipur Martyrs Memorial Committee, Manipur Pari Apunba Lup, Manipur Peace and Integrity Council (3 July 2001), Manipur Students' Federation (13 October 1998), Meira Paibee Women's Association of Kangleipak,[166] Momnu Eerikhombi, National Identity Protection Committee, Poirei Leimarol Apuba Meira Paibee Lup, Satjal (later on Universal Frienship Organization),[167] United Club Organization,

United Committee Manipur (July 2001),[168] United People's Front,[169] Young Horizon and, et cetra.

There were also issue based *ad hoc* or Joint Action Committees. Few committees may be mentioned such as; Manipur Territorial Congress Committee,[170] Dark Day Observation Committee,[171] Nupilan Observation Committee from 1990s,[172] Solidarity Committee on the UN Day Rally in 1999,[173] Manipur Martyrs Memorial Committee,[174] Manipur Defense Rally Organizing Committee in 2000, Meira Paibee Ningsing Numit Observation Committee, and other Joint Action Committees against State terrorism and 'developmental aggression.' There were common platforms to assert democratic rights, human rights,[175] territorial integrity,[176] economic rights, martyrs' day, patriot's day, anniversaries, et cetra. Research centres, study circles, publication units, and media establishments were also created for the production of progressive literatures and democratic propaganda.

The civil societies had been organizers by asserting leadership and winning loyalty at the grass root. They created mass base by asserting unconventional power in handling 'domestic' issues and by addressing certain grievances of peoples. They had been organizers of protests, rallies, demonstrations, blockades, strikes, relief camps, felicitations, sports, functions, meetings, social sterilization campaign, integrity campaign, et cetra. Outside Manipur, they developed contacts and coordination with parallel democratic forces and carried out international campaigns on democratic issues. The present discussion shall focus on the women *Meira Paibee* movement.

Light in the Darkness: *Meira Paibee* Domain

On 15 July 2004, about a dozen meira paibees, stripped themselves in front of 17th Assam Rifles Headquarters at Kangla, Imphal. In the nude, they protested with banners that read 'go back Indian army' and 'Indian Army rape us.' Video footage shows a *meira paibee* protestor rebuking Assam Rifles, 'we are all Manorama's mother, come and rape us... you bastards.'

The immediate cause of the protest was the custodial rape and murder of Thangjam Manorama, a 32-year-old woman corporal of the banned People's Liberation Army, by the personnel of 17 Assam

Rifles. Manorama was arrested from her home on the night of 11 July 2004 after being issued an arrest warrant, tortured, raped, fatally wounded in the private parts to destroy evidence of rape, and her body was disposed nude in the rural fringe in the wee hours of the morning of 12 July 2004. The nude protest, as it has been called, sparked off series of protests, agitations and violent confrontations with the State forces across Imphal Valley. The protest reached its zenith with simultaneous calls for: (a) self-reliance movement of boycotting cold drinks and mineral waters manufactured outside Manipur, (b) non-cooperation movement of boycotting government offices and institutions and, (b) protest movement.

About 24 years ago, in 1980, when entire Manipur was declared 'disturbed' under AFSPA, there was widespread protest against 'disposal of the lives to the Mayang armies.'[177] The birth of *meira paibee* as women vigilant movement against State terrorism has been traced to it.[178] Between 1980 and 2004, *meira paibees* had played crucial roles in the human rights movement. However, the 2004 nude protest was remarkable as it won international attention by deconstructing the moral legitimacy of repressive laws[179] and boosting the morale of agitation.

Composition and structure: Literarily *meira paibee* means 'woman torchbearer.' The term *meira* is also occasionally used to connote initiative, progress, and achievement or to signify a mechanical means for enlightening darkness. Therefore, a *meira paibee*, as an activist, is sometime defined as the repository of hope, whose utmost obligation is to defend and save society from a terror regime. There is an entire literature that construes legends of *meira paibee* by eulogizing it with symbolic attributes of mythical goddesses and woman historical figures.[180]

Most commonly, a *meira paibee* activist, a married woman of the age ranging between 30 and 65 years, working at the grassroot level at her locale, with or without any official responsibility of the organization to which she is loosely affiliated is a woman volunteer who may or may not be a strictly disciplined cadre of any party. Every woman is a potential *meira paibee* who is at liberty to become full time activist for any larger goal.

At the local level each locality has a *meira paibee* unit. Volunteers congregate regularly in *Shanglen* (huts) constructed by them or in local clubs or market sheds. There they decide the timing and nature of human rights vigilance. They sound the alarm or any emergency by banging electric posts or by beating a gong. They have mechanized forms of banging that produce varying rhythms of sound conveying respective message, such as rhythm for *meira paibee* congregation, public meetings and emergencies. They organize periodical torch marches to recuperate their morale and create solidarity.

The local units are grouped under regional bodies or were directly affiliated to apex *meira paibee* organizations operating at the state level. The state level organizations spearhead state level meetings, discussions, protests, rallies, strikes, and agitations to defend human rights. The legal source of fund for the *meira paibee* organizations at all levels is voluntary contributions by the members and donation from others. The rumour about some apex *meira paibee* being funded by insurgents has not been legally exposed.

Reinterpreting the movement: Discussions so far of *meira paibee* have been predominantly centred on the discourse of the human rights. And there are stereotypes of the spontaneity of *meira paibee* movement. These may be analysed to come up with a more inclusive and integrated interpretation.

(1) Firstly, whereas gender analysts interpret the movement as women's collective response to a male dominated military regime that victimized the women most, other human right activists perceive the movement as nothing more than a response to State terrorism. Prof. Arambam Lokendra once lectured that the situation created by the military regime was highly masculine, men dominated and characterized by wild sexual aggression of the Indian army. It left the women with no other choice but to respond spontaneously. A friend of mine who worked for an NGO, on one occasion raised the point that women were the worst affected victims in an armed conflict situation as mothers, sisters, daughters, and wives who lose their children, brothers, fathers, and husbands.[181] The sense of losses prompted women to rise up in defence of human rights. The same line of argument has been carried forward by scholars working on women's movements in Manipur.[182] For them, it is women's assertion

for rights to defend their bodies, psychology, sentiment, and their men from humiliation, oppression, and trauma imposed by a men-dominated military regime. Thus, both the cause and presumed goal of the movement are shown as women-oriented to serve the interest of the women most.

(2) Secondly, pro-liberation protagonists cum human rights activists equally formulate a dichotomy theory that counterpoises 'rights' against 'policy' and show the *meira paibee* movement as spontaneous assertion to defend rights. Here, there is a difference in the way that gender plays out in the argument. For them men, as a result of more vulnerability to extrajudicial torture, killing, forced disappearance and repression, had to restrain themselves from asserting rights, and justice in the public domain. It then became women's responsibility to assert their rights since, on the one hand, they are less prone to brutal repression because of their 'femininity', and on the other, they are equally victims caught in a situation of 'defend or lose'. Both the lines of argument suggest that the feeling of resistance by women against immediate threat of State terrorism is natural. As a result, resistance to aggression takes various forms at the individual or collective levels spontaneously. As far as organized forms of expression at regional and state levels are concerned, these are shown as simultaneous, spontaneous reactions that are merely coordinated by apex organizations.

However, I have a different understanding of these theories. I consider that both the gender and rightist analyses suffer not so much from gendered and rightist reductionism of restricting 'dichotomy' analysis about men *versus* women or rights *versus* terrorism in the respective boxes. There is limitation in interpreting *meira paibi* by detaching it from the larger neoliberal constraints that have been the corollary of diametrical nationalisms, militarization, suppression of democratic dissents, and rights violations. I have seen political aspects of *meira paibee* as AFSPA was a political act, and on the other hand, pro-liberation strategy has contributed a lot to the *meira paibee* movement. Deeper discussion on the idea of spontaneity may clear some of the doubts.

The urgent resistance of an individual victim woman and her

immediate colleagues against immediate threat of State terrorism can be spontaneous, but a movement, such as the *meira paibee* that lasts for more than three decades, is largely a sustained movement influenced by prolonged campaigns and anti-colonial discourse. A protest may express victims' grievances,[183] but it is not independent of being organized. It may not be correct to presume that people are absolutely neutral of any reinforced social value of womanhood, politics, ideology, and spirit of resistance which are socially reproduced, circulated, and consumed at the individual level. Therefore, I attempt to show that the *meira paibee* confrontation with the State forces and other campaign initiatives at local levels, at times undertaken independently as instant responses or sometimes in coordination with apex organizations, though outwardly spontaneous are in reality motivated by the spirit of resistance disseminated by the anti-colonial discourse. This is due to fact that the State, till date, has not invested in people to fight against its own repressive forces or the repressive laws it has enforced.

Resistance or confrontation represents a climax and each of the climaxes presupposes and follows from successful awareness campaign. Between the climaxes, there are a series of informal meetings and discussions that encouraged women to play active roles in the 'conflict situation.' What is crucial is that no individual would dare to claim responsibility of instigating an action for fear of being arrested. Nor would women who confront the State downplay themselves by verbalizing that they were being instigated. Spontaneity as a form of non-orchestrated populism sounds more powerful in political vocabulary as it is being considered non instigated popular action. In this scenario, many choose to call themselves or others spontaneous.

In practice, there is a dialectic between spontaneity and organization. Spontaneity is evident only in the immediate resistance by local *meira paibees* in defence against sudden instances of combing operations, arrest, torturing and sexual harassment. That was a climax on the part of the concerned *meira paibees*. What immediately followed was a more coordinated and organized response by the neighbouring *meira paibees* or regional level response and then state level response. The elements of spontaneity were either merged with or subsumed within the long drawn out strategy of making resistance against the Indian State a tradition. Resistance as strategy presumes repressions that would be brutal and would obviously violate rights. On the other hand, resistance, as a form of inviting repression, is instrumental, directly or indirectly, in construing contradiction between the people and State, which helps in augmenting the 'terrorist' caricature of the State.

Women and nation: *Meira paibees* asserted human rights by targeting the State and its repressions. They acted as the moral centre and symbol of resistance. Their activities augmented primordialist perceptions of women as patriots and defenders of society since the time immemorial. There were speeches, literatures, symbolic statues, events organized and ceremonies dedicated to women who had played historical roles. Perceptions that allude to women as the moral centre of resistance are found in the two domains of 'inner' and 'public.'

Firstly, in the inner domain that is attached to the social value system, sacrosanct qualities are attributed to womanhood. Legends, myths, versions of history and day-to-day usage terms such as *lonna eemani* (language is mother), *eemaleipak* (motherland), *eemagi khomlang lamal singbana pokpagi mahei yallabani* (repaying for the mother's milk makes one worthwhile for having being born), *ayo eema* (exclamatory remark of calling mother out of pain or frightening), et cetra strengthened emotional and social attachment as well as respect for womanhood. They are regarded to possessing inborn 'feminine' qualities required for a civilization to flourish, such as motherhood, cultural repository, community prestige, honour, tolerance, divinity, sacrificing spirit, and statecraft. The 'nation' is personified as motherland, thus identifying the biological body of women with the 'national' territory and that of their modesty with 'national' honour. They should be defended from denial of 'womanhood' and 'femininity' to defend the 'nation' from 'colonial rule.'

Secondly, in the public domain, women being the firmly consolidated groups, play an important role in social, economic, and political activities. They are the human rights vigilant group, and they play important roles in resolving local disputes, social sterilizing campaign against intoxication, robbery, dacoity, crimes, et cetra. They are frequently visible in attending or organizing pro-liberation programmes.[184] They, thus, win respect and the direct or indirect support of insurgents make them socially powerful. Here, I find women expressing 'masculinity' latent in their womanhood, contrary to the understanding of the gender analysts mentioned above. If by femininity people generally meant submissiveness, subjection, and emotionalism as opposed to radicalism, bravery, and sacrificing spirit, then it is curious why Manipuri men let women keep vigil in their locality while they remain indoors for fear of arrest and repression. When men and women were victims in a conflict situation, the valiant roles played by women demanded rethinking of the conceptions of masculinity. The *meira paibees* appropriate the characteristics generally see as male and as part of the public realm through their political activities. If military regime is the masculine domain, then, it is women who, contrary to their supposed submissiveness and helplessness, assert a counter masculinity through open defiance of the regime in various forms of protests, rally, and public mourning for the insurgents killed in encounter.

However, the public domain is also the site where women become victims of repression and sexual harassment. The cycle of repression and protest produces two contradictory ideas of 'war heroines' in democratic assertions and brutally repressed and sexually harassed 'fallen heroines.' The scenes of brutal repression, fallen women coming back home in remorse, victimized women in the hospitals, and relief and support campaigns for them produce a 'terrorist' image of India. The 'fallen heroines' become an emotional issue and play with emotion in mobilizing people to take vengeance for the injuries inflicted upon unarmed 'mothers'. Thus, in all situations of 'rights' versus 'State', the two pre-existing perceptions of womanhood, that is the 'feminine' quality of women as cultural repository and the 'masculine' qualities of women characterized by assertiveness and sacrificing spirit—play off one another and produce a third perception of the 'victimized heroines' that called for immediate relief to defend the helpless 'mothers' in order to defend the nation, its honour, its culture repository, and the 'purity' of community blood running in them. All these factors interplay in hardening the anti-colonial discourse and foster some amount of unity in asserting their 'national feeling'.

The incident of Manorama and the 'nude protest' ignited many to take to the streets and fight pitched battles with the State forces demanding justice and repeal of AFSPA. That phase of agitation had not been fully successful. The State continued with rights violations. *Meira paibees* movement is continued. On 12 April 2009, Nupi Khunnai Meira Paibee of Liwa Bokul Makhong, inaugurated the statue of *meira paibee*. As in March 2009, the Meira Paibee Numit Observation Committee had been investing in constructing a Meira Paibee Memorial Complex 'with an objective to honour and commemorate all dedicated departed *meira paibees* ... (to) expedite the motion as well as commemorate the motion of *meira paibee*s to the future generation.'[185] Their role, along with the other mass fronts, continued to have political functions.

In summing up, the Indian State's commitment to democracy, framed within the framework of the idea of India as a nation, produces two contradictory situations in Manipur. On the one hand, the conscious effort to erase any mark of what Partha Chaterjee calls 'the rule of colonial difference' through guaranteeing constitutional rights allows a certain level of assertions for cultural autonomy, social justice and democratic rights. On the other hand, the neoliberal constraints and militarization had resulted into general economic decline and violation of human rights. If one would agree with Partha Chatterjee that 'postcolonial' India has been marked by bringing together into the political arena the two domains–one of sovereignty and the other of governmentality, corresponding respectively to a discourse of rights and a discourse of policy[186]— then the Manipur insurgency adopted the former in juxtaposition against the later discourse. 'Assertive intelligentsia'[187] could openly form civil organizations and in the name of social service, defending human rights, upholding culture, and redressing the material grievances of the people they could convey anti-colonial polemics.

NOTES

1. Address by the Governor of Manipur Shri B.K. Nehru to the Manipur Legislative Assembly, 30 March 1972.
2. The decade witnessed emergence of political groups viz., Nikhil Manipuri Mahasabha (1938), Praja Sanmeloni (7 January 1940), Praja Mandal (7 March 1946), Krishak Sabha (formed in 1935 as Krishak Sanmenoni) became a political organization in May 1946, Praja Sangha (formed by merging Manipur Praja Sanmeloni and Manipur Praja Mandal on 21 August 1946), Manipur State Congress (4 October 1946), Shanti Sabha (1948) and Manipur Communist Party (September 1948) and Socialist Party (1948) carrying out mass political activities.
3. Manipur State Durbar Resolution, No. 17, 21 August 1946.
4. Kh. Ibochou Singh, 'Responsible government under Manipur State Constitution Act, 1947, Extra Constitutional powers of the Dominion Agent and the Dewan' in *Annexation of Manipur*, Imphal: People's Democratic Movement Manipur, 1995, pp. 162-3.
5. Karam Manimohan Singh, 'Constituent Assembly of India and North East Frontier Agency' in *Annexation of Manipur*, p. 142.
6. Rajkumar Maipaksana Singh, 'Constitutional development of Manipur in a nut shell' in *Annexation of Manipur*, p. 128.
7. Singh, 'Constitutional development of Manipur in a nut shell', p. 128.
8. Singh, 'Responsible government under Manipur Constitution Act', p. 164.
9. Karam Manimohan Singh, *Hijam Irabot and Political Movement in Manipur*, Delhi: B.R. Publishing Corporation, 1989, pp. 337–8.
10. Ibid.
11. Senjam Mangi Singh, 'reaction to the merger of Manipur into the Dominion of India and public responses' in *Annexation of Manipur*, p. 86.
12. N. Lokendra Singh, *The Unquiet Valley*, Delhi: Mittal Publications, 1998, p. 227–8.
13. 'Hill representatives special meeting...Major Khating (Sadar Hills), Manipur State Legislative Assembly Speaker T.C. Tiankham (Thlansip), R. Suisa (Tolloi Hills), Luying Hungyo (Faisti), Tuwalichin (Senbon), DamjaiKhai Waiphei (Churachandpur), T. Luikham (Ukhrul), Buising Kabui (Langkhong), Dr Kampu (Maite), and Kakhanggai (Langkhong Hill)...Meeteis must not decide the fate of Manipur'; *Bharatki Loilam Manipur*, Imphal: Pan Manipuri Youth League, 1993, pp. 71–2.

14. Singh, *The Unquiet Valley*, pp. 227–8.
15. Gangumei Kamei, 'Ethnic responses to merger: a historical perspective' in *Annexation of Manipur*, p. 97.
16. Singh, *The Unquiet Valley*, p. 98.
17. Lal Dena, 'The hill people and the merger of Manipur', in *Annexation of Manipur*, p. 115.
18. Singh, *The Unquiet Valley*, p. 226.
19. Singh, 'Reaction to the merger of Manipur...', p. 91-2.
20. Singh, *Hijam Irabot and Political Movement in Manipur*, p. 358.
21. Dena, 'The hill people and the merger of Manipur', p. 114.
22. *Bharatki Loilam Manipur,* p. 80.
23. Manipur Durbar Resolution No. 3 of 20 February 1935.
24. King's Memo No. 1001-P.1.1, 11 April 1939, submitted to the Manipur Durbar; Annexure, Manipur Durbar Resolution, 15 March 1939.
25. Letter of King Churachand sent to Gimson, on 19 February 1940; File no. 18 C/40, Confidential Programme B, December 1940, R-a/S-C/144, Manipur State Archive (Henceforth MSA).
26. Manipur Durbar Resolution, No. 25 of 30 April 1947.
27. Manipur Durbar Resolution, No. 29 of 4 June 1947.
28. *Selected Works of Jawaharlal Nehru;* Vol. 2, 2nd Series, Delhi: Nehru Memorial Fund, pp. 256–8
29. The Mahasabha by then had became 'a sort of local congress...its adherents sometimes wear Gandhi Caps and go about shouting Congress slogans'; Letter from C. Gimson to Mills, Imphal, 19 February 1940, MSA.
30. Resolution No. 6 passed in a joint sitting of the Nikhil Manipuri Mahasabha and the Manipur Praja Mandal on the 5 April 1947.
31. A front organization of the Indian National Congress for the peoples in Princely States; Bhogendro Singh, 'Manipur the right of Self-Determination, A summary.'
32. Proposed creation of an administrative entity comprising Manipur, Tripura, Cachar and Lushai Hills.
33. In a meeting of the working committee meeting held on the 29 April 1949, the Congress party took a resolution in favour of the integration of Manipur into India.
34. 'Revolutionary nationalist party and Sagolsem Indramani', Imphal: *The Sangai Express*, 24 April 2007.
35. Sagolsem Indramani Singh and Ors. vs. State of Manipur on 26 May, 1954.

36. Note to Minister of States, 15 September 1953, *Selected works of Jawaharlal Nehru*, Vol. 23, 2nd Series, Delhi: Nehru Memorial Fund, p. 233.
37. Ram Manohar Lohia and Ors. vs. V.S. Sundaram on 26 April, 1955
38. R. Constantine, *Maid of the Mountains*, Delhi, Lancers, 1981. p. 91.
39. Maloy Krishna Dhar, *Open Secrets: India's Intelligence Unveiled*, Delhi: Manas Publications, 2006, pp. 122, 124.
40. Calcutta: *Amrita Bazaar Patrika*, Thursday, 6 August 1970.
41. 'Manipur Agitation', Calcutta: *Amrita Bazaar Patrika*, Tuesday, August 18, 1970.
42. Homen Borgohain, 'Manipur: Anatomy of Despair,' *Economic and Political Weekly*, Vol. 17, No. 46/47, November 13–20, 1982, p. 1858.
43. Constantine, *Maid of the Mountains,* p. 94.
44. Nagaland state was created out of Assam State; denial of statehood to Manipur was an independent country before the annexation caused humiliation and frustration among many.
45. Formed on 12 September 1965 during anti-famine agitation.
46. Who were active in statehood agitation.
47. Dhar, *Open Secrets: India's Intelligence Unveiled*, p. 120.
48. *Why Manipuris Fight for Right to Self-determination*, United National Liberation Front, 1996.
49. It was difficult to detect new Burmese and Mizo-Kuki-Chin immigrants through the southern border because of their linguistic and cultural affinity with pre-existing Mizo-Kuki-Chin population.
50. Evans, Sir Geoffery, and Antony Brett James, *Imphal: A Flower on Lofty Heights,* London: Macmillan & Co, 1964.
51. Manipur State Durbar Resolution, No. 1 of 20 July 1946.
52. The Manipur Naturalisation Act, 1947.
53. *Influx of immigrants into Manipur; A Threat to the Indigenous Ethnic People*, Imphal: United Committee Manipur, 2005, p. 131.
54. Ibid.
55. Notice for provisional enrolment of refugees in the electoral roll of the house of people, Notified by P.C. Deb, Reform Officer, Imphal 25 August 1949; document in possession of Padmashree Ningthoukhongjam Khelchandra, Uripok, Imphal.
56. Manipur State Gazette, Extraordinary, No. 84-E-44 10/10/50. 26.
57. Notification No. 8597-601 H.D., 18 November 1950, Manipur Gazette, 29 November 1950.
58. *Influx of Immigrants into Manipur...*, p. 132.
59. Ibid, p. 27.

60. *A Nation and Her People under Siege*; Delhi: The Other Media and Mizzima, August, 2004, pp. 8–42.
61. *Statistical Handbook of Manipur 2002*, Imphal: Directorate of Economics & Statistics, Government of Manipur, 2002.
62. *Influx of Immigrants into Manipur...*, pp. 43–5.
63. Total population of Manipur according to 2001 census was 22,93,896.
64. Comparative analysis of: (a) *Census of India 1991, Series-15, Manipur, Primary Census Abstract, Part II-B*, Directorate of Census Operations, Manipur and (b) *Economic Survey Manipur 2005–06*, Directorate of Economics & Statistics, Government of Manipur, 2006.
65. Dr A.K. Sunder Kumar Singh, 'Distribution pattern of population in Manipur; A geographical analysis' in *Journal of the Geographical Society of Manipur*, Vol. 1, No. 1, Imphal, July-December, 1997, pp. 15–30.
66. Amalendu Guha, 'Little Nationalism Turned Chauvinist: Assam's Anti-Foreigner Upsurge, 1979–80' in *Economic and Political Weekly*, Vol. 15, No. 41/43, Special Number, Mumbai, October 1980.
67. Phanjaobam Tarapot, *Bleeding Manipur,* Delhi: Har Anand Publications, 2003, p. 241.
68. Nari Rustomji, *Imperilled Frontiers*, Delhi: Oxford University Press, 1983, p. 6.
69. Sairem Nilbir, 'The revivalist movement of Sanamahism' in Naorem Sanajaoba, ed., *Manipur Past and Present,* Vol. II, Delhi: Mittal Publications, 1991, p. 138.
70. Gangumei Kabui, 'Socio-religious reform movement and Christian Proselytism', Lal Dena, ed. *History of Modern Manipur (1826-1949)*, Delhi: Orbit Publishers, 1991, p. 103.
71. The national anthem and national song of India.
72. Kangleipak became Manipur in 1724; Paonam Labanggo Mangang, *Kangleipakta Revolution*, Imphal, 1997, p. 9.
73. Dhanabir Laishram, *Chaokhatpa Khunnai amasung Meeyam* (Developed society and the people), Imphal: Centre for Progress of Manipuri People, 1998, p. 113.
74. Rustomji, *Imperilled Frontiers*, p. 2-3.
75. Dhar, *Open Secrets: India's Intelligence Unveiled*, pp. 100-1.
76. Constantine, *Maid of the Mountains*, p. 34.
77. 'Meenei Naithanggi Punshi' (An enslaved life) in Lamyanba; Imphal: Pan Manipur Youth League, October 1974.
78. Labanggo, *Kangleipakta Revolution,* pp. 6–8.
79. *Why Manipuris fight for right to self determination.*

80. Memorandum submitted to the Secretary General, United Nations and the Chairman of the Decolonization Committee (committee of 24) for decolonization of Manipur from Indian colonialism and alien racist regime, enlisting Manipur in the list of the non-self-governing territories of the United Nations and, restoration of independence and sovereignty of Manipur (henceforth RPF Memorandum to the UN), Revolutionary People's Front (RPF), Manipur, 2nd ed., 1999.
81. AMSU took up the foreign national issue agitation from 15th February 1980. Oinam Momon Devi, *A Study of the Students Organization in Manipur as a Pressure Group (1980-1990)*; M. Phil. Dissertation (Unpublished), Manipur University, 1993, p. 61.
82. *Influx of Immigrants into Manipur*, p. 35.
83. Potsangbam Premananda and Huidrom Lokendro received bullet injuries and died on the 17th April 1980; Devi, '*A Study of the Students Organization...*', p. 76.
84. Federation of Regional Indigenous Societies (FRIENDS), National Identity Protection Committee (NIPCO), Ethno Heritage Council (HERICOUN), Information Centre for Hill Areas, Manipur (ICHAM), League of Indigenous People's Upliftment (LIPUL), Kuki Inpi, Tangkhul Katamnao Saklong (TKS), Komrem Union, Zelianrong Union, All Manipur Students' Union (AMSU), Democratic Students' Alliance of Manipur (DESAM), Kangleipak Students' Association (KSA), Students' Union of Kangleipak (SUK), and Students Welfare Association of Kangleipak (SWAK)
85. 'Terror strikes at ISKCON on Janmasthami/four killed, scores injured as gory blast rips apart Ras Lila rendition on Black Wednesday', Imphal: *The Sangai Express*, 17 Aug 2006.
86. 'Killing spree continues; Seven more non-locals shot dead', Imphal: *The Sangai Express*, 19 March 2008.
87. 'RPF condemns targeting migrant workers; our fight is against GoI not Indians', Imphal: *The Sangai Express*, 20 March 2008.
88. 'KYKL refutes, shares thoughts on influx-I, Killing of migrant workers', Imphal: *The Sangai Express*, 28 March 2008.
89. 'JCC of KYKL, UNLF reiterates stand', Imphal: *The Sangai Express*, 05 April 2009.
90. *Bharatki Loilam Manipur*, p. 96.
91. Notification: Office of the Chief Commissioner, Manipur, No. 0001/CC. Of 15 October 1949 (12 Noon); Manipur Gazette, No. 1-E-1; Imphal, Saturday, 15 October 1949; document in possession of

Padmashree Ningthoukhongjam Kelchandra, Unripok, Imphal.

92. Sandeep, 'Institutionalization of insurgency in Manipur', *news@ashanet.org*, 1999.
93. 'Absent at R-Day: Principals axed', Imphal: *The Sangai Express*, 28 January 2009.
94. Resolution of the National Convention on Manipur Merger Issue, 29 October 1993.
95. Wahengbam Memcha Devi, *Administration of Justice 1947 to 1972*; M. Phil. Dissertation, Imphal: Manipur University, 1991, p. 11.
96. 'Legal Notice', dated 1/8/2003, by Sanasam Sarat Singh on behalf of the Universal Friendship Organization based in Manipur (Henceforth *legal notice*); *The Sangai Express*, 5 August 2003.
97. Y. Mohendra Singh, 'Manipur Joining the Indian Union and Transferring the Administration to the Central Government' in *Annexation of Manipur*, p. 171.
98. 'Criticism and constructive submission regarding the study on treaties, agreements and other constructive arrangements between states and indigenous populations', Report submitted by Centre for Organization and Research Education, Manipur to the Sub-Commission on the Prevention of Discrimination and Protection of Minorities, Commission on Human Rights, UN March 1999.
99. RPF Memorandum to the UN.
100. Singh, 'Manipur the right of self-determination...'
101. Naorem Sanajaoba, 'Problem of 1949 Annexation of Manipur', in *Annexation of Manipur*, p. 63.
102. Ahanthem Nilamani, 'The Manipur Merger Agreement, 1949 its legality and constitutionality in the context of Manipur Constitution Act, 1947 and International Law' in *Annexation of Manipur*, p. 140.
103. CORE Criticism and constructive submission.
104. The Declaration on Principles of International Law concerning Friendly Relations and Co-operation among States: to uphold the principle of equal rights and self-determination of peoples enshrined in the Charter of the United Nations.
105. CORE Criticism and constructive submission.
106. Nilamani, 'The Manipur Merger Agreement...', p. 141.
107. RPF Memorandum to the UN.
108. Khaidem Mani, 'The Manipur Merger Agreement and the Manipur Constitution Act, whether the Maharajah of Manipur could enter into the Manipur Merger Agreement – whether lawful or not' in *Annexation of Manipur*, p. 181.

109. This understanding is substantiated by an order of the Supreme Court of India [in Dr Ram Manohar Lohia v/s V.S. Sundaram District Magistrate, Manipur; A.I.R. 1955 Manipur 41 (V42 C 9 Dec)] an excerpt of it which reads, 'under the Manipur Administrative Order 1949, the Manipur State Constitution Act 1947 had been kept intact under para 5 but under clause 7 the existing Legislature was dissolved and the Ministers then functioning ceased to function.'
110. 'A draft policy to protect and uphold the unique historical features, existing historical boundary and also for bringing emotional integration of the people of Manipur to achieve faster economic development of the state' (henceforth UCM draft policy); Imphal: United Committee Manipur (UCM), 2002, p. 4.
111. Devi, *Administration of Justice 1947 to 1972,* p. 11.
112. Singh, 'Manipur the right of self-determination...'
113. Ibid.
114. *Why Manipuris fight for right to self-determination*, 1996.
115. 'RPF Memorandum' to the UN.
116. Address by His Excellency, the Governor of Manipur, Shri B.K. Nehru to the Manipur Legislative Assembly on 30 March 1972.
117. Table 6.1 Central Assistance to State Plans (State wise, VI Plan to X Plan), *Tenth Five Year Plan 2002–7.*
118. N. Mohendro, 'Development experience in Manipur (1891–1969) and the lost article of self-reliance,' 2002.
119. Oinam Sunil, 'Youth's Mental Unrest in Manipur', in *Youth's Mental Unrest in Manipur*, p. 60.
120. RPF Memorandum to the UN.
121. UCM's draft policy, p. 7
122. Laishram, *Chaokhatpa Khunnai amasung Meeyam,* p. 8.
123. Mohendro, 'Development experience in Manipur (1891-1969)...'
124. Dipankar Dasgupta, Pradip Maiti, Robin Mukherjee, Subrata Sarkar, Subhendu Chakrabarti, 'Growth and Interstate Disparities in India', *Economic and Political Weekly*, Vol. 35, No. 27 (1 July 2000), pp. 2413–22.
125. *Manipur State Development Report July 2006*, report of a project sponsored by Planning Commission of India, Institute for Human Development, New Delhi.
126. Laishram, *Chaokhatpa Khunnai amasung Meeyam,* p. 8.
127. *Tenth Five Years Plan*, Planning Commission of India, New Delhi.
128. *Economic Survey Manipur 2005-2006*, Directorate of Economics & Statistics, Government of Manipur, Imphal, 2006, p. 198.

129. P. Khuman Khomba, 'Youth's Mental Unrest in Manipur', in *Youths' Mental Unrest in Manipur,* Imphal: National Research Centre Manipur, 1996, pp. 32-3.
130. N. Joykumar Singh, 'Youth's Mental Unrest in Manipur' in *Youths' Mental Unrest in Manipur,* p. 5.
131. Memorandum of the Forum of Chief Ministers of the North Eastern States Submitted to the Prime Minister on June 21, 2000.
132. Annual Administrative Report of Manipur, 2005–2006.
133. Statement by Dhanabir Laishram Centre for Progress of Manipur Peoples at the UN Working Group on Indigenous Populations 17th Session 26 to 30 July 1999.
134. CORE 'Criticism and constructive submission...'.
135. Mohendro, 'Development experience in Manipur...'
136. *Manipur State Development Report July 2006*, report of a project sponsored by Planning Commission of India, Institute for Human Development, New Delhi.
137. *Agricultural Policy of the Manipur State*, Questions orally answered in Manipur Legislative Assembly Secretariat on Tuesday, 8 May 2007.
138. *Industrial Policy of Manipur*, 1996.
139. *Manipur Gazette*, Monday, December 9, 1996.
140. 'Transforming the Northeast, Tackling Backlogs in Basic Minimum Services and Infrastructural Needs', *High Level Commission Report to the Prime Minister*, Government of India, submitted by the Planning Commission, New Delhi, 7 March 1997.
141. *Manipur State Development Report July 2006*, p. 147.
142. *State of Environment Report Manipur*, 2009.
143. UCM draft policy, pp. 29-30.
144. Ibid.
145. According to Census 2001, Manipur's total population was 22,93,896; 3,79,705 were Cultivators and 1,13,630 were agricultural labourers.
146. 'UNLF spells out agenda on 44th B'day-I', Imphal: *Sangai Express*, 2 December 2008.
147. 'KYKL-UNLF presents contour of its economic programme', Imphal: *Imphal Free Press,* 25 Aug 2008.
148. Puppet of the Indian State.
149. Independence is the first priority: RPF chief; Imphal: *Sangai Express*, 27 September 2006.
150. Constantine, *Maid of the Mountains,* p. 105.
151. Formed on 12 September, 1965.
152. Formed on 29 December 1968; published an anti-colonial periodical journal entitled *Lamyanba.*

153. Formed in 1969.
154. Co-organizer of 'national' seminar in 1993 that invalidated Shillong Accord of 1949.
155. To strengthen emotional and cultural bond among communities.
156. To defend territorial integrity; since 2002 it as invested in the Unity, Development and Peace (UNIDEP) campaign.
157. Unlike Civil Liberties and Human Rights Organization (CLAHRO), it invested in building agitation to defend human rights.
158. To defend integrity; on 31 May 1996 it completed three months campaign.
159. An NGO that espoused human rights and indigenous peoples' rights.
160. Attempted to raise indigenous people's rights.
161. Formed in parallel to AMADA for similar activities.
162. To promote indigenous cultural identity.
163. To strengthen emotional and cultural unity.
164. To repeal Restricted Area Permit and to implement Inner Line Permit against outsiders.
165. To defend territorial integrity and unity.
166. It attempted collective farming under the motto *economic self-reliance*.
167. A Meetei cultural organization; propagated sovereignty through peaceful means.
168. To defend territorial integrity.
169. To defend territorial integrity and democratic rights.
170. On 22 June 1968, it demanded the Indian State to protect territorial integrity of Manipur.
171. 1999; To mourn lost of sovereignty to the British in 1891.
172. To commemorate women war against British Free Trade Policy in 1939.
173. 28 October 1999; organized under the theme of *'Self-determination is our birth right'*.
174. 2000: a Martyrs Memorial Complex was constructed at Cheiraoching Hill in memory of PLA leaders that were killed by the Indian armed forces at Kodompoki on 13 April 1982.
175. 2004; atleast 32 organizations formed Apunba Lup (united front) to agitate against AFSPA.
176. 26 June 2001; AMSU, AMKIL, AMUCO, IPSA, NIPCO, and UPF jointly passed 'People's Declaration' to defend the territorial integrity of Manipur.
177. Petition of the women society of the east 'submitted to the then Chief Minister of Manipur by the Manipur Nupi Khunnai', Imphal East, 16 May 1980.

178. Thokchom Rajen, 'Lamdamsida meira paibeegi eehou' in Macha Leima, *Nupigi Numit*, Special Issue, 12 December 1999, p. 172.
179. Besides the AFSPA there were several 'auxiliary repressive acts' imposed in Manipur such as the Unlawful Activities Prevention Act, The Punjab Security Act of 1953, the National Security Act of 1980 and so on.
180. *Meira Paibee,* Imphal: National Research Centre Manipur, 1999.
181. Nonibala's statement, at the Discussion of Publication on Democracy, 21 March 2003, State Guest House, Imphal, organized by Human Rights Alert, Imphal and American Centre, Calcutta.
182. Mayanglambam Kunjeshwari Devi, *The Women Movements in Manipur*, M. Phil. Dissertation, Manipur University, 1992, p. 64.
183. 'Eikhoigee wakat (Our complaint)', Communication group Manipur Nupee Kanglup Kangleipak (Manipur); Imphal, 27 May 1980.
184. E.g., International Women's Day invitation circulated by All Manipur Women's Volunteer Association, dated 1st march 2000; 'Please take part in the United People's Manipur Defense Rally', pamphlet, dated 18 September 2000; Manipur Dark Day invitation card, 17 April 1999; People's declaration to defend the territorial integrity of Manipur, 26 June 2001; Declaration on Manipur People's Solidarity with the United Nations, 24 October 1999.
185. Meira Paibi Memorial Complex, Imphal, *The Hueiyen Lanpao Daily*, 9 March 2009.
186. Partha Chatterjee, ed., *Wages of Freedom,* New Delhi: Oxford University Press, 1999, p. 16.
187. Susan Bayly, *Caste, Society and Politics in India from the Eighteenth Century to the Modern Age*, Delhi: Cambridge University Press, 2002, p. 148.

3

Coordination and Conflict among Nationalisms

I. INTRODUCTION

India or *Bharat* or *Hindustan*, *Manipur* or *Kangleipak*, *Nagalim*, and *Zale'n-gam* or *Zogam* or *Zoram* were four diametrical nationalisms keeping in a quagmire of *status quo* four respectively constituted diametrical nationalist fronts. Coordination and conflict among these fronts were largely strategic and tactical to accomplish respectively subscribed nationalism. In the event of party fissures within fronts, there were 'internal' party conflicts and the perplexing situation of tactical party coordination across fronts to defend party interest. Firstly, parties might enter into tactical alliance in order to outlive others that were perceived to be immediate party enemies. Secondly, in tactical coordination, nationalism affiliation alone is not the determining factor, as during factional war, immediate party survival was more important than national loyalty.

It is beyond the scope of the book to dwell on minute details of armed insurgent parties. Since most of the information about insurgents, other than occasional reports appearing in the media, could not be accessed, it is difficult to analyse the dynamics of conflict and coordination that occurred every now and then. I shall, however, provide a brief chronology of party formation, party factions, and tactical alliance along and across nationalisms, which had important bearings in Manipur.

Apparently, Manipur in July 2009 had more than 30 armed insurgent parties. Chronologically, the Communist Party of Manipur, formed on 29 October 1948, and its Red Guard, formed in March 1950, carried out armed communist movement till the death of its leader, Hijam Irabot, in September 1951.[1] Irabot felicitated the formation of the United Front Liberation Government of Burma constituted by the Communist Party of Burma, the Burma Communist Party, and the People's Comrade Party and sought its support for Communist Party of Manipur.[2] In 1955, in the Naga Hills and Tuenshang areas, the Naga National Council (NNC) began an armed protracted war against the Indian State to assert Naga sovereignty. By the mid-1960s, NNC cadres were operating in the Northern hill areas of Manipur. In 1964, the United National Liberation Front was formed to fight for Manipur sovereignty. It was followed by the emergence of the People's Revolutionary Party of Kangleipak (PREPAK) in 1977, the People's Liberation Army/ Revolutionary Peoples Front in 1978-9, and the Kangleipak Communist Party (KCP) in 1980. In the coming decades, PREPAK and KCP went into several factions. In the late 1970s, NNC was split and the National Socialist Council Nagaland (NSCN) was formed in 1980. In 1988, NSCN was split into NSCN (Isaac-Muivah) and NSCN (Khaplang) factions. The same year, the Kuki National Army, the Kuki National Organisation, and the Kuki National Front (KNF) were formed to fight for *Zale'n-gam* or Kukiland. In the early 1990s, UNLF split into the UNLF (Meghen) and UNLF (Oken) factions, which engaged in bloody clashes for several years. In 1992, the Kuki Liberation Army (KLA) was formed to fight for Kukiland. In 1993, the Zomi Revolutionary Organization (ZRO) was formed to fight for *Zogam* or *Zoram*. In 1994, the Kanglei Yawol Kanna Lup (KYKL) was formed by merging UNLF (Oken), PREPAK (Meiraba faction), and KCP (Ibo Pishak faction). The party split into Oken and Achou Toijamba factions in 1996 but reunited in mid February 2002. In 1995, the Hmar People's Convention-Democracy was formed to fight for the autonomy and integrity of the Hmar people. In 1997, the Zomi Revolutionary Army was formed with the support of NSCN-IM during the Kuki-Paite conflict of 1997–8. ZRA became the armed wing of the Zomi Revolutionary Organization. In 1999, the Kuki Revolutionary Army was formed, and in 2000, the United Kuki

Liberation Front was formed to fight for Kukiland. In 2004, the Komrem People's Army was formed for the integrity of the Komrem people comprising the Aimol, Chiru, Kom, Koirem, Kharam and Purum communities. On 23 November 2007, NSCN-Unification was formed by some deserters from NSCN-IM. On 30 April 2008, the United Naga People's Council, consisting of the splinter group of NSCN (IM), was formed to restore inter-community peaceful coexistence, in order to safeguard the territorial integrity and sovereignty of Manipur. On 20 May, a Naga based United People's Liberation Army was formed and it supported the territorial integrity of Manipur. On 6 November, a faction of PREPAK formed United People's Party of Kangleipak. The same year, Manipur Naga Revolutionary Front was formed under the leadership of Allen Siro to save the territorial integrity of Manipur. In July 2009, following a desertion on 21 June, a splinter group of KYKL formed the KYKL-Military Defence Force. On 25 February, Zeliangrong United Front (ZUF) was floated on a primary aim to protect the Zeliangrong interest. In June 2011, a faction of PREPAK started operating under the banner, PREPAK (Progressive). The same year, the Maoist Communist Party, Manipur, was formed for the national and social liberation of Manipur.

The Indian State's objective of suppressing insurgency and political dissent has been very clear. In pursuing their objectives, the Indian State's military either confronted or entered into tactical negotiations and ceasefire with various insurgent parties. On the other hand the activities of the insurgent parties can be broadly grouped into three: (a) restorative, (b) chauvinistic and, (c) integrative. Firstly, it could be restorative as in the case of demand for restoration of perceived lost territory. Secondly, it could be 'national chauvinistic' in the sense that communal hatred and ethnic cleansing are being carried out in the name of defending the projected nation. And there is claim for exclusive territorial right over the projected national territory. Thirdly, it could be 'integrative' to consolidate and prevent the 'nation' from being divided into segments. In the course of actions, defections, or desertion to other party, factional clashes within parties, and conflict and coordination between parties were reported from time to time.

The chronology of coordination and conflict amongst insurgent groups is being briefly produced. To begin with, in the 1980s, there were clashes between the NSCN and the NNC and among the various factions of the NSCN. In 1990, RPF along with PREPAK and KCP, formed the Revolutionary Joint Committee. In 1991, UNLF, NSCN (Khaplang), and the United Liberation Front of Assam (ULFA) formed the Indo-Burma Revolutionary Front. In 1993, NSCN-IM formed a United Liberation Front of Seven Sisters, and in 1994, it formed a Self-Defence United Front of South-East Himalayan Region. In the early 1990s, there were clashes between UNLF (Meghen) and UNLF (Oken). During these clashes, the Meghen and Oken factions had a tactical alliance respectively with NSCN-K and NSCN-IM. During the Kuki Naga Clash of 1992–6, KLA was in conflict with NSCN-IM. It was alleged that, in 1997, Zomi Revolutionary Army (ZRA) was formed with the support of NSCN-IM during the Kuki-Paite conflict. Since 1997, NSCN-IM had been under ceasefire with the government. It is being alleged that NSCN-IM made an alliance with HPC-D and some other Zomi and Mizo insurgents against Manipur insurgents. In 1999, UNLF, PREPAK, and RPF formed the Manipur People's Liberation Front. In 2005, the Kuki National Organisation became an umbrella organization of several Kuki-Chin-Mizo insurgent groups[3] and entered into Suspension of Operation with the Indian army. In 2008 Kuki-Mizo based umbrella organization called United People's Front[4] entered into Suspension of Operation with the Indian army. In 2009, UNLF and KYKL formed a Joint Coordination Committee. In 2009, RPF forged an alliance with CPI (Maoist) of India. Since 2011, Zeliangrong United Front (ZUF), despite being Naga, has been clashing with NSCNs. In July 2011, the Coordination Committee was formed by KCP, KYKL, PREPAK, PREPAK (Progressive), RPF, UNLF, and UPPK. But UPPK defected to the Indian army in 2013. It has been alleged that certain factions of KCP were working in close alliance with the Indian army even from jail with the support of the police. In May 2013, the United Revolutionary Front (URF)[5], KCP (Lamphel),[6] and KYKL (MDF) entered into a Memorandum of Understanding with the Indian army.

II. TIMELINE OF DIAMETRICAL NATIONALISMS

Nationalisms involve struggle for territorial control. Anthony Smith argues that possession of territory or a recognized homeland is an essential goal of nationalism.[7] In this regard, Anderson is of the view that, in most of the colonial countries, the nationalists' 'nation-state' had to be grounded firmly in a territorial and social space inherited from the pre-revolutionary past.[8] Hobsbawm, however, questions the very idea of territorial 'inheritance' and he says that, for most Asian countries, 'national territories' were usually constructed out of territorial demarcations made by the European colonial powers that had also brought together the populations within such territories under a common administration.[9] I would like to argue that, in Manipur's context, the idea of inheritance is relevant in the case of the Indian State that controls Manipur on the basis of pre-Independence treaties and documents. Manipur integrationists may also be considered to be inheriting certain colonial territorial perception since the existing boundary that they intend to defend is a larger or small product of colonial boundary settlements. However, Anderson's understanding is relevant for the established countries that are being rightly or wrongly referred to as nation-states. Insurgency for sovereignty calls for a different explanation. Insurgents had used colonial accounts primarily to substantiate that their nation is different from others' and that seeds of communal divisions were transplanted by the colonial rulers. On the contrary, assertions for *Nagalim*, *Zale'n-gam,* and *Zogam* suggest resistance to Smith's pre-revolutionary inheritance.

1900–20

Manipur in 1901 shared boundaries with Myanmar in the east, Naga Hills in the north, Cachar (in Assam) in the west and Lushai Hills (in Mizoram) and Myanmar in the south-west.[10] Apprehension about 'territorial disintegration' seemed absent. Sporadic raiding among hill village communities and low scale protest against colonial rulers, creation of different administrative regions[11] for 'tribes' and 'non-tribes' did not seem to be a threat to integrity. Or simply, the idea of integrity had not developed. The formation of Naga Club in 1918 in the Naga Hills and the Thadou-Kuki rebellion of 1917–19 seemed to have no impact on Manipur integrity issue. However, there were territorial assertions vis-à-vis colonial boundary demarcations. In 1908, the Manipur State Durbar opposed the Lt. Governor of Assam's decision by which Manipur was forfeited from the right to claim any share in the Barak River Fishery.[12] Other than this, there is no reported fear of 'disintegration'.

1921–40

Sporadic and localized parallel community formations along linguistic and cultural lines were shaping among Zelianrongs (Tamenglong District), Meeteis (Cachar in Assam) and certain sections of population (Nagaland). Firstly, in the Naga Hills and Tuenshang Areas by late 1920s Naga Club had organized Angami, Kacha Naga, Kuki, Sema, Lotha and Rengma communities. A memorandum to the Simon Commission, dated 10 January 1929 expressed their desire to create Nagaland by incorporating communities which they had not known then.[13] Secondly, in present-day Tamenglong District, there was Zelianrong movement (1927–31) led by Haipou Jadonang to create Kabui Raj, later on identified with Naga Raj. After Jadonang was executed on 29 August 1931, a woman leader, Gaidinliu, fled Manipur and spreaded the movement into the Cachar and Naga Hills.[14] Later, Gaidinliu had to face adversaries in defending her *Heraka* cult[15] and her Kampai (soldiers) clashed with the NNC in the 1960s. But the movement boosted incipient Naga formation in the 1930s. Thirdly, there was Meetei religio-cultural revivalism against Hinduism led by Naoriya Phulo at Jaribon village (Assam) in 1930, which began to have impact in Manipur from the mid-1940s.

In parallel, Manipur monarchy asserted territorial claims over the hills. In January 1928, Manipur Durbar demanded direct governance over hill districts,[16] and it was reiterated to the Butler Committee. The Durbar also demanded that, for strategic reasons, the Manipur boundary should be established in writing.[17] In November, the Durbar reiterated restoration of the Kabow Valley.[18] In the mid-1930s the Durbar members opposed separate annual budgets for hills and non-hills.[19] On 21 December 1938 it asserted to control the hill budget.[20] On 1 April 1939 and on 8 March 1945 it demanded amalgamation of hill-valley administration.[21]

1941–50

Manipur integrationists in late 1940s were apprehensive about territorial lose. They opposed Sir Coupland's plan to form Northeast Frontier Agency by merging Manipur and other areas under one administration.[22] They felt 'Manipur will be totally segregated from the hills and thus become an incomplete geographical entity.'[23] Their concern for territory was mentioned in January 1947 before the Chamber of Princes.[24] In May 1947, the Durbar demanded evacuation of Burmese forces from Manipur.[25] The visit of King Bodhachandra in October and November to Shillong was meant to raise 'reversion of the Kabaw Valley to Manipur.'[26] The Joint Boundary Mission with the Burmese government in December 1947 was aimed at defending the boundary between the two 'nations'.[27] In late 1848, Manipur integrationists protested the inclusion of Manipur in the proposed *Purbanchal* state within India.[28]

In the meantime, Manipur integrationists were attempting consolidation across communities and adopted the Manipur Constitution 1947 and the Manipur Hill Areas Administration Regulation 1947. They also played roles in forming the popular government of 1948. The Constitution Making Committee members were drawn from different communities[29] to ensure 'the integration of the hill and valley administrations.'[30] They adopted the Manipur State Hill (Administration) Regulation 1947 that recognized local self-government in the hills. The constitution was based on voluntary federalism and was adopted on a trial basis of five years.[31] The first Legislative Assembly in 1948 was formed by members comprising 32 Meetei, 4 *panggal* or Muslim and 16 'tribal' elected representatives. Integrity was proclaimed by the King.[32]

However, parallel community formations were gaining momentum in the Lushai Hills, the Naga Hills, and the Tuenshang areas.

Firstly, the Mizo Union was formed in 1946 in the Lushai Hills to defend Lushai customs and land rights. But 'the Lushai (Mizos) want[ed] the Kuki of Manipur and other areas in their boundaries.'[33] They demanded that 'Chin Hills Regulation, 1896 and Bengal Eastern

Frontier Regulation 1873 should be retained.'[34] In 1947, the Mizo Union asserted 'right of territorial unity and solidarity and self-determination within the province of Assam in free India.'[35] Similarly, Kuki-Chins in Burma demanded to include Naga Hill areas, the Arakan Hill District, and the Paletwa Township in Chin Hills in their proposal.[36]

Secondly, in the Naga Hills and Tuenshang areas, the Naga Club formed in 1918 was rechristened as the Naga National Council in 1946. Many asserted that they were not part of India and wanted freedom.[37] The NNC agreed to form an interim government under the protection of Dominion of India for funds, development and defence for ten years after which the Naga people would decide on self-determination.[38] Despite disagreement on some points,[39] the NNC signed the Nine Point Agreement with the Governor of Assam, Sir Akbar Haydari in June 1947. The agreement acknowledged territorial interest of NNC as, '...present administrative divisions should be modified so as to (1) bring back into the Naga Hills District all the Forests transferred to the Sibsagar and Nowgong Districts in the past, and (2) bring under one unified administrative unit, as far as possible, all Nagas.'[40]

These two trends had tremendous impact in Manipur. According to Lal Dena, 'all Hmars living in different parts of northeast India, particularly those in Manipur opted for integration with Mizoram. (They) boycotted the first Manipur general election of 1948 to join the *Mizo Sorkar*.'[41] Amongst the Mao Community, Athiko Daiho in 1946 advocated 'complete secession of hills from Manipur and the formation of Lushai Hills, Somra Tract; Chin Hills Naga Hills, et cetera, into a federated hills.'[42] He founded the Naga National League (NNL) in the Mao areas to fulfil the dream.[43] In early 1948, the League expressed cooperation with NNC to merge certain hill regions of Manipur with the Naga Hills.[44] In the first week of March 1948, a committee was set up to desist from paying revenues to the Manipur government.[45] The League boycotted Manipur elections and appealed to the Indian State to defend the self-determination of Mao and 'other allied Nagas of Manipur.'[46] Manipur government resorted to repression, leading to the killing of three, bullet injury to four, and arrest of Daiho and N. Modoli on 27 August 1948.[47] Although the communist leader Irabot applauded 'revolutionary movement of the Mao Nagas'[48] diametrical nationalism opposed to Manipur became clear. Communal assertions were gradually developing. But the Indian State subscribed to the recommendation of 1947 which stipulated, '(in Northeast areas) ...the present boundaries have, we find, been in existence for many years and we feel that there is time for a separate commission set up by the Provincial Government to work on the problems involved.'[49] Therefore on 26 October 1949 the Dominion of India defined 'whole of the area which, immediately before the commencement of this order, is comprised within the state of Manipur.'[50]

1950–70

On 16 May 1951 NNC reportedly secured 99.9 per cent vote for self-determination in a plebiscite in the Naga Hills and Tuenshang Areas. On 25 January 1952 NNC launched civil disobedience against general election. When the Indian State began armed repression, the NNC launched a protracted armed struggle in 1955. On 2 April 1956, the NNC inaugurated Federal Government of Nagaland.[51] In the meanwhile Naga People's Convention was formed at Kohima in 1957[52] to broker peace. The Indian State adopted the Naga Hills-Tuensang Areas Act on 29 November 1957 to defuse the NNC. In 1959, the Makokchung convention, organized by the NPC, proposed and adopted a Sixteen Point Agreement that included integration of contiguous Naga inhabited areas under one administration. The NPC, after negotiations with the Indian State, signed a Sixteen Points Agreement in July 1960. The agreement intimated to form the State of Nagaland comprising the Naga Hills-Tuensang Areas and recognized 'the wish for the contiguous areas to join the new state.'[53] The State of Nagaland Act, 1962 was passed and statehood was inaugurated on 1 December 1963. In this scenario, the Nagaland Baptist Church leaders' initiative for peace was the formation of a Peace Mission on 24 February 1964. Responding to the Peace Mission, there was a bilateral agreement between the Indian State and the FGN on 6 September 1964. The Nagaland Assembly on 12 December 1964 resolved to urge the Indian State 'for integration of Naga areas.'[54] The same demand was reiterated by the Nagaland Assembly again on 28 August 1970.[55] On 21 October 1970, the Naga Integration Central Committee resolved to observe widespread Naga Integration Day throughout 'Naga areas' on 20 November.[56]

In Manipur, due to Central rule from 1949, 'which did not have any democratic base, created a political vacuum in the hills of Manipur... naturally, the Nagas joined the Naga Nationalist Movement.'[57] In 1954, Daiho proposed to the State Reorganisation Commission to create a hill state comprising Manipur, Naga Hills and Lushai Hills.[58] When R. Suisa became an Outer Manipur MP (1957), he organized the Nagas of Manipur. On 22 October 1957, the Manipur Naga Convention was held at Ukhrul to speed up Naga integration and to form the Manipur Naga Council. It could affiliated Zelianrong, Anal Union, Mao-Maram Union, and Tangkhul Long by the time of the second convention on 30 November 1958.[59] During the ceasefire period in Nagaland in the 1960s, 'activities of the Naga Federal Government became very active in Manipur's Ukhrul, Mao and Tamenglong areas.[60] Naga Integration Committee (NIC) was formed in Manipur. On 26 July 1968, NIC submitted a memorandum to the Prime Minister demanding integration of the Naga area of Manipur with Nagaland.[61] The same demand was raised to the Prime Minister in September 1969 by NIC, which subsequently published a booklet entitled *Why not South Nagaland by the Forgotten Nagas*. The first Convention of the Nagas of Manipur held under Session Chairman, James L. Kilakhe and Secretary Peter Pheiray, at Mao Gate in Manipur on 16 May 1970 resolved the Naga people to live together in one state.[62]

Among the Kuki-Chin-Mizo groups, the Paite National Council at its general meetings in 1957 and 1960[63] asserted to unite Chin people. On 30 May 1960 PNC submitted a memorandum to the Prime Minister demanding 'unification of the Zomis of India, Burma and Pakistan under one Country.'[64] In 1960, the Kuki National Assembly submitted a memorandum to the Prime Minister stating that Kuki areas had accidentally been included in Manipur.[65] In 1964, the Kuki National Assembly and Manipur Mizo Integration Council passed a resolution to create a single administrative unit for Kuki and Mizo peoples.[66] A convention of Kuki-Chin-Mizo organizations was held from 15 to 18 January 1965 at Kawnpui in Churachandpur to secure 'a 'Mizoram State', comprising all the areas inhabited by members of the Mizo tribe.'[67] The ninth General Assembly of Hmar National Union was held at Hmar Kholia (Cachar in Assam) from 13 to 17 January 1966 with Shri H. Thonglora as the chair. On 24 and 25 February 1966, a meeting of the Simte National Assembly was held at Dumen Village, in Churachandpur, under the president-ship of Kachindes Simte.[68] On 24 March 1966, a public meeting of the Mizo National Front was held at Ratu (Mizoram) about 10 miles from Tipaimukh in Manipur. It was resolved that the MNF would attack Simol Tou and Tipaimukh simultaneously. On 26 August 1966, a meeting of PNC was held at Tuitemun Village in Jiribam (Manipur) under the president of Zelu Chin of Chingmun. The memorandum of MNF (Mizoram) submitted to the Prime Minister on 30 October 1965 reasserted integration of the Mizo peoples.[69] According to Chaube, 'in 1965 Laldenga, the Mizo National Front *supremo* lured the Kuki youths of Manipur towards formation of a Greater Mizoram (including parts of India, Burma and Bangladesh) at an all-party Conference at Churachandpur (in Manipur).'[70] Accordingly, Mizo Integration Council was formed in Manipur at the time of the talks between MNF leaders and the Indian State. In 1967, violence occurred in the south Manipur hills in league with the MNF on the issue of enforcement of Manipur Hill Areas (Acquisition of Chiefs Rights) Act of 1967.[71]

Manipur integrationists were alerted by 1950. The Constitution (Scheduled Tribes) Order, 1950 and subsequent amendments, VIth Schedule of the Indian Constitution, Manipur (Village Authorities in Hill Areas) Act, 1956, Manipur Land Revenue and Land Reforms Act, 1960,[72] and the Union Territories Act of 1963 which recognized special provisions for hill areas of Manipur[73] were perceived as pro-tribal and divisive. The activities of the Kuki-Chin-Mizo and Naga organizations had worried them. Suspicion about the creation of Nagaland state in 1963 and Naga integration initiatives of the Nagaland Assembly and humiliations for lost of Kabaw Valley to Burma in '1953' and devaluation of Manipur under Part C State status were interplaying. They began forming several organizations, including insurgent groups, to assert territorial integrity. According to Constantine, the United National Liberation Front was formed in 1964 to achieve 'liberation of Manipur and restoration of the Kabow Valley and parts of Assam.'[74] Revolutionary Government of Manipur's concept of Manipur included 'areas of the Sibsagar District and parts of Cachar' (Assam).[75] UNLF was worried that NNC activities were increasing in Mao, Tamenglong, and Ukhrul areas during the ceasefire in 1960s.[76] In 1965, the All Manipur People's Convention and All Manipur Students' Union protested threat to the integrity of Manipur. On 17 September 1965 All Manipur People's Convention submitted a memorandum to the Indian State expressing apprehension about potential lose of territory due to suspension of operation with the FGN/NNC.[77] Manipur Territorial Congress Committee on 22 June 1968 demanded an assurance by the Indian State to protect territorial integrity.[78] On 26 December 1968, Manipur People's Party was formed 'to safeguard the territorial integrity of Manipur and ethnic identity of the people.'[79] On 28 December 1968 Pan Manipur Youth League was formed to 'strengthen the relationship of Manipuris, to promote unity, understanding and organized life.'[80] After its first conference in Imphal, a mammoth procession was organized demanding restoration of the valley (Kabow) from Burma.[81] In 1970, a book entitled *Boundaries of Manipur* authored by Dr Chandramani was published.[82]

1971–90

On 22 January 1972, the general meeting of Naga Integration Central Committee, at Shajaoba, at Mao in Senapati District reiterated integration of contiguous Naga areas.[83] However, the integration movement was delayed by some dynamics. In Nagaland, the NNC was weakened by Phizo's escape to London since 1960, the house arrest of Vice President Imkongmeren in January 1975, increasing repression by the Indian State, and political polarization among Nagas. When the Shillong Accord of 11 November 1975 was interpreted as the NCC accepting the Indian Constitution,[84] it led to factionalism within the NNC. The National Socialist Council of Nagaland (NSCN) was formed on 31 January 1980 and it immediately engaged in armed clashes with the NNC. Furthermore, communal sectarianism within the NSCN resulted in even more factions. On 30 April 1988, a faction led by Khaplang carried out a coup and the NSCN was split into the NSCN (Isaac Swu & Muivah) and NSCN (Khaplang) factions.

In the meanwhile, in Lushai Hills, as a follow up of Mizoram Accord on 30 June 1986 that was signed between the Mizo National Front and the Indian State,[85] the state of Mizoram was created in 1987. The Accord failed to ensure unification of Mizo inhabited areas across states.[86] A section of disillusioned Hmar people formed the Hmar People's Convention (HPC) in 1986. From April 1987, the HPC carried out a protracted armed struggle to create an independent state consisting of Hmar inhabited areas of Mizoram, Manipur, and Assam.[87] In the meanwhile, Kuki Tribes Reorganization Demand Committee was formed in Manipur. On 28 April 1987, the Committee submitted a memorandum to the Indian State demanding to include 'the Kuki Tribes in the scheduled Tribes lists.'[88] Some sections of Kukis formed the Kuki National Organisation and its armed wing Kuki National Army in 1988[89] to bring together all the Kuki-inhabited areas in the Kabaw Valley (Myanmar) and in Manipur under one administrative unit called *Zale'n-gam.*[90] The same year on 18 May, another Kuki organization, the Kuki National Front (KNF), was formed[91] primarily to fight the NSCN-IM and to create Kukiland. On 20 May, delegates of Kuki-Chin-Mizo who met at Champhai (Mizoram) formed Zo Re-unification Organisation (ZORO) for unification of the Zomi people.[92]

As far as Manipur integrationists were concerned, they suspected the Manipur (Hill Areas) District Councils Act of 26 December 1971 that allowed considerable autonomy in the hill districts. However, the Northeastern Areas (Reorganisation) Act, 1971, dated 30 December 1971 and the grant of Manipur statehood on 21 January 1972 seemed to have temporarily diverted their attention until the Naga Shillong Accord of 1975 became controversial for its territorial extent. The Supplementary Agreement to the Shillong Accord on 5 January 1976, which stipulated that the 'arrangement [of peace and deposition of arms] at agreed place[s] would be made in Manipur'[93] worried them. The apprehension was logical as Naga insurgents had been active in Manipur during the ceasefire period. In Nagaland, Member of Parliament Ranu Saiza and charismatic leader Rani Gaidinliu openly demanded merger of Senapati, Ukhrul, Tamenglong, and Chandel districts with Nagaland. In order to counteract, the Manipur People's Party (MPP) organized conference in July 1978 and resolved to defend Manipur integrity. The MPP memorandum to the Indian State, dated 4 October 1978, demanded protection of integrity. In the meanwhile, insurgent parties such as PREPAK, RPF/PLA, and KCP, which asserted territorial integrity, were formed. However, there seems to be relative silence on the integrity question in the 1980s due to other sensitive and overlapping issues such as imposition of AFSPA to entire Manipur since 1980, human rights assertions, the Meetei revivalist movement, anti-foreigner agitation, Manipur language recognition agitations, and factional clash among Naga insurgents, et cetera.

1990–2000

Kuki–Naga Clash

In 1991, Kuki integrationists in Myanmar launched armed protracted war to create Kuki-homeland. State repression led to the uprooting of several Kuki villages[94] and fleeing of many to Manipur and Mizoram states. It led to Kuki territorial assertion gaining momentum in Manipur: for example, another outfit, the Kuki Liberation Army (KLA), was formed in 1992. The stage was set for a violent dispute on the question of territory and six years of Kuki Naga Clash (1992–6).

Narratives of the Kuki-Naga Clash are propaganda articulated by diametrical camps. According to the Kuki National Organisations, the clash was sparked off as a result of a quit notice dated 22 October 1992, served to the Kukis by the United Naga Council.[95] According to G.S. Oinam, the NSCN (IM) was extorting a 'land tax from the Kukis.'[96] The Naga People's Movement for Human Rights, however, says that the Kukis were creating a homeland out of Naga areas in Manipur,[97] Nagaland, and Assam.[98] In April 1994, Glenn T. Morris wrote,

> (clash erupted) in May 1992, in the town of Moreh (in Manipur), where elements of the Kuki National Organization began to impose taxes on the Naga residents and merchants of Moreh. Subsequent oppressive acts by the KNA led to the Naga abandonment or Kuki destruction of nine villages in and around Moreh. Eventually, either spontaneous Naga village self-defence (rechristened as Naga Lim Guard) or elements of the NSCN-Muivah responded to the KNA taxation, resulting in intense armed battles in the area.[99]

In the following month, *Economic & Political Weekly* published a different narrative that reads

> NSCN imposed a land tax on the Kuki settlements in Manipur, and it also declared that Kukis (a signatory to the Naga Club memorandum of 1929) would not be included in the list of ethnic groups that would be part of an independent Nagaland. As a consequence, the Kuki retaliated by openly declaring their different racial descent and expressed aspirations for an independent Kuki homeland by forming the Kuki National Organisation ...The Kukis had always resented the tax levied on them by the NSCN and the formation of KNA emboldened the Kukis, especially those settled in Chandel district of Manipur bordering Myanmar, to refuse payment of the tax...Therefore, a conflict ...[100]

Perhaps, diametrical nationalisms were the factors of the conflict that made many vulnerable sections suffer the most in the long run. The role of the Indian army was suspected. NPMHR, in April 1994, charged that a combined force of the KNA and the Indian army had invaded Tingpui Laimanai Kabui village on 5 September 1993.[101] It was suspected that the State was taking revenge on Nagas through the Kuki insurgents.[102] The NSCN (IM), on 27 July 1994, condemned what it termed 'the treacherous use of the nomadic Kuki terrorists by the Indian government in butchering the innocent Naga.'[103] Kuki National Organisation, however, charged that the Indian army and Naga insurgents were in collusion, as NSCN-IM cadres in Indian army uniform were carrying out widespread attack on the Kukis.[104] The Revolutionary People's Front, however, targeted the Indian army for being a silent spectator during the Kuki-Naga clash.[105] There were rumours about some Manipur insurgents giving training and guarding Kuki villages to protect them from the NSCN-IM. There were also rumours about Mayang traders amassing huge profit during the conflict by selling gunpowder, bullets, and licensed shot guns to the warring camps. These charges and rumours had important bearing on communal perceptions.

Kuki–Paite Clash 1997–8

In 1992, Hmar People's Convention and Mizoram government negotiated and a memorandum of settlement was signed on 27 July 1994. Dissatisfied with its outcome, a section parted ways with the over ground HPC and formed Hmar People's Convention – Democracy in 1995.[106] Two years before, the Zomi Reunification Organization (ZRO)[107] was formed in 1993 to integrate the Zomi people in Chin state (Myanmar), Chittagong Hill Tracts (Bangladesh), Mizoram, and Manipur under an imagined *Zogam*. In the meanwhile on 20 May 1993 and 1995, memorandums of the Zo Reunification Organisation (ZORO) to the President of the US and the UN member nations sought help for unification of the Mizo/Zomi peoples.[108] Accordingly, the ZRO also carried out a memorandum campaign and submitted it to the Indian Prime Minister on 6 September 1993.[109] On 9 August, it circulated pamphlets asking Zomis to unite.[110] On 2 September 1995, the leaders of the Paite National Council, the Simte Tribe Council, the Tedim-Chin Union, and the Vaiphei National Organisation signed an agreement to intensify efforts towards re-unification of Zomis under the ZRO. Unity initiatives involved territorial claims, collection of taxes or funds, and control over resources, et cetera. It was temporarily halted as a result of Kuki – Paite clash from June 1997 to October 1998.

Kuki-Paite clash was sparked off by killing of eleven Zomis by Kuki National Front (president faction) on 24 June 1997 at Saikul in Senapati District. To retaliate ZRO formed Zomi Revolutionary Army and Zomi National Volunteers as armed wing and overground front respectively. According to Zomi National Volunteers, to re-unify Kuki-Zomi peoples the term Zomi became a nomenclature accepted by the Zous, Simtes, Vaipheis, Paites and Tedim-Chin tribes, while the Thadou-speaking group of tribes denies it and maintains the term Kuki as their nomenclature, 'the KNF (P) applies criminal force to induce the Zomi tribes to accept the nomenclature Kuki.'[111] Differences led to dispute over area control of taxation and membership. Therefore the Saikul incident sparked off communal clash in other parts of Manipur, particularly in Churachandpur District. Killing and displacement[112] continued until a ceasefire was signed on 1 October 1998 to respect status quo of different nomenclatures, membership and taxation.[113]

GoI–NSCN (IM) Ceasefire Trajectory

NSCN (IM) was admitted to the Unrepresented Peoples and Nations Organization in 1993 and on 30 July Flemish Support Group for Indigenous Peoples expressed solidarity to the Naga question. On 14 September 1994 Nagaland Assembly resolved to upheld Naga integration. Manipur Assembly on 24 March 1995 condemned the Nagaland Assembly resolution and resolved to defend Manipur integrity. Manipur integrationists formed Committee for Peace and Integrity (COFPAI) and carried out three months integrity campaign from March to May in 1996. In 1996 United National Liberation Front circulated a booklet that stipulated that Manipur had been an ancestral territory.[114] The same year, Revolutionary People's Front's memorandum to the UN charged the Indian State as impairing territorial integrity and sovereignty of Manipur.[115]

In early 1997 Manipur integrationists were worried by the ceasefire negotiation between GoI and NSCN-IM. Manipur Assembly on 14 March 1997 resolved to defend territorial integrity. When three months ceasefire between GoI and NSCN-IM was effective from 25 July 1997 the Indian State was silent on Manipur integrity. Therefore, All Manipur United Clubs Organisation declared 'the time has come for all the people of Manipur to stand up against the divisive forces which are bent upon creating fear-psychosis amongst the innocent people and turning Manipur into a killing field.'[116] A unprecedentedly massive public rally was organized in the Imphal Valley on 4 August 1997 to defend territorial integrity.

In 1998 NSCN (IM) demanded formal extension of ceasefire to all Naga inhabited areas. It boycotted 'elections on 19 and 23

February 1998 and (demanded) praying for pacifism through the hoisting of white flags throughout the length and breadth of *Nagalim*.'[117] General Secretary Thuingaleng Muivah reaffirmed, 'the cease-fire area coverage has to be extended to the Manipur side also.'[118] In the meanwhile Kuki National Organisation published a booklet entitled *Zale'n-gam: The Kuki Nation* in 1998. The booklet argued for multi-national theory for Manipur and asserted Kuki homeland.[119] The Manipur Assembly on 17 December passed a resolution to defend Manipur integrity.

On 2 March 1999 NSCN–IM proclaimed, to use the term *Nagalim* in place of Nagaland.[120] It released a map of *Nagalim* depicting 1,20,000 sq. km. areas incorporating Karbi Anglong and North Cachar Hills District (Assam); parts of Golaghat, Sibasagar, Dibrugarh, Tinsukia, and Jorhat districts in Assam; parts of Dibang Valley, Lohit, Tirap and Changlang districts of Arunachal Pradesh and Tamenlong, Senapati, Ukhrul, Chandel and Ukhrul districts of Manipur. From 31 May to 2 July it convened Consultative Body Meeting of mass organizations to assert solidarity in the struggle for self-determination.[121] There was also alleged NSCN (IM) hand in the formation of Kuki Revolutionary Army (KRA) in December 1999. While these were on, the ceasefire was extended for one year from 1 August. Manipur integrationists responded with integrity 'expeditions' in the hill areas, patriotic programme, sports, and cultural events to defend integrity.

On 4 April 2000, the Naga People's Movement for Human Rights reiterated to the Senators and representatives of USA that *Nagalim* covered all Naga inhabited areas. In June, the NSCN-IM demanded the Indian State to extend ceasefire to all Naga inhabited areas.[122] The Indian State insisted that there could not be a formal ceasefire, but that an informal one could be extended.[123] The NSCN-IM threatened to withdraw from the ceasefire. Manipur integrationists suspected that ceasefire was practically extended to Manipur. On 28 September 2000, Apunba Manipur Kanba Ima Lup and National Identity Protection Committee organized a rally and asserted their integrity.[124] In October, there was tension arising out of reported encroachment into the Dzuckou Valley by the Nagaland Government.[125]

2001

In early 2001, Manipur integrationists were on routine integrity cultural programmes. For instance, AMESCO and Kabui Dhama Sabha Manipur jointly organized Zelianrong festival Gan-Ngai for 'peace and betterment of our future generations.'[126] However, integrity tension suddenly erupted. On 7 March, the NSCN-IM threatened to withdraw from ceasefire unless it was extended to entire *Nagalim.*[127] On 8 March, the NSCN-IM circulated an open letter 'to Our Meetei Brothers and Sisters'[128] that warned, 'We do not believe in forced brotherhood, forced union, forced integration, and forced marriage.'[129] On 19 March, Kohima Declaration was adopted to launch a campaign against all draconian laws in operation in *Nagalim.*[130] In response, the Manipur Assembly on 22 March resolved to oppose any threat to the Manipur integrity. NSCN–IM on 12 April urged upon Meeteis 'to see that their national case is well founded so that the dangers involved in using unruly tribe or group for expediency against the Nagas may be safely abandoned before it is too late.'[131] A memorandum signed by civil societies in India, submitted to the President of India on 24 April, demanded peace between the Indian State and NSCN-IM.[132] By 23 May, the NSCN (IM) was able to influence European Parliament to send an *ad hoc* parliamentary mission to conduct an enquiry for political solution to Naga question.[133]

On 14 June, the ceasefire was extended 'without territorial limits.' Immediately in Manipur, a general strike was called by the All Manipur United Club's Organisation and then by the All Manipur Students' Union for 72 hours from the midnight of 15 June. On 18 June, lakhs of peoples in the Imphal Valley took to the streets. Protestors set ablaze several government offices, including the Manipur State Legislative Assembly building, Assembly Secretariat, the CM's Bunglow, and other government and parliamentary party buildings. During repression, 14 persons were instantly killed in firing and several hundreds were injured. On 26 June 2001, the AMSU, AMKIL, AMUCO, IPSA, NIPCO, and UPF passed a resolution called the 'People's Declaration' to defend the territorial integrity of Manipur. Manipur integrationists raised black flags in the Imphal Valley as a mark of defeat and protest. Kuki integrationists took part in the protest on the ground that any attempt to extend the ceasefire in Kuki areas would jeopardize the political interest and existence of the Kukis.[134] Naga integrationists, in the meanwhile, organized a convention on 28 June in Senapati and adopted the Senapati Declaration to welcome extension of ceasefire without territorial limit. White flags were raised by Naga families in the hill districts.

The ceasefire protest in the Imphal valley gained momentum and spread to Assam and Arunachal Pradesh. Due to pressure, the Prime Minister on 24 June and 8 July gave assurances that the words 'without territorial limits' would be reviewed and territorial integrity of the Northeast states would not be disturbed. In Manipur, the Manipur Peace & Integrity Council and the United Committee Manipur were formed on 1 July and 3 July respectively to fight for integrity. On 27 July, the Indian State announced deletion of the three words 'without territorial limits'. It was widely welcomed by ceasefire protestors in Manipur, Assam, and Arunachal Pradesh. However, the announcement ignited protests in Nagaland and other Naga inhabited areas. Manipur integrationists sensed victory and white flags were hoisted in the Imphal Valley. Naga integrationists responded with black flags as signs of mourning and defeat. On 23 October 2001, the United Naga Council submitted a memorandum to the President of India demanding unification of all Naga inhabited areas.[135]

Manipur integrationists intensified integrity campaigns. A series of conventions, seminars, meetings, campaigns, events, cultural programmes, and publications to spread propaganda were held. The Integrated People's Progressive Union (IPPU) organized 'a three-day seminar on the impact of administration on mutual relationship of Manipuris', from 3 to 5 September 2001 with a motto to establish peace, harmony, and unity. A compilation entitled *Manipur Fact File 2001* called on the people for integrity. AMUCO published a booklet 'to erase and efface communal, sectarian and chauvinist ideologies, which are exploitative and oppressive in nature and are obstructing progress and development.'[136] In October, AMESCO organized a grand intercommunity feast-cum-interaction and exchange programme under the theme of integration for peace and coexistence.

2002

In January 2002, the United Committee Manipur organized a certificate distribution ceremony in honour of those who were either killed or injured in repression during what they termed the 'Great June Uprising' of 2001. It began an initiative to construct a 'Great June Uprising Memorial Complex at Kekrupat where the corpses of those killed during the June 2001 agitation were cremated.'[137] On 28 March, it called on the State to explain the operation of NSCN-IM cadres in Manipur. On 24 April, it insisted the State to declare statewide holiday on 18 June to commemorate the 'Great June Uprising Day'.[138] On 18 April, the UCM laid the foundation stone of the complex. In May, it organized a leaders' meet and a resolution was adopted to coordinate all the communities to discover origins to bring a harmonious society. On 7 May, a section of Manipur integrationists submitted a memorandum to the Prime Minister of India opposing proposed inclusion of hill districts in the VI Schedule of the Constitution on the ground that it would promote communal clash and territorial disintegration.[139] In the meanwhile, a Convention of Ethnic Reconsolidation was held on 16 May to form an organization called Ethno Heritage Council (HERICOUN) to strengthen inter-community unity.[140] On 20 May, the UCM invited community organizations[141] and a resolution termed *Apunbagi Wasak Warep* was adopted to defend territorial integrity. On 30 May AMUCO called on people to observe Protest Day on 14 June and Unity Day on 18 June. On 12 June 2002, the Manipur assembly resolved to defend territorial integrity. At the same time, AMUCO and AMSU called for a protest on 14 June under different themes: *Manipur Meeyambu Machet Tana Thugainaba Hotnabagi Mayokta Leppa Numit*[142] and *Eekheng Tahankhiba Numit*[143] respectively. The UCM, then, insisted the Manipur Government declare 18 June a Great June Uprising Day and a state holiday. Manipur State conceded to the demand. On 18 June, programmes were organized under different themes such as the Great June Uprising Day by UCM at the newly constructed complex, Unity Day by AMUCO, Integrity Day by the government, and under different themes by others. At the year end, UCM drafted a 'Draft Policy to Protect and Uphold the Unique Historical Features, Existing Historical Boundary and Also for

Bringing Emotional Integration of the People of Manipur to Achieve Faster Economic Development of the State.' It was submitted to the Indian leaders and publicly circulated.

In the Imphal Valley, integration initiatives produced two interplaying trends: (a) increasing civil society roles in hosting integrity programme, and (b) growth of 'integrity consumers.' The second trend is interesting. For instance, on 15 June an application submitted to UCM reads,

> I, Rameshkumar, although originally not a Meetei, am now a real child of Manipur. I have no place to live in other than Manipur. I have been converted to a Meetei and my surname is Yumlembam. My wife is also a daughter of the Meetei .... Therefore, requested you to kindly settle the dispute between me and my landlord (probably because he had played important role in the integrity campaign held dear by the UCM).[144]

In an application dated 18 July 2002, the Sitlhou Council India of Motbung in Sadar Hills invited UCM to take part in an Obsequies Ceremony cum Memorial Stone Erection of Pu Thangkhomang Sitlhou and requested UMC to sponsor a video camera to cover the programme.[145] In August, the Sandang Shenba Maring Youth Club of Maring Community asked for financial assistance for organizing XIX Cultural Meet in August 2002.[146] In the same month, the All Manipur Muslim Institute sought for medicines and food for flood affected Muslim people of Haoreibi in Ningel.[147] When MC Mary Kom won second gold medal in the World Women Boxing Championship, the Komrem Students' Union Manipur (of Kom community) requested UCM to bear charge of reception hall and sound system.[148] When a team of Kangchup Chiru Youth Club was qualified to take part in State Level Churachand Football Meet and, therefore, 'representing the Senapati District for the first time', UCM was requested to provide fund.[149] When the Peace Organising Committee was formed to organize the All Manipur Christian Get Together for Peace to be held at the United Baptist Church in Tamenglong on 9 and 10 February 2004, financial assistance was sought from UCM.[150] Nupi Khunai Chaokhat Lamjinglup, Moreh, and Chandel Districts demanded 'donation to the organization's free education scheme from class I to VIII at the Government High School.[151] Maring

Students' Union (of the Maring Community) requested for video to cover Golden Jubilee Celebration of Maring Students' Union.[152] A letter dated 22 January 2004 and signed by a member who claimed to represent Kuki Inpi, was submitted to the UCM; the person sought for a personal assistance of Rs 30,000 in order to purchase a second hand motorcycle for integrity mobilization.[153] On 6 February 2004, Seven Village Development Action Committee of Heinoukhong, Chandel District, requested AMESCO to construct a sports complex (play ground) for the seven villages at Heinoukhon region.[154]

Several similar applications, demands, and requests were discovered in the offices of AMUCO, UCM, and other prominent organizations. The addressee organizations that played 'apex' roles in integrity campaigns were being asked to consider the applicants. Whether the trend was an indication of mass/community base expansion of the concerned addressee or simply opportunists' consumerism in the name of integrity or a combination of both, require a different type of research. Manipur integrationists, however, presumed their legitimacy as 'apex' from such consumerism.[155]

2003

Arrest of NSCN-IM leaders

In early 2003, AMUCO was busy in an integrity campaign under the theme *Live Together, Struggle Together and Grow Together*. It installed green flags inscribed with the message, *Punna Hingminnabagi Leepunna Manipurgi Ngamkhei Ngaklee.*[156] White banners imprinted with *Let us strengthen the bond of living together* and *Let us safeguard the unity & integrity of Manipur* were widely distributed. In the meanwhile on 16 January 2002, some organizations and women *meira paibees* resolved to seek freedom from India if there would be territorial disintegration. On 20 January, All Political Party Delegation from Manipur submitted a memorandum to the Prime Minister of India demanding protection of territorial integrity.[157.] The same day, the MAPI Council released a pamphlet with maps depicting Manipur in 1500, 1883, and post-1949. A convention organized on 23 January at Gandhi Memorial Hall Imphal resolved to defend integrity and named the following communities as the indigenous peoples of Manipur, namely, Aimol, Anal, Baite, Chin, Chiru, Chothe, Gangte,

Guite, Hmar, Inpui, Jenmei Liangmei, Kabui, Kharam, Khoimu, Khongjai, Koirao, Koireng, Kom, Lamkang, Lufao, Lushai, Mao, Maram, Maring, Mate, Meetei, Mizo, Monsang, Moyon, Moyon, Ngaithe, Ngamei (Angami), Paite, Pangal, Paomei, Purum, Ralte, Rongmei, Soibu Misao, Sukte, Sumte, Tangkhul, Tarao, Thadou, and Zou.[158] And there were routine integrity programmes to host functions on 14 and 18 June, 4 August, et cetera.

In early October 2003, communal tension erupted centred on the proposed visit of NSCN (IM) leaders to Tamenglong District. A few days before, on 28 September, AMKIL and NIPCO organized 3rd Manipur Integrity and Solidarity Day and reiterated to defend territorial integrity. And a memorandum was submitted to the President of India on 5 October. On 6 October, NSCN (IM) reiterated its commitment to *Nagalim* and stated, 'map of Manipur should not be a factor in deciding the political future of the Nagas.'[159] There was weeklong media browbeating on that issue. It was escalated to a protest by Manipur integrationists on 6 October, when police arrested NSCN-IM leaders[160] at Tulibari village on IT road in Senapati District. The NSCN (IM) leaders were planning to attend a public meeting on 8 October to campaign for *Nagalim*. They were released immediately under the advice of the Indian State, and escorted up to Mao by a Special Task Force of State Police. The people of Senapati also accompanied the NSCN (IM) leaders upto Mao in around 50 vehicles including buses adorned with white flags.

The unconditional release sparked off weeklong protest by Manipur integrationists. On 7 October United Committee imposed 18 hours general strike condemning 'intrusion of NSCN (IM) cadres.'[161] Provocative statements were framed against Manipur State, namely, 'Manipur sold away by a weak Chief Minister', 'Government working to disintegrate state', 'Government's double standard,' et cetera. AMSU charged Manipur State for 'being hand in glove with the Naga rebel group in trying to disintegrate Manipur.'[162] AMUCO charged the Indian State for, 'sinister design ... to disintegrate the people on ethnic and communal line.'[163] They charged that ceasefire had been arbitrarily implemented in Manipur.

Political parties and MLAs joined the protest although Manipur insurgents had attempted to synchronize integrationist emotion and anti-colonial discourse. On 9 October, Manipur Forward Youth Front announced a protest on 15 October, that is, the day in 1949 when Manipur was annexed. AMUCO decided to launch series of agitation against alleged divisive policy of the Indian State. When UCM called on the people to protest from 12 October, the State imposed indefinite curfew and foiled the plan. On 13 October, Manipur Cabinet resolved to defend territorial integrity. On 14 October, UCM convened a Leaders' Meet that resolved to agitation from October 16 to 20. It reiterated restoration of pre-merger status for Manipur in case the ceasefire agreement would be extended to Manipur. On 16 October, a lengthy meeting presided over by Chief Minister O Ibobi was held to strengthen a coalition to launch integrity campaigns. UCM, however, went ahead with agitation. Under the pressure, on 17 October, political parties including SPF reiterated to press on the Indian State to ensure territorial integrity. On 20 October, AMUCO appealed communities to be united. On 22 October, Manipur Cabinet reiterated to protect territorial integrity. However, UCM announced a three day civil disobedience from 22 to 24 under the theme *Cease of duty for safeguard of territorial integrity of Manipur.* AMSU joined the agitation and hoisted black flags at educational institutions. On 25 October UCM organized all political party meeting at the State Guest House and resolved to defend territorial integrity. Subsequently, on 26 October, a joint memorandum was submitted to the Prime Minister of India intimating 'deep concern about any speech or statement by the Prime Minister that may affect the territorial integrity of North east states namely Manipur, Arunachal Pradesh and Assam in the light of the ongoing peace talk with the NSCN (IM).'[164]

Naga integrationists were also alarmed. They responded with provocative statements. On the following day of the arrest of NSCN-IM leaders, Naga Hoho condemned the arrest as an attempt to sabotage Naga peace process. It categorically charged that Meeteis who were living for Manipur needed to realize the national aspiration of the Naga people. On 9 October, Naga People's Organisation demanded resignation of all the Manipur Naga MLA's and Ministers. On 14 October, Naga National Council reiterated that Nagas would continue to fight till they achieve proper recognition of a free and independent *Nagalim*. In response to UCM's statement on 13 October that had said that Muivah (Gen. Secy. of NSCN-IM) could become Chief Minister of Manipur if he would live for the integrity of Manipur, Naga integrationists termed the UCM initiated protest as immature and at the same time urged not to distort Naga history. Naga Integrationists intimidated Manipur Naga MLAs to sign on a declaration paper pledging support to integration of *Nagalim*.

The declaration paper was circulated through United Naga Council and the dateline of submission was 25 October. Eleven Manipur Naga MLAs (including seven ministers) were indecisive and waited till the eleventh hour of the dateline. In fact, on 7 February 2002, the MLAs had taken an oath to support *Nagalim* and the ceasefire if they were elected to the Manipur Assembly. How the oaths were obtained and under what process was a different issue. On the occasion of Federal Assembly meeting at Tadubi on 17 July 2003, the UNC had resolved to seek written statement from the MLAs to confirm their oath. According to a UNC circular on 18 October 2003,

> in case if any non-compliance by the said date, it will be deemed that the terms of agreement of the declaration had been wilfully breached and as per the provisions contained therein, the UNC will issue all necessary directives and take appropriate follow-up steps so that the desires and aspirations of the Naga people are not held to ransom and sabotaged at this crucial juncture for the sake of individual interest.[165]

In response, the eleven Naga MLAs signed a memorandum addressed to the Prime Minister of India seeking an early solution to the Naga question. On 25 October, A. Aza, a Naga MLA holding the portfolio of Youth Affairs and Sports Minister, however, conveyed that the seven ministers had not signed the declaration, although the press had quoted their unstinted support to political integration of the Nagas as well as the ongoing peace process. On 28 October, Chief Minister of Nagaland Neiphiu Rio submitted a memorandum to the Prime Minister demanding amalgamation of all Naga inhabited areas under single administration. The Prime Minister responded, 'at present there is no political consensus on changing the boundaries here.'[166] Tensions and media browbeating got subsided after the visit of the Prime Minister. Manipur integrationists continued with routine integrity campaigns. On 26 November 2003, an Inter Community Cultural Festival under the theme *Cultural Exchange for Communal Harmony and Integrity* was organized at Pallel in Chandel District.[167] The Nagaland Assembly reaffirmed integration of Nagas under one administration.

2004

The year 2004 was apparently silent on territorial issues. Manipur integrationists continued routine integrity campaign till the middle of the year, when several months-long agitation against Armed Forces Special Powers Act suddenly erupted. Pent up fury against serial killing carried out by the police during that year's Holi festival and the custodial rape and murder of Miss Manorama by Assam Rifles on 12 July resulted in an emotional outburst and the nude protest of 15 July; repression and casualties amongst agitators, however, continued. It seems the AFSPA issue had subsided other issues.

2005

Assertive rituals of June 18

In the third quarter of May 2005, integrity tension erupted when Manipur integrationists protested operation of NSCN-IM in Ukhrul District. It became serious when, on 27 May, a memorandum signed by Manipur Naga MPs and MLAs demanded integration of Naga areas.[168] The UCM demanded legal action against the signatories and charged the Indian State as responsible for divisive politics. To defuse UCM tension, the ruling Secular Progressive Front, on 2 June, resolved to protect territorial integrity. UCM, however, insisted on the Manipur MLAs to make public declaration to protect territorial integrity. CPI (M) and opposition parties joined UCM in the protest, demanded action against the concerned Naga MLAs and destruction of NSCN-IM camps in Manipur.

Adding fuel to the fire, the media, on 7 June, reported that the Indian State was examining any possibility of setting up a Border Commission for Naga inhabited areas. Although NSCN (K) condemned NSCN (IM) and categorically stated as early as 23 May that 'the Nagas were wasting their common sense on the issue of integration which is a deleted issue,'[169] the media report was taken for granted as the pretext to intensify Manipur integrity campaign. Integrity protagonists rebuked the State, articulated patriotism and attempted to expand mass base particularly in Imphal Valley. They prepared for grand integrity rituals in June.

Unrest escalated when UCM, on 8 June, referred to 18 June as a state holiday and the UNC opposed it. On 10 June, UNC denounced the decision of Manipur State of declaring 18 June a state holiday. According to UNC, the holiday hurt Naga sentiment and disturbed the ongoing ceasefire. UNC geared up to organize mass protest on 16 June under the theme *Solidarity Rallies–Towards Naga Unification*. The following day, All Naga Students' Association Manipur issued caution to Manipur Naga Ministers, MLAs and MP against doing anything that might damage Naga interest. In the meanwhile, AMUCO organized a Protest Day ritual on 14 June. The same day, NSCN (K) announced a ban on the proposed UNC rally of 16 June and the 24-hour blockade scheduled for 21 June. Despite the ban and staged managed security restrictions imposed by the State the UNC rally was successful in Ukhrul, Senapati, Chandel and Tamenglong Districts. The rallies submitted memorandums addressed to the Indian State through the District Headquarters. Manipur integrationists were humiliated and they demanded action against the concerned officers on the charge of dereliction of duty by allowing UNC rally and receiving the memorandums. UNC, however, clarified that they were not against any organization nor against any community but the agitations had been solely targeted at the Manipur State for taking immature decision. AMUCO blamed the State for the tension and raised anti-colonial discourse. On the other hand, the NSCN (IM) demanded the Indian State to resolve Naga integration within a proposed federal set up.[170]

On the eve of 18 June, Manipur State set up three police helpline posts and a decision was taken to deploy state police and four companies of CRPF to maintain law and order. On 18 June, Manipur integrationists organized 'integrity rituals' and the State maintained strict silence on the issue of holiday. Government offices in the hill districts remained open for the day. However, the UNC went ahead with a 24-hour blockade from midnight of 19 June and ANSAM carried out indefinite economic blockades from 21 June onwards. While AMUCO reiterated that economic blockades could not be a solution, the MAPI Council condemned the blockades as being against the spirit of peace and warned of divisive policy pursued by 'some vested interest.' On 23 June, the Manipur State Assembly reaffirmed its pledge to protect territorial integrity.

The ANSAM agitation was not lifted till 10 August. But the responses in the hill districts were a mixture of support and opposition.

Firstly, the Churachandpur District Students' Union, dominantly composed of Kuki-Chin-Mizos, extended moral support to ANSAM. On 25 June, the Kohima-based Consultative Committee for Peace appreciated Manipur Naga MLAs who had submitted the 27 May memorandum. On 27 June, the All Tribal Students' Union Manipur extended support to ANSAM. The same day, goods laden trucks meant for supply to Manipur were burnt down. On 3 July, the Naga Students' Federation warned Manipur State to consider the demand of ANSAM or face negative consequences. On 13 July, ANSAM asked Manipur Naga MLAs to resign. On 20 July, probably in retaliation against the State's policy of escorting over 200 trucks to fetch essential commodities, the Irang Bridge on National Highway 53 was bombarded by blockade supporters.

Secondly, prolonged economic blockade created opponents. Food stock was running out and prices of essential commodities were skyrocketing. Most daily wage earners were not earning and were economically threatened. Nagas who coexist with others in and around the Imphal Valley were apprehensive about risking their lives and properties in case of communal clash. Many in the hills demanded a peaceful solution. Due to pressure, Manipur State sent invitations to ANSAM for a dialogue. On 17 July, an all-party meeting chaired by the Chief Minister of Manipur resolved to seek for an intervention by the Indian State. ANSAM was also facing pressure of State repression including 'wanted tags' on their leaders. Others were also pressing them for peace. As a result, few rounds of talks were held in Manipur and Delhi. Finally, economic blockade was lifted on 10 August.

2006
Education Affiliation Controversy

Naga civil societies took decisions on 9 August 2001 and 4 November 2005 to launch non-cooperation against Manipur State. Accordingly, by 25 March 2005, UNC and ANSAM were prepared to agitate to introduce Nagaland Board of Secondary Education curriculum in the Manipur portion of *Nagalim*. On 12 June 2006, Nagaland State intimated the matter to the Union Ministry of Human Resource Development. Naga integrationists protested the Manipur Secondary Education Act 1972 on the ground that it prohibited any school under the Board of Secondary Education Manipur from affiliating to any Board or Council outside Manipur. On 10 July 2006, they raised *Bye Bye BSEM* and *Welcome NBSE* and consigned to flames thousands of BSEM text books. The chairperson of NBSE, however, on 14 July, clarified that no affiliation could be granted to schools located in Manipur at that point of time. But in the third week of June, a delegation of Naga Students' Federation were lobbying in Delhi to implement their proposal.

On 25 July in Manipur, the UCM sent a memorandum to the Prime Minister seeking for a clarification on the matter. The Kuki Students' Organisation on 25 July opposed ANSAM's initiative as the four hill districts in question were proportionately possessed and represented by both Nagas and Kukis. The same day, NSCN (K) issued a warning of strong action against any civil organization which would be a partner in the ANSAM's campaign. The following day, UNC, Naga Women Union Manipur, NPMHR, and ANSAM urged upon Manipur integrationists not to interfere in their initiatives as latter's protest would not in any way halt their way.

The following weeks there were media browbeating between NSCN (K) and NBSE affiliation protagonists. On 7 August Manipur State sent a representation to the Union Minister of HRD demanding that no board of another state should infringe on the jurisdiction of the board or council of another state. Kuki Movement for Human Rights (KMHR) and KSO opposed the affiliation initiative and sought for a definite clarification from the Union Ministry of HRD. They warned that Kukis were majority in the hill districts of Manipur and that Nagas did not have rights to arbitrarily speak for the whole hill districts of Manipur. However, under the pressure of UNC and ANSAM, five elected Manipur Naga MLAs on 8 August sought for an early intervention of the Prime Minister of India as a special case to effect affiliation. On the night of 20 August, the office of the Zonal Education Officer in Ukhrul was ransacked and properties were destroyed by UNC and ANSAM supporters.

On 23 August, a postcard campaign, signed by Naga students demanding affiliation to NBSE and addressed to the Prime Minister of India, was kicked off in Ukhrul. On 26 August, student rallies were organized in Chandel, Ukhrul, Senapati, and Tamenglong districts and memorandums addressed to the Prime Minister and NBSE were submitted through the respective District Headquarters. On 6 September, UNC issued a directive to ANSAM and other affiliated organizations to implement a ban on the Meetei language and Meetei audio-video products such as CDs, cassettes, et cetera, in the Manipur portion of *Nagalim* with effect from 17 September 2006. Over 28 Government High Schools were ransacked in Ukhrul districts and effigies of the Chief Minister and Education Minister of Manipur were burnt. On 8 September, ANSAM issued warnings to the CD/cassettes parlours to take note and comply with the UNC directive as it was aimed at to check dilution of Naga history from the impact of Meetei influences. On 28 September, two passenger buses that had number plates inscribed with Meetei script were vandalized in Senapati District. While Meetei Erol Eyek Loinasillol Apunba Lup (MEELAL) condemned the act, AMUCO, on 2 October, stated that the unfortunate incident was the outcome of a chauvinistic conflict between two groups of people, one, who worked for the political gain of some politicians by engaging Meitei/ Meetei in the conflict, and the other who could not see anything beyond Meetei/Meitei.

On 10 October, Manipur media reported that more than 868 students from 30 private schools in Ukhrul had left for Dimapur (Nagaland) the previous day. On 5 November, Naga Students'

Federation reported that 'a staggering 3665 Naga students from Manipur would appear matriculation examinations in Nagaland for which the process of enrolment and filling up of examination forms are on in full swing.'[171] While those students were preparing themselves to take the NBSE exam, cadres of NSCN (K) on 3 February 2007 intercepted a Kohima-bound bus carrying 51 Manipur Naga students, forced them out, and pushed the vehicle down a hill in Thonglang area of Tamenglong district. Thereafter, the affiliation issue was silent for a few months. It rose up again on 4 July when 11 government schools were torched in Senapati, Chandel, and Ukhrul Districts; the act was justified by ANSAM the following day. At the same time, the UNC endorsed ANSAM's NBSE affiliation movement. However, the arson was widely protested by others. On 9 July, HERICOUN, MEELAL, and Threatened Indigenous People's Society and Democratic Students' Alliance organized a protest against the justification of arson by ANSAM. On 18 July, ANSAM reiterated justifying of the NBSE affiliation movement. The following day, suspected ANSAM volunteers seized thousands of Meetei audio and video CDs from parlours in Ukhrul.

On 14 September, Nagaland State adopted a legislation to allow schools from other states to get affiliated to the NBSE. The following day Manipur State adopted a decision to press for an ordinance to nullify the decision of the Nagaland State and sent a delegation to appraise their stand to the Indian State. Manipur integrationist organizations such as DESAM and UCM reacted against the decision of Nagaland State. But Naga organizations such as UNC, NWUM, NPMHR and ANSAM celebrated victory. On 19 September, Manipur Cabinet decided that, in the event of any school or educational institute violating the cabinet decision, those students would not be allowed to pursue higher education in Manipur and they would be prohibited from seeking service under the Manipur State. An ordinance to ban any school in Manipur from affiliating to other states was submitted to the Governor. While the matter remained unresolved, a joint memorandum of ANSAM and All Private School Forum of Tamenglong, Ukhrul, Chandel, and Senapati (APSF-TUCS) sought from the Secretary of Education of Schools, Manipur to issue a No Objection Certificate (NOC) credentials to the private schools operating in the 'Naga dominated' four hill districts in Manipur.

2007

Moreh Town Tension

A lucrative border trade had been flourishing in the town of Moreh bordering Myanmar. Due to certain policies of the State, by the mid-2000s, Kuki-Chin-Mizo insurgent parties operating in that area were operating more freely. Other insurgents were also operating, most probably in disguise. Incidentally, most of the Kuki-Chin-Mizo insurgent parties were seeking autonomy and exclusive homeland within a federal structure. There were clashes of interest among insurgents for area control and other economic and tactical reasons at Moreh. Moreh had been incorporated in the *Zale'ngam* vision and there had been efforts by the Kuki-Chin-Mizo civil societies to flush out Manipur insurgents from *Zalen'gam* and *Zogam*. In December 2006, a declaration rechristened as Moreh Declaration was adopted to press upon concerned governments to 'shift away base camps of non-Kuki-Chin-Mizo insurgent groups beyond agreed areas of operation. [172] In a memorandum submitted to the Indian State on 5 March 2007, the Kuki Students' Organisation appealed that Kuki inhabitant areas of Manipur, bordering Myanmar, were the most neglected areas. It argued that due to porous borders, those places had become a haven for the UNLF. It demanded setting up of permanent battalion bases for Assam Rifles at all strategic locations for the safety and safe passage of the people and proper functioning of government administrative mechanism.[173]

Against this backdrop, a tension erupted in the town of Moreh in June 2007 as a result of a killing sprees unleashed by UNLF and KNO. On the morning of 9 June, the UNLF shot down five Kukis[174] on the charge of being KNO cadres. In retaliation, KNO killed six Meetei labours[175] of Khurai in Imphal. The people of Khurai in particular, and across communities in general, protested the killing. The victim families refused to accept the corpses until a memorandum of understanding was signed with the Manipur State on 12 June. Moreh town was closed down for weeks. Fearing communal clashes, many who were living in Moreh took refuge in

Myanmar. Manipur State imposed curfews and additional forces were deployed to deescalate tension. On 13 June, a Memorandum of Understanding was signed between Manipur State and representatives of Meetei Council Moreh, Hill Tribal Council, Meetei Muslim Council Moreh, Tamil Sangam and others to create a secure atmosphere and cooperation among communities at Moreh. Moreh Market was resumed to normal commercial activity on 19 June. A Coordination Committee for Peace and Normalcy in Manipur was formed to provide relief and a unity rally was jointly organized by community organizations. Gradually, the tension subsided.

The Moreh incident needs to be contextualized in an atmosphere of diametrical nationalisms. A press release circulated by the United Peoples' Front[176] said that the prevailing charged atmosphere in the area was due to differences between two armed groups that had indulged in killing and counterkilling of innocent civilians, thereby, turning it into a communal violence-like situation.[177] The Revolutionary People's Front had cautioned that collateral damage to civilians on account of the conflict between KNO and UNLF and the resultant act of sowing seeds of communal animosity between Kukis and Meeteis would be a blunder. In other words, the Moreh killings were illustrative contour of collusion and conflict among parties that had different national imagining. The primary interest to establish area control in order to extract revenue had interplayed with diametrical nationalisms. Killings were justified on the basis of nationalism and victims were branded as enemies. According to UNLF, Indian armed forces were working in cahoots with KNO and that those five Kukis that they had killed were cadres of KNA. It seems that right to life was arbitrarily denied to the projected 'national' enemies. KNO had similarly responded in a communal manner. According to KNO, the unfortunate killing of 11 persons was a direct consequence of UNLF's intrusive presence in Kuki territory and their indiscriminate activities. Taking sides with KNO, NSCN (IM), which had been trying to claim stake in Moreh, asserted that those incidents of violence had 'partly exposed the plans of UNLF and Manipur State since Kukis were denied to live peacefully in Moreh and its surrounding areas soon after UNLF succeeded in collaborating with Burmese army. Charges and countercharges were pitted against one another. In the process, each of the diametrical fronts attempted to organize 'camp followers' around them. But the victims were innocent civilians, striving for their respective economic livelihood. Terrorism in the guise of nationalism had brought misfortune to them.

III. PARADOX OF NATIONHOOD

Many are caught in the viscous cycle of conflict generated by diametrical nationalisms towards making *Indian, Kangleipak or Manipur, Nagalim, Zale'n-gam, Zogam* nations. However, in the above context official nationalism precedes 'nation' and the national claims remained paradoxical. Different individuals affiliated to different nationalisms were intermixing and the borders based on nationalisms are overlapping across communities. The paradox is exemplified as peoples are being mechanically encapsulated in one-nation theory, which merely articulate superficial nationhood cloak but fail to diffuse psychological cohesion towards any officially imagined nation. I shall analyse it.

Kangleipak

Kangleipak (sic. Manipur) protagonists construed a colonial image of the Indian State. They refuted the Sanskritized history on the ground that Manipur had no long historical and cultural ties with Hinduism or India in the past. They traced the origin of Manipur in the primordial past, comparable to both British and Indian 'national' histories. According to late Prof Sanajaoba Manipur '... had her defined territory, population, successive governments, external relations with neighbours, economic centralization, common official language, common ancestry for two millennia and above all, a full-fledged constitutional system, equipped with judicial mechanisms.'[178] In order to fit into national 'criterion' within the framework of international instruments prescribed by the UN and other international conventions, the Revolutionary People's Front asserted that 'the basic parameters of an independent state, as stipulated by the Montevido Convention, 1933, namely, (a) territory, (b) population, (c) government and (d) capacity to maintain external relations, had been found in the state of Manipur.'[179] They concentrated on (a) continuous reproduction of anti-colonial discourse challenging the Indian national history, and (b) articulation of a one-nation theory for Manipur positing against the divisive discourses of *Nagalim* and *Zalen'ngam* histories.

Firstly, the people of Manipur are being depicted as having common racial and genealogical origin; different from the Indians (Mayangs). They are being considered aboriginal or indigenous and different from 'outsiders'. To substantiate the argument, they selectively refer to the cosmology, legends and traditions inscribed on Meetei *puya*s and other oral accounts maintained by the Kabui, Mao, Maram, Meetei, Tangkhul, and Thangal.[180]

Secondly, there is constant effort to identify citizenship with Manipuri language, that is, 'anybody whose mother tongue is Manipuri language ... belongs to the Manipuri people...'[181] The argument is that, amidst dialectal plurality, there exists a common language that binds the people into one.[182]

Thirdly, there is constant articulation of cultural similarities and assimilation among peoples.[183] It argues for pristine cultural ethos and that primeval instinct transmitted down through traditions and social practices are common to all. They cite cultural artefacts, audible and visible social constructs such as ritual and customary practices that are being deemed common.[184]

Fourthly, Manipur is being shown as a historically evolved, stable community based on common territory.[185] Historical documents such as agreements, negotiation, procedures, maps, survey reports, and chronicles are referred to in order to argue that a 'national' territory of Manipur had been fully established for half a millennium.'[186]

Fifthly, the people of Manipur are being shown as playing an important collective role in state formation throughout the history as they had lived under 'federation evolved out of the *autochthonous* groups.'[187] Peoples and community leaders have played an important role in the making of a democratic Manipur; in the Constitution Making Committee in 1947, the responsible government of 1948, and the post-1950 governance. The people have been collectively exposed to external invasion and internal fractures due to colonial divisive policy.

Methodologically, the one-nation theory constitutes a polemical historiography based on selective reading of sources in order to articulate political agenda. The primordial polemics suffers from anachronism as it traces the genealogy of the post-1949 Manipur in the pristine ancient past. The weaknesses may be discussed as follows:

Firstly, contemporary Manipur was construed as an inviolable 'national' territorial entity without detaching it from the pre-existing official landscapes demarcated by the British colonial monarchy from 1826 to 1947. The boundaries were designed by rulers from above. Were there voluntary consents of the inhabitants affected by it? History of the ruled, autonomous or unadministered communities, feudal oppression, arbitrary demarcation of boundary, rebellion and suppression, et cetera, and resistance against forced demarcations have been out of focus. This is reductionism driven by certain territorial hangover.

Secondly, the idea of primordialism is conceptually challenging as a result of forced locating of a nation in the pre-1947 Asiatic socio-economic context. Under Asiatic socioeconomic conditions, there were self-sufficient and isolated tribal and feudal village communities. It remains questionable if a single legislation in the span of a wink of time[188] led to the magical transformation of the material conditions for a mechanically structured colonial 'political community' to be fully evolved into a nation. Logically, Asiatic condition and modern nationhood are two different historical conditions, the former preceding the later.

Thirdly, post-1949 symbols and visual representations for Manipur arbitrarily incorporated cultural artefacts connected to the royalist insignias and certain numerically dominant community. These are proven antitheses to the idea of democratic novelty based on common invention based on consensus. In a communally sensitized social relation, hegemonic embodiment or underrepresentation of a certain community creates social fissures and makes the idea of oneness self-contradictory.

Fourthly, there are conceptual confusions exemplified in self-defeating illustrations. For instance, if Manipur had to be called a nation because there was cultural exchange and intermarriage among communities; the same relation between Meetei and Mayang or between Manipur and other Indians may lead to assuming India as a nation. If official Manipuri *lingua franca* is to be considered an important ingredient of nationhood, as the scheduled tribes offered it as second language, how does one define the national affiliation of Manipuris who adopt Hindi or English as a second language? If Manipur had to be considered a nation based on cross community elite representatives in the Manipur Constitution Making Committee and Assembly elections, post-1949 elite representatives to the Indian bourgeoisie democratic State had to be cited to conclude that Manipuris are unanimous in being psychologically Indian.

Finally, justification of rebellion on the presumption that the people were sovereign in the past sounds apolitical. Every community in Manipur possesses history or narrative of sovereign past, real or imagined, free from the jurisdiction of an overarching Manipur administration. In that case, shouldn't all the communities or clans or localities be allowed to re-establish their sovereignty if the war for Manipur sovereignty had to be based on the idea of reclaiming certain presumed sovereign past? On the other hand, the one-nation theory had not spelt out the mechanism to accommodate the perception of a sovereign past, real or imagined, inherited or perceived among the coexisting communities. The theory is being challenged by the counterpoising theories of *Nagalim* and *Zale'n-gam*.

Nagalim and Zalen'ngam

Nagalim and *Zalen'ngam* protagonists posited against one another over territorial assertion on the one hand, and on the other hand, collectively posited against the *India* and *Kangleipak* agenda. The two theories are interwoven in constructing divisive discourses between tribes and non-tribals. It describes the Nagas and Kuki-Chin-Mizos as tribes and claimed for exclusive rights over the hills that comprises 90 per cent of the entire geographical area of Manipur. The Meeteis are being cited as exploiters leading to deprivation and marginalization of the tribes. The two forwarded respective one-nation theories for *Nagalim* and *Zalen'gam.*

Firstly, according to *Nagalim* protagonists, the Nagas had always been a sovereign nation occupying an area of 1,20,000 sq. km. of Patkai Range in between longitude 93° E and 97° E and latitude 23.5° N and 28.3° N. *Nagalim* is located at the tri-junction of China, India and Burma,[189] bounded in the North by China, in the West by Assam, in the South by the Manipur Valley, Mizoram, and Chin Hills (Burma), and in the East beyond Chindwin River and along its tributary Uyu River (Burma).[190] In order to claim aboriginal title and claim for exclusive territorial rights, *Nagalim* is being romanticized as the only land first settled and continued to be settled by Nagas alone.[191]

The *Nagalim* agenda refute the existing territorial boundaries as arbitrary and mechanical. For instance, 'to the Nagas, the very creation and existence of the state of Manipur has been perceived as an instrument of suppression of their rights and insult to their dignity.'[192] Manipur is identified with the Meetei and they argue, 'the Nagas have nowhere at any point of time given their allegiance to the Meeteis or their Maharajas to decide their future, orally or through an agreement.'[193] They articulate that Nagas and Meeteis were two different peoples since 'Naga people have their own culture and history, which they all wish to appreciate and learn.'[194] They condemn the one-nation theory for Manipur since it is 'nothing but lies ... there is no reason for the Meeteis to be overlording the Nagas.'[195] Therefore, they would not allow Manipur officials to visit the disputed Dzuko valley where Manipur had an official stake.[196] They would never tolerate what they termed 'Kuki homeland (Zale'n-gam) to be carved out of the Naga areas of the four hill districts of Manipur (Chandel, Senapati, Tamenglong and Ukhrul), parts of present Nagaland and Assam where the Kukis inhabit.'[197]

The euphoria of a primordial sovereign *Nagalim* is being construed. The assumption that they had never been governed by 'others' may somehow be relevant to the British unadministered areas. But it was in a different historical time and cannot be universally applied to all the communities that today constitute the Naga nomenclature. For instance, they argued that present-day Manipur was a result of colonial crafting. If they had to resist the colonial crafting and Meetei 'colonialism', then the rhetoric of being unconquered would become self-contradictory. On the other hand, lack of unity and common political psychology, which refutes one-nation theory, is reflected in the consolidation propaganda that calls for unity vis-à-vis divisive policy, which is 'viewed as a heinous crime against Naga nation on one hand and total violation of the law of nations on the other.'[198] A nation can be mechanically divided on policies and interests but not from being a nation. The 'law of nation' cited above is a craft of the protagonist's own volition. The 'law of nation' for the Marxists is bent on historical materialism. A nation is a stage of development, moving away from tribalism to the higher stage of a stable community based on modern cohesive factors. But the Nagas reiterated for being tribes. At the same time, tribalism, that is considered to be characterised by sectarianism and internecine bloodshed along tribal lines, is being considered an impediment to Naga integrity.

Secondly, *Zale'n-gam* or 'land of freedom' or Kukiland 'is the ancestral land of the Kuki people,'[199] where they 'originated, on which they were raised, developed, excelled and fought valiant battles (for survival).'[200] The imagined *Zale'n-gam* inhabited by Kuki-Chin-Mizo groups comprises 'contiguous' regions in Northeast India, Northwest Burma, and Chittagong Hill tracts in Bangladesh.[201] In Manipur, *Zale'n-gam* comprises half of the geographical area of Manipur, that is, Chandel and Churachandpur districts, Sadar Hills (in Senapati District) and vast tracts in the Ukhrul, Tamenglong, and Senapati Districts.[202] Their sovereignty is traced in the past, 'prior to the advent of British colonialists, there was complete self-rule and independence in *Zale'n-gam.*'[203] Their forebears had lived exclusively and gloriously in *Zal'e-gam,* possessing 'unique' customs, culture and traditions.[204] Their territorial claim refuted Naga exclusive territorial claims over Chandel, Tamenglong, Senapati, and Ukhrul Districts. They issued caution against threat by potential migration of Meeteis and others in *Zalen'ngam.*

The primordial one-nation theory for Kukis bypassed British colonial reports that argue for immigration of the Kukis and their 'nomadic' economy.[205] According to history, the British adopted the policy of founding Kuki settlements in several strategic areas adjoining the Imphal Valley[206] in the aftermath of the incorporation of Kuki irregular levies in expeditions.[207] *Zalen'gam* writers are silent on this. Instead they engage in formulating a multi-national theory for Manipur. Manipur is being defined as a land of different nations that 'have nothing in common.'[208] The differences are expressed in territorial terms, and as such, *Zale'n-gam* 'do not lay claim to any Naga or Meetei territory; they only seek the integrity of their ancestral lands.'[209] On the other hand, they identify Manipur with present Imphal Valley and Meetei. *Kangleipak* and *Zalen'ngam* 'were parallel sovereignties that existed side by side and were complementary to each other.'[210] In juxtaposition to *Nagalim*, *Zale'n-gam* protagonists asserted that Kuki-Chin-Mizos were rulers of the Manipur hills. They 'had received tax and tributes from the Tangkhuls and Kabui Nagas.'[211] However, *Zale'n-gam* had fallen as a result of British invasion and the subsequent divisive policy. 'Much against the interest for preservation, consolidation, and promotion of our ethnic identity, the British colonial rulers after subjugating us our ancestral homeland was divided, so were ... distributed like cattle sold and separated.'[212] They compared themselves with the Jews and the Kurdish that were being presumed forced scattered and killed in genocides. They lament about an enfeebled *Zale'n-gam* seeking for rejuvenation through integration of Kuki-Chin-Mizo nation.

They perceived immediate threat from what they termed Naga 'design of territorial expansionism'[213] and Meetei 'chauvinists' who used *Zale'n-gam* as launchpad to carry out activities against the Kukis and the Indian army.[214] In addition to the threat, they were apprehensive about community defections. The 'Anal, Moyon and Monshang, Chiru, Chothe, Lamkang, and Maring people, who belong to the Old Kuki categorization were manipulated to adopt Naga as a political identity by the NSCN-IM operating in Manipur'.[215] They considered that statehood for *Zale'n-gam* would bring solution to all these.[216] To achieve it they would go to the extent of forging alliance with the State and at the same time bidding a 'farewell party to the Meeteis (Manipur) in the same way the Manipur Nagas are doing.'[217]

To sum up, the divisive discourses discussed above were deliberate and literarily overlooked community composition of the hills and valleys. They also tried to cover up internal mistrust, assertions, dissension, and lack of oneness. To be more precise, imagined *Nagalim*, *Zale'n-gam*, and *Zogam* nationhoods on the surface of the Earth were inhabited by diverse linguistic, if not dialectic, and cultural communities. *Prima facie* the Nagas and Kukis are in the continuous process of making into stable political communities as long as sectarianism along tribal or clan lines are continued.

The Nagas in the Manipur such as Rongmei or Kabui, Liangmei Zemei, Tangkhul, Mao, Maram, Maring and Tarao, and Thangal communities are considered as predominant members. The Anal, Moyon, Monshang, Lamkang, Tarao, Chothe, Chiru, Koireng, and Kharam communities are considered having linguistic affinity with Kuki Chin and cultural affinity with the Nagas. They are inclined towards Naga political identity.[218] Due to socioeconomic and geopolitical factors, 'Anal, Kom and Thangal had identified themselves as Nagas.'[219] In their cases, a shift away from colonial anthropological meaning to political meaning seems to be taking place. The Kuki Recognition Committee in 1987 upheld that Chiru, Chothe, and Kom belonged to the Kuki nomenclature.[220] The Kuki was mentioned as original signatories to the 1929 Naga memorandum submitted to the Simon Commission. But their name was no longer visible in the Naga-Akbar Hydari Accord of 1947 and afterwards. The withdrawal of Kuki doesn't create a stabled Naga nation. In the words of Jamir in 2000, 'We were actually a group of heterogeneous, primitive and diverse (communities) living in far-flung villages that had very little in common and negligible contact with each other.'[221] 'Localism and (communalism) are among the chief problems that have dogged Naga efforts at nation building or the concept of 'Naganess' or 'Nagahood'.'[222] There was a widespread rumour that some Nagas in Nagaland do not want some Naga communities from Manipur to be recognised as Nagas. For instance, the NSCN-K issued quit notice to the Tangkhuls on the ground that 'the Tangkhuls, the so-called the elder brother of Meeteis who are trying to adopt a new identity as a Naga is only a paradox of phobia. The Nagas never knew the Tangkhuls before 1990 and were only foreigners to Nagas who never knew Nagas but only spoke Manipuri and were Manipuris to the Nagas.'[223] The Changs, Konyaks, Sangtams, Khiamniungans, Yimchungrus, and Phoms peoples in Nagalnd were demanding a separate state called Frontier Nagaland or Eastern Nagaland. They opposed holistic recognition of the Mao and the Rongmeis peoples in the scheduled tribes list of Nagaland. Among the Kuki-Chin-Mizo groups, the Kuki-Paite clash from June 1997 to October 1998 occurred over the alleged 'dispute in ideology and acceptance of a common nomenclature'[224] on the one hand, and on the other hand, the perpetuation of clan-based armed organizations needs deeper study to unfold dynamics of consolidation and negation.

To conclude, there has been a paradox of nationhood as claimed in the course of diametrical nationalisms. However, the diametrical nationalist fronts are involved in struggles to consolidate peoples into their respective imagined nationhood by attempting to make national ideology as above all other loyalties. These are carried out in the name of constituting a strong central national authority in order to develop economic rationality and for rapid material development of the 'national' citizens. In this scenario, the diametrical objectives of *India* or *Bharat* or *Hindustan*, *Manipur* or *Kangleipak*, *Nagalim*, and *Zale'n-gam* are in *status quo.* Coordination and conflict among these fronts were largely strategic and tactical to accomplish respectively subscribed nationalism.

NOTES

1. Karam Manimohan Singh, *Hijam Irabot and Political Movement in Manipur*, Delhi, B.R. Publishing Corporation, 1989, p. 326
2. Rajendra Kshetri, *The Emergence of Meetei Nationalism,* New Delhi: Mittal Publications, 2006, pp. 63-4
3. The organizations under KNO are Kuki National Front (Military Council), Kuki National Front (Zogam), United Socialist Revolutionary Army (Old Kuki), United Komrem Revolutionary Army, Zomi Reunification Front, Zou Defence Volunteer (ZDV-KNO), Hmar National Army, Kuki Revolutionary Army (Unification), Kuki Liberation Army (KLA-KNO) and Kuki National Army (KNA).
4. The organizations under UPF include Kuki Revolutionary Army, Kuki National Front, United Kuki Liberation Front, Kuki Liberation Army (KLA-UPF), Zomi Revolutionary Army, Kuki National Front (S), Hmar People's Conference/Democratic and Zou Defence Volunteers (ZDV-UPF).

5. Formed by KCP (Lanheiba), KCP (Chingkheiganba) and KCP (Sunil Meetei)
6. Comprised KCP (Lamphel), KCP (City Meetei) and KCP (Taibanganba)
7. Anthony D. Smith, *Theories of Nationalism*, London: Duckworth, 2nd ed., 1983, p. XIII
8. Benedict Anderson, *Imagined Communities, Reflections on the Origin and Spread of Nationalism*, London, Verso, revised ed., 1995, p. 2

9-10. E.J. Hobsbawm, *Nations and Nationalism since 1780*, *Programme, Myth, Reality* (henceforth *Nations and Nationalism*), Cambridge: Cambridge University Press, 2nd ed., 1997, p. 138

11. *Administrative Atlas*, Delhi: Registrar General of India, 2005, p. 4
12. *Rules for the Management of the Manipur State*, File, Confidential, Government of Eastern Bengal & Assam, Political Department, Political A. September 1907, Manipur State Archive (Henceforth MSA).
13. *Manipur State Durbar Resolution* (Henceforth MSDR) No. 12 of 13 July 1908.
14. *Naga Memorandum to Simon Commission*, 10 January 1929.
15. Rani Gaidinliu case file 1930-35, R-1/3-B, 35, MSA
16. Press statement by the Haipei Rani Gaidinliu Birth Anniversary Celebration Committee, 2007
17. MSDR, 1 January 1928.
18. Ibid.
19. His Highness the Maharajah Memo No. 715 I-I; MSDR No. 1, 28 November 1928, Imphal.
20. MSDR of 27 June 1938.
21. MSDR No. 1 of 21 December 1938.
22. MSDR No. 28 of 7/8 March 1945.
23. The joint conference of the Nikhil Manipur Mahasabha and Manipur Praja Mandal, 5 April 1946.
24. Singh, *Hijam Irabot and Political Movement in Manipur*, p. 197.
25. Ibid., p. 277.
26. MSDR No. 22, 18 May 1947.
27. Singh, *Hijam Irabot and Political Movement in Manipur*, p. 277.
28. Minutes of a Joint Border Meeting held between the representatives of the Burma Government and the Manipur State on 17 December, 1947.
29. A pitch battle between protesters and police on 21 September had led to the killing of a police officer and injury to many others.

30. Apart from British and Meetei representatives, there were Md. Quaze Wali Ulla (a Panggal or Manipuri Muslim), Daiho (Mao Naga representing Tamenglong region), Suisa (a Tangkhul Naga representing Ukhrul), Teba Kilong (Temenglong region), TC Tiankham (Churachandpur region), Thankoupao Kipgen, (Southeast area).
31. Manipur State Constitution Making Committee Resolution of 14, 25, 27 and 29 March 1947.
32. Minutes of the meeting of the Constitution Making Committee held on 29 March 1947.
33. Proclamation of King Bodhachandra, 18 October 1948.
34. *Report of the Sub-Committee on Northeast Frontier (Assam) Tribal and Excluded Areas*, Annexure IV, Appendix C, No. OA/24/Cons/47, Constituent Assembly of India, Council House, New Delhi, the 4 March 1948 (Henceforth Report of the Sub-Committee on Northeast Frontier (Assam) Tribal and Excluded Areas).
35. Letter of Peters, Superintendent, Lushai Hills, L.L. Peters, 4 August 1947, * No. 69237-76 G of 21 August 1947.
36. Memorandum submitted to His Majesty's Government, Government of India and its Constituent Assembly through the Advisory Sub-Committee by the Mizo Union in 1947.
37. *Report of the Frontier Areas Committee of Enquiry*, Camp Maymyo, 21 April, 1947.
38. Statement of Mr Jaipal Singh, Constituent Assembly, 30 July 1947; Delhi, *Constituent Assembly of India*, Vol. IV.
39. *Report of the Sub-Committee on Northeast Frontier (Assam) Tribal and Excluded Areas.*
40. *Constituent Assembly Debate*, Annexure III, Appendix C, 28 July 1947.
41. The Naga-Akbar Hydari Accord, 1947.
42. Lal Dena, 'The unresolved issues of the Hmar.' http://www.manipuronline.com/Features/June2002/hmar11_2.htm, accessed on 15 July 2002.
43. Lal Dena, 'The Hill People and the Merger of Manipur', in *Annexation of Manipur 1949,* People's Democratic Movement, Manipur, 1995, p. 115.
44. Singh, *Hijam Irabot and Political Movement in Manipur*, p. 202.
45. Ibid., p. 304.
46. U.A. Shimray, 'Naga Integration Movement: A Historical Perspective'. http://www.kanglaonline.com/index.php?template=kshow&kid=585, accessed on 25 June 2009.

47. Singh, *Hijam Irabot and Political Movement in Manipur*, p. 304.
48. Shimray, 'Naga Integration Movement: A Historical Perspective.'
49. Singh, *Hijam Irabot and Political Movement in Manipur*, p. 322.
50. *Report of the Sub-Committee on Northeast Frontier (Assam) Tribal and Excluded Areas.*
51. Imphal, *Manipur Gazette*, Wednesday, 26 October 1949, No. 219.
52. *Naga Resistance and the Peace Process*, Delhi: Other Media, 2001, p. 10.
53. S.C. Jamir, *Bedrock of Naga Society*, Nagaland Pradesh Congress Committee (I), 2000.
54. The Sixteen Point Agreement Arrived at Between the Naga People's Convention and the Government of India in July 1960.
55. Annexure 7, Resolution of Nagaland State Assembly; *Manipur Fact File 2001,* compiled by All Manipur College Teachers' Association, Imphal, 2001, p. 54.
56. Ibid.
57. Shimray, 'Naga Integration Movement: A Historical Perspective'.
58. Gangumei Kamei, 'Ethnic Responses to Merger: A Historical Perspective', in *Annexation of Manipur 1949,* Manipur: Peoples' Democratic Movement, 1995, pp. 98-9.
59. Ibid.
60. S.K. Chaube, *Hill Politics in Northeast India*; Patna: Orient Longman, 2nd ed., 1999, p. 212.
61. R. Vashum, *Nagas' Right to Self-determination*; Delhi: Mittal Publications, 2000. pp. 87-8.
62. Shimray, 'Naga Integration Movement: A Historical Perspective'.
63. Ibid.
64. Held at Hanship village from 10 to 13 October 1957, at Mualnuam village from 6 to 8 February 1960, at Hiangtam Lamka Village from 27 to 29 May 1960.
65. http://www.sialkal.com/home_doc_PNC.htm, accessed on 25 June 2009.
66. Interaction with Hareshwar Goswami, May 2005.
67. http://www.dipr.mizoram.gov.in; accessed on 25 June 2009.
68. Ibid.
69. File, Fortnightly confidential 31st Reports 1964-66, Imphal: Government of Manipur, MSA.
70. Memorandum submitted to the Prime Minister of India by the Mizo National Front General Headquarters, Aizawl, Mizoram on 30 October, 1965.
71. Chaube, *Hill Politics in Northeast India.* p. 213.

72. Ibid.
73. Extends to the whole of the State of Manipur except the hill areas.
74. Section 52 of the Union Territories Act of 1963.
75. R. Constantine, *Maid of the Mountains*, Delhi: Lancers, 1981, p. 95.
76. Ibid, p. 104.
77. Ibid, p. 95.
78. A three-day seminar on impact of administration on mutual relationship of Manipuris, Organized by Integrated People's Progressive Union (IPPU), Imphal, 2001, pp. 9-10.
79. Letter No. 10/PM/1373-6 of June 22, 1968 of Manipur Territorial Congress Committee.
80. S.K. Sanaton, ed., *Manipur's Integrity and Manipur Peoples' Party*, Imphal, Organising Committee 35th MPP Foundation Anniversary Celebration, 2002, p. 3.
81. Constantine, *Maid of the Mountains,* p. 118.
82. Ibid., p. 122.
83. *Bharatki Loilam Manipur*, Pan Manipuri Youth League, 1993, p. IX.
84. Shimray, 'Naga Integration Movement: A Historical Perspective.'
85. The Shillong Accord of 11 November 1975 between the Government of India and the Underground Nagas.
86. Mizoram Accord of 1986.
87. Ibid.
88. Dena, 'The Unresolved Issues of the Hmar.'
89. Memorandum Submitted to Prime Minister Rajiv Gandhi by the Manipur Kuki Tribes recognition Demand Committee on 28 April 1987.
90. The first batch of the cadres, under the command of Thangkholun Haokip, was trained by the Kachin Independent Army (KIA) in Myanmar.
91. Land of freedom.
92. Under the leadership of Ranco Thangboi Kuki.
93. 1st World Zomi Convention, 1988. http://www.zogam.org/documents.asp?article=documents_213; accessed on 25 June 2009.
94. Supplementary Agreement to the Shillong Accord on 5 January 1976, regarding implementation of Clause II of the Shillong Accord of 11 November 1975.
95. G.S. Oinam, 'The Kukis', Kuki International Forum, 2006.
96. Manifesto of the Kuki National Organisation.
97. Oinam, 'The Kukis'.

98. Chandel, Senapati, Tamenglong and Ukhrul Districts.
99. Press statement of the Naga People's Movement for Human Rights, Imphal, 17 September 1993.
100. Glenn T. Morris, 'Race Wars in Nagaland, Brahmanic Kautilyan Policies of Divide and Rule, Nagaland: Still Fighting After All These Years', Fourth World Bulletin, April 1994, Reproduced by the NSCN-IM on 14 April 1994.
101. Vibha J. Patel, 'Naga and Kuki: Who is to Blame?' in *Economic and Political Weekly*, Vol. 29, No. 22, Bombay, 28 May 1994, pp. 1331–2.
102. 'Naga Nation', 16 April 1994. http://nscn.livejournal.com/.
103. 'The Nagas Struggle for Freedom & Justice' in *Justice and Peace*, Boston, MA 02127-1093, 28 May 1994.
104. The Statement of the NSCN (IM) to the UN Working Group on Indigenous Populations, 12th Session at Geneva on 27 1994.
105. Memorandum submitted to Dr Kofi Anan, Secretary General, United Nations Organization, Geneva, by the Kuki National Organisation in May 2005.
106. http://www.e-pao.net/epRelatedNews.asp?heading=2&src=140607 accessed on 14 June 2007.
107. Dena, 'The Unresolved Issues of the Hmar'.
108. ZORO, formed in 1988 for Zomi Re-unification gradually lost credibility after the constituent parties Zomi National Congress and People's Convention fought state assembly elections by violating a Charter of Agreement signed in 1988. Therefore ZRO was formed in April 1993 at Phapian (Kachin State).
109. Memorandum submitted to the Secretary General, United Nations by the Zo Reunification Organisation (ZORO) on 20 May 1993.
110. Memorandum submitted to the Prime Minister of India by the Zomi Reunification Organization (ZRO) on 6 September 1993.
111. Appeal issued by the Publicity Wing, Zomi Reunification Organisation (ZRO), 9 August, 1993.
112. Root Cause of Kuki-Zomi Conflict; A pamphlet published by the Zomi National Volunteers, 1997.
113. A nutshell on Kuki Occupied Territories, 2003, Kukiforum.
114. Text of Final Peace Accord between Zomis and Kukis for Restoration of Peace and Normalcy, 1 October, 1998 on behalf of Kukis and Zomis respectively by the representatives belonging to Zomi, Kuki, Meetei, Thadou communities, and Government of Manipur.
115. *Why Manipuris Fight for Right to National Self-Determination,* United

National Liberation Front, Manipur, 3rd ed., 2001

116. 'Memorandum submitted to the Secretary General, United Nations and the Chairman of the Decolonisation Committee (committee of 24) for de-colonization of Manipur from Indian colonialism and alien racist regime, enlisting Manipur in the list of the non-self-governing-territories of the United Nations and, restoration of independence and sovereignty of Manipur' by the Revolutionary People's Front, Manipur; (henceforth RPF Memorandum to the UN).
117. Pamphlet circulated by the AMUCO in July and August 1997.
118. Speech Delivered by Isak Chishi Swu, President, Government of the People's Republic of Nagalim, 21 March 1998.
119. Deepak Dewan, 'Breach of Trust: An exclusive interview with Thuingaleng Muivah', Delhi, *Northeast Sun*, 1 July 1998.
120. Haokip, P.S., *Zale'n-gam: The Kuki Nation*; Kuki National Organisation, private circulation, 1998.
121. Proclamation by the President of the People's Republic of Nagaland, 2 March 1999.
122. Message of Gratitude, NSCN-IM, 1 July 1999.
123. Press Statement of NSCN-IM Stand on Extension of ceasefire, 21 June 2000.
124. *Nitin Gogoi,* 'Government rejects NSCN demand for extension of ceasefire to other Northeastern states'; NSCN-IM, 3 August 2000.
125. Pamphlet released by AMKIL and NIPCO on 18 September 2009.
126. 'Situation in Nagaland Manipur border villages under Control', *Sangai Express*, Imphal, 8 October, 2000.
127. Gan-Ngai Festival Invitation; State Level Celebration on 8 January 2001 at Kuki Inn.
128. Statement of the collective leadership, Statement issued by the NSCN-IM leadership on 7 March 2001.
129. Letter to Our Meetei Brothers and Sisters, NSCN (IM), 8 March 2001.
130. Ibid.
131. 'The Kohima Declaration', 19 March 2001.
132. Statement of the Collective Leadership of the NSCN (IM), 12 April 2001.
133. 'Memorandum' submitted by Naga Civil Societies to the President of India on 24 April 2001.
134. 'Motion for a Resolution on Nagaland Pursuant to Article 47 Par I of the Rules of Procedure', tabled by Olivier Dupuis and Gain

Franco Dell' Alba on Behalf of ARE Group, http://www.radicalparty.org/humanrights/nag_res.htm, accessed on 25 June 2009.

135. 'Memorandum submitted to the Prime Minister of India', submitted by the Kuki Students' Organisation Delhi demanding Withdrawal of Centre-NSCN (IM) Ceasefire Extension beyond Nagaland, 27 June 2001.
136. 'Creation of Meghalaya, Mizoram and Nagaland', Lok Sabha Unstarred Question No. 3252, to be answered on 21 December 2004.
137. *Unity, development and peace in Manipur: Findings and proposition of the first phase of public dialogue on Unity Development and Peace in Manipur*, Imphal, AMUCO, 2001.
138. 'Application to the Superintendent', Department of Archaeology, Government of Manipur, Ref. No. L/1/UCM/AC, dated 13 March 2002.
139. 'Memorandum to the Chief Minister of Manipur', submitted by the United Committee Manipur on 24 April 2002, File, UCM, Ref. No. 3/1/Memo/2002.
140. 'Memorandum submitted to the Prime Minister of India', submitted by the Manipur Land Revenue and Land Reform Act Extension Demand Committee, 7 May 2002; Ref No. Fax 3029545.
141. 'Proceeding of the Convention of Ethnic Reconsolidation (Before forming HERICOUN)', Imphal, Thursday 16 May 2002.
142. Executive members of the Baite National Convention Council, Komren Union Workers, Mate Tribe Council, Minority Youth Development Organization, United Committee Manipur, Vaiphei Tribes Union, Young Mizo Association, Zeliangrong (Naga) United Club's Association, Manipur, and Zou Union (Manipur) had attended the program organized at Gandhi Memorial Hall in Imphal on 20 May 2002.
143. Lit. *Protest Against the Policy to divide the people of Manipur into fragments.*
144. Lit. *The day when bloodshed was compelled.*
145. 'Application by Rameshkumar to the UCM', File UCM, 15 June 2002.
146. 'Application', Ref. No. 1/3/S.C. 1-2002, 18 July 2002.
147. 'Application submitted to the United Committee Manipur by the Sandang Shenba Maring Youth Club', Imphal.
148. 'Application', Ref No 11(c)/AMMI/2002, 29/8/02.
149. 'Application', 3 November 2002.
150. 'Application', Ref. No. 41, 31 August 2003.
151. 'Application', 22 January 2004.
152. 'Application submitted to the AMESCO', 8 February 2004.

153. 'Application submitted to the AMESCO', February 2004.
154. 'Petition to United Committee Manipur', 22 January 2004.
155. 'Application', 6 February 2004.
156. E.g., 'Sir ... in this regard, I as a citizen of the state would like to suggest that the UCM being an apex body of the people of the state may initiate steps to organize meetings / conventions at various levels to find out that the root causes which led to the present situations where the territorial integrity of Manipur is under threat and accordingly evolve concrete action programme or agenda to be taken up to strengthen the emotional & social relation among the various indigenous communities of Manipur', Letter to UCM submitted on 21 August 2002, by K. Bhogendrajit, Lairikyengbam Leikai, Imphal.
157. The bond of coexistence defends the boundary of Manipur.
158. 'Memorandum submitted to the Prime Minister of India, New Delhi' by All Political Party Delegation from Manipur on the protection of the Territorial Integrity of Manipur, 20 January 2003.
159. Meeyamgi Warep, Imphal, Convention at GM Hall, 23 January 2003.
160. 'Peace Talks Have Nothing to do with Manipur's Integrity', NSCN (IM); Imphal: *Sangai Express*, 7 October 2003.
161. The Home Minister (Kilo Kilonser), AK Lungalang, Deputy Kilonser K Chawang, Tatar David Pere, and Captain of the NSCN (IM).
162. 'Protests Galore, UCM Calls 18 hr General Strike', Imphal: *Sangai Express*, 8 October 2003.
163. Government working to disintegrate State, AMSU; Imphal: *Sangai Express*, 9 October 2003.
164. Press statement of AMUCO; File, No 3/2/SP (AMUCO)/ PR/ 2003-28.
165. PM urged not to give any statement on territory issue, Imphal: *Manipur Mail*, 27 October 2003.
166. Notice issued in the name of Azang Longmei, General Secretary, United Naga Council, Senapati, 19 October 2003.
167. Vajpayee rider on Greater Nagaland, Imphal: *Sangai Express*, 30 October 2003.
168. Invitation to Inter Community Cultural Festival 2003, Organized by RPDF, REACH-M, ATWO & PAACWA (Pallel mixed community organization).
169. Sushanta Talukdar, 'Siege within', Delhi: *Frontline*, Vol. 22, Issue 16, 30 Jully-12 August 2005.
170. Integration of Naga inhabited areas is a deleted issue: Mulatuno,

Imphal: *Sangai Express*, 24 May 2005.

171. Amitabha Roychowdhury, 'Resolve core issue of integration, IM tells GoI', New Delhi, 17 June 2005. http://e-pao.net/epRelatedNews.asp?heading=1&src=180605; accessed on 18 June 2005.
172. '3665 State Students Enrol to NBSE', Imphal: *Sangai Express*, 5 November 2006.
173. Adopted on the occasion of the Seminar on Kuki National Reconcialation, held from 30 November to 2 December 2006 at Moreh, organized by Kuki Students Democratic Front (KSDF), Kuki People's Congress (KPC) and Kuki Women Human Rights Organization (KWHRO).
174. KSO Memorandum to the Prime Minister of India, Imphal 6 March 2007.
175. Doumang Haokip (30) of Moreh Chawangphai, Tongkhullen Sitlou of Moreh Ward number 7, Canaan Veng and Pastor Henjam Lungdim of Moreh Moljol.
176. Likmabam Bungo (25) of Khurai Sajor Leikai, his younger brother Bungcha (22), Oinam Nilmani (30) of Khurai Konsam Leikai, Thingbaijam Johnson alias Itomcha of Khurai Sajor Leikai and Yanglem Romesh alias Pikpa (23) of Khurai Konsam Leikai. Arambam Tomba (60) of Khurai Chaithabi Leirak was rescued by the police.
177. A conglomerate of various Kuki-Chin-Mizo armed groups.
178. UPF, ZSF, others yearn for peace; Imphal: *Sangai Express*, 12 June 2007.
179. Sanajaoba, 'Why India cannot disturb Manipur boundary of 1947? uti possidetis juris', 2001.
180. RPF memorandum to the UN.
181. Sairem Nilbir, 'The Relation between the Hill and Plain People's since Time Immemorial', pp. 22-3.
182. Singh, 'Manipur the Right of Self-determination, a Summary' (n.d.).
183. P. Lalitkumar Singh, 'The People of Manipur,' 2001.
184. *People of Manipur rises to save unity and territorial integrity*, Imphal: United Committee Manipur (UCM), 2002.
185. Ibid.
186. 'Memorandum on the protection of the Territorial Integrity of Manipur' submitted to the Prime Minister of India, by All Political Party Delegation from Manipur, 20 January 2003.
187. 'As one can easily verify from Henry Yule's map of Manipur in

1500 A.D., down to James Johnstone's Map in 19th century and to Surveyor General of India's map of Manipur, 1984 A.D. They have been corroborated and recognized by other countries in their official maps and records', *People of Manipur rises to save unity and territorial integrity.*

188. 'Criticism and constructive submission regarding the study on treaties, agreements and other constructive arrangements between states and indigenous populations', Report submitted by Centre for Organisation and Research Education, Manipur to the Sub-Commission on the Prevention of Discrimination and Protection of Minorities, Commission on Human Rights, UN, March 1999.
189. Such as Rules for the Management of Manipur State and the Manipur Constitution Act 1947.
190. Concise Background information on Nagaland (Nagalim). http://www.angelfire.com/mo/Nagaland/, accessed in April 2002 (dead link now).
191. Achan Ramsan, 'The basis of territorial integrity and history: a quest for justice in retrospection.'
192. Naga Peoples Convention, Senapati Declaration, 28 June, 2001.
193. Ramsan, 'The basis of territorial integrity and history: a quest for justice in retrospection.'
194. Naga People's Convention, Senapati Declaration, 28 June, 2001.
195. Statement of Support by Gloria Kim, President and Mughali Achumi, General Secretary, Naga People's Friends Network Korea on 18 August 2006.
196. Statement of Support by Gloria Kim...
197. 'Naga tribe not to allow Manipuris to enter Dzuko', Imphal: Imphal Free Press, 17 February 2006.
198. Press statement of Naga People's Movement for Human Rights, 17 September 1993.
199. 'Who is the author of division among the Nagas and their territory?', NSCN-IM, September 2006.
200. P.S. Haokip, 'Ideological Aspects of Zale'n-gam'.
201. *Manifesto of the Kuki National Organization.*
202. Ibid.
203. P.S. Haokip 'Greetings from Zale'n-gam, the Kuki nation!' 10 April 2006.
204. Haokip, 'Ideological Aspects of Zale'n-gam'.
205. 'Brief History of Kuki', http://www.ksdf.org/about_kukis.asp accessed on 24 December 2006.

206. *Manipur Administration Report, 1908-1909.*
207. Sir James Johnstone, *Manipur and The Naga Hills*, Delhi: Manas Publications, reprint-1990, p. 26.
208. Letter from Mr J.E. Webster, Chief Secretary to the Chief Commissioner of Assam to the Secretary to the Government of India, Foreign and Political Department, Shillong, 27 June 1919.
209. 'Memorandum submitted to His Majesty's Government, Government of India and Its Constituent Assembly' through the Advisory Sub-Committee by the Mizo Union, 1947.
210. KNO's 'Memorandum to the Prime Minister of India', 2006, Ref. ZG/GEN 02-671/06, 9 August 2006.
211. P.S. Haokip, 'The Zale'n-gam and Kangleipak Equation' in *Zale'n-gam: The Kuki Nation*, 1998.
212. *Manifesto of the Kuki National Organisation.*
213. 1st World Zomi Convention, Aizawl, Mizoram, 19-21 May 1988.
214. KNO's 'Memorandum to the Prime Minister of India', 2006.
215. KNO's letter to Gen Than Shwe, Chairman, State Peace and Development Council, Burma 2006.
216. An introductory statement concerning the Kukis on the occasion of the United Old Kuki Army joining the Kuki National Organisation, Ref. No. ZG/IS 02-06/07, 4 December 2007.
217. KNO's 'Memorandum to the Prime Minister of India', 2006.
218. Luntinsat, 'Kuki-Meiteis: Not Border Fencing but Farewell Will', KSDF.
219. Gangumei Kamei, 'Origin of the Nagas' in *Nagas at Work*, Delhi: Naga Students' Union Delhi, 1996, pp. 14-5.
220. http://themanipurpage.tripod.com/culture/peopleofmanipur.html, as accessed on 15 March 2009.
221. Memorandum Submitted to Prime Minister Rajiv Gandhi by the Manipur Kuki Tribes recognition Demand Committee on 28 April 1987.
222. Jamir, *Bedrock of Naga Society.*
223. B.G. Verghese, *India's Northeast Resurgent: Ethnicity, Insurgency, Governance, Development*; Delhi: Konark Publishers, 1996, p. 95.
224. *On Naga Hoho's Naga Integration*, Naga Socialist Council of Nagaland, (Khaplang Faction), 2002, p. 8
225. *Root Cause of Kuki-Zomi Conflict*, A pamphlet published by the Zomi National Volunteers, 1997.

4

People's Democratic Aspiration

I. INTRODUCTION

The conflicts in Manipur are modelled and perpetuated under an overarching neoliberal political economy. Firstly, it is apparent that the solution sought by the Indian State is bent on integration trajectory without rooting out the system responsible for creating a colonial situation. The colonial system is manifested in unrestrained militarization to defend capitalist control over resource, market, and labour on the one hand and 'communal unrest' amongst peoples under puppet regimes and sectarian collusive forces on the other. Secondly, it is also apparent that most insurgent parties are bent on a neoliberal model. In the process, in July 2010, the capitalist forces, without consulting the public, further penetrated the latest extent of extracting license in a 'secret manner', for unrestraint control of 3,850 Sq. km. in the name of Oil Exploration & Drilling, which is almost one sixth of total area of Manipur. Most political writings also got structured in the system. Most writings have failed to (a) define the State and its political economy, (b) analyse the material interest and community composition of the ruling class, (c) discuss the ideology and policy of the leadership, (d) analyse the dynamics of collaboration and conflict among the elites, and (e) provide progressive vision to address the issues related to economic livelihood, security, socio-cultural growth and peace. This chapter shall discuss the dialectics of negative repercussion of neoliberal nationalism and the democratic aspirations of people in the grassroots.

II. POPULAR ASPIRATION OF LEI-INGKHOL

'Lei-Ingkhol is our homeland; we were born, our deaths were cremated and social life is built here,' expressed an aggrieved elder denizen (late) Ahanthem Ibomcha. 'For five decades my life is built around the village for survival and security,' lamented handicapped leper Ms Matumbi and she blamed, 'why the selfish rich and powerful want to destroy us to construct capital project.' On being asked about joining the protest, Mr Rocky, a daily wage labour retorted 'we are helpless because the government may kill us in fake encounter if we protest the project.' These were the main concerns raised in April 2005, but seldom published in the media when the contractors were scrambling for profit from the Capital Project. They resisted, hold the ground firmly despite arrest and casualties in repression, and defended the village for some years.

Gradually they lost morale of unity and spirit of resistance. Therefore, on 15 June 2013 a team of police and civil servants siege Lei-Ingkhol. They made alarm of combing operation, forced everyone into indoors, but surveyed the village at gun point. 'It was like a sudden combing operation. While we were forced indoors; every house and family head were photographed,' recounted Anil Maimom, president of village youth club. 'They verbally warned about eviction by 15 July but did not tell anything about compensation and rehabilitation,' said Geetchandra, general secretary of Joint Action Committee against the Eviction of Lei-Ingkhol. According to Ms Ngambi, 'We had wanted to raise an alarm to assemble the women for security, but the police pointed gun and no one could reach the alarm post.'

Few years back, the Manipur State cabinet made a reiteration, dated 16 December 2010, to acquire Lei-Ingkhol village (village) to construct components of the controversial Capital Complex or Capitol Complex. Land acquisition notifications had created tension in Lei-Ingkhol. The spirit of resistance was high and the village was resolutely resilient. From February 2005 to September 2006, they resolved to defend their village from government projects. However, on 15 June 2013, they were considerably weakened and demoralized. They desisted from bringing notice to their plight through the media. Nor did they seek the support of civil societies to resist.

But the 15 June siege raises several questions. Should civil administration function in this manner of flexing muscle power and informal threat to the common people? Can't democratic consensus precede imposition of policy at gunpoint? Many feared to say 'no' to eviction. Isn't this 'silence' a manufactured consent under duress? Although the Lei-Ingkhol question has not been seriously addressed by bourgeoisie intellectuals and neoliberal civil societies in Manipur, the dialectics of 'resistance' by villagers and 'manufactured consent' by the State invoke deeper questions about people's democratic aspirations against the backdrop of neoliberal constraints. While on the one hand the State have been aggressive in implementing its project; on the other hand the insurgent forces have failed to invest in saving the village. In this scenario, the Lei-Ingkhol issue have unveiled the failures of both the State and the insurgent fronts towards fulfilling the expectations of the people who have wanted to defend their village from destructions..

Flashback

On the rainy night of 12 September 2006, Chief Minister (henceforth CM) of Manipur Okram Ibobi, his staff, and the then Union Minister of State for Labour Oscar Fernandes made a surprise visit to Lei-Ingkhol Village (henceforth village). The CM, who had many times was invited to visit the village, was gloomy for reasons he alone knew. An official visit at night appeared fishy as it was untimely for sightseeing and media coverage. Oscar's verbal assurance to defend the village was, however, perceived a big victory by those who had been on indefinite relay hunger strike from 7 June 2005 onwards. He wrote to the village on 7 November 2006:

> I have taken up the matter with the Chief Minister Manipur and (he) has assured me that he will look into the matter and take an appropriate action soon. You may kindly carry this to the agitating Villagers to suspend their relay hunger strike immediately, since I have visited the Village earlier and I know the problem in person...

Lei Ingkhol was a suburban village officially located about five kilometres from the capital city at Village No. 8 Mantripukhri, Sheet No. 2, Tahsil Imphal Eat II. Originally marshy with wild bushes and reeds, hitherto isolated and neglected for fear of diseases and superstitions, it was first settled in the late 1940s by socially ostracized lepers and tuberculosis patients. In the course of time, families expanded and migrant labours and landless families settled on it.[1] In May 2012 the village was inhabited by 610 persons (291 men and 319 women), 93 per cent of the population belonging to the Meetei people and were organized into 116 families. The total 134 income earners in the village comprised of 90 wage labourers, 24 lower grade State employees, and 20 marginal stall keepers and petty shop owners. Poverty level was high and there comprised of 35 BPL cardholders and 22 Annapurna Yojna cardholders. There were 186 students who were mostly enrolled in government schools that were in degenerative conditions. Most families were built on small plot of land but could not afford to obtain *patta* (ownership registration). However, in its established form, the village being located adjacent to the hill slope and a rivulet had been noted for scenic beauty, favourable climate, rich natural resources, and prospects of tourism. Pertinent to the land grabbing trend elsewhere, a collusion of contractors and bureaucrats decided to construct certain components of Capital Project such as official quarters, squares and parks by destroying the village.

Capital Project

The Capital Project is a Rs 434.06 crore construction project financed by the Indian State under Special Plan Assistance scheme since 2004–05. The SPA fund opens up avenue of scramble for profit among commission seekers comprising political elites, contractors, bureaucrats, and others who indulge in accumulation of wealth through misappropriation of public fund and bribery. Bureaucrats and other elitist staff, who subscribe to luxurious and splendiferous living, were also eager to have new well furnished quarters with facilities in Imphal. All of them wanted to have a fortified elite zone. The CP was accordingly planned to construct new Assembly Hall, Secretariat Building, High Court Complexes, et cetera. Lei-Ingkhol had to be destroyed to construct components of high court such as residential bungalows for the Chief Justice, other judges, judge's library, residential quarters for officers and staff of the Registry, High Court Guest House with recreation centre, Medical

Dispensary, Bank, Post Office, Telephone Booth, Railway/Air Ticket Reservation Counter, High Court Officers and staff training centre, PWD Office for maintenance of building, 75 cubicles for the Advocate's Chamber, et cetera. with enough space for parking vehicles for the lawyers and the litigants.[2] To give a shade of 'people', a People Forum structure was included without actually defining it.

From the beginning, the project had been controversial for lack of transparency, public accountability, and displacement and destructive tendencies. Selection of construction site had suffered from hastiness, arbitrariness and violation of prescribed norms.[3] The blue print of the project had been altered and changed from time to time. Installation of the foundation stone for an Assembly Hall in the Kangla Fort premise was protested and it was done without obtaining clearance from the Archaeological Department. When the project was shifted at Chingmeirong there was protest as the *Kairang Khong Wetland* was filled up and foundation stone was inaugurated by the Prime Minister Dr Manmohan Singh on 20 November 2004 without clearance from the Union Ministry of Environment and Forest. Arbitrary eviction notices were issued to acquire land from Thangmeiband, Chingmeirong, and Tharon village.[4] According to the report of the Citizens' Concern for Dam & Development;

> Public Hearing Notification (No. PCB/Engg/35/97-98) regarding Capital Project was announced by Manipur Pollution Control Board (MPCB). The Notification was dated 7th January 2005, however it was published on 13 February 2005 only. The notice also did not mention where the EIA/EMP reports will be available to the general public. On 17th February (MPCB report) is not fully ready and that it should be ready on 21st Feb ... It was only on 22/23 of February that the EIA/EMP was made available after a letter from a registered NGO was produced. By the time the report came only 20 days was left for the public to comment on the report. The EIA was only in English language. There was no local language version of the EIA. ...The Rapid EIA Report was prepared by MPCB and the Hearing will also be conducted by MPCB itself. An EIA/EMP can be conducted by an external/Independent agency and not by the state pollution control board. ... Page 1–5 is irrelevant information. ... The 6th Page has a heading Capital Project that just listed the project components only

> and nothing about each of the component itself. There is no description of the project, in fact, a Detailed Project Report does not seem to exist on which an EIA can be based. A proposed site plan exists but this has not been given to the public.[5]

When there was widespread protest, the Manipur State changed the site and on 20 April 2005 a press release was issued to acquire 111.06 acres of land in the Mantripukhri area including the Lei-Ingkhol Village. Lei-Ingkhol opposed the decision and carried out several forms of protests, including road blockade and pitch battles with the police. Despite protest the main route of the village was permanently blocked in 2006 without adequate alternative arrangement. Despite assurance by Oscar the Manipur Cabinet took a decision on 16 December 2010 to destroy the village. In January 2011, the wooden bridge constructed by the villagers for the purpose of transportation was destroyed at gunpoint. It was followed by the siege of 15 June 2013 and an eviction order with the dateline of voluntary evacuation fixed for 15 July 2013.

The 15 June terror suggests use of force to impose 'consent' and acquire land at any cost. There was also a policy to divide the villagers and weaken their bargaining power. Coupled with psychological threat, disunity silenced them, which further helped the State in falsely fabricating the village 'consent' and justifying eviction. The justification, however, did not undo displacement impacts at the receiving end. Eviction on 15 July was postponed for sometime. According to Nilachandra, a village activist, 'although each family may be allotted a small plot there hasn't been any official announcement of adequate compensation and collective rehabilitation.' The irony is that eviction order had preceded negotiation and rehabilitation, which exposed a lapse in formality and a bypass in procedure for building consensus and arranging rehabilitation. It was undemocratic.

Where would the villagers go after displacement? Would the poor be able to buy land and construct homes at their own cost? Would they ever live together again as a collective entity? How would the trauma inflicted on the young children be rehabilitated and who would take the responsibility to do so? Where had those political leaders gone who had promised to defend the village during the election campaign? Why was the State reluctant to offer adequate compensation and a rehabilitation package so that the integrity, dignity, livelihood, and survival of the village as a collective entity were being ensured?

Developmental Aggression

The 20 April 2005 Cabinet decision was a repetition of arbitrariness and authoritarianism. Firstly, the village was not consulted before being included in the Project. On the contrary, brutal repression had created bloodshed, and physical and psychological insecurities to the villagers. Secondly, piecemeal construction of projects in different areas could evade Environmental Impact Assessment/ Environmental Management Plan (EIA/EMP) norms but did not ruled out overall destruction. Thirdly, the sudden change of site and size of structure meant a fluctuating Capital Project (CP) at the behest of project mongers. The original blue print for 32.76 acres had required acquisition of more land as the Chingmeirong Maning Lampak was not larger than 27 acres.[6] But the project area was suddenly expanded to 111.06 acres in Mantripukhri areas in addition to 27 acres at Chingmeirong. Fourthly, militarization of the project site and restrictions imposed on the public to the extent of imposing prohibition on taking photograph of foundation stone that was laid near roadside suggested suspension of democratic rights, dialogue and consensus. Fifthly, destruction of pre-existing infrastructures,[7] that is, adding burden to the poor economy suggested personal profit motives of a vested collusion.

The arbitrary decision of 20 April 2005 was the result of two interplaying trends: (a) accumulation of private wealth in the name of development, and (b) agenda of a fortified elite zone (FEZ).

Firstly, the Manipur rulers did not directly create capital by investing in constant and variable capitals. But they grossly indulged in wealth accumulation through misappropriation of public fund, extraction of commission and bribery. They were shareholders in the CP. They destroyed pre-existing infrastructure in order to (a) extract commission out of the total expenditure to be incurred in the eviction/demolition process and at the same time distribute among themselves unaccountable materials derived from destruction/demolition, and (b) extract commission and materials from reconstruction/relocation of the demolished infrastructure to new sites. Therefore, the CP was not constructed at a site where there would be no controversy, no displacement, and less destruction.

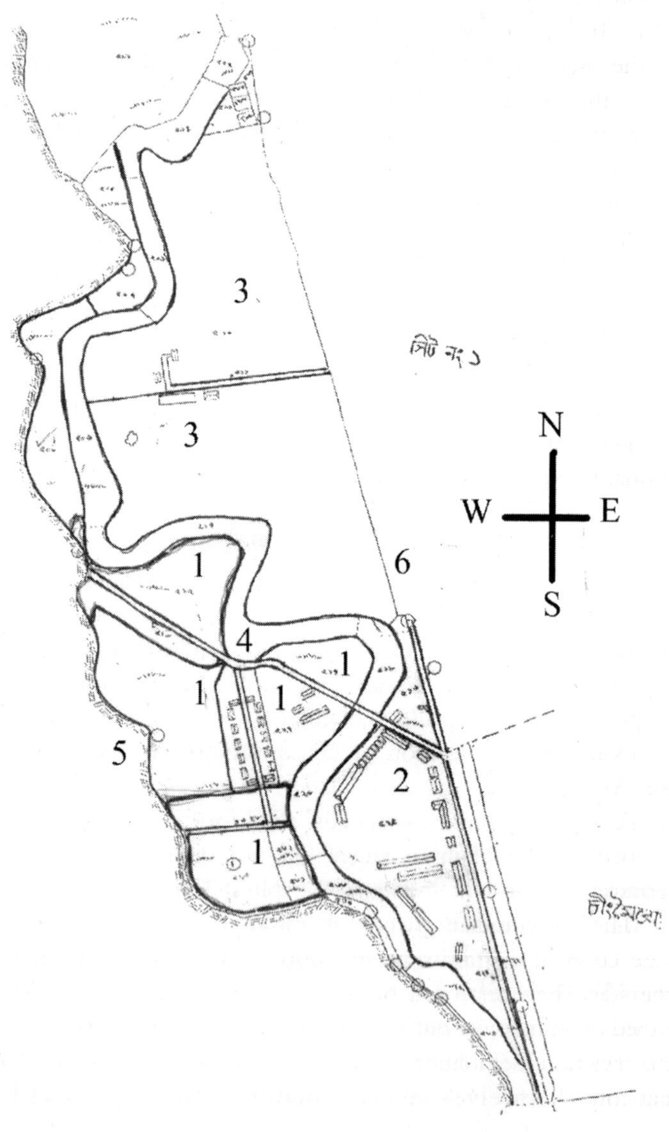

Secondly, as the illustration shows, the entire enclosed area constituted the CP site in the Mantripukhri area. In the last decade agricultural lands in and around the Mantripukhri area were acquired to construct State offices and institutions.[8] Indication No. 6 is the National Highway No. 39, which is likely to be shifted away in near future. Indication No. 5 is the hill range, acting as the natural fort on the western site. Indication No. 4 is the Irong Rivulet that passes through the entire area in the middle. No. 3 is the area of the destroyed Manipur Agricultural Farm. Indication No. 2 is the area of the destroyed PWD Store House campus. Indication No. 1 is Lei-Ingkhol Village. Adjacent to the indication No. 3 on the Northern side there is a CRPF station. At few kilometres distance away from it there is an Assam Rifles station located on the foothill. At a distance very close to the indication No. 2 on the southern side there is a police station and an Assam Rifles post. On the foothills of the indication No. 5 there is a route that could be used for regular frisking and flag march by troops.

The entire area is located at about 5 km from the heart of the Imphal City. The area is noted for its scenic beauty and moderate breeze. Vast tracts of land stretching from Indication No. 3 on the foothills and on the eastern side of the National Highway have been purchased by rich bureaucrats, contractors, businessmen and political leaders. Since the land covered by Indication No. 2 alone would be used for the construction of High Court Complex, rest of the area would be used for the construction of the structure of People Forum and quarters. Ground levelling of several acres had been carried by removing earth from the hill adjacent to the CP site. As experience suggest the land will be grabbed by or allotted to the powerful rich. Logically, a belt of elite housing complex clubbed together and defended by the natural wall and security barracks will be established in the long run.

The vested profit interest of the collusion of project mongers were covered up by using developmental jargons. Repression and intimidation were used to discourage protest, and local leaders were bribed directly or indirectly to divide opinion and to create confusion and frustration among the villagers. However, it has been very clear that controversies and protests centred on Tipaimukh Dam, Mapithel

Dam, Khuga Dam, attempted land grabbing at Kyamgei to construct NIIT, Airport expansion on the agricultural land in Changangei area, oil exploration and drilling, et cetera, had arose for want of transparency, accountability, and democratic process in projects. The CP, its destructive and suppressive tendencies had to be seen in this context. Lei-Ingkhol submitted 'most humble prayer to save us, our homes livelihood, social security, emotional ties, religious belief and religion-cultural practices, interpersonal relationship and honour from displacement, marginalization, destruction and humiliation.'[9] However, the CM did not listen.

Protest

Chronologically, protest was first registered on 21 February 2005 when Lei-Ingkhol Youth Development Organisation, individuals from Tharon Village, Thangmeiband and Tarung Village organized a joint sit-in-protest to defend the village. It was reiterated on 12 April and the following day Joint Action Committee against Eviction of Lei-Ingkhol (henceforth JAC) was formed to initiate agitation. On 20 April JAC launched sit-in-protest and sought the help of civil societies. On 21 April JAC organized a public meeting and a resolution was adopted to continue agitation.[10] The same day a memorandum was submitted to the Governor seeking for his intervention to defend the village. On 22 April JAC convened a joint meeting with civil societies and a resolution was passed to intensify protest. The following day JAC submitted memorandums to civil societies, local committees and individuals seeking for their support. On 26 April, a memorandum was submitted to the CM to exclude the village from CP.[11] The following day JAC sought for a meeting with the CM. The request was turned down. On 29 April, a joint meeting convened by JAC decided to meet the CM at any cost. On 30 April a protest was carried out in front of the gate of CM's Bungalow. The CM informed to a JAC delegate that he would take a decision only after visiting Lei-Ingkhol. But he did not ensure any date to visit. On 4 May, JAC carried out half road blocked on National Highway 39 (henceforth Highway). On 5 May, memorandums were submitted to the President, Prime Minister and Home Minister of India and a cycle rally from village to the

CM's home at Thoubal was organized. Protest pamphlets were pasted on the residential walls of the CM. On 6 May, Highway was half blocked. On 8 May, a cycle rally was carried out from the village to a rural village Tangkham via Pangei. On 10 May a symbolic rally was carried out from the village to the Capital Project Foundation Stone site at Thangmeiband. On 15 May, JAC protested the visit of the then Guwahati High Court Chief Justice B.K. Roy to the High Court Construction site adjacent to the village. On 2 June, the JAC announced to carry out road blockade on Highway 39 from 6 a.m. of 6 June. On 6 June, the JAC carried out Highway blockade from 6 a.m. It was brutally suppressed at around 8.30 a.m. On 7 June, JAC announced an indefinite relay hunger strike. In September, a delegate of JAC visited Delhi and submitted memorandums to the political leaders and. On 12 September 2006, Oscar Fernandes visited Lei-Ingkhol.

Politics of Blockade

The blockade has been upheld by many in Manipur. The government had condemned it for certain demerits. According to an official statement released in May 2007, in 2004–5 the total lose due to bandhs and blockades was Rs 246 crores. In 2005–6 the total loss due to bandhs and blockades was Rs 553.23 crores. A total of Rs 520.73 crores was reported lost during 2006–7 (Till January 31, 2007) due to bandhs and blockades.[12] Despite huge lose many opted to impose blockades when peaceful democratic assertions could not achieve positive result. Normally, the government listen to public demand only when the demand could create *disturbance.* Blockade creates *disturbance,* hence *normalcy,* in the existing context.

Lei-Ingkhol did not begin with blockade. The JAC started with protest demonstration, press statement, and memorandums. But the State was adamant. Despite protest, on 28 April 2005 the state Cabinet reiterated to construct the project at any cost. The same day State officials visited High Court Complex construction site. When an appointment to meet the CM was denied, on 30 April, two truckloads of residents made a surprise landing in front of CM Bungalow from different directions. The police erected barricades and blocked them. It was after browbeating and tussles with the police that a delegate was finally allowed to meet the CM for a short while.

The CM's verbal assurance was not satisfying. Rumours about forced eviction were widespread. It was a time when evictions were frequently published in the news. Bulldozer driver Gopal, a resident of village working in PWD, spread a rumour of eviction as he was being asked by officers to get bulldozers repaired to carry out eviction in few days. A clerk, N. Rajen, who was working in the High Court Bench, informed the village about a sanction order being approved by the High Court to begin CP construction. Many from neighbouring localities were also spreading rumours of forced eviction any time without compensation.

The JAC had to adopt means to win public sympathy and also to exert pressure to the State. Blockade, that is, *disturbance* became an option. Why? Gandhian non-cooperation movement and sit-in-protest would have been a choice had it not been for the numerical inferior labour community in the unorganized sectors. Rights are not going to be ensured because those are enshrined in the *statute* but because rights were defended. If Mao Tse Tung had suggested for the armed struggle to defend rights; for Lei-Ingkhol blockade was a militant middle path between Gandhian non-violence and Maoist gun-shots. *Disturbance* was opted to ensure repression and casualty so as to draw public attention, sympathy and support. It was also a means of raising the issue above other overlapping issues in the media.

The first blockade on the Highway was attempted on 4 May 2005 at around 11 a.m. The villagers, who hitherto had been less exposed to protest culture, were ideologically instable, psychologically weak and practically inexperienced. When the first detachment of police arrived they were taken aback. When more police arrived and intimated repression some began retreating. JAC convinced them to pretend fearless as retreat would mean defeat. In the meanwhile, JAC negotiated with the police and confined the blockade to half of the width of the Highway till 4 p.m. On 6 May, another half blocked was carried out from morning till evening. On 2 June, an ultimatum to carry out a complete road blockade on 6 June was announced. Between 4 May and 6 June, the JAC had organized several campaigns, cycle rallies, rallies, public meetings and petitioning to the Indian State. Many had expressed solidarity. However, the CM was adamant. On 11 May, Manipur Cabinet resolved to shift away within three days the Leprosy Hospital at Lei-Ingkhol to a far place called Lamlai and agricultural laboratories near Lei-Inkhol to other places. On 15 May 2005, an official team including the Chief Justice of Guwahati High Court and CM visited the proposed High Court Complex construction site. On 31 May, the state Cabinet reiterated its earlier decision to construct CP in the Village.

In the meanwhile, the protest had been costly. Most villagers had been confined in the village for many days as they had suspected eviction at any time. The labourers had not gone out to earn. Students had not been attending classes. CIDs and police had been frequently intruding. Survey teams had been regularly visiting. Rumour of forced eviction had been spreading. Although there had been solidarity from many, no effective pressure had been built to shake the 'regime'. At the same time there had been some progress in the consciousness, spirit and confidence. Pent up apprehension about forced eviction, fury against the rulers, self-confidence in assertion and sense of humiliation had been interplaying. They had wanted to assert loudly that they had not accepted the project. The support for blockade ensured by 'apex' civil societies such as All Manipur United Clubs Organisation and United Committee Manipur on 1 June, although they did not contribute anything on the scheduled date, had boosted the morale of the villagers.

The night of 5 June was an emotive situation. The *wakat lampak*[13] was fully crowded. Assembled in several small groupings, buzzing among themselves, each villager was curiously waiting for decision and action plan of JAC. They were also worried. AMUCO and UCM had not shown any sign of support as they were busy with the 18 June ritual. The leaders of 'apex' *meira paibee* organizations were merely conveying goodwill message. The villagers were left to either lead themselves or to withdraw. But will they fight? Out of the total population of 518 in June 2005 only about 100 were capable for the street. The rest were lepers, children, aged, child bearers, girls and men who must not be at the forefront. Out of the 100 capable, half were women *meira paibees* and the rest were boys. The village was cast with emotional gloom as casualty was presumed in repression. When the boys were lined up, Parikhomba's mother cried and appealed JAC to spare her only son. JAC then disbanded all until further announcement in few moments. It was reminded to all that the blockade would be a violent one and casualties would be inevitable. Government employees were asked not to be at the frontline as they might lose their jobs. Those who were responsible to the families might not be at the frontline. N. Ranjan, Bokun and some others withdrew. However, Parikhomba turned down his mother's pleading and joined the frontline. Finally, names of the volunteers were announced.

The villagers asked the leaders to go into hiding from that night. They must not be at the forefront as their arrest or casualty would be a setback to the agitation. Three fronts were planned. First, women *meira paibee* front would occupy the southern flank, block traffic coming from south, confront police and make a show for media coverage. They would hold ground at the tri-junction near Sangakpham bazaar. In case of repression they might escape by taking the route leading to the hill on the west. Second, boys would stretch themselves in detachments of three and cover a kilometre distance on the Highway. The northernmost flank would block traffic coming from the North. They might use stone and sticks to block government vehicles defying blockade. That would convey a message and private vehicles would not dare to take the risk of defying blockade. In case of repression they might escape towards the west and reach the hill and hide. Third, those who would stay back in the village were assigned to dig out holes on the roads approaching the village to obstruct police vehicles. They were suggested to contact civil societies and media in case if the first and second fronts had fallen under brutal repression. At around midnight, after hours of tactical planning, the assemblage was dismissed.

On the morning of 6 the first and second fronts were deployed as it was planned. From 6.30 to 8.30 a.m., the highway was blocked. There was heavy deployment of police. They intimidated the agitators to retreat or face repression. The women hold the ground firmly despite some altercation and minor tussles with the police. In the meanwhile there were three unexpected happenings. First, among those who had stayed back, Mr Ranjan and Bokul felt regretted, therefore, took a different route and started pelting stone to vehicles. Second, the aged and handicapped lepers felt regretted, took a different route and formed a sited human barricade on the middle of the Highway somewhere in the middle distance of northern and southern flanks. Third, a team of girls felt regretted, assisted in digging hole on the road and then went to Mantripukhri area. There they won some support from Mayang and Panggal residents. While these were happening the boys at the second front began to break window panes of vehicles. Exaggerated news of the attack was self propelling. Vehicles plying in the blockade zone were temporarily at freeze. The JAC leaders disguised as pressmen moved freely and coordinated the agitators.

The agitators were outnumbered by police. Repression began around 8.30 p.m. The women tried to defend and fought for some moments with their sticks but were dispersed by heavy tear gas and baton charge. Some of them were chased upon, caught, singled out and deliberately injured by point blank firing of rubber bullets and mock bombs. Mr Rajen and Bokul were caught while stone pelting, flogged, handcuffed and locked inside a police van. The boys were chased after but the police were blocked on the way by the sited human barricade of the aged and lepers. While the police spent few minutes in locking them in police vehicle, the boys had successfully escaped. In the meanwhile, the girls and women who had fraternized with Mayangs and Panggal supporters, independently of JAC, carried out a second attempt of blockade. They were repressed and two were arrested.[14]

Media coverage of the blood tinted face of Ms Pakpi, her multiple injury on the heads, fallen *meira paibees*, and the arrest of aged and lepers had drawn attention. The following day All India Radio, Imphal hosted a debate on the issue. Lei-Ingkhol became a headline in the news for few days. Supporters were growing in numbers. The bloodshed became an important point of reference in memorandums and campaigns. It was proven that blockade and bloodshed was much more than mere defiance of authority or resilient *disturbance* as suggested by the State. They were means to relocate certain suppressed political voice to the central stage of political bargaining. Blockade, therefore, constitutes a *normality* intricately rooted in Indian destructive projects enforced by an adamant bourgeoisie State in Manipur.

Terrorism

The manner Capital Project has been enforced using repression, militarization, and subjecting techniques which had prolonged terror impacts on the receiving end has called for serious thought on the notion of security and terrorism.

Firstly, Lei-Ingkhol had never experienced a prolonged terror situation before. To them the State Cabinet, CM, land surveyors, CID personnel and policemen were creating an atmosphere of physical and economic insecurity, causing casualty, social subjection and displacement for more than eight years. It was suspected that there was terror propaganda to justify militarization. A bomb was exploded on 24 October 2005 at 8.30 a.m. near the then diversion point of the road leading to the village. The timing and site of the blast, the manner it was planted in sand dune, absence of clarification from the insurgents, and militarization of the CP site after the blast let many to suspect that the blast was carried out by State secret agent to justify militarization of the project site, installation of watchtowers facing the village, and frequent visit by police to obstruct social scrutiny of projects and also to discourage regular visit of democratic activists in the village. Few years after, one Sitaram a Mayang trader who married local woman Meme, was fatally killed in mysterious ran down by an unknown vehicle on Highways. After about a year a rumour charged him a secret agent in planting the bomb. On the other hand there was another rumour that suggested that the bomb blast was perpetrated by rival contractors to obstruct the work progress of one Bikram, a contractor who had obtained work order. While these rumours had not been proven, the bomb blast had negative terror impact in the village.

Secondly, the protest was too expensive for the labour class who live on daily wages. In addition to bearing the expenditure of meetings, campaigns, demonstrations, et cetera, for more than a year, most villagers were compelled to take leave from works to take part in the protest. Wage labourers were unpaid for being on leave or lost contract jobs for being irregular.[15] The destruction of their main road increased the cost of transportation as they had to take a different lengthy crude road. In that sense the Indian leaders' notion of eco-terrorism[16] can be borrowed and applied in the context of Lei-Ingkhol since the impact of CP has been economic deprivation, pauperization, and inherently destructive and displacement of the villagers. It was an attack to their economy creating disruption and insecurity so that they finally become subservient to the directives of the CP mongers.

From Fear to Adventurism

Some developed the senses of heroism, gamming, and exhibition during the course of agitation. Initially they were timid and expressed helplessness. Once they were on correct political track they found supporters, overcame fear and isolationism, and developed self-confident in their activity. Some became heroes and were referred to by others in the story of people's struggle.

One day in April 2005, Master Tum Tum, now a youth, was on hiking. His parents were poor and could not afford to send him to good schools. He spent most of his time loitering with neighbourhood children of his 'class'. He was afraid to protest eviction as the police would come and kill.[17] Similarly, Mr Rocky, then a bachelor but now a father of two children belonged to migrant labours of 1980s. He said there would not be any option than voluntary evacuation. Protest was totally unthinkable of since Lei-Ingkhol was a small village that can be subdued by the smallest detachment of armed police. He was afraid to take part in any form of protest on that issue.[18]

Like Master Tum Tum and Mr Rocky most of the residents were not ready to protest openly for fear of repression. State employees feared most for losing their job in case their roles were exposed.[19] The executives of Lei-Ingkhol Youth Development Organisation and women association Lei-Ingkhol Khunsem Leimarol Apunba Lup opted for mercy appeal to the CM.[20] They devoted in legal advice from lawyers who may file case for compensation in case eviction was inevitable. Above all, many feared that protest would infuriate the CM and it might sabotage the chance of winning his sympathy. They approached their MLA and other officials for mercy to support.

The mercy appeal was proven a failure and the Cabinet decision of 20 April was announced. Thereafter they reluctantly began to organize for press conferences and invited civil societies. They believed that apex *meira paibee* organizations and civil societies alone could lead a protest. They were at times too timid to directly approach civil society leaders. Someone had to lead them to meet civil society leaders. They addressed with the respectable term *ima* (lit. mother) to any member of the apex *meira paibee* organizations and prayed for her leadership. The subjective conscience of being inferior and incapable was deep rooted.

The apex civil societies and *meira paibee* organizations, however, had a different policy. They expected the *locale* to raise issues in their own capacity. The apex would visit, encourage, guide and provide support if possible. In case the *locale* could create an effective standard of agitation the apex would coordinate branches and networks to assist the *locale*. The effective standard could be possible only after simultaneous task of rigorous internal organization and protest. For Lei-Ingkhol, the effective standard presupposed self confidence, spirit of resistance and acculturation with protest. Therefore, series of interactions with *apexes* were held. Village delegates were deputed to neighbourhood localities and public gatherings to speak and mobilize others.

Initially the villagers were reluctant to be assertive. They were persuaded. It was feigned to them that blockade would be staged managed in consultation with police. Both media and police would be informed one day before blockade. When the police would arrive for repression JAC would demand for peaceful court arrest. But the blockaders must hold the ground firmly, raise slogan and express aggressiveness without indulging in violence. They should enjoy protest and play valiant role as expression of bravery, courage and relentless struggle even by a coward would have media impact.

When half blockade on Highway was enforced on 4 May 2005 the police was informed to provide protective measures. The contents of the petition sounded absurd. However, for a moderate form of protest instituted by a community of incapables, such petition was meant to create confidence in them and it was a tactics of training. It was also a trial of potential and a call for safety and negotiation. The blockade was peaceful. Initially there were reflections of confusion and timidity. They became active after JAC had negotiated with the police to carry half-blockaded only till 4 p.m. They were organized into two sitting columns stretched in the middle of the Highway with two banners on the front and the rear rows. They raised occasional slogans and circulated pamphlet to the strangulated traffic. They were relieved from reaction by the traffic and police repression. Vehicles lowered down speed and passed off calmly. Passengers would either lean out heads to read the banners or stretch out hands for pamphlet. The blockaders sensed social recognition and became self-confident and heroic. The boys then began halting vehicles and explain the protest or throw in pamphlets. Some of them distributed pamphlets to the police. It was the beginning of an unprecedented adventure and they enjoyed doing it. There was unanimous decision for carrying out second half blockade on 6 May 2005.

The qualitative transformation into adventurism was revealed in the two cycle rallies that were carried out by the boys on 5 and 8 May. In the beginning none of the boys were ready as they feared exhaustion and police restriction. After a long lecture only Rocky rose up. He was applauded and singled out. Thereafter five more boys volunteered and were merged with Rocky. 5 May was scheduled for cycle rally covering one way distance of about 50 kms from the village to the permanent residence of CM at Athokpam in Thoubal district. The meeting was adjourned. Thereafter cycles were gathered. As most cycles of the poor were in bad condition a temporary repairing workshop was erected. While the preparation was underway, former cyclist Mr L. Sanjoy was passing stories of adventurism in cycle rally. Many boys and even children were moved by his story and they approached JAC to enlist their names. As the number swelled in, JAC convened a meeting to select only the capable.[21]

Early morning of 5 May the residents were assembled. LIKLA had prepared food for the rally boys. A flag off ceremony was organized and with the blessing of JAC the boys began their journey. On reaching the crowded junction of North AOC, about 3 km distance from the Village, they parked their cycle in a row and banners were fixed onto it to attracted attention. The boys entered into shops, circulated pamphlet and received donation. Thereafter, the rally resumed. On reaching the Kangla Park area, about 1 km distance from North AOC, commandos halted the boys. The valiant heroes at the North AOC were all of a sudden panicked ridden. The commandos asked them to return home. At that point of time, JAC convinced the boys the significance of courting arrest. The commandos alerted that a cycle rally could not be carried out without prior permission. If order was defied the boys would be arrested and tried according to the law. JAC then politely appealed the police to make preparation for voluntary court arrest. The commandos, however, declined to accept court arrest on the ground that JAC was simply trying to politicize it. The matter was conveyed to their higher authority. Finally, the police permitted to go ahead with the cycle rally by taking a different route other than the VIP road.

Thereafter the boys changed the route leading towards Wangkhei area. On reaching Palace Compound the boys showed interest in meeting the titular 'King of Manipur' Leishemba Sanajaoba. They rode into the royal compound, parked the bicycles, and stood at the royal gate. The King was still in the bed but JAC convinced the royal attendant to allow the boys to meet the King. With the permission of the King the boys entered in the palace. But the palace looked somewhat ruin and wanting renovation. Inside the palace, there was a darbar hall. Chairs were laid in a circular row and there was a throne on the southern side of the wall facing towards the front door at the North. Adjacent to the durbar hall on the western side was a room where a team of Ching Tam Apunba Sheishaklup[22] was accommodated. The boys interacted with the team and the King. The King was also affected by the proposed eviction to convert the palace into a historical site. After sometime, the King while in parting donated few packets of bread for the long journey.

On the way the boys halted at several places, circulated pamphlets and received donation. They received donation from the members of civil societies such as the MAPI Council and COHR. On reaching

Lilong Bazaar in Thoubal District, Mr Aslam Khan, the then vice president of TIPS presented packages of fast food. At Thoubal Bazaar the boys lined up their bicycles, spread banners, circulated pamphlets and received donations. At Athokpam they pasted protest pamphlets on the fencing walls of the CM, local clubs and other constructions and raised protest slogans against CP. Thereafter, the boys returned to Thoubal Bazaar and had afternoon meal in a hotel. Thereafter, the return journey began. On entering into the village, the boys raised victory slogans. They were welcome by with heroic salutes. The cycle rally was in the news headlines the following day.

Adventurism in cycle rally was circulated with exaggeration. Many parents were moved by it and approached JAC to enlist their children for the next. After disqualifying many, four more boys in addition to the previous cyclists were enlisted for the next rally on 8 May, to cover one way distance of about 18 km stretching from village to Tangkham Village via Pangei Bazaar.[23] This time the boys were more experienced in campaign and fund collection. At Pangei bazaar they parked in a row and fixed banners onto the bicycles. While some of the boys were circulating pamphlets in and around bazaar area, a section that was attracted on the sight of beautiful girls indulged in door to door campaign in the interior of the surrounding localities. They were happy with cordial reception and offering of food and water. As they spent time in enjoyment a search team had to find and bring them back. But they all discovered pleasure in it. At Tangkham Village they interacted, circulated pamphlets and established personal contact. They sought for soap and towel from the house of Ms Binokumari. Thereafter they had afternoon meals near a foothill, and enjoyed swimming and bath in the public pond. At dusk the boys returned to the public playground of Tangkham, made contacts with others and returned home.

In summary, many discovered pleasure, masculinity and adventurism in the protest culture. Fear was relatively overcome and many developed self confident in the activity. Adventurism had political impact as it attracted public attention. They were able to carry out the public rally on 10 May and on 6 June they imposed full blockade on the Highway.

The Mediator as Brokers

There were professionals who attempted to take personal advantage of the 'crisis hour'. They played tricks with hoax prescriptions at high cost of money. There were self styled mediators who had visited the village using the pretext of extending support to overcome the plight of the village.

First, there were advocates who wanted to draft memorandums and also encouraged litigation with the intension to extract advocate fee. However, there were problems. Litigation would confine the issue within the legal framework and it could not undo the mandate of land acquisition defended by the Land Acquisition Act 1894. On the other hand the encroacher tagging on the village by the administration further weaken legal arguments in favour of the villagers. The legal would only be helpful for seeking an injunction to delay eviction. Finally, JAC resolved to withhold from legal approach for some time. However some persons secretly proceed with legal proceeding with the hope to ensure some protection. Advocate fees were regularly paid but the court finally dismissed that 'the plaintiffs are not entitled to the reliefs claimed in the suit.'[24]

Second, one Ms Yumnam Indrani, a charismatic middle class woman from a different locality, quite unpopular for being a self styled mediator had generated a rumour in the village about government plan to reallocate the village at a place called Wangkhem in Thoubal District. The villagers must accept it or lose everything. She asked for negotiation. Many were moved by her suggestion to reallocate. Normally her plan was if both sides would come to settlement under her initiatives, she would charge negotiation fee from both. One day JAC summoned her and told her that JAC was not ready for any kind of compensation but resolved to defend the village. Thereafter she did not turn up again.

Third, there were spiritual custodians known as the *maibas/ maibees* who would act as mediators between people and god(s). It would suggest that for a community of people that had not completely done away with superstition but were ignorant about the temporal causes of political economy and the power of popular struggle in changing government decision, they sought divine intervention to console psychological inferiority. Perception was widespread that divine intervention would help in political victory. Some members of the Lai-Committee, JAC and LIKLA approached different *maibees,* paid ritual fees and spent enormous money in offering to deities. On one occasion the villagers were asked to light evening candles. In another occasion every family was asked to make black dolls and hang it upside down to defeat evil designs of the State. After 6 June blockade a shrine was constructed in the protest ground at the instigation of a *maibee.* And she was paid well. In such situation spiritual professionals found consumers and profiteered through sale of presumed divine mercy at high cost of price. But the god of the CM seemed more powerful than the gods of the poor as finally the CP had won.

RPF's Campaign

Ms Suno's son and Mr Gopal's son were insurgents. Why were their parties not defending the village? Byron, a retired PLA cadre was not playing enough roles. So the villagers were unhappy with them. Suno was silent about her son. Gopal had been uncooperative except spreading rumour of eviction. Therefore, when his son was arrested not a single villagers had cooperated in his release. These were the common sense circulated in the village.

However, insurgency campaign during the 'crisis hour' was witnessed on two occasions.

First, one Idhou, a self proclaimed RPF 'cadre' conveyed to JAC about his visit. When he was seated amidst a small gathering of JAC members there was ere silence with a mixture of fear, respect, confidence and expectations for him. This was the normal psychological impulse of laypersons towards an unknown insurgent. He came fully prepared with knowledge about the village, the names of landowners, their size of landholding, working condition of NGOs, hospitals, project plans of the State, et cetera. After exhaustive discussion he assured to convey the demand of village to his superiors for appropriate actions. Thereafter, he either visited the village periodically or met with JAC leaders separately at some other appointed places. But no visible help was directly coming.

Second, one day a stranger visited with two associates. They called on Byron, had long discussion and left. Next day he visited again with two different associates. This time he approached me to enquire about the issues. He approached in a friendly gesture and told me that his wife Marina and I were childhood friends. I was surprised as I had not heard about Marina for more than seven years since 1997. The last time I met her was at a private bank run by my friends Suresh and Premajit, which had gone into bankruptcy years ago. The stranger told me that he was also present when I had visited the bank. After some discussion he disclosed to me that he had been a RPF recruiter and the associates were selected for Basic Military Training at the PLA camp. I was surprised! Then he told me that he had visited the village to see if there were youths willing to join underground because of frustration with the State. Then he gave me long advises so that educated person like me should not think only for prestigious job and money, but also think about contributing to the freedom movement. His approach was interesting. He began with personal story to invoke emotional attachment and familiarization and thereafter suddenly shifted to campaign tactics. To him every individual was a potential cadre and his objective was to lead everyone to the BMT camp. Even if he could not recruit anyone it seems he left a party name whomsoever he interacted. Was he a real recruiter or an imposter? Was he a cadre or a casually hired recruiter? What was his name?

The visits of Idhou and the recruiter had profound psychological impact for some time. Most villagers perceived that insurgents were more powerful and committed than civil society leaders. Many had the illusion that insurgents could defend the village. They speculated that Idhou would do something for them, even to the extent of shooting down some cabinet ministers and the police who are terrorising them. However, there had not been any feedback from the party. Had Idhou retired, surrendered, killed, jailed? Had he sided with the State or had he simply disinterested? After 2005 he was never seen again. The trust that people had in him and his party gradually diminished. It begs a question; what is the mass line of the insurgents?

Cosmetic Solidarity

Despite widespread solidarity covered by the media the protest was not achieving the targeted goal. The blockade of 6 June had proven that the village was let alone to defend itself. Thereafter protest was deescalated from radicalism to relay hunger strike. Street demonstrations were not to be seen again. Petitioning was however shifted to Delhi. JAC continued press releases and solidarity statements from others till September 2006.

The question is why was the CM not responsive to the demand? Was it sheer highhandedness and autocracy? What perpetuated his highhandedness? In the struggle between highhanded State and democratic movement, the highhandedness was perpetuated by relative weakness of the popular assertion. Micro analysis of cosmetic solidarity substantiates the point.

To begin with, the solidarity statements of the civil societies had been cosmetic from the beginning. They did not directly involve in the struggle. The apexes merely encouraged JAC to go ahead with protest. Sometimes they merely handed over a bunch of blank letter heads of other local organizations. JAC was asked to write whatever they considered suitable in those letterheads and post it to the media. As a result most solidarity statements by 'others' were manufactured by JAC without the knowledge of the concerned 'others'. It was not certain if those others really exist or were they aware of the issue.

Most of those who were familiar with the issue through the media and had condemned the project had neither visited the village nor organized peoples to join it. When AMSU led some students of Kid's Corner to the village on the plea of taking part in the relay hunger strike, the students were unaware of the issue they were supporting. The effort of AMSU was thankful but a qualitative initiative to make people aware of the issue was missing. These students were mere camp followers obeying certain command.

There can be no denying that some civil societies had frequently visited the village. Some of them had extended political and logistic supports. The first press conference at night was assisted by Umakanta of TIPS. The protest in front of the CM bungalow was lead by E. Johnson of IPSA. Jiten Yumnam of CCDD donated pamphlet. Jiten and Ms Leirik of Kanglamei attended the public rally of 10 May. Members of COHR frequently interacted with the residents. AMUCO donated certain quantity of relief package. UCM and MSF had facilitated in raising the issue at public gatherings organized by them.

However, sectarianism among civil societies had made impossible a stringent united front. There were suspicions and browbeating against one another. At times, a particular organization A suggested JAC to insist organization B to join protest on the ground that B was in good term with the State. Condition was imposed on JAC that A would join the protest only when B had taken part in it. When JAC with all its effort was able to win the support of B, A simply withdrew support on the ground that it could not work together with B as B was in good term with the State. A was simply betraying JAC.

Another betrayal was the June 6 blockade. UCM and AMUCO were the most powerful apexes that had suggested for the blockade. Had they not assured full support it was unthinkable of JAC to lead the blockade alone. JAC believed in them and called the blockade. However, UCM and AMUCO waited for each other to respond first and in their diplomatic tussle they deliberately withdrew support at the last moment. Therefore, all the joint statements that were passed in joint sittings existed on papers only.

The JAC lost faith to the apexes, particularly after 6 June, although it welcomed their solidarity and visits. Before June 6 LIKLA that was affiliated to Kangla Mei had informally distanced away as its support was below expectations. JAC considered UCM as irresponsible and refused to attend any programme organized by UCM in that month. In the meanwhile they approached for support from the hill village communities. Mr Thameng and his wife belonging to the Zou community were sent to the northeast at Saikul sub-division in Senapati district to contact and seek the help of Kuki chiefs and if possible Kuki insurgents. A team of Mrs. Yumsangbi (a Kabui Naga converted to Meetei), Mrs. Heitonbi and Mrs Naganbi were sent to the north at Luwangsanggol Village in Senapati District to organize Thanggal community and also to seek the help of Naga insurgents if possible. JAC also sought the help of two Naga CID officials Mr Pungam Keishing and P. Salew Joseph who frequently visited the village to inspect the 'crisis hour.' They were convinced that the CP was destructive in the Imphal Valley and that it could have been constructed in the hill districts. The objective of JAC was to shift away the CP and defend the village. With their support JAC met the then MP Rajya Sabha Mr Rishang Keishing and appraised the issue. JAC also met some hill based civil societies. But they were not enthusiastic about having the CP in the hills.

After 6 June a delegation of JAC was sent to Kangpokpi Sadar hills in Senapati District to seek the help of Kuki leaders for another round of effective blockade on Highway. Other Naga organizations and Delhi based civil society organizations and democratic forces were also approached. However, their support could not be materialized at the last moment due to bigger overlapping crisis that engulfed Manipur, for example, ANSAM initiated a 54-day economic blockade. Money was also a big problem. Campaigns and network building was very expensive. The small village dominantly inhabited by the poor labour could not bear expenses for larger politics. In short, no united force strong enough to create effective disturbance vis-à-vis the state could be created.

Consumers *sans* revolutionary ideology

If revolution is the ideological underpinning of insurgency; revolutionary activity is expected wherever an insurgent is sheltered. If insurgents are fugitive for security reasons; at least certain minimum amount of revolutionary expressions in the casual conversations with trusted colleagues, revolutionary interpretation of current burning issues, promotion of revolutionary literatures, and investment in democratic activities are expected from them. If some revolutionaries are outlawed fugitives; over-ground comrades are expected to operate under lawful banners, spread revolutionary consciousness and strategically expand mass base among different sections of people by working with them on relevant local concerns, consistently organize different levels of members into different levels of organizations, and bring up political movement to higher stages. These seemed to be missing at Lei-Ingkhol!

In mid 1990s one Mr Ibomcha, Deputy Home of UNLF was taking shelter for some years. He was mistaken for a *maiba* (priest) as his visible activities were spreading Meetei patriotism, spiritualism and performing religious rituals. Sagolsem Byron was a retired PLA cadre,[25] late Mangsidam Kairangjaoba was a cadre of KYKL, Chanambam Bobby was with one or the other insurgent party,[26] and Ahanthem Naoba was a cadre of UNLF (now retired).[27] There were hearsays about secret others taking shelter in the village from time to time. All of them, other than sharing to their friends the romantic guerrilla adventurism and sufferings of fugitive livelihood, which attracted some of their peers, had not contributed much to the discussions that could have revolutionary impact. They had no political and economic programmes to organize people.

At the level of civil societies the women *meira paibee* LIKLA was affiliated to apex organization Kangla Mei for some years since early 2000s. Later on it showed allegiance to other apexes such as Poirei Leimarol Meira Paibi Apunba, Nupi Samaj and others. The local club LYDO and some youths had closely worked with UCM in 2002–03. During the 'crisis hours' of 2005–06 JAC established new contacts with TIPS, HERICOUN, AMSU, NIPCO, AMKIL, MAPI Council, MSF, AMUCO, COHR, and IPSA. However, these contacts were more personal and tactical but less ideological.

The civil societies were supposed to raise and interconnect local issues with other larger democratic issues. They were expected to organize the local, create units, nominate local leaders to coordinate with apex, conduct regular political and ideological classes, and expand local political base. During 'crisis hour' they were expected to spend more time in the village, carry out door campaigns, circulate propaganda literatures, and lead the movement. These expectations were not fulfilled in the case of Lei-Ingkhol. Civil societies, other than CCDD had not drafted a pamphlet for circulation on the Lei-Ingkhol question. Their statements and speeches about CP and destructive projects were bent on legal approach and failed to correlate class questions, character of the State, role of the elites, dialectics of capitalist projects and militarization, et cetera. Nor did they initiate systematic and regular study circle with the villagers on their issues to relate it with the larger people's democratic movement.

The normal form of contact that an apex had established with the village was inconsistent, casual and tactical. It was only when an issue had appeared that a delegation of apex would visit the village, called on leaders, handover pamphlets or invitations to them, and just went back. They did not reappear until another issue had come up. In this scenario hawkers who regularly circulated newspaper and interacted with villagers had wider personal contact than an apex. Logically villagers' response to an apex was largely personal and individualistic. An individual would attend a programme organized by an apex not because he/she was politically aware or committed but because of personal obligation with the invitee.

In some cases individual response to the call by apex was motivated by adventurism and personal gains. For instance, when UCM was preparing for 'the Great June Uprising' in 2002 many village youths had volunteered in fund raising drive and other activities. UCM at that point of time was the most popular civil society in the Imphal Valley. The youths, apart from emotional attachment with the integrity question and 18 June incident of 2001, were primarily moved by senses of heroism and adventurism for being associated with UCM. They carried UCM inscribed identity cards wherever they went, produced it and exacted donations, misappropriated a portion of the fund, called themselves activist and had pride in repeating it.

However, misunderstanding with UCM erupted on some issues. Firstly, villagers opposed UCM's plan to reserve a portion of hill considered to be owned by the village for constructing Zelianrong cemetery. Secondly, there was allegation by UCM that a self styled secretary of the village had misused the name of UCM while misappropriating money for extracting earth to fill up *Kekrupat* to construct 'the Great June Uprising Memorial Complex'. Thirdly, by 2003 the activities of UCM was perceived *mundane* and many did not renew membership. Fourthly, during the 2005 agitation the response of UCM was delaying and half-hearted. Villagers felt betrayal when UCM withdrew from direct involvement in the blockade of 6 June. Many, therefore, refused to take part in the 18 June programme hosted by UCM at Kekrupat in 2005. The point is the village perception of 18 June 'rituals' was less political or ideological impulse, but by way of personifying the 'ritual' with some individual leaders or organizations. They thought AMUCO and COHR were more helpful during the 'crisis hour' and willingly attended 18 June 'ritual' organized by them. The loyalty was continued for few years until the personal bond was strong. By 2010 their participation became nil.

They were mere camp followers responding to invitations to show personal loyalty. Most were unaware of the theme and underlying issues of the programme they were attending. In public meetings the technical words and complex theoretical discourses delivered by professional speakers were difficult to digest. They remain conceptually, theoretically and politically less organized. The village organizations were loose and the members had multiple or shifting allegiance to apexes and electoral candidates. They worked simultaneously with AMUCO, NIPCO, AMKIL, Poirei, Kangla Mei, CADA, MSF and others from time to time based on issues. A member of JAC appealed to COHR for stipend to become active volunteer but he also worked with the Indian National Congress. The village was against the government during 'crisis hour' and had condemned political parties for not supporting them. But during the general elections (2007 and 2012) they took money from electoral candidates and almost clash one another for the sake of the candidates. By 2009 some of the boys who were active in the cycle rally and had hated the State were recruited to Village Defense Force, Indian army and the Indian Reserved Battalion.

Lapse of common guiding principles and progressive political outlook had paved the way to *anarcho-individualism*; opportunism and sectarianism had kept them disunited in the long run. The spirit of resistance became a past never to repeat again. They had succumbed to the divisive policy. Couple with psychological threat, disunity was a factor for absence of resistance and eviction was justified. But what have the insurgents and civil societies done for the village? To sum up, when Capital penetrate into Manipur in the guise of grant, investment, economic packages primarily for the construction of dams, roads, military installations, office buildings and institutions; practically it sponsored local puppet regimes to indulge in repression and let the exploiters enjoy free control of resources and other forms of destructions. It seemed that most of the insurgents had taken bourgeoisie democratic revolution[28] line and had been shareholders of the capitalist project. Most of them were comparatively blind to the plight of the peasant and working families who were victims of oppressive regime. Lei-Ingkhol is gone.

III. HOLIDAY POLITICS

A holiday is a formalized ritual constructed in recognition of the presumed historical significance of an event or practice or person and manifests in itself an institutionalized subjection of the people through imposition of certain degree of cultural uniformity. A holiday, therefore, is invention of tradition aimed at subjecting a population to meanings associated with the constructed practices or symbols. It is an attempt to integrate cultural sentiment of a projected community under a common practice that is, to continuously defend an imagined collective identity. However, in a heterogeneous society if such invention embodies or articulates community oriented tradition type, it becomes an artefact of contest vis-à-vis pre-existing traditions or invites the growth of contending traditions. I shall analysis it based on the unrest in 2005 centred on *18 June*.

In 2005 the All Naga Students' Association Manipur (ANSAM) commenced an 'indefinite economic blockade' from 21 June on Highways passing through Manipur against Manipur State's decision to declare 18 June as Manipur Integrity Day and state holiday. The agitation had destroyed offices, private vehicles, and public bridge and had disrupted economic livelihood. It was only on 10 August, after fifty two days of blockade that ANSAM and the Manipur State, under extreme pressure from various civil societies in Manipur and beyond came to an agreement and lifted the economic blockade from 12 noon the following day.

The economic blockade had drawn the attention of various critics who focused primarily on the justifiability of economic blockade as a form of protest against the observation of 18 June as a holiday. The critics either defended or challenged the sagacity of declaring state holiday in commemoration of 18 June but failed to contextualize the politics that had developed over the years within the parameters set by the State's cultural policy of declaring holiday. Holiday politics escaped critical observation and discussions that were primarily centred on 18 June could not come up with a consensual solution to the crisis. The seeming return to peace following the lifting of the blockade could not erase public apprehension about another cycle of unrest centred on 18 June.

Holiday politics

State's holiday lists in Manipur illustrate that there had been a mixed commitment towards upholding (1) Indian nationalism, (2) Manipur patriotism and (3) democracy. The 'mixed commitment' can also be interpreted as reflection of certain undemocratic and hegemonic underpinning in policy making. It also reflected continuous tussle between community rights and the State's response to the communities. An analysis of the mixed commitment becomes necessary.

Firstly, the Indian State had created 'national' rituals such as the Republic Day and the Independence Day not merely to celebrate achievement of 'independence' and 'republic' but also to disseminate a sense of citizenship and civic fraternity among the people under common 'national' celebration. In 1980s Manipur witnessed heavy investments by the State to ensure pomp and shows and maximum participation in these celebrations. The Republic Day parade marched through the main routes of Imphal city. Large numbers of students, military and paramilitary forces, sports players, cultural troupes and tableaux representing regions, communities and departments took in the Republic Day parade. There were sky diving and aeronautic shows to attract more audience. There were free transport arrangements for audience. In a similar way, the Independence Day was characterized by observation of holiday and functions where the aesthetic ramification of the unfurling of the Indian 'national' flag along with presentation of orchestrated 'national' song served 'national' propaganda.

Secondly, Manipur State's commitment to disseminate Indian

nationalism, however, did not desisted it from practically collaborating with the insurgency agenda of promoting Manipuri patriotism and initiatives to defend the territorial *status quo*. In this 'regionalism' interplayed in the invention of official rituals that incorporated selected traditions or events whose origins could be traced in certain community past. Holidays were scheduled in order to create receptive consumers[29] to facilitate grand celebration/ observation of invented traditions such as the Houchongba, Death Anniversary of King Gambhir, Khongjom Day, Patriots' Day, Women's War, and Irabot's Day.[30]

Thirdly, the commitment to democracy had allowed certain amount of community cultural autonomy and assertion of community identity artefacts. The autonomy, however, had not allowed to infringe on the State and its policy. Therefore, there was a dialectics of community rights and State policy characterized by collaboration of the two on certain common interest. The dialectics, however, perpetuated communal shaping when it went through a process of attributing priority to certain selected community artefacts. For instance, the Manipur gazetted general holiday list 2001 had listed thirty three holidays. Eleven holidays primarily aimed at arousing Indian nationalism and Manipur patriotism were meant to be observed by all.[31] Fourteen holidays were closely related to Meetei culture.[32] Gaan-Ngai and Lui-Ngai-ni were celebrated by Nagas; Idul Zuha, Idul-Fiter and Milad-un-Nabi were meant for Panggal (Manipuri Muslim); Good Friday and Christmas were for Christians across communities and; only Kut for Kukis. The restricted holiday list of the same year had listed thirty two holidays. Out of it, twenty two holidays[33] were related to Meetei culture; Christmas eve, Post Christmas and New Year Eve were related to Christians; Shab-e-Quadar Shab-e-Baraat and Muharram were meant for Panggal; Mahabir Jayanti, Budha Jayanti and Guru Nanak Birth Day are meant for Mayangs and; Netaji Subhas Chandra Bose (Birth Day) could be be observed by any one.

In actuality, cultural *status quo* and mutual respects as later on emphasized in the 'draft cultural policy'[34] were practically less adhered to as reflected in the lists. Protagonists of 'minority' politics could charge that the lists reflected favourable treatment of the State, to the numerically dominant Meetei community and numerically inferior but politically and economically influential Mayangs. It needs to be seen that sacrosanct community identity is embodied in each holiday no matter one may try to depict non-communal origin. Interestingly, most of the holidays were arbitrarily decided by the State or were the result of effective pressure by concerned groups. However, in a highly contested situation where the Indian State was perceived as Mayang hegemony and Manipur patriotism was interpreted as Meetei dominance the holiday policy had left the room open to communal fabrications and tension based on these at various levels. Politics of 'negation' and 'assertion' centred on holiday became evident.

Firstly, politics of negation is characterized by outright rejection of official ritual and holiday. The legitimacy of negation is derived from the construction of hegemonic character of the ritual and the communal meaning associated with a holiday. I have mentioned ANSAM agitation against 18 June holiday. Boycott of the *Indian* Republic Day and Independence Day by insurgents are other examples. The boycott of these two holidays had repercussions in spreading liberation consciousness which interplayed with Manipur patriotism embodied in counter rituals[35] and disseminated a sense of popular negation of the symbols or rituals that symbolized the hegemony of the Indian State. It had an impact. Popular enthusiasm about these rituals seemed declined to a considerable scale. The State had to shift the venue of those rituals from open public spaces to more fortified and enclosed functions in the Kangla Fort attended by troops, sponsored cultural troupes and some officials. Similarly schools, colleges and other private institutions though they remain closed on the Independence Day no longer organize grand rituals as celebrated elsewhere. It seems that the totalising meaning of Indian integration supposedly conveying through observing 'national' days had been deflated and any forceful attempt to superimpose such rituals had substantiated undemocratic authoritarianism of the Indian State. Authoritarianism provided the defiant groups with the mass base to disseminate anti-colonial polemics.

Secondly, the politics of assertion exhibits community rights playing important roles in shaping State's cultural policy. Communities or cultural groups with strong representation consciousness had created narratives about their respective 'day' and agitates for inclusion of 'it' in the holiday list. Powerful lobbies got listed and the weaker were neglected. The politics of assertion to get listed, therefore, was not dissociated from the normative pattern of the State's cultural policy of imposing homogeneity. On the other hand it led to numerical addition of holidays in the list. The assertive communities, therefore, instead of doing away with the loopholes of the policy became structured into it and perpetuated the policy.

Analysis of Meetei revivalists and Zelianrong[36] assertions explains a lot.

Firstly, Meetei 'revivalists' had opposed religio-cultural practices associated with Hinduism and counter-asserted what they construed 'purely' Meetei. And they used the democratic platform provided by the State as their launch pad. Due to their pressure the State on 13 October 1975 declared Lainginthou Sanamahi Mera Chaorel Houba[37] day a general holiday; included Sanamahism[38] in the column of religion in the 1981 Census; declared Sajibu Nongma Panba[39] day as restricted holiday in 1981. Sajibu Nongma Panba and Eemoinu Eeratpa were included in the general and public holiday list of the year 2000.[40]

Secondly, Zelianrong community agitated against the State's attempt to delete Gaan-Ngai festival from the holiday list.[41] Had it not been for Zelianrong's strong political influence among civil societies and the strategic control of Highway 53 the State would have not conceded the demand. Similarly there is pressure by Kukis to declare holiday on 17 March to commemorate Anglo-Kuki War[42] and by Zelianrongs to declare holiday on 29 August to commemorate death anniversary of Haipou Jadonang.[43]

These few examples reveal that the politics of assertion presupposes enough community resources and successful mobilization to sustain prolong assertion. The smaller or weaker communities who could not exert sufficient amount of pressure were often denied from being listed. The holiday policy therefore can be construed as augmenting dichotomy between listed and non-listed identities corresponding respectively to greater and smaller traditions or dominant and inferior communities. It generated communal stereotypes and social distancing among communities.

Communal reading of holidays

Culturally, each community possesses peculiar formalized rituals and cultural traits. In principle communities enjoy constitutional safeguards to promote respective identities. Politically in the context of diametrical nationalisms, where communal propaganda plays significant role in the consolidation, communal sentiment prevails. Community members are being invested to become receptive to communal propagandas that construe the idea of dehumanized 'self' vis-à-vis hegemonic neighbouring 'others'. In this scenario communal interpretations of the holiday lists can have significant impact on shaping communalism. One needs critical reading of the listed holidays.

Firstly, some holidays are closely connected to reinvented community pasts. These pasts could not be dissociated from fabricated communal meanings as the 'ritual' forms and narratives had community orientation. We many focus on: (a) Houchongba, (b) Death Anniversary of Chinglen Nongdrenkhomba (Gambhir), (c) Khongjom Day, (d) Patriots' Day, and (e) Women's War.

(a) Houchongba festival is considered very old and many traced its origin in the 1st century A.D. According to the available sources such as the royal chronicle called Cheitharol Kumbaba and British accounts Houchongba is a 'tribute gathering ritual' patronized by 'Meetei' king, when all the vassals, if not subdued chiefs, turned up at the palace to pay tribute to the king, received gifts from him and enjoyed with drink, dances and 'masculine' shows. The festival, therefore, had a feudal origin. The current celebration has continued to retain certain aspect of the feudal past with the king occupying the centre stage.

(b) Death Anniversary of King Chinglen Nongdrenkhomba (Gambhir) has been observed in order to commemorate the conquest of Cachar (Assam) and liberation of Manipur in 1826 from seven years Burmese occupation. The observation became prominent along with the promotion of legends that embellished Chinglen's love for motherland, selfless endeavour for liberation, and efforts to defend 'territory' and death due to alleged heart stroke on hearing the news of forced transfer of Kabaw Valley to Burma by the British in 1834. The death anniversary is aimed at arousing Manipuri patriotism to defend Manipur territorial *status quo.*

(c) Khongjom Day has been declared a general holiday in recognition of the widespread perception of the heroic sacrifices made by Manipuri soldiers, particularly major general Paonam Naol (Paona Brajabashi) who had fallen at the Battle of Khongjom during Anglo-Manipur War in 1891. It has been widely held that Naol, despite of the inferior position of the Manipur soldiers both in numerical strength and arms power, did not retreat till the last breath. There has been a legend that depicted the invincibility of Naol because of mystical power. But he had resolved to be killed for two reasons; he could not save the life of his dearest student-soldier Chinglensana from the enemy and he perceived that the defeat of Manipur was inevitable.

(d) Twelve December has been declared state holiday in commemoration of the launch of Women's War (Nupi-Lan) against British trade on rice in 1939. The agitation went on for months with women vigilant groups imposing ban on functioning of rice mills, boycotting market in British Reserves, dumping carts transporting commercial rice and fighting pitch battles with the State troops. It culminated into movement for responsible government. The legacy of Nupi-Lan has been continuously circulated along with the legends of *meira paibee* movement against State terrorism. There had constructed a Nupi-lan Memorial Complex with statues installed on a high platform depicting women agitators snatching rifles from the British soldiers.

These holidays were meant to be observed across communities. However, the manner the rituals has been organized shows that the protagonists and State were yet to free themselves from contentious communal hangovers of embellishing communal meaning to these days. These are being discussed as follows:

(a) Khongjom Day (23 April) has Meetei Hindu orientation. The first recorded ritual organized in 1957 constituted among others singing of Hindu gospels such as Radhe Shyam, Hari Nam, and Hare Krishna Hare Ram. In 1966 Anna Utsob was offered to Lord Krishna. Subsequent observations were opened with recital of Hindu scripture Gita and offering of oblation in the Khongjom River. Usually series of *sanskirtans*[44] were performed at the foothill of

Kheba Chngkhong. Such cultural performances were carried out by the Manipur State Kala Academy under the patronage of the State. The Manipur State Kala Academy could have escaped from being charged Meetei-centric had it refrained from performing rituals centred only on Meetei Hindu cultural themes. The State could have maintained secularism had it not instructed the Academy to perform *sanskirtan*. The patriotic drama entitled Khongjom War has been centred on Naol's war efforts in particular but contained several overstretching dialogues on Meetei 'masculinity' and patriotism. It has been annually staged under the patronage of the Department of Information and Public Relations.

(b) In the similar fashion the Patriots' Day drama[45] had failed to emphasize the roles of other communities in defending Manipur from external invasions. Though the Manipur State Archive in its compilation entitled *Manipur who is who 1891*[46] had included the name of three Nagas[47] among the twenty seven war convicts their names were listed in the last and the narratives against their names failed to connect them with the war except that they were punished on the charge of killing a fugitive British who was hiding from Meetei soldiers.

(c) The dominant version of narratives of the Nupi-Lan 1939 has been concentrated more on the events on 12 December 1939 and the role of Meetei women in the subsequent agitation. The popular conception of the event failed to acknowledge the role of Kabui and Panggal women.[48] Community embellishment of the event has been deep rooted.[49] Notable singer late Kh. Joykumar had praised the valour and sacrificing spirit of the Meetei women[50] and connects such qualities with the event. In short the State had failed both in doing away with community meaning attributed to those rituals and in refraining from organising community oriented rituals.

Secondly, Kuki and Zelianrong assertion for inclusion of Anglo-Kuki War Day and Jadonang Day[51] in the holiday lists may be discussed.

(a) There is no doubt that those events were historical and had occurred at certain colonial period. Like others they also deserve accommodation in the holiday lists. This is the line of argument that Anglo Kuki War Patriots Memorial Foundation[52] and the

Zelianrong Union for Cultural Association Manipur[53] had been forwarding. Whereas Kukis had been lobbying petitions and propaganda, Zelianrongs had reached the climax of imposing economic blockade on national Highways.[54] There is no need of trivialising significant historical roles in the past played by leaders who attempted to consolidate fuzzy identities into enumerated politico-cultural identities.

(b) However, these events had bitter historical memories and can be communally interpreted. Vulnerable Kabuis and Meeteis were the prime target of Kuki raids.[55] On the other hand it is being charged that Jadonang had indulged in instigating anti-Meetei and anti-Kuki stances.[56] Jadonang was arrested by British on 19 February, 1931, tried by a British court, charged with murder of four Meetei traders and executed on 29 August, 1931 in Imphal. At the same time recent protagonists of these events had also indulged in articulating the demand from community perspectives. Therefore, the demand appears to be mere repetition of inventing tradition to create communal stereotyping towards exclusivist politics.

Except the Khongjom Day (23 April), there seems to be no open negation of the State patronized rituals that had been discussed above.[57] The absence of open negation, however, does not rule out potential communal politics centred on these rituals. It seems that many had incorporated historical memories to promote patriotism but those had culminated into wild expressions of chauvinism. Many listen to 'irrational' community sentiment/identity and constructed golden age myth about the past rather than doing away with communal misinterpretations in the present. The invented pasts are artefacts in the making; there are embodiments in each, a particular version of history that confronts with other similarly crafted communal counter histories.

Symbols of feudal pasts had been reinstated in some of the listed rituals and holidays. The feudal regime was oppressive and exploitative. But when feudal regime and tribalism had co-existed, the context was not as communal as one perceives and interprets from today's perspective. However, we live in a present where the past has been constantly communalized. In this situation Houchongba festival can be perceived as communal hegemony.

Obviously, connecting the lord-subject festival under feudal regime with the 'present jubilant' to assert integrity can have negative meaning and become anti-thesis to mutual respect.

Historically, Chinglen, Koireng and their forefathers were historical figures. They had fought wars against 'enemies' and had many times saved the lives of the subjects. There were loyal subjects who had enjoyed relative degree of security under their regimes. Their defeat at the hands of the Burmese and the British had led to oppression and suppression under 'foreign' rule. However, like any other rulers elsewhere they had fought for throne and were also exploitative. Kings had practised brutal phambal lan[58] on weaker principalities and vulnerable villagers. The past was, therefore shameful from today's perspective of democracy, secularism, equality and fraternity. As different communities they were; there was no single forefather. As different communities we are; constructing golden age myth of the feudal forefathers and rejuvenating the legacy of conquests and rule pertains to carry communal meaning and it can be problematic.

What is the implication of constructing controversial historical memories of the past when the past fail to deliver justice in the present? What is the logic of expecting the past to unite the people when there has been failure to deal with the existing problems which are due to the deliberate ignorance of fighting for equal distribution of opportunity to collectively develop and grow? The past cannot justify the present inadequacies nor could it correct the people from committing further mistakes. Ultra patriotism would crumble and demean the very essence of co-existence and interdependence. One doesn't have to rely on the miracles of an imagined past to lead the people towards progressive future.

Different interpretation

Politics of assertion or negation under diametrical nationalisms explains the logic of ANSAM's economic blockade. To recall, 18 June was a violent event in 2001, an immediate outcome of 'conflict triangle' involving the Indian State, Manipur integrationists and *Nagalim* patriots. It marked the outburst of month long violent expression of pent up fear, frustration, apprehension, hatred and mistrust against Bangkok Ceasefire Agreement (BCA) signed between the Indian State and NSCN-IM on 14 June 2001.

Manipur patriots perceived a victory when the Indian State announced deletion of 'without territorial limit' from the BCA. The seeming victory was celebrated with waving of white flags[59] and dancing and singing. The *Nagalim* patriots did not lose in the contest[60] but they raised black flags and mourned defeat to arouse community feeling towards Naga consolidation. On the other hand, AMUCO and UCM subsequently intensified their integrity campaign with the distribution of integrity banners and the construction of 'The Great June Uprising Memorial Complex' respectively.

In the following year, Manipuri integrationists resolved to organize 18 June to commemorate the 2001 agitation. Manipur State on 12 June 2002 reiterated to defend integrity. AMUCO and AMSU called for mass sit-in protest on 14 June under the themes; *Manipur Meeyambu Machet Tana Thugainaba Hotnabagi Mayokta Leppa Numit*[61] and *Eekheng Tahankhiba Numit*[62] respectively. UCM, then, insisted that the Manipur State declare 18 June 'Great June Uprising Day' and a holiday. Manipur State conceded to UCM's demand, worked out necessary security arrangement for 14 June and 18 June declared 18 June a holiday. The stage was set ready for observing the 18 June under different banners such as the Great June Uprising Day by UCM, Unity Day by AMUCO, and Integrity Day by the State, et cetera.

Whatever be the intension of the organizers there has been strong community assertion inherent in the nature of the construction of the memorial and the 18 June at Kekrupat.

Firstly, the reinstated public memory in an already communalized situation when Manipuri patriotism has been rightly or wrongly identified with Meetei patriotism became a communal symbol for the simple reason that the memorial and the rituals were never dissociated from communal misrepresentations. It became the reference point of counter narratives that construed out of it living testimony of the hegemonic other.[63]

Secondly, though non-Meeteis took part in 18 June, numerical dominance of the Meeteis, who turned up in mourning costume, overshadowed the presence of others.[64] For instance, the language of the wake up song called *yakairol* , the speeches delivered and the rites performed were largely Meetei originated; the entire observation can be interpreted as Meetei oriented. The guard of honour by sword-holders dressed in Meetei warrior attire invoked communal sense of Meetei masculine assertion in the feudal past. The history of the integrity of Manipur, which have been articulated to defend the territorial *status quo* or one nation theory can be perceived as largely Meetei centric, as such history have been largely based on the sources selectively reproduced from the Meetei royal accounts and the sacred texts known as puyas.

Scientifically, 18 June is an invention, an objectified symbol of concocted victory and defeat in the politics of resistance and consolidation. Constructed visual logo installed as a replica of territorial integrity, in its artefact form was a language that refuted the 'dichotomy theory' propounded by the 'dissenters.'[65] It was a resistance against disintegration. However, insertion of 18 June in the domain of the State, that is a common platform where everyone has a rightful claim, allows the contending others to initiate counter-politics in the same domain. Incorporation of 18 June by the State was either self-defeating or deliberate divisive ploy. In the overall analysis, the State's holiday lists exemplified favourable treatment to dominant pressure groups.

Apart from the listed holidays and those that were being asserted, there are several others that are likely to become assertive in the near future. These may be categorized as those connected with governmental departments,[66] those concerning human rights,[67] those connected to Manipur patriotism,[68] those organized by community organizations,[69] et cetera. There are many more community festivals of the smaller communities that are not covered by the press. Will the State delete some in order to accommodate new ones or prevent new ones from being assertive? As Manipur is composed of sensitive communities or cultural groups, enlisting of all in the holiday list to respect all sentiments will leave the people with few working days. On the other hand, the State cannot do injustice to the smaller communities or cultural groups by failing to enlist them. The solution then does not lie in arbitrary deletion or insertion of a holiday. The solution lies in doing away with the existing holiday lists. There is need of a cultural policy based on a 'balanced representation system', where only common symbols or rituals based on mutual consents are recognized. A new holiday calendar has to be formed collectively. This could be a progressive attempt, a step towards building a new society.

IV. CONCLUSION

The State was indulging in (a) displacement and destruction in the name of development, (b) policies that were apparently granting concessions and were responsive to the demands of dominant pressure groups, and thereby, more or less ignoring the aspiration of weaker groups, and (c) highhandedness and authoritarianism that had encouraged violent and radical assertions such as blockades and destructive assaults. Being frustrated with the State, many had joined insurgency.

However, the liberation movement could not make a leap forward due to diametrical nationalisms, communalism, sectarianism, and[70] opportunism. The mass fronts were failing in creating revolutionary consciousness across communities. Their ideological line and political strategy were confusing. They were dominantly bent on neoliberalism. The contacts they had developed at the *locales* were largely personal and *ad hoc* in character. They had not created revolutionary mass but only half-hearted camp followers who had acted on sentiments and personal loyalty. The camp followers were loosely organized pressure group and were neither revolutionary nor radical reformists.

The bulk of the camp followers constituted the most vulnerable section as a result of (a) 'developmental aggression' in the name of projects, (b) armed conflict among the diametrical nationalist forces including the Indian State, (c) communal conflict, self-defeating strikes, and economic blockades, and (d) overall constraints imposed by the neoliberal regime. Despite divisive trends and sectarianism many camp followers across communities had shared experiences and interdependence due to social and economic factors. This was clearly manifested particularly in the urban areas of Imphal Valley and in the twilight zones where communities had shared boundaries and economic cohesion. The primary concerns of the bulk of these camp followers were economic and cultural. They responded to all forms of nationalisms in some way or the other depending on their immediate material and emotional concerns. They were consumers *sans* revolutionary ideology. In the absence of a powerful and revolutionary force, they remained in a state of dilemma and without progress.

NOTES

1. Statement of Y. Giridhon (70), a leper and first generation immigrants, dated April 2005.
2. File No. HC, III-83/2004/1801/G, 26 May 2005, from the Registrar General, Guwahati High Court, Guwahati, to the Chief Secretary, Government of Manipur, Imphal.
3. Statement of Yumnam Jiten, Citizen's Concern for Dam & Development, April 2005.
4. (1) Notification by District Collector, Imphal West, No. DC (II)/6/186/LA/MLAs/2004, 11 January 2005.
   (2) Notification by District Collector, Imphal East District, No. DC (IE)/12/52/2004, 20 January 2005.
   (3) Press statement of Tharon Village Authority sent to the ISTV Network, Imphal, 12 November 2004.
5. *A Critical Analysis of the Capital Project, Manipur*, Imphal, Citizens' Concern for Dams and Development, 2005.
6. M/s Raj Rewal Associates, New Delhi was hired as consultant for this project and it drew the blue print for the whole project.
7. Such as agricultural infrastructure, P.W.D. Store House, Cold Storage, Soil Testing Laboratory, Seed Stockades, Trial & Multifunction, Tissue Culture Laboratory, Fruit Processing Factory, Mushroom Laboratory, Model Floriculture, Fruit Preservation Factory, T.B. Hospital, Leprosy Hospital, Destitute Children Home, Lower Primary School, Mental Hospital that had been under construction and Community Care Centre.
8. Apart from acquiring 50,000 sq ft of land for construction of IT Park, 27.12 acres of agricultural land was acquired and fenced for construction of an IT-Special Economic Zone (IT-SEZ). The President of India, Smt Pratibha Devisingh Patil inaugurated the Information Technology (I.T.) Park, Manipur on 11 March, 2011;

Manipur DIT Times, Vol. 1, Issue 1, May 2011.

9. Memorandum of the JAC Lei-Ingkhol to the Chief Minister, Manipur, dated 26 April 2005.
10. Resolution of the Meeting organized under the aegis of JAC Lei-Ingkhol on 21 April 2005.
11. Memorandum of the JAC Lei-Ingkhol to the Chief Minister, Manipur.
12. Economic loss due to bandhs, Legal action on Govt's mind; Imphal: *Sangai Express*, 25 May 2007.
13. Lit. Protest Ground. The name was adopted after the protest began from 21 April. Otherwise it was crematory site. After 21 April at temporary roofed structure was erected and the residents spend day and night in a roster system not only to exhibit protest but also to keep a vigil. Mostly women stayed under it during the night.
14. 6 June 2005; Ms N. Pakpi, Ms S. Ibeni, Ms N. Borni, Ms K. Yumsangbi, Ms A. Bino, Ms S. Rakhisana, Ms Sh. Shanti (pregnant), Mr W. Gunamani, Mr N. Rajen, Mr Sitaram and Mr Bokul suffered casualty. Eight leper women, N. Matumbi, Punimashi, Memcha, Nupimacha, Sanahanbi, Soro and Tombi were picked up by the police. Miss Nanao and Ms Shanti were arrested in the second attempt.
15. Mr Nilachandra, Joint Secretary of JAC Lei-Ingkhol, who had worked in a bakery, had to leave the job, interview in September 2006.
16. Statement of Khagen Das, an MP from Tripura, in the Rajya Sabha, 28 November 2001, Session 194.
17. Interaction with master Thiyam Tum Tum, April 2005.
18. Interaction with Rocky, April 2005.
19. Interaction with N. Ranjan, a clerk in the Guwahati High Court, Imphal bench, April 2005.
20. Decision of the LYDO & LIKLA, 15 April 2005.
21. N.M. Meetei, L. Sanjoy, K. Rocky, N. Basant, N. Yaifaremba, G. Boy, O. Bobby, A. Inakhunba, S. Abu, N. Lanngamba, T. Pari, L. Iraijao, S. Sanayai, S. Motilal, L. Naobi, L. Ranjit, S. Gandhi were selected by the JAC.
22. United Hill and Valley Singing Club.
23. G. Dhaneshwor , W. Sanatomba, Sh. Bungcha and Budhachandra.
24. Judgment, dated 31 December 2010, Civil Original Jurisdiction Suit No. 10 of 2005/20/09, Civil Judge (Sr) Division No. II, Manipur East.
25. The entire family had become fugitive due to repeated police atrocities.
26. Had retired but left home again because of repeated police atrocities

27. Had married, invested in small business; but police continue to torture him from time to time.
28. Manipur freedom movement from India.
29. The experience of receiving meanings and imaginative pleasure; Kosaku Yoshino, ed., *Consuming Ethnicity and Nationalism, Asian Experience,* Hawaii: University of Hawaii Press, 1999, p. 2
30. 30 September; birth day Hijam Irabot (30 September 1896–26 September 1951), who carried out communist armed struggle and died in the jungle in 1951.
31. New Year's Day, Republic Day, Death Anniversary of King Gambhir, Player's Day, Khongjom Day, May Day, Patriot's Day, Independence Day, Gandhi Jayanti, Irabot Day and Nupi-Lal.
32. Imoinu Iratpa, Yaosang, Yaosang 2nd Day, Yaosang 3rd Day, Meetei Cheiraoba, Cheiraoba, Kang, Kanglen, Mera Chaoren Houba, Durga Ashtami, Janma Ashtami, Diwali, Ningol Chakkouba and Mera Houchongba.
33. Uttarayan Sankranti, Sarasati Puja, Shiva Ratri, Yaosang 4th Day, Bijay Govinda halankar, Baruni, Kongba Leithong Phatpa, Shilhenba, Jalakeli, Akheri Chahar Sumba, Harisayan, Jhulon Houba, Jhulon Loiba, Radha Ashtami, Heikru Hitongba, Tarpon Houba, Tarpon Loiba, Mera Waphukpa, Gobardhon Puja, Gosta Ashtami, Kwak Jatra and Mera Wayungba.
34. 'Manipur Culture Policy, a Draft', Department of Arts and Culture, Government of Manipur, November 2002.
35. Black Day or Gloomy Day or Protest Day.
36. A nomenclature of Zemi, Liangmei and Rongmei (Kabui) communities.
37. A ritual dedicated to the Meetei supreme god Sanamahi.
38. Meetei uphold Sanamahi as their supreme God and the religion popularized by the revivalist school is considered as Sanamahism.
39. Meetei new years.
40. Sajibu Nongmab panba (New Year) falls on the 1st day of the Sajibu month; Emoinu is the goddess of wealth and prosperity.
41. Post harvest festival of the Zelianrongs
42. Between 17 March 1917 and 20 May 1919 Kukis rose in rebellion against British war policy of recruiting kukis in the Manipur lobour corps, to be sent in foreign countries as labourer for digging trenches, carrying loads and building base camps during the First World War.
43. Jadonang was a traditional doctor-cum-priest belonging to the Rongmei Naga of Tamenglong District, Manipur. He launched a

movement for the socio-economic regeneration of the Rongmei community and other culturally closer communities such as the Zemis of North-Cachar hills and the Laingmeis of Southern Naga Hills; Rajkumari Tamphasana Devi, *Zelianrong Naga Movement (1927–1980): A Study in Some Aspects of Ethnic Process in Northeast India*, a PhD thesis submitted to Manipur University, Canchipur, 1998. p. 76

44. Performance of Hinduism oriented ritual songs sung mostly in Sanskrit language with cymbals and drums.
45. Entitled *Bir Tikendrajit,* annually staged on 13 August is centred on the theme of the Anglo-Manipur war of 1891 and the role played by prince Koireng and general Thangal in that war.
46. Kh. Sarojini Devi, ed., *Manipur Who is Who 1891*; Imphal, Manipur State Archives, 1990.
47. Chirai, Chowkami and Gowho.
48. Nationalist journals began to emphasising multi-community composition of the women agitators; *Macha Leima, Nupigi Numit*, Special Issue, Imphal, 12 December 1999, p. 17–25
49. Many, including the *Meeteis*, think that it was an agitation exclusively launched by *Meetei* women.
50. In his song entitled *Malemda saknaribaa Meetei Nupeegi Nupi-Lal* (World famous women's war of *Meetei* women).
51. The government bent on *Zelianrong* pressure and declared a half holiday on *Jadonang day* in 1981. Nothing seem to progress beyond that for many years.
52. Holiday appeal; www.e-pao.net, news archive, 15 May 2005.
53. ZUCAM ultimatum; www.e-pao.net, news archive, 10 August 2002.
54. 'ZUCAM bandh'; www.e-pao.net, news archive, 24 August 2002.
55. Lal Dena, *History of Modern Manipur* (*1826–1949*), 1st ed., Delhi: Orbit Publishers, 1990, p. 131.
56. Devi, *Zelianrong Naga Movement* ... p. 87.
57. Some people demanded that Khongjom day should be observed on 25 April and to shift the venue to Tenggol Lampak.
58. A king would wage *coronation war* immediately after getting onto the throne in order to express his might over the subjects.
59. The central government, on 27 July, agreed to delete the three words *without territorial limit* from the general clause of the Bangkok Agreement.
60. Ceasefire has been practically extended in Manipur.
61. Lit. *Protest Against the Policy to divide the people of Manipur into fragments.*
62. Lit. *The day when bloodshed was compelled*
63. For the *Nagas* it was an insult to the presumed defeat.

64. Except the symbolic participation of delegates of community organizations who shared the presidium of the convention
65. Manipur as composed of historically antagonistic communities.
66. Anti-Terrorism Day, 21 May; Information and Public Relations Day; Kargil Divas to victory in Kargil War 1999; Manipur Statehood Day; Manipuri Language day; May Day; Sericulture Day; World Environment Day; World Health Day; World Heritage Day; World No Tobacco Day; World Population Day; World Telecom Day; World Theatre Day; World Tourism Day, etc
67. Disappearance Day, 26 May; Hiroshima Day on 6 August; International Human Rights Day, 10 December; International Women's Day, 8 March; Nupigee Phidam Phirepnaba Numit, 24 January; UN International Day in support of Victims of Torture, 26 June, etc.
68. Anti-Military Repression Day, 15 July to commemorate self-immolation by Pebam Chittaranjan and nude protest against AFSPA; 1891 Exile Memorial Day, 23 November; Arambam Samarendra Death Anniversary on 10 June; Dedication Day, 24 July to commemorate self-immolation attempt by five MAFYF volunteers against AFSPA; Hunger Marchers' Day, 27 August to commemorate the killing of four students by police during agitation against famine in 1965; Kajao Memorial Day, 25 May to commemorate execution of Kajao by British in 1891 for spearing death British political agent in Manipur; Manorama Death Anniversary to commemorate the custodial rape and killing of Manorama by Assam Rifles; Meira Paibi Day on 28 May and 29 December; Realization Day on 17 April to commemorate killing of two students by police during anti-foreigner agitation in 1980; National Dedication Day to commemorate the death anniversary of King Narasingh.
69. Rani Gaidinliu Memorial Day of the Zelianrong community to commemorate Zelianrong movement under the leadership of Ms Gaidinliu; Kuki Black Day on 13 September to mourn 1992–6 Kuki-Naga clash; Puya Meithaba Day of the Meetei 'revivalists' to mourn the burning of Meetei Scriptures under the instigation of a Bengali preacher in the 18th century.

Conclusion

From the Marxist point of view, *India, Manipur* (Kangleipak)*, Nagalim,* and *Zale'n-gam* were not nations. Either India or Manipur has been a structurally constituted political community ruled by the elite under the constitutional framework of the bourgeoisie State. Nation-formation has not been completed due to the constraints of the neoliberal regime that rely on divisive forces for their own survival. There has been threat to the administrative integrity and territorial *status quo* as pro-liberation groups attempted to create different nations. At the same time, the elitist attempts to forge different scheduled tribes to create *Nagalim* or *Zale'n-gam* suffered from polarization due to geographical, linguistic, economic, sectarian, and chauvinist factors. In this context, where diametrical nation-formation processes have prevailed, official nationalisms preceded nation. Armed conflicts among diametrical national fronts and sectarian or chauvinist communal assertions were emanated in the course of mechanical dissemination of nationalism and the enforcement of policies to fulfil party agenda.

Conceptually, the UN's recognition of a member as 'nation-state' presupposes a nation but it had not formulated a convincing and universally applicable definition of nation. Generally, a 'nation-state' has been presumed to be the coming together of a nation with a State. It begs for some questions. For instance, what is a nation? Which nation have constituted what form of State, under what specific condition and for what specific purpose? And, when or why or how a nation and State have become corresponding to one another? What became apparent has been that the UN's 'nation-state' in most contexts had remained a political jargon of the capitalist States that had restricted the rights to self-determination of peoples in autonomy model within their territorial border. But the size and shape of bourgeoisie State territories were not permanent. The fact that the size of the Indian territory had been fluctuating due to expansion and 'encroachment', substantiates the point. Bourgeoisie 'national' maps are changing, so as is the composition of 'nation' under their rule. In this sense, the UN's decolonization agenda cannot be abrogated, as the normative process of nation-making is continued by many pro-liberation groups across the globe.

Theoretically, Marxist historical materialism suggests that a nation is a historically constituted, stable community of people, formed on the basis of a common language, territory, economic life, and psychological make-up manifested in a common culture. In the context of India, the claim of nation had been a fabulous fiction to cover up neoliberal interests of the rulers. The State had continued to indulge in all forms of cosmetic favouritism, deceptive propaganda and brutal tactics to diffuse nationalism or to brainwash many to make them familiarize with orchestrated 'national' populism. The insurgents, although appreciative of the pro-liberation agenda against exploitation and misrule, mimicked the model of the Indian State in their nation making attempts. *Prima facie* diametrical nationalisms exemplify absence of Anders's 'imagined community' reflecting an absolute psychological cohesion across communities or political sections towards a common nation.

The Purpose of Being India

In 1947, political power of British India was transferred to the monopolistic capitalist groups of Tata, Birla, Dalmia, Singhania, Bhatt, and comprador section of Bombay bourgeoisie, capitalists from among Gujaratis and Parsis, Marwari moneylenders, Tamil usurers, et cetera,[1] who were intimately linked to the princes, landlords and British capital. They adopted a capitalist socio economic system where social relations were based on commodities for exchange, in particular private ownership of the means of production and on the exploitation of wage labour and resources.

The system had been perpetuated through means of suppression, subjective psychological propaganda, and other sectarian and counter-progressive tactics that kept many divided and caught up in a vicious cycle of self inflicting conflicts along communal and territorial interests.

Territorial annexation was a prerequisite since Capital, which had been both a pre-condition and an outcome of capitalism, had required a territorial base to thrive on. Although territorial expansion could be obstructed due to competition and rivalry among the capitalists of different countries, the Indian bourgeoisie took the advantage of imperial interregnum[2] in South Asia in the immediate years after end of the Second World War and they expanded their territorial base wherever possible. Apart from blackmailing or bribery[3] or intimidation or military tactics to annex territory, they also spread integrity jargons and 'national' propaganda to cover up forced annexation and military occupation. The Indian Constitution, till date, approves territorial annexation,[4] but it has no provision for the right to secession.

The Northeast, which was inhabited by economically backward tribal and peasant communities, apart from strategic calculation,[5] had been important for (a) labour, resources (water, uranium, oil, coal, precious stones, minerals, plantation, flora and fauna, tourism, carbon credits, and forest products), and market, (b) creation of a buffer vis-à-vis presumed Chinese social imperialism, and (c) development of a military stockpile and commodity stocked to carry out commercial interest in Bangladesh, Bhutan, Burma, Laos, Cambodia, Vietnam, Thailand, Indonesia, et cetera. They therefore annexed the Northeast. Interestingly, whether a territory should be annexed to the extent of using military force as it were in the cases of Hyderabad, Kashmir, Manipur, et cetera, or should be kept as a subordinated neighbour as it were in the cases of Sikkim (now annexed), Bhutan, and Nepal[6] or should be shown favourable treatment as it was in the case of Burma (at the cost of the controversial Kabow Valley as claimed by Manipur and the ongoing Burmese built ups) was worked out meticulously to fulfil the vested material interest of the Indian rulers.

Dialectics of Capitalism and Militarization

Capital is based on exploitation; militarization is a corollary of it. The militant approach by the bourgeoisie forces for territorial control had culminated into wars for occupation of Kashmir, delimitation of the McMohan Line and series of armed skirmish along international borders. In the Northeast, the sudden forced annexation of the tribal and 'political communities' that had been established under respective polity or State parallel to the Indian State had created the objective conditions of resistance.[7] The resistances ranged from communist armed resistance,[8] tribal resistance, national liberation movements, and democratic assertion against destructive projects. To suppress resistance and democratic assertions, the Indian bourgeoisie adopted a militant policy. The Northeast was governed through governors and military officials for several years until reliable local regimes were installed. The Assam Disturbed Areas Act 1955 and the Armed Forces (Assam & Manipur) Special Power Act, 1958 were imposed. The AFSPA interplayed with other repressive legislations such as the Land Acquisition Act 1894, Prevention of Seditious Meetings Act, 1911, Indian Penal Code and Criminal Laws, Unlawful Activities Prevention Act, 1967, National Security Act, 1980, Prevention of Terrorism Activities Act, 2002,[9] et cetera. Interwoven deceptive jargons such as 'national security', 'counter-terrorism', and 'law and order problem' were circulated widely to cover up subjugation, exploitation, and suppression.

Collusion of Forces

The army and paramilitary forces became operative with impunity under AFSPA. They occupied and converted several strategically important hilltops, tourist centres, grazing grounds, communal lands, institutional and religious campuses, et cetera, into barracks (including those in the residential areas). War hysteria in the operational zones had serious repercussion on the social mobility for economic livelihood. Troops imposed a typical war economy in the operation zones in the remote rural areas, for example, forced rationing of supplies and Military Civic Action Programmes. Militarization had undermined the role of civil administration, that is, military rule was more dangerous than the corrupt civil administration. It was not expected of any democratic country. The MCAP didn't bring qualitative transformation in the means and relation of production. On the contrary, there was correlation of militarization of capitalist projects (such as dams, mining, mining, oil drilling, forests, office buildings, et cetera), and democratic assertion of civil and economic rights. The MCAP did not address the core economic needs of the people. But its objective have been to show some kind of service delivery, to use it as a propaganda means to show themselves as friendly to the people. In practice, such propaganda could cover up military occupation to some extent. At the same time, such adh-hoc cosmetic service delivery could divert attention by creating a clique of beneficiaries amongst a section of the population. Such clique of beneficiaries could also be subsequently used as tactical underpaid irregular agents.

There were hordes of police, rifles, and underpaid auxiliary forces that were recruited on contract basis (for example, Village Volunteer Forces, Special Police Officers, Village Defense Forces, et cetera) that operated under the unified command structures of the Indian army and enjoying certain amount of impunity in actions. Several educated middle-class youths were recruited to the police through bribery, that is, normally at exorbitant prices paid by selling off or mortgaging away properties. To recover the dues and lured by money and the prospect of promotion to higher ranks, they indulged in widespread bribery, extortion, harassment, and fake encounters. To keep their morale high, the State covered up their crimes and defended them politically.

There were batches of gangsters operating either from jail or under the command of state forces. They included funded 'counter'-groups and 'surrendered' groups who used the cloak of the revolutionary and indulged in rampant extortion, looting, killing, harassment, and terrorism. There were communal warlords and conservative reactionaries who were stakeholders in the corruption nexus with the political barons, bureaucrats, contractors, and project mongers. They misappropriated public funds, displaced peoples on the pretext of development, exploited labour, drained the wealth of the people, and perpetuated misrule. They carried out communal campaigns to cover up class exploitation and diverted attention from genuine democratic issues.

Debacles of Imperialist Globalization

The first two decades of the twenty-first century had been remarkable in terms of increasing collaboration of the Indian big bourgeoisie with the imperialist cartels and finance institutions. They could penetrate the Southeast Asian underdeveloped countries for market and resources. They had directly or indirectly played a role in serving US imperialist interest in Afghanistan, Iraq, and elsewhere. They indulged in collaborative-cum-competitive relations with the Chinese social capital in post-LTTE Sri Lanka, Myanmar, Bangladesh, Nepal, Bhutan, et cetera. They had been investing in the commercial projects spreading across the extensive 'Mekong-Ganga' river belt stretches. In the Northeast, apart from other multinational companies and Indian bourgeoisie banks, the ADB finance intrusion had been gaining momentum. As a war pre-emption drive, they had permitted the US army to conduct a series of military exercises in the jungles of Mizoram to adapt to guerrilla warfare. There has been alleged US FBI operations in Meghalaya. The issuance of Protected Area Permits was lifted from the Northeast in 2011, probably under the pressure of the European Union, largely to promote foreign strategic analysts in the guise of tourists.

On the other hand, the Indian big bourgeoisie had successfully withheld heavy industrialization in India. India had been comparatively reduced to a warehouse and market for foreign capitalist technologies and commodities, and an exporter of assembled commodities. The economic goal of *India Shining* had been predominantly visible in the tertiary construction subsectors and in other secondary manufacturing sectors such as assembling of automobiles, expansion of telecom networks, et cetera. To maximize extraction of Capital, millions of tribes and peasants had been forcibly displaced at gunpoint from their lands to promote imperialist assembling units. At the same time, a vast chunk of peasants had been deprived of investment and had been impoverished due to forced extraction in order to fulfil imperialist quota of food grains and other agrarian products.

In Manipur, the Indian bourgeoisie had created a subordinate ruling class composed of chiefs and landlords, usurers, contractors, commission agents, corrupt officials, petty merchants, et cetera, that was dependent on the Indian bourgeoisie for political and economic power. The latter did not directly create Capital through investment in constant and variable capitals. It indulged in accumulation of wealth through misappropriation of rent (in the form of central grants) received in return for exploitation of Manipur by the Indian bourgeoisie. The contradiction or polarization within the Manipur ruling class had been reconciled through creation of revenue blocks and electoral constituencies where they contest for power. It produced unsuccessful counter-elites who strived to use communal propaganda to create for them communal revenue blocks and 'alternative administration arrangements'. They all adopted militant models in pursuing extraction of wealth and exploitation of labour.

From the beginning, the Indian State, in order to govern subjective conscience along communal lines, had created certain perceptions, if not propaganda sources, that were prepared from anthropologists' paradigm.[10] Subsequently, rules were framed[11] to create administrative revenue areas along tribal or ethnic lines. The structural incorporation of caste/tribal reservation systems, and other material incentives, funding of cultural assertion, researches, publications, et cetera, had promoted writings on tribes and ethnics from the middle-class intelligentsia. The trend received a major thrust by the post-1990 global instruments such as United Nations declarations of the Decade for Eradication of Colonialism (1990 to 2000), Decade of the World's Indigenous People (from 10 December 1994), adoption of Indian Protection of Human Rights Act 1993, establishment of the UN Permanent Forum on Indigenous Issues (2000). All these had provided opportunities and encouraged NGO sectors to streamline middle-class sections towards ethnic or tribal or indigenous issues. All these had been reformists trying to find some form of reconciliation within the neoliberal system and not the creation of revolutionary class.

In the meanwhile, increasing penetration by the State, market forces, immigration, and job opportunities could not phase off structural crisis leading to inequality and unrest. The State invested in cosmetic reformism to divert attention and militarization, leading to suppression, repression, and insecurity. The situation had catalytic impact in generating frustration and disillusionment about livelihood. The material condition of peasant rebellion and wage labourers' assertions was looming. The local ruling class indulged in two-way strategies to retain their political and economic power. On the one hand, they carried out sectarian and communal propaganda to cover up their role in the crisis of the regime. On the one hand, they played the leadership role to curve out exclusive revenue blocks for unrestrained control over land, labour, funds, and resources. All these are interwoven into one with communal interpretation of economic grievances and misrule. Most peasants and wage labourers were thus communally organized.

Concurrent to the penetration by the State and market forces, parallel community formations under different nomenclatures, cultural assertion or revivalism, sense of lost of freedom and 'national' identity, and spread of democratic ideas, there had been insurgency groups ranging from those who raised freedom from India to those who sought for ethnic/tribal/communal autonomy. While some had been pro-Manipur, there had been others that asserted diametrical nationalisms. They had commonality in regards to articulation of (a) the one-nation theory to consolidate respectively projected 'nation', (b) anti-colonial discourse against projected national enemy, and (c) divisive discourse as responsible for internal contradiction.

To sum up, at present, the conflicts in Manipur are modelled and perpetuated under an overarching neoliberal political economy. Firstly, the pro-liberation assertions are largely perpetuated by the Indian capitalist constraints. It is apparent that the solution sought by the Indian State is bent on Indian integration trajectory without rooting out the system responsible for creating a colonial situation. The colonial system is manifested in unrestrained militarization to defend capitalist control over resource, market and labour on the one hand and 'communal unrest' amongst peoples under puppet regimes and sectarian collusive forces. Secondly, it is also apparent that the ethno-national forces that articulate territorial integrity or exclusive ethno-nation, under the leadership of middle class capitalism aspirants are bent on the neoliberal model. They either confront or collude with different local ruling groups depending on the issues, but all of them have commonality in communal orientation in certain forms or the other.

National and Social Liberation

Politically most of the tribes and 'political communities' in Northeast had inherited and continuously reproduced respective notion of sovereignty, political freedoms and rights. However, annexation, capitalist onslaught, and communal politics had kept them perpetually dependent, exploited, and misruled. Constitutional rights to life, economic livelihood, and democracy were kept under suspension. They were forced to elect corrupt and exploitative regimes that denied them the right to referendum of unpopular political representatives and corrupt officials. Their economic hardships had increased due to exploitation, destructive projects, restrictive forest laws, militarization of economic zones, market monopoly, and lack of incentives, et cetera. In Manipur, the number of people killed in fake encounters, convicted, intimidated, tortured, jailed, and forced disappeared by the State forces as result of mistaken identity, personal reasons, for their political ideology and democratic dissent has been increasing. State propaganda continued to misrepresent peace, development, and democracy. Freedom and growth were hardly realized by the majority of the people.

Many were less critical to the neoliberal regime and the *modus operandi* of the local collaborators. Instead, many opted to play with communal sentiment and seek for sectarian solution. In the process, capitalist forces got further penetration to the latest extent of extracting license in a 'secret manner' without consulting the public in July 2010 for oil exploration and drilling, which is almost one sixth of total area of Manipur. Recently, in Manipur the issue of collective assertion against potential displacement, environmental destructions, and militarization got temporarily diverted away during a short-lived communal flare up centred on alleged assault of an actress Miss Momocco by a cadre of NSCN-IM on 18 December 2012 in Chandel. The propaganda of 'national' enemy interplayed with communal sentiment during protest and counter-assertions. The issue of sexual assault or human rights was diverted away and instead territorial integrity and ceasefire politics became forefront. Many innocents were assaulted and properties destroyed.

Finally, it is crucial to realize that communal propagandas, chauvinist claims, and sectarian agendas are crucial in diverting revolutionary consciousness and leading peoples towards bourgeoisie reformism and counter-revolution. Against this backdrop, the market forces continue with structural control by juggling with the deceptive jargons of unity, peace, and development. The ongoing ceasefire politics by the State and 'ethno national' models of the pro-liberation forces needs to be analysed to find out if these are mere reformist structural adjustment without rooting out the root causes of subjugation, exploitation, suppression, poverty, and insecurity. We need an answer as to how long the insurgent groups would continue with the neoliberal model of the Indian State. How will they reconcile with diametrical nationalisms? What are the preventive measures to reconcile increasing class contradictions among the ranks and files? What is the goal of freedom struggle? What can they offer more than what the Indian State has been doing with cosmetic packages? What is their revolutionary vision and strategy? Are nations to be curved out in the name of revolution but ended up with creating havens of class rulers? There is a need for a change—a change in the perspectives of revolution and insurgency. People clamour for a world order free from subjugation, exploitation, and suppression. That calls for a revolution towards development, peace, and democracy.

NOTES

1. A.M. Dyakov, 'The National Question in the Indian Union and Pakistan', *Revolutionary Democracy*, Vol. IX, No. 2, New Delhi, September 2003.
2. Japanese, French, British powers were considerably weakened in Northeast and the adjoining Southeast Asian regions.
3. Privy purse and other royal prerogatives for submissive princes/ kings.
4. *Constitution of India*, Part I, Article 1.
5. (a) Statement by Shri Ari Bahadur Gurung and Rev J.J.M. Nichols Roy in the Constituent Assembly of India, respectively on Wednesday, 23 November and Saturday, 19 November 1949.

6. V.N. Khanna, *Foreign Policy of India*, 4th edn., New Delhi: Vikas Publishing House, 2001.
7. There were submissions by several landlocked tribes and communities that had lacked unity, consciousness, political leadership, and means of resistance.
8. Communist Armed Revolutionary Movement in Manipur (1949–51).
9. Repealed on Thursday, 9 December 2004.
10. Report of the Sub-Committee on North-East Frontier (Assam) Tribal and Excluded Areas; Constituent Assembly of India, Council House, New Delhi, 28 July 1947.
11. Such as the Constitution (Scheduled Tribes) (Part C States) Order, 1951 (and subsequent amendments).

Appendix

MANIPUR ADMINISTRATION ORDER 1949

The Manipur Gazette, extraordinary published by the authority.

No. 1E1, Imphal, Saturday, Oct. 15, 1949. Government of Manipur. Orders by the Chief Commissioner.

Notification: Office of the Chief Commissioner, Manipur. No. 0001/CC. Of 15 October 1949 (12 Noon)

Manipur administration order 1949 issued under Notification No. 219-P in the Gazette of India dated the 15th Oct, 1949, incorporates the provision that as from midday of Saturday the 15th Oct, 1949, the Ministers of Manipur State shall cease to function and the legislature will stand dissolved. It is therefore hereby notified that with effect from midday of Saturday the 15th Oct, 1949, the aforesaid Ministers shall relinquish charge of the portfolios held by them and with immediate effect all the portfolios are taken over by the Chief Commissioner.

The legislature also as stated in the order shall stand dissolved with effect from midday of Saturday the 15th Oct, 1949.

Rawal Amar Singh
Major General, Chief Commissioner of Manipur.

MANIFESTO OF THE NATIONAL SOCIALIST COUNCIL OF NAGALAND, 1980

Preface

The concept of 'Human Race', internationalism and the myth of nations could in no sense deprive the Nagas of the basis of being a family and a nation of their own existence. This self-determination is their righteous cause and Nagas shall always be the people of this noble cause. It *is,* however, to be submitted that, notwithstanding the feat of patriotism and valour, Nagas found themselves being self-defeated now and then. It is purely due to, in the first *place,* parochialism practised in the highest circle of national affairs. Also, the path the people have to tread was not illuminated, the *sine qua non* of clarity of the way to their salvation was absent. The masses were, by and *large,* led along in the name of nation alone. It is the bounden duty of every sensible citizen to be concerned about the necessity of evolving the sure way to save the nation from such treacherous mess of conditions. It is time to enlighten the people and meet them with a clear-cut Manifesto that they be led out of their precarious helplessness, that potentials may be sublimated and channelized towards the salvation of their country.

Oking
31 January, 1980

Isak Chishi Swu

Executive Chairman
National Socialist Council of Nagaland

Manifesto of The National Socialist Council of Nagaland

Nothing is more inalienable for a nation, big or small, than her sovereignty. No moment, either, is more challenging for a people than the time when their free existence is challenged. The Naga National Council has failed. The sovereign existence of Nagaland is more at peril than ever before. It is high time for the revolutionary patriots to declare their national principles, their views and their aims.

I. Nagaland and The Naga National Council

We live in a world of constant change. But the forces causing the change are not always the same. They develop and perish according to the different given conditions, stages and times.

To us, the forces that defend the righteous cause of the sovereign national existence and further the just cause of the people along the inevitable course are alone patriots and revolutionaries. All forces standing in opposition to this are traitors and reactionaries, in that they try to pull the wheels of history back. All the reactionary traitors lean upon one another, all revolutionary patriots stand as one, supporting one another; there is no via media.

The Naga National Council was the only authentic political organisation of the people of Nagaland. It was this council that boldly took up the historic national trust, that is, the safeguarding of the right of the sovereign existence of Nagaland. With all its resoluteness, the Council faced ups and downs and was never deterred by setbacks here and setbacks there. It had withstood the bitter period of the past three decades or so, turning neither to the right nor to the left - although there had been marked degeneration in its integrity and vigour. Our country could exist and we owe it to the National Council and to the thousands of patriots who have unsparingly laid down their lives and to the unprecedented endurance of the people, thanks to the leadership the Naga National Council had given to the people in their past national trials and tribulations till the time of its failure to condemn the treacherous ministry and the Accord of treason of 1975.

The sober reality, however, is that our country is still under heavy occupation of the enemy troops. What are we to do with this? The enemy will never withdraw of its own accord. In no circumstances should we allow ourselves either to count on the sensibleness of the enemy. Because it is always suicidal. History has sufficiently warned us against the repetition of such error. Politics is successful but only when backed by arms. We are safe so long as we fight to save ourselves. Therefore, we have to fight and back the enemy out at all hazards. If negotiations, however, would be indispensable, they should be done only from a position of strength. Any attempt, therefore, at negotiated settlement at the moment would undoubtedly mean doing away with oneself, if not, it is traitorous in motive.

Facts must be acknowledged in spite of whatever turn the world might take; people must know what is what. The enemy is superior, therefore, our war will have to be a protracted one. We are in the course of active defence. Who will lead us through this long war? It is the most decisive issue. It has got to be reasoned out.

True, facts must be admitted and it is a fact that the most ignominious sell-out in the history of Naga people ever since the time the first bullet of freedom was fired, is beyond dispute the notorious 'Shillong Accord'. That Accord deserved an outright official and open condemnation by the

Ministry that surrendered arms and consented to such sell out.

This failure left the country in a dangerous political mess. Nation-wide danger was thus brought about. Any earnest appeal in a time like this for guidance, and letters of determination to fight to the last were never vouchsafed; no imperative given. The helpless unyielding were left entirely to themselves.

Of course, being resolute in purpose, we were able to make shift for ourselves. Any bold and genuine act of competent people in the forefront, in the name of the National Council, to save the country from the tragedy of the Shillong Accord by condemning it and the Ministry concerned was adversely reacted to. Any correct and required stride given in the matter of policy to salvage the country from the dead-end of the leadership was often brushed aside. The aloofness of the leadership from the people all through the .difficult years, despite the earnest appeal of the people to come back and lead them, was justified on selfish considerations. Dissensions, misunderstandings and failures naturally arising therefrom were often imputed to the people. Essential men were often toppled by intrigues and their lives were treated as mere stuff. Only relatives were confided to and the hard-won glory and honour of the nation and the sacrifices and untold sufferings of thousands of patriots and the people, were appropriated and the highest office of national trust was used for the glory and gains of a family or two and their relatives. Any criticism to that effect was dealt with at gun-point, family and relatives were placed above the nation. Who can deny all this? Indeed, the truth is suppressed; that is the problem.

What is more, the delegation of downright traitors was warmly welcomed and met time and again before the eyes of the whole world. The use of the exalted name of the only national institution by the traitors was deliberately consented to and resolutions of anti-national aspiration were countenanced. Apparently, modalities and terms for another fresh capitulation are being worked out in close collaboration with the rank traitors. Surely traitors are collaborated with, patriots despised. Traitors are propped up, patriots condemned and the principle of unholding the freedom of every inch of Nagaland is deliberately withdrawn. These are the unfolding realities of the day and not of long ago. Because traitors are always from within and they lean upon one another in due time. One naturally wonders, if such conduct of affairs would commend itself. What can such state of affairs assure to the people? Nothing but danger. It is only heading for fresh capitulation from the highest level. But this is Nagaland and we are the people, we claim your promise; where is it?

Indeed, the· Naga National Council is spent; it has turned out to be treacherous and reactionary. Any effort to revolutionise it is stifled. It has neglected to carry its solemn national trust through to the end. It has totally failed. The resort being made to "peace" and "unity" is simply a desperate attempt at covering up and making virtue of their obvious treason. No matter in how many ways you would try to pass yourself off as saviour, you would be discovered. We declare the issue is sharp between the reactionary traitors on one side and the revolutionary patriots on the other. No identity exists between the dross and the grain whatever. Lovers of the nation and the people are driven to a state where a breakthrough is a must and it has to promptly done if Nagaland and the Naga people are to be saved at all for what is their due on earth. Truly, the historic moment of saving Nagaland from the failure to the Naga National Council has come as the most crucial challenge to one and all.

II. On Policy

Every problem has a solution and to effect it, there is always the most realistic way. In the words of Chairman Mao, "Policy is the lifeline". Therefore, any problem that is not handled precisely in the way the objective conditions warrant, is bound to meet with failure. It is policy that decides the outcome of any contest apart from strength. Thus, the question of making the right approach is above all others, to be pondered over in the light of practical investigations.

(a) Policy and the Leadership

The defeat of a people is not always brought about by the superiority of the adversary in strength but through incorrect leadership and the pursuit of unfounded policy. We should take this fact into serious consideration in order to avert the danger of self-defeat. A people that fails to admit the maxim that national victory is impossible without correct policy and correct leadership, is doomed to ultimate ruin. It is not uncommon that often leaders act at the dictate of their feelings and whims and suffer setbacks one after another, for any policy that is independent of the objective conditions is without basis and as such, is bound to suffer failure. Policy could only be realistic when it is based on the actual conditions of the people concerned and the enemy, and the world in general.

It is, therefore, not a matter of one's choice but that of necessity that leadership should have correct assessment of any situation through close investigations. It necessitates that he should be at the core of the situation, that is, he has to be with the masses, mobilising and working in close association, to lead them through all the critical states with policy that is warranted by the conditions. It is in this way that the people could appreciate the wisdom of the leadership and his concern for the nation. They could confidently rally round him. Moreover, they could learn the knack of analysing problems and discover the right and the wrong for themselves. They could also acquire practical experience to handle the situation, enhance confidence in themselves and raise their cause. Such perfect harmony between the people and the leadership makes them invincible.

It is deplored that the leadership acted, in the past long period of nation-saving, completely independently of the actual conditions and in total isolation from the people. No amount of attempts to explain away the aloofness of the leadership on the ground that he was sent out by the people could hold water any longer. Obsolete views should be shaken off. We should be realistic because it is the politics of saving the nation and not that of justifying one's position.

We do not think it proper either, on the part of the leadership, to stay away from the people even when there is fatal danger at home and against the appeal of the people to come back and illuminate their way. It should also be borne in mind that when he failed to understand the people and vice versa, both would lose their bearings. However· far he may make his way ahead, however high he may soar, he is bound to be pulled back and be down if he does not pull the people along with him. He should see that there is not adverse gap between him and the people. Indeed, in a problem of this nature, nothing could be accomplished apart from the people.

The contention that a particular leadership staying in a foreign land has sustained the existence of Nagaland thus far and that he alone will bring the final victory too, needs immediate correction. It explicitly means that a policy, though it has no bearing on the objective conditions, could be correct and a nation could be saved without the support and sacrifices of the people. This is the basic erroneous conception that has bred internal strives which have brought the Nagas down to this ebb. Such a view categorically rules out the support of the people and ignores their untold sacrifices.

It has placed the leadership who has lost the confidence of the people above the people, above the nation and above righteousness. This section of the people, in no way, stands for the national cause since it is the line of direct negation. They are treacherous; they have to perish with the leader whom they blindly worship. Probably, their leader would bring them the golden plate of Nagaland's freedom from the hidden deep blue sky. Facts are stubborn and have no regard for anyone, although we acted often times in deference to the elders. Things are now more in perspective and Nagas are no longer in their 1950s. We have to put an end to the reactionary mentality of interpreting the correctness of policy in terms of personality. We are revolutionaries; we do not believe in fantasy and absurdity; neither could we ever be persuaded of the talisman of any helpless leadership. We shall not fly in the air; we shall walk on the ground and work with the people, for it is our experience that correct policy could only be determined in the right perspective of a given situation and correct leadership could emerge only in the course of the struggle along with the people.

In addition, the conduct of national affairs through the intermediary of the family and relatives through the past years has naturally alienated the people and the Government. The refusal of the leadership to keep correspondence with the Home Government on official terms and his meagre and perfunctory pieces of advice, the correspondence between him and his family and near relatives, who are mostly traitors, often despising the home authority, the subjection of Government communications to the virtual censorship of the family, who maintain an air of hauteur, the practice of viewing the home situation in the light of self-motivated information from the family and his ultra vires utterances on some national issues - have made a mess of everything in us. Such arrogation to themselves of the authority to conduct affairs exclusively and the shameless, self-made notion of being above others in respect of nationality and ownership of Nagaland, has deliberately relegated altogether the people and the nation far to the background.

Who can question these facts? Nagas are made to see a strange centre of power, being created out of the family and relatives of the leadership and a few others with whom he has apparently formed an aristocratic circle, above the Government, above the people and above Nagaland. He has practically forgotten the people and their immeasurable sacrifices. He does not count on the people's support but seeks the backing of his men who are mostly traitors. Accordingly, he has acted irrespective of the involvement of the question of national principles. The people are alienated; he has dug a chasm between himself and his henchmen on the one side and the people of Nagaland on the other.

It will be a wonder of wonders if such policy is .to be the wisdom to save a nation. Of course, if one knows the people, the people would know him to; if despise the people, the people would certainly despise him too; if one respects the sanctity of National cause, the nation would honour him too; and this is the way of the world. We are revolutionary patriots; we do not allow ourselves and our people to be imposed upon be empty rhetoric. We are vehemently opposed to the politics of any form shall be done away with and the nation's integrity safeguarded. We cannot bluff heaven and earth too long; the people know who is who and what is what. We will never relinquish Nagaland to anyone. It is high time to sum up our past and take a concrete approach to the problems confronting us. Nagaland has got to be liberated from prejudices, injustice and from all sort of aristocratic snobbery.

(b) Rectification of Basic Erroneous Views

Since the inception, there has been a persistent view that it is too much for the Nagas to resist the colossal invading might of India and Burma, and that some sort of settlement by peaceful means should be arrived at. Unfortunately, the failure to grasp the reality of the problem has made many a well-intentioned national worker turn opportunist.

While admitting elements of truth in this view, one should as well fully realise the national danger involved in the possible inference to be made from it. The issue is not a contest of strength but of upholding our historic right against the aggressive forces. In this society of human frailty, we do not discount the impact of might on any issue. Nevertheless, the trend of viewing the world from the angle of power alone, ruling out the question of right and wrong, obviously leads to the conclusion that the weak are born to be ruled by the strong and the poor by the rich.

In other words, the world is for the monster and not for the people. This view represents the mentality of the lower nature of man, especially when taken over by an aberration. It makes the existence of human society meaningless. Men of sense look at problems from the viewpoint of right and that decides more approvingly the outcome of conflicting issues. The strong make might their resort. They are more easily prone to the use of force in settling problems. They are able to do much harm and can even annihilate many of the weak and win battles; but it is perseverance and the act of undaunted confrontation with the eventuality of death for the truth one knows that win the war in the long run.

Victory is, thus, not in the power to kill but in the fearlessness to face death for a just cause. The logic that strong win over the weak is foul if it is taken at its face value without taking consideration the other side of the experience of the history. The strong are often defeated by the weak if they preserve for their just cause to the end. The outcome of the U.S. Vietnamese war may serve as a clear example.

The rulers of India and their strong men could not understand Nagaland and her people. They only knew the Nagas were "naked" and on this account, despised them and disregarded all their historical rights. However, 'Naked Nagas' also have their homeland and it has never been conquered by the Indians nor by the Burmese. Neither have the Nagas ever joined the Indian Union nor that of Burma by consent. As the Indians and the Burmese took recourse to force, Naga people knew for certain that the problem had involved the challenge on our stand on the basic issue of principle, to face which, we have come into being. Indians demanded 'total surrender'. They also boasted stating that to finish the Nagas was a matter of a day, and took pride in it. The generals and the strong men who were the hope of India were sent one after another into Nagaland to conduct the unprecedented theatre of cruel war. Hundreds and thousands of troops operated and ravaged the land, indiscriminately putting out thousands of lives. The resorted to endless devices of torture and killing.

They did their worst. But are the Nagas finished and are they no more now? Have the Indians won the war? By no means. They had to change their stand from 'total surrender' to negotiations; the 'one day' has turned out to be a quarter of a century. The Shillong Accord, by virtue of which India claimed victory, is a dead letter. From the relentless resistance of the people, totally condemning the Shillong Accord and its predecessors, it is proved that any agreement that may be entered into on Indian terms can never be the solution to the problem.

However, it is clear that India would muster all the traitors and organise them into an active puppet front to attain their objective which is expressed in lucid terms by Morarji Desai, a one-time Prime Minister of India, as "I will exterminate the Nagas without any compunction". But the prospect of winning the war in the years to come is still worse as the force that fights a wrong cause can never be strong. The longer they fight the greater would be their loss, for it is a mere false hope that is encouraged by the acts of the traitors to nurture. Moreover, it is evident from the present-day phenomena that India, not to speak of forcing the Nagas into the Union, would not be able to hold together all its component parts for all time to come; the discontented peoples and nationalities are bound to rise up to save themselves from perishing altogether in India· society where suppression, discrimination and all sorts of corruption abound. India would soon be bound up with her internal turmoil. The mighty problem of poverty and hunger shall loom ever more. India can gain no ground to defeat us.

As regards the possible settlement of the problem, it is an ill-time by all considerations, because our adversaries, relying on their might, are intransigent and are not prepared to recognise the fact of our distinct existence. Whatever solutions they might talk about are nothing but terms of surrender. Secondly, though we have been able to establish ourselves on more solid ideological grounds, at present, we are not able to present ourselves formidably to make the adversaries admit that we can fight a long war to their detriment.

And so to seek a solution in a time like this would evidently be suicidal. An honourable solution is only in our preparedness to fight a protracted war to the victorious end. Our righteous cause would unfailingly back us up; it cannot be otherwise. Although might, in its own way, can be formidable, it is the truth and our resoluteness for it that would inevitably triumph in the long run.

(c) Principles of Expediency

It is principle on which the meaning of life takes root. When it is shaken, everything is forced afloat on the evil side of the world; the purpose of life is discarded and society is set out of scruples. The conduct of such a permissive society is governed by the philosophy of the Fallen Angel. It is beyond forbearance to see the fate of any people being wafted on towards that end.

It is by keeping the principles that objectives are attained through policy and the meaning of life is pursued to its reality. To save a nation or a society one must, above all, be established on the solid rock of principle. We should know that whenever expediency is stressed there is always the danger of principle being sacrificed. It is like running with both feet off the ground leading to a fall. Opportunities get circumscribed where expediency is resorted to.

We, Nagas, have suffered much from this, we have to struggle to come round from such grievous hurt. It stems, in the main, from failure to know the exact prowess of the country. When the enemy's power is over-estimated, there is always a fear which consequently leads one to embark upon unfounded, feeble policy through which the adversary could come to know of him and have the advantage of taking the offensive on all fronts. It is most dangerous when we do not know both ourselves and the adversary, until we know the adversary, paradoxically we cannot know ourselves either as we are, to deal with him.

The leaders at home did not believe in the resisting power of the people, they did not comprehend the fact that, for all setbacks, the force of the people could make its way to the final victory. They feared that continued fighting would bring terrible consequences, nay, that India could even annihilate the people of Nagaland and argued - "what would freedom mean if people are finished; it has, therefore, involved the question of humanity." They accordingly discouraged fighting and the efforts to strengthen the defence line. The cause of the nation was no more in them. They carried within them only the defeated hearts.

It is also open secret that they had been playing an underhand game with the enemy to get the area of their occupation free from military operation and directed the spearhead of the operation to the stalwart patriots to soften them in their line. Unfortunately, many a well-intentioned national worker became victim of it. They always overestimated the enemy in spite of his practical inability to crush us in the past twenty-five years and made importunate, fear-ridden overtures here and there which they considered expedient at the time when Nagas were worst situated.

This nature of unrealistic and ill-timed approaches exposed our helplessness to the adversary. He had got what he wanted. Now knowing for sure that Nagas were no longer in a position to hold their own both in battle and at the negotiating table, the Government of India launched a timely offensive and successfully had his terms dictated. It was, it should be acknowledged, a splendid catch hauled ashore. In their vain attempts to foist the treacherous Accord on the people, they have employed all sorts of political black arts, calling heaven and earth, now here, now there. They do not cease to talk at large of their act - "Our conscience is clear; we have done it to save our nation". Words of valour and honour are profusely used in their politics of prostrate capitulation.

We wonder if a man could fight better with a monster by jumping into his jaws, nay, by permitting to be swallowed deep into the stomach, than from a free position. Are we to experiment upon the sovereign existence of Nagaland by concluding an agreement of treason, and bury it for expedience's sake? Is this expedient, as claimed by the Accord makers, who once boasted of themselves as the oracles of the country? It is no more than saving one's own life, at the expense of the nation. Your philosophy is—"let it be, even though everything of the nation is lost, if I am saved."

Nagaland would not be so cheap as it was disposed of in your agreement. You will come to know the hard fact that Nagaland belongs only to the people and you cannot defraud them of it. The leadership who still harbours the notion that people could be led by the nose has overshot himself and has fallen astern of time. We, the revolutionary patriots, shall at no time view our free Motherland through the eyes of a traitor. Whatever noise you may make, it will be only your helpless cry from the bottomless pit into which you have jumped of your own doom is sealed there.

On the whole, we cannot approach the world without clarity, neither could we ascertain the actuality of any condition through fear. Accurate appraisal of what the enemy and ourselves can and cannot do is essential for prudent dealing. Whatever might be the superiority of the enemy, there is no power on earth that dares annihilate the Nagas.

Therefore, we should never allow ourselves to be carried away by the baseless view that the adversary could wipe out the whole population. This is a mere phantom projected through the fear-ridden shallow politicians, now traitors, to intimidate the people into accepting their line of capitulation. We should not yield to blackmail of whatever kind. We should never lose sight of the truth that victory is in our resoluteness and correct policy, for Nagaland can definitely fight for the just cause of her freedom so long as the opponents are able to fight the wrong, being mindful of the fact that overestimation of the adversary causes fear and makes one commit right opportunism, while underestimation leads him to be presumptuous and makes him commit left opportunism. It is the correct reassessment of the actual condition that makes a correct approach possible.

III. Nagaland and the Influx of Indian Capital and Indian Nationals

The pouring in of Indian capital in our country, for political reasons, has shattered the Naga people into a society of wild money. It accumulation in the hands of the reactionary traitors and the rich has accelerated the process of exploitation and suppression of the people. The appropriation of the vast means of production, distribution and exchange and other means of profit-making by this exploiting class and by the Indian parasites has drawn a distinct line between them and the people. The struggle between the two classes would ever assume greater magnitude with the exploiting class and the Indian defending all the time the untenable status quo and the people directly opposing it. This antagonism is not a small problem and no Naga would be free from it.

In addition, the involuntary influx of Indian Nationals from over-populated India into our country has set all Nagaland under constant threat of eventual submersion. In this connection, it may be recalled that before the year 1947, there was not a single Indian in Nagaland. It has now more than two hundred thousand Indians. If, with a greater ratio of influx, another twenty years would go, what would be the state of affairs? The expropriation of vast tracts of public land and other means of capital-making everywhere by the exploiting class by using the Indian nationals as labourers and their votes in the election contest have given a clear aspect of certainty to the constant and rapid exploitation of the Naga people at large by the reactionary traitors and the Indians.

The massive exploitation of mineral resources by the Central Government of India with the bureaucrats and the exploiting reactionary traitors in the puppet state power and the constant flow of swarms of Indians into the small area of Nagaland, will in a short period of time completely overwhelm and uproot Nagaland, depriving thereby the Naga people of all jobs and their just due and of their means of life. Because exploitation has no temperance. This is how a people is exploited to the worst of fates - the fate of becoming the helpless exploited foreigners in their own motherland. What does this lost world hold for the Naga people? Nagas are, indeed, faced with the irreconcilable fate from which we have to deliver ourselves. But deliverance from such imminent doom decisively calls for a revolutionary force.,

IV. Nagaland and the Effete Indian and Burmese Culture and Their Faiths

Along with the occupation of Nagaland by sheer military might, one started witnessing the process of Indianisation of the Naga people on full massive scale. The rulers of both India and Burma knew well that force alone could never serve their purpose of making the Nagas the component parts of their communities. As they knew that anything Indian or Burmese was detestable to the Nagas, they had to undergo a tough course of time to have the Nagas assimilated to their culture and ways to life. Persuasion was not possible either, only the process of subjecting them to assimilation was essential. For this reason, massive introduction of decadent Hindu culture and literature and those of the Burmese, in the social and individual life of the Naga people through public institutions and mass media, started all Nagaland pervasiveness. Thus being conditioned entirely to and swamped by the waves of Indian and Burmese influence, one could only see the precious varieties of the Naga· people in jeopardy of eventual extinction.

New Problems bring new omens. The spread of Hinduism and the queer noises have reached our homeland. Although, as doctrine Hinduism is not a recruiting force, it is not to be easily dismissed, since it is backed by a Hindu Government. The forces of Hinduism, viz., the numberless Indian troops, the retail and wholesale dealers, the teachers and the instructors, the intelligentsia, the prophets of nonviolence, the gamblers and the snake-charmers, Hindi songs and Hindi films, the rasogula makers and the Gita are all arrayed for the mission of supplanting the Christian God, the eternal God of the Universe. The challenge is serious, there is no hiding, no pretension.

The preachers of the Gospel, the holy men of God and the demagogues, are you prepared to resist these surging waves of the Hindu would upon our country? This danger flows from India and the vulnerability of the Church leaders and the pliable demagogues has added to the problem. To join the Indian Union as they insisted, is to allow ourselves to be drowned and perish in these waves of dead doctrine. Whereas to defend Nagaland's Independent Existence as we have been doing with our lives and our all, is to assure ourselves safety from the doom of Hinduism.

This is simple logic. The failure of the Christian leaders to grasp the way the evil forces work and their failure to face them in the way they should has, indeed, placed Nagaland on a most serious trail. We are not only confronted with a war of physical force but also with the more dangerous insidious war of assimilation. A war of such nature does not admit of a shallow approach; it demands of us thorough combat.

We live in a sophisticated world but our religious leaders take a shallow view of it. They do not apprehend the fact that the hard realities are always beneath the surface. In spite of the long political bloodshed, they have never realised the immense significance the politics of defending one's own national freedom has on the question of spiritual salvation. They believe in the illusion that the constitutional sanction of India would safeguard the freedom has on the question of spiritual salvation. They believe in the illusion that the constitutional sanction of India would safeguard the freedom of their faith. They failed to realise that any written constitution could be thrown overboard by the majority whenever expediency arose. The recent "Freedom of Religion Bill, 1978" introduced in the Indian Parliament which forbids further conversion to Christianity, is a clear example to this effect, and .it would serve as an eye-opener to all those who trust in the constitutional guarantee.

Yet the Church leaders would persist in joining the Indian Union of their own volition. You, good fellow, want us to resign ourselves to the wrong world which, to us, is the hardest of all. This is very wrong and *you* have done it. Harmful brains work harmful things. Preachers of all ranks have gone after the blessing and the 'awards' of Indian bosses. Spiritual uprightness is pushed into the background, pliable demagogues are out, dressed in 'dhoti' with that queer red mark of foreign goddess on their broad foreheads, preaching reverence for cows-half absorbed, full devil O Nagaland, whither goeth thou!

One is urged to ask, if Jesus, the Christ, is not sufficient to save the Nagas and the world and how the question of taking help from the Hindu goddess has ever arisen. The keeping of a substantial area of Nagaland and the Naga people therein under the so-called Arunachal Pradesh exclusively for the influence of Ram Krishan Mission over the innocent· is a long-range design to wreck the Nagas among themselves on different religious faiths and thus perpetuate their occupation of Nagaland.

Furthermore, the abundant amenities of life accorded to them are only sinister seeds of dissension being sown in the Naga family. Whatever it may be and wherever they may be. Nagas are Nagas and we shall prove the evil of this policy before long. India's "Ahimsa", "All Roads Lead to Rome", and "No Religion Has the Monopoly of Righteousness" are, no doubt, masterpieces of philosophy. The time has come for you and for us either to shrink back or prove through. God wants us right now to stand for Him. Now is the time to hold firm our ground with Christ and face the stick and carrot policy and persecutions of all Indian type. Real sacrifices of the soldiers of Christ are called for to make our country for Him and for Him alone. 0 men of God, lead us to Saviour Christ, for He alone is the Way, the Truth, and the Life that leads to God, the Father. Our Saviour taught us saying, "and thou shall be hated of all nations for my name's sake". Truly, it is time we pose the question, "Who is on the Lord's side?" Come for Christ, come for Nagaland's freedom. We are here and you will find us here always. Or you go for India and Burma and their goddesses. There is so third way, for "he who is not with me is against me and he who does not gather with me scatters."

V. Nagaland and the Party System

A country is always to be saved by its population but population as such is not a force until it is organised and brought into solidarity. It is, therefore, first and foremost that there should be solidarity and single organisation of the people. In other words, a nation is most secure when its citizens are kept instituted against any possible influence of the anti-national elements. Party politics proceeds in the main, from party interests, and as such permitting party politics in any form in times of national emergency, is in many ways obviously affording opportunities to the opponents to have a hold on some of the antagonistic parties. Any force that may have that tendency to disintegrate the solidarity of the people must be removed at the first opportunity.

In a country like Nagaland, particularly at the present time, party system could never accomplish anything except leading to ruination. It would mean only the game of the traitors and the exploiting class. The stage where there could be conductive practice of party system is still a long way off. The nature of the problem with which we have been confronted necessitates concerted efforts of the people through an organisation, if our country is positively to be saved from danger of any kind. The dictatorship of the people through an organisation is, therefore, indispensable.

Nevertheless, it is to be admitted that the constructive criticism of any erroneous policy is as much indispensable as the dictatorship of the people itself. Hence, the dictatorship of the people through a single political organisation and the active practice of democracy within the organisation is unquestionable for the salvation of Nagaland. Will not party system then be essential in normal times hereafter? Whether it is normal time or nor the kind of existence that our society will have cannot approve of parties of anti-nationals and exploiting class. In short, there can be no room for anti-people elements to function in our society.

The damage done to the healthy body politic and the upright characteristics of the Naga people as a whole, through the practice of Indian party system by the traitors, is beyond easy description. In their contest for the rein of state power all the parties involved in it indulged in all evil practices. To win the favour of the Central ruling party, 'the mithun' and 'the cock' alike promised in their words the annihilation of what they called 'hostiles' and the 'miscreants'. At the same time to ingratiate itself into indirect favour with the dupe the national defenders, 'the cock' showed superficial leniency to the common people and to those unfortunate national workers who fell victims of arrests. Both favour the inflow of Indians and exploited them for votes.

The accumulation of Indian money in their hands and the corrupt ubiquitous practice of bribery and the purchase of votes for money has left the people to the tender mercy of money. It is money that words, it is money that represents the 'Assembly'. All are shaken down before money that has no sentiment and are taken over. These 'parties' are formed mostly out of the traitors and the deserters from the Naga National Council. Now the notorious Shillong Accord makers in direct collusion with these parties, paradoxically, in the stolen name of the people, are merrily pulling the NNC back to their traitor's home, to save and enhance their parties and status at the expense of the National right. It is because they all are status mongers and renegades; they have no ideas to give up. Quo vadis, NNC! You cannot conceal for long years your treacherous inclination; you cannot shift the blame on to the people. We advise you to stop presuming upon the people's forbearance of you. We, the Nagas of today, do not permit any easy calculation on us.

The mithun and the cock, the 'honest brokers' and the hypocrites, the holy men of peace and the prophets of nonviolence, and the latest Accord makers, all without exception have joined hands with one another in the noble enterprise of instituting the modern most Vanity Fair in the puppet society where freedom, power and reality of life all end up in money, wine and women. Is this the system of society the Nagas are to seek their salvation from? Certainly no. On the contrary, this is a system that must be done away with and the Nagas delivered from this neither gloom for a society of higher order free from the fear of domination exploitation and suppression.

IV. The Indo-Burma Issue with Nagaland and the Means

The fate of a nation is never decided by spinning a coin. Neither our means is determined by the influence of any divine principles nor by our wishes. To us, there is no violence or non-violence as such in respect of policy, but it is the nature of the objective conditions that has to do with the means. To break a stone we use a hammer, to reap, a field we use a sickle and to deliver Nagaland from the preposterous occupation of Indian and Burmese military might, we need arms.

When Gandhiji was there the Nagas were happiest to talk of the Indo-Naga issue and even came to initial agreement. But the authorities post-Gandhiji tore up the agreement and the worst was forced upon the Nagas thereafter. Shooting down the Nagas at will started despite peaceful approaches. In the circumstances, the Nagas could not be expected to face Indian bullets with Gandhiji's Ahimsa. Nagas had to fire back in self-defence.

At any rate, could we make it the turn of Nagaland to be devoured? Never reason with a monster. Gandhiji's Ahimsa posed to the liberal Englishmen might have led into the gas chambers if it had been posed to Hitler, the Fuehrer. We shall in no case meet invasion of our country with non-violence. It is coward's politics, heading only for the jaws of the monster. Force to force, reason to reason. It is your aggression on us that had given rise to this spell of armed conflict; it is your killing of us that had touched off bitter retaliation. The problem is with you, it is not with the Nagas.

A political issue needs a political solution. The issue between India and Burma on the one side and Nagaland on the other is a political one. Therefore, it requires a political solution. But India and Burma seek military solution and this is the crux of the problem. Our freedom is forced into the battlefield; we have to pick it up with the gun. How long India and Burma continue their occupation of our homeland, that long we are bound to fight. We permit no power on earth to disturb our home and dictate terms to us.

And to you, who shout aloud for 'peace' and 'unity' we make our position unequivocal. If peace is the issue, we are of peace and that with freedom, and not for the peace you mean in capitulation. If unity is the question, we are definitely for unity but on the correct line alone. Those who shouted 'peace', 'unity', 'compromise', 'reconciliation', 'humanity' and so on: where have they all gone? These and more are the slogans of the traitors and the hypocrites combined. No nation is ever rescued by high sounding empty slogans. It is arms that save a nation. We are revolutionary patriots; we shall hold the fast to our gun. He who lays down his gun, lays down his freedom. This is the Gospel truth of our politics. We declare we will never lay down from our hands our arms, our freedom and our country.

VII. Nagaland and the Policy of Self-reliance

No country is prepared for the worst until its people are settled down to the practice of self-reliance. In other words, the people that have no determination to struggle by themselves have practically no motive force to sustain the meaning of life they have to live; they are left a drift only waiting for the unknown destiny to be driven to. It is the practice or relying on oneself that gives reality to one's existence.

The most dangerous harm affecting our politics today is that *ab initio* the people were made to believe in foreign help for their survival. This policy of setting the people on the hope of external help sapped the initiative to save themselves. Such policy is opportunist and treacherous in that the people are driven to despair and capitation when things would not turn out as they expected. We have to see to it that people are educated and built up on the realistic line. Without putting into practice the principle of self-dependency, the essence of being revolutionary vanishes.

The revolutionaries being mindful of the truth that their efforts alone are decisive, have to struggle to stand on their own feet. They should be well established with the people as one and teach them to realise that their future is assured only in their preparedness to save by their own efforts and abandon the idea of making external aid decide their course. They should also cultivate themselves to make the best of the conditions they are in and struggle against the unconducive tendencies, such as, indulging in tastes, acting at the dictate of whims or being dissipated, which the revolutionary state or condition can never approve.

It is hard to consolidate ourselves on foreign assistance. There could be no consolidation of our position without the practice of self-reliance, and without consolidation, it is idle to think of the final victory. We have to struggle and it is in the course of struggle that we acquire the existence essential for surmounting the inevitable problems on our way to final victory. Consolidation of home-front by our own efforts and the determination to fight through to the end could certainly win the favour of other countries and make their help worthwhile. He who does not realise the significance of the practices of self-reliance could not be a revolutionary patriot to the last.

Upholding the principle and shouting that 'Nagaland belongs to the Nagas' alone will not do. It requires of us far beyond that. Every vigorous effort must be made to realise it. We should not believe in parroting the principle; we must be prepared with the people and practically chart out way through. Mere words should not be our strategy, Nagaland had experienced enough of it; it has not yet recovered from the crisis of faith created by the strategy of bombastic utterances.

However, without the centralised system it is quite a problem to achieve anything good. It is in the centralised system that unity could fostered and save the country from the persisting internal nuisances and fight for the freedom of every inch of Nagaland. The policy of relying on ourselves could also be best implemented in this system. We should also change our tactics and strategy. Persistent fighting, as in the past, is an area where the enemy could do better; it should not be encouraged. We should find out the weak point of the enemy and consolidate ourselves there and that should be our base area. In this way, we can wrestle and have initiative almost all the time in our hand in dealing with the enemy, however superior he might be.

VIII. Nagaland and the Policy of United Front

The problem before us is how to confront an enemy of superior force and defeat them. The practical wisdom of the leadership lies in solving this problem. In order that the adversary may be defeated, he needs to be confronted on all fronts, which is pretty well impossible for a much weaker opponent. We should, however, know that we are not alone, because it is the world of conflicting historical forces.

Therefore, the question of the strategy of United Front with all the forces that could be united with it in some way or other cannot be dispensed with. In other words, we should by no means ignore or underestimate the necessity of a united front so long as there is the danger of isolated forces being defeated one after another. We should learn to help one another so that we are able to stand against the common enemy. Two men are always stronger than one and fighting on several fronts is more effective than fighting on a single front. We should be so united that there is coordination in our action.

There should be firm coordination with the forces that are within the enemy line too, and struggle to wreck the enemy from within. Enemy forces are most effectively disintegrated only when they are confronted from within and without. The old style of fighting single-handed like a bull should be avoided. We are to see the conditions around are jointly exploited against the enemy. Until that is done, we cannot claim that we are confronting him precisely in the way by which he could be defeated. It amounts to leaving the field to the opponent alone with all the initiative in his hands to defeat us.

We have to rectify our policy from being indifferent or opposed to the formation of a united front. We are revolutionaries; we should not be confined to ourselves alone, we should not just fight about without the tactics and strategy of winning over the enemy. We should even forgive the traitors and the mistake of being on their side provided they repeat of their mistakes and cooperate with us in the task of saving the nation of us all. We declare will unite with all the forces, God-fearing and Godless, that can be united with and fight against the monster in packs.

It is a pity that the leadership persistently harps and counts on the tantalising boon of some particular imperialist country and bosses and the sensibleness of the adversary by making antagonistic pronouncements against the countries which are sympathetically sharing with us the weal and woe. We cannot refuse to ask ourselves: By so doing, has he gained them as he calculated? Definitely no. It is just beating about the bush. As a matter of fact, he is held up in a predicament by his own boomeranging. The option before him how is either to go on parroting the principle or come back empty-handed. And then, *en route* to? Disloyalty to friends in their critical time has done much damage to mutual confidence. When open war broke out between our friends and our adversary, the leadership betrayed cooperation for the wanton purpose of winning the favour of the adversary. The ambivalent policy of the enemy was often miscalculated. Wounds caused by such perfidy are not easily healed. Friends are wounded, the adversary is gladdened and strengthened against us.

This is a total failure of policy, resulting from the inability to know the forces that would be on our side and the forces that are against us. It is the failure to understand Nagaland and the world around. It is self-isolation and self-antagonism; it is rightist and cowardice; and treacherous in the ultimate analysis. It is a self-defeat on both fronts, internal and external: It is a sad thing that we are led into such adverse state of affairs. The good old times are gone, we cannot call them back. We have to have the damages repaired, however long it may take, and bide our time. The world is not ended here; it keeps evolving. We should endeavour to adapt ourselves to and catch up with the forces at work. It is not for the world to wait for us; it is for us to struggle and to keep pace with the march of time. We should also correct ourselves from the past mistake of being out of step with the forces that are in our favour.

IX. Nagaland and the System of Socialism

What existence must our society have in this material world is the cardinal issue before us. We are to know that it is the world where there is the problem of exploitation of men by men and we are not an exception to this. It is altogether due to the system we live in. Therefore, it is true that the problems of disparity and poverty, and the concomitant evils, which have resulted from exploitation cannot be solved by any amount of benevolence and benefactions. It is the system that has to be abolished and lead the people into a new one where there is freedom from the fear of economic exploitation and political domination suppression. Of course, we shall not struggle for the stage of perfect equality, simply for the factual reason of impossibility.

Nagas are living in a society of free enterprise and it is this system that amply affords the reactionary traitors and the rich a free hand to exploit the poor and the masses in general. The naked armed invasion on us by India and Burma marked the beginning of enormous influx of Indian capital and its prominent role and activities in our society have created wild conditions. The concentration of capital in a few hands and its constant investment for acquiring more capital has set the whole society into a tremendous swing of exploitation of the Nagas by all Nagas and by the Indian parasites.

The existence of class distinctions is more prominent than ever before. The exploiting classes consists mainly of the reactionary traitors, the bureaucrats, a handful of rich men and the Indian vermin. They have practically no concern for the masses nor for the survival of the nation, but interest themselves in exploitation of the people and retention of their status. Their identification of interests with those of the exploiting rulers of India has led them to be identified with the Indians in various walks of life; and as they are accomplices, the Government of India is always behind them. On the other hand, the masses are the victims; they bore the brunt of the long attack. It is undoubtedly to their unyielding endurance that we own the survival of the nation today and it shall be so for all time to come. They are also the victims of exploitation; they are daily exploited everywhere. The contradictions that exist between the two classes are such that there could be no meeting point whatsoever.

From the above brief analysis, two outstanding points emerge: In the first place, the free existence of Nagaland is a must for the salvation of the people. In the next, the abolition of exploitation of the people is imperative if people are to assure their future.

The fact that the sacrifices and the efforts of the people alone could withstand and save the nation from external invasion is beyond dispute. But in spite of this standing fact, we are posed with the question. For whom would the nation, saved by the sacrifices and the efforts of the people, be? No doubt, it would be for the people alone. However, the actuality of this would be borne out solely by the system that would be implemented.

To us, it is definitely SOCIALISM alone that can assure the fairest deal to the community as a whole as it is the only social and economic system that does away with exploitation and oppression. Moreover, we are profoundly convinced of the course of human society to Socialism, that is, the inevitability of Socialism from the struggle of the two irreconcilable classes. Without this salvation in Socialism, we promise no future to the people; we betray them to no hope; they are made beasts of burden.

However, to achieve the salvation of the people in Socialism, the dictatorship of the people through a revolutionary organisation is indispensable. It is because the revolutionaries alone stand out for the political freedom of Nagaland, against the system of exploitation of the Nagas by the Nagas, and further the cause of the people to Socialism, where virtually all the means of production, natural resources and their distribution, transportation and communication, and other essential functions are to be owned by the state or by the community as a whole. It is only in the dictatorship of the people through a Revolutionary Council that the principle of people's supremacy is upheld to its meaning, the free existence of Nagaland could be safeguarded and Socialism could be realised. Therefore, any force opposing it would obviously amount to being antinational and anti-people.

X. Nagaland and the National Socialist Council

The world is changing fast but the Naga National Council has failed to keep pace with changing conditions. It has not understood the world and Nagaland; it has isolated itself from the people; it has not promised the people any future from the danger of the forces of domination, exploitation and assimilation. All the old forces have yielded and are drowned without a trace and any contrary claim is just a claim to save one's own face, and not to save the nation. All have fallen and Nagaland remains to be saved. Where is the way to save our nation now? Where is the Council that upholds the cause of the sovereign Nagaland and the salvation of the people?

We declare we are revolutionary patriots. Let no traitorous nor reactionary bounds be on us. To us the sovereign existence of our country, the salvation of our people in Socialism with their spiritual salvation in Christ are eternal and unquestionable. It is because life has meaning and that is in freedom alone. Only the revolutionary patriots are diametrically opposed to all the antinational, anti-people forces. Because: We refuse Nagaland to be gotten for gold; we refuse Nagaland to be weighed in terms of silver, sine and women; we refuse Nagaland to be valued for one's status. Indeed, our Nagaland shall forever refuse to perish together with any leadership or organisation that has failed and betrayed her cause that has not promise of future for her people. Time moves on, and we have to move along, although the Naga National Council does not, for we have to redeem Nagaland. Therefore, in this reconcilable world, our National Socialist Council declares:

(a) National Existence

We stand for the unquestionable sovereign right of the Naga people over every inch of Nagaland whatever it may be and admit of no other existence whatever.

(b) Political Institution

We stand for the principle of people's supremacy, that is, the dictatorship of the people through the National Socialist Council and the practice of Democracy within the organisation.

(c) Economic System

We stand for Socialism. Because it is the only social and economic system that does away with exploitation and ensures fair equality to all the people.

(d) Religion

We stand for the faith in God and the salvation of mankind in Jesus, the Christ, alone, this is "NAGALAND FOR CHRIST". However, the individual freedom of religion shall be safeguarded and the imposition of this faith on others is strictly forbidden.

(c) Means

We rule out the illusion of saving Nagaland through peaceful means. It is arms and arms alone that will save our nation and ensure freedom to the people.

(f) Self-reliance and the Policy of United Front

We stand for the practice of the principle of self-reliance and for the policy of United Front with all the forces that can be united with.

Sons and Daughters of Nagaland

Ask not what the Maker has in store for us. In His righteousness. He has given us all that is ours. Let us understand our country and our freedom and hold them fast, for what have the people that doubt their freedom and that of their country? They are only fit to be ruled, nay, they are already ruled. They are the people to be pitied most. Without her freedom Nagaland too has nothing. Truly, when freedom falls, everything falls. Your country is challenged; your freedom is in peril. Arise and look! It is time; it is our today; we should never fail her, for no amount of sermons and lamentations can save her tomorrow. We have chosen Nagaland and her freedom forever; we will never part with them. Indeed, it is the war we have to fight; it is the war we have to win. We shall accept no summons to bow down; our Nagaland shall never put her hands up. We shall live only in freedom. This alone is the way to our salvation. Praise the Lord! We hold the promises of history.

LONG LIVE NAGALAND!
LONG LIVE THE NATIONAL SOCIALIST COUNCIL
OF NAGALAND.

MANIFESTO OF THE KUKI NATIONAL ORGANISATION

The Kuki National Organisation is a revolutionary movement based in Zale'n-gam: land of freedom, the ancestral territory of the Kuki people…

The Kuki National Organisation is a revolutionary movement based in Zale'n-gam: land of freedom, the ancestral territory of the Kuki people. The ancestral Zale'n-gam comprises the contiguous region in Northeast India, Northwest Burma, and the Chittagong Hill tracts in Bangladesh. Zale'n-gam is the land where the Kukis originated, on which they were raised, developed, excelled and fought valiant battles for its preservation and protection. Following the 'Kuki Rising, 1917-1919' (OIOC), which was a culmination of resistance to British colonialists' aggression that began in 1777, Zale'n-gam was divided between India and Burma by the colonialists. Despite the historical injustice resulting in the division of Kuki territory without their consent, and the consequent separation of their people, successive generations of Kuki have not forgotten that they are one nation. They have neither abandoned nor faltered in the pursuit of their right to regain freedom.

The Kuki National Organisation, on behalf of the Kukis, of the present and future generations, pledges to restore the ancestral Kuki territory to its rightful status. The Manifesto and ideology of KNO is based on the resolution of the Kuki chiefs, who fought against the British in the 'Kuki Rising, 1917-1919'. The resolution reads:

At all cost, we should fight against the British for the preservation of our independence, and for the protection of our land, culture and tradition (in JC Higgins' letter No 1243, 7 November 1917, to the Chief Secretary of Assam).

The zeal and sacrifice of our forefathers made nearly one hundred years ago remain fresh in our hearts and minds. Not daunted by the might of the world's most powerful imperialists of the time, they fought them to preserve the territorial integrity of Zale'n-gam. Their fortitude and tenacity continues to inspire KNO in its obligation to restore Zale'n-gam to its status, which is the birthright of the Kuki people. KNO pledges to pursue its goal through means that are noble and which do not compromise the integrity and commitment demonstrated by our ancestors.

The Kukis were a sovereign nation before the advent of the British...

Prior to the advent of the British, the Kukis were in their own right a sovereign nation. Kuki polity, based on chieftainship, functioned with a full complement of governing bodies, such as *Semang* (Home Minister), *Pachong* (Defence & External Affairs), *Lhangsam* (Minister, Public Relations & Broadcasting) *Lawm Upa* (Minister of Youth, Economic & Cultural

Affairs), *Thiempu* (Priest), *Tollai Pao* (Law and Order Enforcement Minister). At the national level, this governance is known as the Kuki Inpi. The pattern is replicated at the *Lhang* (district) and *Gamkai* (state) level. Integral to Kuki polity is the *Inpi*, the apex body, in which each Kuki Chief is a member.

The Inpi met to execute policies and programmes, and as matters of importance, such as which affect the security and safety of the entire Kuki nation arose. One such instance took place in 1917: the Kuki Chiefs from the entire length and breadth of Zale'n-gam held a series of conclaves at Chassad, Jampi, Longya, and Khongjang. At these conclaves they resolved to rise against the British to protect the sovereignty of Zale'n-gam. To mark their resolve for a concerted effort, the Kuki Chiefs performed *Sajamlhah* and ate the heart and liver of the mithun or bison killed for the occasion, symbolising commitment from the depth of one's heart or core. As is customary, portions of the meat are sent to every Kuki village Chief not present on the occasion. The tradition of *Thingkho le Malchapom* (hot king-sized chilly tied on to smouldering firewood) was launched, signifying a declaration of war against the British. *Thingkho le Malchapom* was sent to every Kuki village to convey that an offensive against the British has begun. This practice, which also indicated the Kukis were fully prepared, enabled the united Kuki Rising of 1917-1919.The traditional Kuki Inpi, which remained latent since India gained independence from Britain, was revived following the fresh lot of crises faced by the Kuki people from 1980s and 1990s.

The relationship between the Kuki Chief and the Meitei *Ningthou* (Raja or Chief) was one of mutual respect and understanding. They stuck together through thick and thin, helping each other in times of external aggression. An eloquent ancient Meitei aphorism bears testimony to this relationship: *Chingna koina pansaba, Haona koina panngakpa, Manipur sana leimayol....* (Rough translation) *Encircled by the range of hills, secured all around by the people who dwell therein; Oh Manipur, thou golden land.* The aphorism clearly demarcated Kuki and Meitei territories. The 'people' or 'Haona' refer to the Kukis, who were masters of the hills, where they received tax and tributes from the Tangkhuls and Kabui Nagas; Manipur sana leimayol, the golden land, refers to the ancestral Meitei territory consisting the valley, which lay safely surrounded by Kuki hills and their braves.

Contrary to some academics' view, the Kuki Chiefs were not *'vassals'* of the Meitei Ningthou, neither were they ever treated as such. The Kuki Chiefs were independent and benevolent autocrats, who kept their territory secure and intact. In the words of JH Hutton, The Kukis were ruled by their own organized chiefs and treated as they had been in the past at any rate, by the Manipur State as allies (Introduction to William Shaw's book, *Notes on Thadou Kukis* (1929), written by JH Hutton, July 1928, p 3). The Kukis protested the transfer of hill administration to the Manipur State Durbar and made clear their stand by stating: The hills were never a part of India prior to the annexation of these frontier hills (Statement of KNA, 1947). This position was reiterated by KNA: **The unchallenging fact is that, if the British government left the country, then naturally the Kukis should be free** (Memorandum to the Prime Minister, 1960).

The freedom loving Kukis were politically subjugated by the British, but morally they remained independent and this manifested itself from time to time...

The aggressions of the British on Kuki territory, which began in 1777 culminated in the Kuki Rising of 1917-1919. The British Government let loose a reign of terror on the Kukis both during and after the Kuki Rising. To this day bitters tears are shed when experiences are related of the torture, oppression, and extent of losses in terms of property and lives suffered at the hands of the British. The intensity of Kuki defiance is cited by Maj Gen DK Palit (1984, 62) in *Sentinels of the North-East*: rather than attend a Durbar the Political Agent of Manipur organised to discuss the issues that incensed the Kukis, Chief Ngulbul of Mombi (Lawnpi) and Chief Ngulkhup of Longya sent a message that they have **'closed the country to the British.'** In today context, Chief Ngulbul and Chief Ngulkhup's dominion is the Chandel district of Manipur.

In spite of the cruel suppression meted out by the British, our forefathers' courage, hope and love for freedom did not falter, and this manifested periodically through WWII. Shakespear (1929, 224, *History of the Assam Rifles*), wrote that the events of the Kuki Rising of 1917-1919 covered the **'entire hills of Manipur'**; Meluri Sub-division and Peren District of present-day Nagaland; and in Eastern Zale'n-gam, of present-day Burma, up to the river Chindwin and the Kale-Kabaw Valley. This concerted offensive led by the Chiefs is a tribute to the traditional Kuki polity, which is embodied in the Inpi. The Kuki Rising is also significant as it highlighted the historicity of Kuki Polity and Kuki unity across the present-day international boundaries of India, Burma and Bangladesh. The British government, cognizant of this fact, and dreading the strength of a united Kuki people, had a system of border meetings between officers of Manipur and those of Somra Tract in Upper Burma, Chin Hills, Naga Hills and Lushai Hills. After obtaining detailed accounts of the Kukis and fully assessing their strength, the British Indian Government began reorganizing administrative regions to divide and control Kuki territory.

By the Act of 1935, Government of India, Burma was separated from India in 1937. This deft imperialist masterstroke split Zale'n-gam between British India and British Burma, without Kuki consent. In the words of William Shaw (1929, 50), **'The unprepared Kukis could not, however, openly challenge the Britishers but had to wait for an opportune time when they could re-assert their freedom.'** The opportunity to regain their freedom came in World War II. In this Great War the Kukis and the Indian National Army fought on the side of Japanese. The Kukis entered into a political agreement with the INA and the Japanese army regarding the future of the Kukis after the war ended.

In a booklet (written in the vernacular) Manipur a Kuki te leh Christianity (1984), Pu Jamthang gives an account of the agreement between the Kukis and the Japanese held in present-day Burma at Koija (north of Homalin) and Zalen (south of Homalin) camps, on 5 Oct and 12 Oct 1943, respectively. The number of Kuki Chiefs and elders present on the occasion was 310; Imperial Japan was represented by 3 Japanese officers, namely Ezemia, Nokamisan and Nakamisang. A translation of the text regarding the treaty at Koija and Zalen camps is as follows: **The Kukis and the Japanese killed a mithun or bison to formalise the treaty. They ate the animal's liver and heart (symbolising deepest commitment to the treaty) and declared that a tiger devour either party that reneged!**

The points of the Kuki-Japanese agreement are as follows:

a) In war time, Kukis would help the Japanese in combats against the British, provide local guides, intelligence, provisions and other materials
b) In the course of the war, the Imperial Japanese army would respect the dignity and honour of the Kuki people
c) Following victory of the Axis powers, the Kukis would regain independence, as was prior to the advent of the British, and Japan would facilitate in the process of Kukis rebuilding their nation

The victory of the Allied forces and subsequent independence of Burma, India and Pakistan resulted in Kuki territory being incorporated within the three state-nations. The British not only divided our ancestral lands, but also divided us into 'Old Kuki' and 'New Kuki' with the sole intention to subdue and prevent us from becoming a strong and united nation.

India and Burma have interpreted the peaceful movement of the Kukis since 1940s as a sign of weakness, and as a result, failed to address their issues…

Unyielding to the forced division of Zale'n-gam, the Kuki National Assembly was formed in 1946 to demand independence from India. Within Burma, as a mark of protest, the Kuki people did not participate in the widely acclaimed Panglong Agreement of 1947, held at Panglong in the Shan state. The Panglong Agreement was a conference, which was attended by certain Members of the Executive Council of the Governor of Burma, and representative of the Shan States, the Kachin Hills and the Chin Hills – but not the Kukis. Despite the enforced circumstances of the Kukis, their mode of expressing grievance and seeking redressal in India and Burma has been non-violent. However, this gesture has not been appreciated by the respective governments of both countries; they appear to interpret the peaceful movement of the Kukis since 1940s as a sign of weakness, and have ignored the Kuki question. The governments of India and Burma have failed to protect the lives, liberty and property of the Kuki people. In other words, the basic human rights of the Kuki people have been denied in their own lands. These, and other grievances, have been patiently borne to a point where forbearance ceases to be a virtue. Our anticipation for the concerned governments to take proactive initiatives has so far proven futile. We are therefore obligated to consider, deliberate and articulate our political goals, which is our inherent right and sacred duty to posterity.

In the Indian Union, the states are organized on ethno-linguistic lines in recognition of the existing mosaic of ethnic identities, languages and cultures. The right to govern their own affairs within their traditional territory has been denied to the Kukis, whilst it has long been extended to other ethnic entities in the Northeast. As a result, the Kuki inhabited areas of Manipur Hills, Karbi-Anglong and North-Cachar Hills of Assam and Tripura remain grossly underdeveloped and the people live in abject poverty. Fair developmental programs have consistently been denied to Kuki inhabited regions by the state machinery dominated by the majority communities. The long years of neglect and sufferings of the Kuki people under these state governments, dictated by the interests of the majority communities, have rendered the Kukis economically, socially and politically backward and deeply vulnerable. Please note: **'Unity in Diversity'**, the basis of Indian Polity, can work only when the diverse communities are on the same pedestal and can relate to each other with mutual respect.

The Kukis have been subjected to political adversity and their neighbouring communities have taken advantage of their consequent vulnerability. This fact was highlighted by the Kuki National Assembly in 1960: **'Unless strong measures are immediately taken up for self-preservation, namely establishment of a separate state of their own within the Indian Union, they will surely succumb sooner or later to**

a process of extinction and extermination, which has been threatening them very seriously.' The Indian government has not addressed the Kuki issue and thus continues the saga of the Kuki people's never-ending sufferings and struggles. From 1950-1990, the Tangkhul people of Ukhrul District in Manipur carried out selective and systematic elimination of Kuki chiefs and elders, totalling 42. This was done to implant a fear psychosis among Kukis so that they may leave their hearths and ancestral lands. In the process, 64 Kuki villages were uprooted, which are now occupied by the Tangkhuls. In an ever-worsening scenario, on 22 October 1992 **'Quit Notice Served by United Naga Council (UNC) to Kukis'** was issued, signed by RK Thekho, president of UNC, Imphal. Copies of the notice were distributed to all Naga villages, Sub Divisional Offices/District Commissioner Offices of the Manipur state government, and to the Editors of Manipur Mail and Manipur News for publication. As a result, from 1992-1997, the NSCN (IM) led by Thuingaleng Muivah, a Tangkhul, launched the infamous Kuki genocide. The casualties totalled over 900 Kuki people dead (a significant number of them women and children), 350 uprooted villages, and more than 50,000 people displaced.

The degree of human rights violations committed by the NSCN-IM is reflected in the statement of Yambem Laba, a noted journalist from Manipur:

The Naga cry against human rights abuse perpetrated by the Indian army for over fifty years was, completely overshadowed by one incident of Zoupi village on 13 September 1993.

The above remark refers to one of the many incidents in which NSCN (IM) cadres at gunpoint tied up and massacred 107 Kuki men (87 died at the spot; 20 later succumbed to injuries), butchering them with matchetes and spears. In fact the Nagas served notice to the Kukis to quit Zoupi village by 15 September. In spite of the people leaving the village on the 13th, two days ahead of the deadline served, they were butchered. This reveals the treacherous mentality of the NSCN-IM.

In addition, Dr Isak, Medical Officer of Chandel, who conducted the post-mortem of one of the three women raped and killed by the NSCN (IM) guerrillas at Moltuh village in 1992, reported:

Face blindfolded. Gang raped before being killed. Throat split up with knife. Left portions of the skull completely battered up. Left breast badly bruised. A piece of stick measuring about seven inches was found inserted in her vagina.

Pu Tobu Kevichusa, Secretary of Naga National Council statement at the funeral service of Pu Mangkholen Hangsing, IAS, Commissioner of Taxation and Excise is noteworthy:

Isak and Muivah, the leaders of NSCN (IM), have proclaimed among the international community that the Government of India have killed innocent Nagas and abused their human rights. On the contrary, here is a stark example of their role of engaging in fratricidal activity by killing blameless people like Mangkholen to benefit their sectarian policy.

The atrocities committed on the Kukis and on those who stand for justice clearly violate not only basic human rights, but also contradict NSCN-IM's slogan, 'Nagaland for Christ'. Rather surprisingly, many people – both within India and in the international community – are more concerned with Nagas' self-determination and violations of their human rights by the Indian security forces without ever a thought regarding the NSCN (IM)-led Naga violation of human rights against the Kukis! The KNO possesses and will produce at the appropriate time, concrete evidence of NSCN (IM)'s brutal murders and other atrocities. These include photographs of those killed and mass graves of slain Kuki villagers (where it was impossible to have individual burials), dates and places of killings and a list of Kuki villages uprooted.

Ever since the 1950s and 1960s, the Kuki people have submitted numerous memorandums demanding a separate state and also appealed for protection and restoration of their uprooted villages. Unfortunately, the government of India and Burma have so far chosen to ignore the Kuki people's positive overtures. The indifference of the Government of India has resulted in escalation of atrocities against Kukis that beggar description. The government, instead of addressing the Kuki question, has kept up its negotiations with NSCN-IM, the perpetrators of Kuki genocide, while completely evading talks with KNO. In August 2005, KNO signed the Suspension of Operations with the Indian Army, which represented the Central Government, in order to facilitate political dialogue with Government of India. To date, talks between Government of India and KNO have not begun. This speaks volumes about the indifference and extreme callousness of the GOI towards the Kuki people and their problems.

In the meantime, capitalizing on the vulnerability of the Kukis, the Meitei insurgent outfits have infiltrated Kuki areas in large numbers, where they have set up bases and wantonly indulged in inhuman harassment and torture of Kuki villagers. They also launch attacks on Indian Security Forces, mindless of the reprisals on civilian Kukis, and engage in laying anti-personnel Landmines to the detriment of the village folks. Many Kukis are therefore either killed or incapacitated by landmine explosions. The Meitei insurgents who have understanding with the military junta are also operating from Burmese territory. The Government of India remains a mute spectator to these sufferings of its Kuki citizens and has failed utterly to protect them.

In Burma, the Kuki people have been subjected to persecution and torture by the state machinery dominated by the majority Burmans, ever since the 1962 military coup under General Newin. The Government of Revolutionary Council headed by General Newin had since 1967 forcibly evicted more than 20,000 Kuki villagers in Kabaw Valley during the iniquitous 'Khadawmi Operation' led by U Muang Maung into neighbouring India. The pretext for the eviction was either non-possession of National Registration Cards or possessing bogus ones. The rightist military introduced the system of National Registration for citizens soon after it assumed power in 1962. This was intended primarily to deprive citizenship to ethnic minorities, including millions of ethnic Tamil Indian Businessman in and around Rangoon. Besides, the Registration Cards, meant to be issued free of cost were illegally sold at a high price. From the early 1980s there have been renewed attempts at displacing the Kukis and transplanting ethnic Burmese population in the Kabaw valley. Some existing examples of such transplanted settlements are Ongchija, Tanan, Myothit, Nanaungow, Mantong and Ywatha, which were deliberately set up by the military junta. Besides such acts of discrimination, the junta has been extracting forced-labour from Kuki villagers in the Kabaw Valley and dispossessed the Kukis of many of their villages. Construction of new churches has also been categorically stopped.

The military junta in Burma has also persistently pursued a policy of Burmanization of periphery minority ethnic communities. This has been carried out through a process of assimilation, acculturation, suppression and forcible imposition of the Burmese language and the Buddhist religion. In the course of action, Churches of many Kuki villages in Myanmar has been burnt down. The pastors and community leaders have been tortured, and villages forced to move in order to set up Burmese (pro-military Junta) settlements or Army bases. The State Law and Order Restoration Council, which grabbed power in the post 1988 democratic uprising, intensified the persecution and eviction of Kuki citizens. The State Peace and Development Council, the new face of the Junta, despite promises to restore democracy, has displayed no change whatsoever in their approach towards the ethnic nationalities. Neither has the military's disdain and mockery of democracy and national reconciliation diminished.

The Kuki National Organisation's objectives and policy: Re-Unification of our ancestral lands divided between India, Burma and Bangladesh...

The Kuki National Organisation is committed to self-determination for the Kuki people in their ancestral lands. The KNO's present definition of self-determination is the right of the Kukis to govern their own affairs within a defined territorial entity (Statehood), one in India (Western Zale'n-gam) and another in Burma (Eastern Zale'n-gam) as a first step towards re-unification of the Kukis. Our forefathers, the patriots of the Kuki Rising of 1917-1919, fought the British colonialists to preserve Kuki polity and the people. In like manner, KNO stands for statehood to secure the ancestral lands of the Kuki people, their identity, culture, customs and traditions. These fundamentals are essential to promote an all round development of our people. KNO will steadfastly strive to achieve these noble objectives. The objectives are based on the historicity of Kuki ancestral polity and territory. The KNO calls upon the entire Kuki populace around the world to come together as a nation whose people share a common origin, culture, customs and traditions. We also appeal to every capable Kuki to contribute his or her strength in the struggle we have embarked upon to redeem our national pride and heritage and to establish freedom, liberty, security and welfare, which is our people's right in Zale'n-gam.

The present political objectives of KNO—statehood for Kuki ancestral lands, each within the Union of India and Union of Burma—provide clear evidence of our conciliatory stance towards the respective governments. We urge the governments of India and Burma to pay heed to the numerous pleas and memoranda that have been placed before them to date and expedite the process of granting statehood to the Kuki people. KNO has opted for a conciliatory stand and anticipates the governments of India and Burma will reciprocate meaningfully.

The KNO also call upon the United Kingdom to facilitate this process and thereby help remedy the present predicament of the Kukis and the state of their ancestral territory for which they are historically responsible. We appeal to Germany and Japan, the partners of the Kuki people during World War I and World War II, to extend due moral and political support for the realization of KNO's objectives.

With statehood and its vital elements of self-governance, its inherent infrastructure and other provisions, our socio-economic and political condition that was destabilized by the British and neglected by the successor states would appropriately be restored. A new era of peace and development that shall dawn upon the Kuki people once our objectives are realized will create conditions that engender peaceful co-existence with our neighbouring communities, which is essential to develop a symbiotic relationship and join the global march towards progress.

The KNO adheres to a reconciliatory approach towards our neighbours, particularly the Nagas and Meiteis. With regard to the Meitei people, the Kukis, aware that the ancestral lands of both peoples, the Hills and Plains, were being clubbed together as a single entity by the powers that be, and vigilant of the possibility therefore of both peoples losing their ancestral territories, national freedom and sovereign inheritance to the emergent Indian state-nation if the Manipur Ningthou were to sign the merger proposal, vehemently opposed it. The Meiteis failed to appreciate such statesmanly opposition of Kuki Chiefs to Manipur being annexed in 1949 into the Indian Union, and instead continue to make every effort to trivialize this significant effort made by the Kukis to preserve both peoples' political and territorial inheritance. Furthermore, when the NSCN (IM) launched the ethnic cleansing of the Kukis in the hills of Manipur in the 1990s, both the revolutionary and civil society groups of the Meiteis did not intervene to prevent the Kuki genocide. We therefore urge our one-time Meitei brothers to withdraw their armed cadres from Kuki territory. They are also urged to immediately abandon setting up landmines in Kuki territory. The KNO are signatory to the Deed of Commitment to ban landmines, an initiative of Geneva Call, Geneva.

The NSCM (IM)'s aggression on the Kukis from 1990s that went beyond traditional warfare has left an indelible mark on the minds of the Kuki people. The KNO would like to remind them of a statement made by the Kuki National Assembly:

While our heartfelt sympathy and good wishes go to the Nagas for the achievement of their demand, they may at the same time be cautioned not to come in the way of the same demand of the Kukis (Vide- A Kuki State: A Memorandum of the KNA to the Prime Minister of India, 1960).

The KNO, therefore urge both the Nagas and Meiteis that as partners in observing and claiming human rights, let aggression and intimidation be shunned, and civilized and charitable conduct be our crowning glory. The KNO, in order to create peaceful co-existence among the Kukis, Nagas and Meiteis within their respective territories, is open to a tripartite dialogue. For this to succeed the later two communities must relinquish their territorial acquisitiveness and hegemonic policies.

The KNO presently adheres to a policy of pursuing our objectives in an amicable manner. The dove with two olive branches on our Website's Homepage symbolizes our goodwill towards all. The symbol also makes clear our intent to achieve a harmonious resolution of differences with the governments of India and Burma. Given the Kuki people's history of opposition to British colonialism to preserve the integrity of our ancestral lands, KNO's appeal for Kuki lands to be accorded statehood, one in India and another in Burma, is rational and legitimate. Fulfilment of the rights of the Kuki people for self-determination in this respect within a reasonable time frame will ensure our goodwill to endure. **The KNO shall be duty-bound to consider alternatives to our present approach if the governments' apathy and negligence persist concerning Kuki aspirations.**

God Bless Zale'n-gam, the Kuki nation!

MEMORANDUM OF THE REVOLUTIONARY PEOPLE'S FRONT, 1999

'Memorandum submitted to the secretary general United Nations and the chairman of the Decolonisation Committee (committee of 24) for de-colonisation of Manipur from Indian colonialism and alien racist regime, enlisting Manipur in the list of the non-self-governing-territories of the United Nations and, restoration of independence and sovereignty of Manipur'. Revolutionary People's Front, Manipur 2nd Edition, 21 September 1999.

To
The Secretary General, United Nations AND
The Chairman, Decolonisation Committee (Committee of 24)
Geneva/New York Headquarters.

MEMORANDUM: Submitted on behalf of all the dependent and colonised people of Manipur representing the Meitei and the Meitei cognates viz., the Nagas, the Kuki-Chins for granting and restoration of independence and de-colonisation of the State of Manipur from the present colonial Administering Power of India, which has occupied Manipur since 15 October, 1949, till today.

Prayer

1. For supervising and examining historical materials/records relating to the illegal annexation and colonisation of Manipur by India
2. For terminating the foreign and colonial regime of India over Manipur
3. For international appraisal of the illegal and unjustified annexation of the Nation-State of Manipur in 1949 AD
4. For giving international recognition to the National Liberation Movement of Manipur, which continues since the time of annexation in 1949 till today, and allowing the people of Manipur to exercise their inalienable right to self- determination in conformity with the UN General Assembly Resolution 1514(XV) of 1960 and other subsequent resolutions
5. For all necessary and elaborate steps, appropriate measures towards complete de-colonisation of Manipur and cessation of subjugation of her people to the earliest, and lastly, for holding emergent as well as periodic sessions of the De-colonisation Committee in Imphal city in 1999; and
6. For enlisting Manipur in the list of the non-self-governing territories of the UN by enlarging the existing Mandate

Respected Secretary General/Chairman,

0.1. This is a factfully updated petition of the prayer submitted on 11 December 1996 to the Chairman, UN De-colonisation Committee. We, the undersigned representatives of the Revolutionary People's Front (RPF), a front of the national liberation movement in the State of Manipur, which is currently a constituent State of the Republic of India, furnish the following facts, based on historical, political, socio-economic materials as well as legal and constitutional materials for your immediate consideration and urgent international supervision of the colonisation and dependence of the people of Manipur by the colonial power of India with the help of a colonial occupation army, which continues the ongoing repression, suppression, torture, extra-judicial murder and subjugation of the people of Manipur under a permanent colonial process and colonisation in different forms. Since time immemorial, Manipuris call Indians as Mayangs i.e., foreigners.

0.2. We fully appreciate the de-colonisation process, adopted by the UN since 1960 and the emergence of a hundred independent sovereign states in conformity with the de-colonisation process. The de-colonisation process was initiated by the Special Committee on the Situation with regard to the Implementation of the Declaration on the Granting of Independence to Colonial Countries and Peoples (De-colonisation Committee hereafter) vide the UN General Assembly Resolution 1654 (XVI) of 27 November, 1961, the UN GA Resolutions 1810 (XVII) of 17 December, 1962, 2621 (XXV) of 12 October, 1970, 35/118 of 11 December 1980, 40/56 of 2 December 1985, 45/33 of 20 November, 1990, 46/181 of 19 December, 1991, and the UN GA Resolution 52/78 of 10 December, 1997.

0.3. It is pertinent that the UN GA Resolution 52/78 of 10 December, 1997 has mandated the Special Committee for "the Eradication of Colonialism in all Territories that have not yet exercised their right to self-determination, including independence", "to formulate proposals for the elimination of the remaining manifestations of colonialism" and "to recommend to the General Assembly the most suitable steps to be taken to enable the populations of those territories to exercise their right to self-determination and independence".

0.4. The Special Committee at its 1484th meeting, held on 6 February 1998 has accepted to review the list of territories to which the Colonial Declaration of 1960 has applied. The Special Committee has continued its review of the list of Territories to which the Declaration is applicable and it also "intends to continue to review the list of Territories to which the Declaration is applicable".

0.5. The non-self-governing territory of Manipur, illegally annexed and placed under military occupation since 15 October, 1949 deserves a legitimate place in the list of territories under the supervision of the Special Committee to enable the people of Manipur to exercise their inalienable right to self-determination, independence and sovereignty. The facts of colonisation and subjugation are furnished below under the relevant headings:

I. Historical Evidence

1.1. The State of Manipur, which lies in the latitude range of 23°83^2 and 25°68^2 (North) and in the longitude range of 93°03^2 and 94°78^2 (East), is one of the earliest States in the continent of Asia, including the Indian sub-continent. This ancient Asian State was known by different names to different countries that is - 'Poirei Meitei Leipak' or 'Kangleipak' to the indigenous people of Manipur or Meiteis; 'Kathe' or 'Ponnas' to the Burmese; 'Hsiao Po-lo-mein' to the Chinese; 'Cassay' to the Shans; 'Moglai' to the Cacharis and Bengalis and 'Mekle' to the Assamese (as well as to the British in the 18th Century) in the pre-Christian period. Its location is identified with places within the jurisdiction of Tugma, Triglipton, Mareura and Kirrhadia as per the sources of Ptolemy. The Manipuris, themselves knew the State by as many as 22 names in different ages and at different times. The early state of Pragjyotishpur or, Kamrup or, present Indian state of Assam has been for millennia a buffer between State of Manipur and State of India known as Bharat for millennia. All the available maps available with India depict Manipur as an independent state till the annexation in 1949.

Genealogy of Manipur Kings

(Source CHEITHAROL KUMBABA, the Royal Chronicle of Manipur)

Sl. No.	*Name of King*	*Period (AD)*
1.	King Nongda Lairen Pakhangba	33 - 154
2.	King Khuiyoi Tompok	154 - 264
3.	King Taothingmang	264 - 364
4.	King Khui Ning-ngonba	364 - 379
5.	King Pengsiba	379 - 394
6.	King Kaokhangba	394 - 411
7.	King Naokhamba	411 - 428
8.	King Naophangba	428 - 518
9.	King Sareimang	518 - 568
10.	King Urakonthouba	568 - 658

11.	King Naothingkhong	663 - 763
12.	King Khongtekcha	763 - 773
13.	King Keirencha	784 - 799
14.	King Yaraba	799 - 821
15.	King Ayangba	821 - 910
16.	King Ningthoucheng	910 - 949
17.	King Chenglei Epan Lanthaba	949 - 969
18.	King Yanglou Keiphaba	969 - 984
19.	King Irengba	984 - 1074
20.	King Loiyumba	1074 - 1122
21.	King Loitongba	1122 - 1150
22.	King Atom Yoiremba	1150 - 1163
23.	King Iwanthaba	1163 - 1195
24.	King Thawanthaba	1195 - 1231
25.	King Chingthang Lanthaba	1231 - 1242
26.	King Thingbai Selhongba	1242 - 1247
27.	King Puranthaba	1247 - 1263
28.	King Khumomba	1263 - 1278
29.	King Moiramba	1278 - 1302
30.	King Thangbi Lanthaba	1302 - 1324
31.	King Kongyamba	1324 - 1335
32.	King Telheiba	1335 - 1355
33.	King Tonaba	1355 - 1359
34.	King Tabungba	1359 - 1394
35.	King Lairenba	1394 - 1399
36.	King Punsiba	1404 - 1432
37.	King Ningthoukhomba	1432 - 1469
38.	King Kyamba	1469 - 1508
39.	King Koiremba	1508 - 1512
40.	King Lamkyamba	1512 - 1523
41.	King Nong-en-faba	1523 - 1524
42.	King Kabomba	1524 - 1542
43.	King Tangjamba	1542 - 1545
44.	King Challamba	1545 - 1562
45.	King Mungyamba	1562 - 1597
46.	King Khagemba	1597 - 1652
47.	King Khunjaoba	1652 - 1666
48.	King Paikhomba	1666 - 1697
49.	King Charairongba	1697 - 1709
50.	King Garibaniwaz (Mayamba)	1709 - 1748
51.	King Chitsai	1748 - 1752

52.	King Bharatsai	1752 - 1753
53.	King Maramba	1753 - 1759
54.	King Chingthangkhomba	1759 - 1762
55.	King Maramba	1762 - 1763
56.	King Chingthangkhomba	1763 - 1798
57.	King Labyanachandra	1798 - 1801
58.	King Madhurjit	1801 - 1803
59.	King Chourjit	1803 - 1813
60.	King Marjit	1813 - 1819
61.	King Takuningthou (Heerachandra)	1819 -
62.	King Yumjaotaba	1820 -
63.	King Gambhir Singh	1821 -
64.	King Jay Singh	1822 -
65.	King Yadu Singh (Nongpok Chinglen Khomba)	1823 -
66.	King Raghav Singh	1823 - 1824
67.	King Nongchup Lamgaingamba (Badhra Singh)	1824 -
68.	King Gambhir Singh (Chinglen Nongdrenkhomba)	1825 - 1834
69.	King Chandrakirti (Ningthempishak)	1834 - 1844
70.	King Nara Singh	1844 - 1850
71.	King Debendra Singh	1850 -
72.	King Chandrakirti, KCSI	1850 - 1886
72.	King Surchandra	1886 - 1890
72.	King Kulachandra	1890 - 1891
73.	King Churachand Singh, KCSI	1891 - 1941
74.	King Bhodhachandra	1941 - 1955

The international community would note that not a single Indian (Hindustani) king had ever ruled Manipur either directly or indirectly. The Indian history is of no concern to the people of Manipur till 1949. This is corroborated by the history of India positively and invariably

1.2. The State formation was completed in the early Christian era, when as many as seven principalities amalgamated themselves to constitute the earliest Meitei State (Nagas, Kukis were Meitei Cognates), which territorially fluctuated but extended beyond the present territory. The earliest settlers were the ancient Meiteis of the present valley area, Meitei cognates re-named by British as the Nagas and Kuki-Chins. The Nagas and Kuki-Chins are proto-Meiteis. The early Meitei State which is presently known as Manipur is a State of three major ethnic group of Mongolian race, namely, (i) the Meitei (valley Manipuri), Hill Manipuris re-christened by the colonial British as (ii) the Nagas and (iii) the Kuki-Chins. There was a centralised Constitutional Government since 429 AD, according to a renowned Meitei Scholar late Oinam Bhogeswar, whose works are found in plenty in Manipuri, i.e., Meitei language. The history of Manipur had been documented in a royal chronicle known as "Cheitharol Kumbaba" (33 AD to 1950 AD). The English translation is available in the Indian Office Library, London, and other Archives of the United Kingdom, which still preserve a large number of historical documents, treaties and other official records pertaining to the relation of the State of Manipur with the British Government since 1762 AD till 1949 AD. These materials, including local and native, may be closely examined as historical records by the De-colonisation Committee in order to form an objective and positive view of the people of the State of Manipur for at least three centuries so that the official and colonial perspectives of the Administrative Power of the Indian State alone may not form the sole basis for any objective appraisal. Early and medieval Indian history has never included present Manipur as its component till India's illegal annexation of Manipur in 1949. Even the Indian colonial historians admit this.

1.3. A centralised Constitutional Government had been functioning in the early State of Manipur invariably from 1100 AD, when the Meitei monarch Loiyumba had promulgated a political Constitution known as "Loiyumba Shinyen", the translation of which is enclosed herewith as an Annexure (Annexure No. I). Several European states did not emerge as stable entities at that point of time.

1.4. The aforesaid constitutional Government continued from 1100 AD till the international conflict arose in between the Manipuris and the Burmese in the 18th and 19th centuries AD, when the Manipuri king Pamheiba alias Garibaniwaj invaded Burma in the 18th century several times with as many as 30,000 warriors. A large part of the Manipur territory was later ceded by the colonial power of India to Burma (now Myanmar) - the Kabo (or Kabow) Valley, that had been a part of the Manipur Territory till the early part of the 19th century. The British gave annual revenue of Rs.5000/- to the Government of Manipur on behalf of the Burmese till Indian occupation of Manipur in 1949. The Government of India, which had annexed Manipur in 1949 unlawfully and unconstitutionally, ceded the Kabo valley to Burma (present Myanmar) after signing a secret Indo-Burma Treaty in 1953. The provision of the secret treaty are not yet made known to the people of Manipur as well as to the citizens of India. The colonial government of India holds up "Right to information" to the occupied territory and people of Manipur on this account. The colonial government operates like a Mafia on Kabo Valley.

1.5. After Burmese military occupation of Manipur for seven years in the period from 1819 to 1825, complete sovereignty was restored to Manipur following a bilateral treaty Treaty of Yandaboo, signed in 1826 in between the British Crown representative and the representative of the Burmese Government. By this treaty, the Burmese power in Asia and the imperial colonial power of the British Crown had accorded multilateral international recognition to the independent and sovereignty of the early State of Manipur. In 1835, the British set-up in Manipur a Political Agency, which was supposedly a Consulate in that period and it continued for a long time. The British power and the Manipur power had continued the friendly relationship by mutually opening Political Agency. The Manipur Power opened the Political Agency of Manipur in the British Territory at Lakhimpur (Cachar) as well as at Calcutta. The Anglo-Manipuri friendship was established for the first time in 1762, when a treaty had been signed between the representative of Maharajah Jay Singh (alias) Bhagyachandra of Manipur and Mr. Harry Verelst, Chief of the Chittagong Factory on behalf of the British Crown on the 14th September, 1762 (Annexure No. II). The treaty is a testimony to the independent, sovereign political Status of Manipur (known to British as Meckley). The basic parameters of an independent state, as stipulated by the Montevido Convention, 1933, viz., (a) territory, (b) population, (c) government and (d) capacity to maintain external relations, had been found in the State of Manipur. Manipur had, therefore, been recognised as sovereign state in as early as 1762 AD. The present Indian state did not exist in 1762.

1.6. There was mutually protective Anglo-Manipuri arrangement in between the Manipur Power when the British Viceroy had a summit meeting with Maharaja Chadrakirti of Manipur in August, 1874. By this arrangement in between the Manipur and the British powers, both the contracting parties had agreed to assist one another in the mutual and reciprocal interests of both the powers. The relationship broke down in 1891 March, when the aggressive British army had initially been defeated by the Manipuri army on 24.3.1891 and the Manipuri army had finally been defeated on 25 April, 1891. However, the British Queen did not annex Manipur to her empire (Annexure III). At her worst situation, Manipur remained an international protectorate.

1.7. Subsequently, the British had military occupation in the State of Manipur till 1907 by totally disarming the Manipuris to the last man. However, the Queen did not annex the State of Manipur as part of the British Colony to the British territory for the several reasons (Annexure

No. III). The British Parliamentary Proceedings on the subject would be found in the Hansards of U.K. in June and July 1891. Even after the defeat of Manipur, it had not been annexed to or colonised by the British although the British Crown considerably interfered in the local administration of Manipur by assuming the latter as an International Protectorate. Manipur was not a part of India in this period.

1.8. From the Manipuri perception, it was a political intervention in Manipur's political sovereignty. Manipur had been labelled as a Native State in the sub-continent of India from the British perspective. Thereafter, in fact, from the Manipur perspective, Manipur had never been a constituent of India, as this Asian State of Mongolian race and Mongolian population is completely different from the other so-called Native States of the Indian sub-continent, which are truly the realm of the Aryan and Dravidian races. Further, the leaders of the Indian freedom fighters and the Congress Party, led by Aryan leaders like M.K.Gandhi, J.L.Nehru and Sardar Patel had consistently defined the Native States of India as a blood- relation State, which means an Aryan or a Dravidian State. Since, Manipur is a Mongolian State, it had never been a part of Ancient State of the present British-created India. It is quite clear that no Mongolian State could ever be considered as a constituent State of the Aryan and Dravidian peoples, who are racially integrated. The Manipuris are alien race, subjugated, occupied and oppressed by the foreign Indian rulers. The colonial officials of India made attempts to dilute the independence of Manipur by citing her as one of the 560 native states.

II. The Manipur People – A PEOPLE

2.01. The 2 million indigenous Manipur people comprising of 31 population groups (clans) speaking Tibeto-Burman or, Sino-Tibetan language having their common pedigree from a common Mongolian ancestor constitutes a PEOPLE or, nation absolutely distinguishable from the Indian or, the MAYANGS as they are so known to the indigenous Manipur people - the Manipuri people in a composite-territorial sense.

2.02. The indigenous Manipur people being the first settlers or, autochthones in the present territorial state, presently occupied by the Indian colonial regime and her occupation army, had organised their own history and nation-state since 33 AD, independent of the historical experience of Indians.

2.03. No pre, proto-history, ancient and medieval history of India including broad-based works of history written by India's first prime minister Jawaharlal Nehru viz., Glimpses of World History, Discovery of India, Autobiography, have mentioned Manipur and her indigenous people even once. Even the history books, re-constructed with a view to incorporating India's recent illegal territorial acquisitions and pre-1949 Maps included in the text books do not include Manipur. This gives testimony to the self-evident fact of Manipur people being alien, dependent and foreign to the Indian People.

2.04. The royal chronicle of Manipur—"CHEITHAROL KUMBABA", which had recorded the genealogy of Manipur Kings since 33 AD and proto-history of Manipur as recorded in "KANGBALOL"—which had noted the first proto-historical King Kangba of the then Manipur, had not mentioned any historical ties of Manipur with India. The historical records of neighbouring countries like Tibet or, Burma (Myanmar) have invariably corroborated the absence of Manipur—India historical ties, if any.

2.05. None of the Indian kings—Bharat, Ashoka, Chandragupta, Akbar to the last Indian emperor Bahadur Shah had any links with Manipur, let alone their temporary sway and administration. The British crown who ruled India since 1858, in similar tradition, did not rule Manipur till the lapse of British intervention or Paramountcy in 1947. Manipur had remained an international protectorate of the British till 1947.

2.06. The native states of India save Manipur had been the successors to the Sikh, Hindu or, Maratha empires, notwithstanding the British consideration and treatment of Manipur like any other Indian states.

2.07. The status of the Manipur people as a 'PEOPLE' is decided by the following criteria: *Firstly,* the indigenous Manipur people being Mongolians are racially different from the Indian who are Aryan-Dravidians. Dr. Sunitikumar Chatterjee, the most renowned Indologist in his major work—'Kirata Jana Krti' admits this distinction. *Secondly,* Dr. Grierson in his most authoritative volumes of the Linguistic Survey of India, had recorded that the Manipur people are speakers of Tibeto-Burman language, unlike the Indians. *Thirdly,* as corroborated by all historical accounts of both Manipur and India, the people of these two countries had been distinctive, different and alien to each other in the last several centuries. *Fourthly,* Manipur state had remained independent of India till the latter had unlawfully and coercively annexed the former. *Fifthly,* the Manipur indigenous people have been subjugated, dominated and oppressed by an alien, foreign government of India.

2.08. Following the unlawful Indian annexation of Manipur, the demographic composition of Manipur has been dramatically altered during the half-a century old foreign, Indian occupation of Manipur. No better testimony could be addressed to this population grafting issue than by what the government of Manipur admitted in 1984 corroborated by the government of India's occasional statements on the subject. Subsequently, the pre-dominantly Mongolian population of the state has been considerably altered.

2.09. The Manipur people as a 'PEOPLE' had not been consulted at the time of Indian annexation of Manipur in 1949 (see Annexation *infra*). This denial of popular consultation gives evidence of the Indian colonial behaviour.

2.10. The Manipur people, who had not exercised their inalienable right to self-determination in 1949 has not abdicated this right in any sense of the term. This right of a people has to be exercised as yet.

2.11. The government of India is run by the executive constituted by a President, a Union Cabinet of about 50 ministers, the Indian army led by hundreds of generals, an apex court - the Supreme Court of India and several creatures of the Constitution. No Manipur people had ever been inducted into these top echelons of power during the last half-a century. In a parliament of 793 Members of Parliament, only three members hail from Manipur. Besides the local government and assembly have been held so as to masquerade a representative form of government at the local, state level. Similar elections have been held in East Timor also by Indonesian government. Manipur is a *de facto* non-self-governing territory since the Indian annexation in 1949 and the Manipur indigenous people are non-self-governing people.

2.12. However, the state-of-the art colonial propaganda has successfully projected the non-self-governing people and territory of Manipur as one having a fully representative form of government and internal democracy, by stating that local elections are being held periodically, whereas, these farcical colonial elections, processed under the nose of the world's third largest army institutionalising large-scale corruption and bribery have not reflected the genuine wishes and aspirations of a people, let alone a plebiscite or referendum. 3,000 Indian dailies and powerful electronic multi-media cover-up the genuine aspirations of the non-self-governing indigenous people of Manipur. The Indian Colonial machinery has successfully divided Manipuri People into Meiteis, Nagas, Kukis so and soforth, thereby encouraging balkanisation of the 2000-year-old territorial integrity of Manipur, whereas the boundary of Manipur can never be disturbed or altered to the prejudice of Manipur under 'UTI POSSIDETIS JURIS' rule of International Law, that has been recurrently affirmed by the International Court of Justice.

2.13. The colonial, non-self-governing status of Manipur people would remain unredressed as such, unless the UN includes Manipur in the mandate for de-colonisation by incorporating her in the list of non-self-governing people, through the good offices of the Special Committee on De-colonisation and the Fourth Committee of the UN General Assembly. The contemporary development of International Law has to take the publicists seriously. Jorri Duursman in his work—"Fragmentation and the international relations of Micro-States" observes - "Peoples who find themselves in similar circumstances as colonies will enjoy a complete right of self-determination even if they are not specifically mentioned in the list of Non-Self-Governing or Trust Territories." (Cambridge University Press, 1996 ISBN 0 521 56360 7, page 83).

2.14. The UN Declaration on Principles of International Law concerning Friendly Relations and Co-operation among state, 24 October 1970 (UN GA Resolution 2625 para. 6) provides that

"6. The territory of a colony or other Non-Self-Governing Territory has, under the Charter, a status separate and distinct status under the Charter shall exist until the people of the colony or Non-Self-Governing Territory have exercised their right of self-determination in accordance with the Charter, and particularly its purposes and principles."

The above-mentioned principle is applicable to Manipur, which is a *de facto* colony or, Non-Self-Governing territory of colonial power—India. The UN and its members have the obligation to de-colonise Manipur either by enlarging or, modifying its mandate or, by way of appropriate intervention in order to eradicate colonialism in its wholeness.

2.15. The UN shall be performing its Charter obligations, provided it sends a visiting or fact-finding mission to Manipur on a war-footing, before it takes a decision on this petition and a decision could be taken after giving a full hearing to both the colonised people and the metropolitan colonising power—India.

2.16. The government of India, on her own had accepted that the word "Peoples" applies to a large compact group, who made a conscious demand for the right of self-determination (see UN Doc. E/CN.4/SR. 2256 (1952)p.5). The 2 million-strong indigenous Manipur people in their compactness within the territory of Manipur, invariably constitute the 'People', as defined by India. The government of India should, therefore, initiate the process of self-determination (both internal and external) for the indigenous Manipur People before 2000 AD.

III. Military Siege and Illegal Annexation

3.01. Manipur King Maharajah Bodhachandra Singh had acceded only three subjects of defence, external affairs and communications to the then dominion of India as per the agreement or treaty signed on 11.8.1947. It was preceded by an earlier agreement, known as the Standstill Agreement.

The agreement was signed by the Manipur Maharaja with a political entity—pre-independent India which did not have treaty-making power as on 11.8.1947 and as such the validity of the Accession Treaty is doubtful and questionable since India became legally independent and sovereign only on 15.8.1947, following the Indian Independence Act, 1947. Manipur became independent as per Section 7(1)(b) of the Indian Independence Act, 1947 (Annexure No. IV). By a proviso of Section 7(1)(b) and (c) of the aforesaid Act, whatever prejudicial relation Manipur had with the British Government before independence had been denounced and repudiated at the time, when Manipur adopted her own 1947 Constitution for installing a popular democratic government of the state with a constitutional monarch, as titular figurehead. The promulgation of the Manipur State Constitution Act, 1947 (Annexure No. V) and the Indian Independence Act, 1947, had washed out the obligation if any arising out of the Instrument of Accession. Manipur state has not been bound by the agreement accordingly.

3.02. In a number of Privy Purse cases and similar other cases, the Supreme Court of India had closely examined the political status of the native States of India in the pre-1947, 1947 and post-1947 periods before their merger to India. It had consistently as well as categorically held and decided in its rulings given since 1954 till 1993 that the Native State is fully independent and sovereign in 1947 during the relevant period (Annexure No. VI). Therefore, it is evidently clear and irrefutable that Manipur, which was considered as native State even from the British perspective, had become fully independent and sovereign on and from 15.8.1947. Further, its political status was an independent and sovereign ancient Asian State, which retained its independent and sovereign political status till 14.10.1949, although it did not join the United Nations. Being a land-locked, primitive state, the rulers lacked the information for seeking access to the UN.

3.03. As per the UN GA Resolution 2625 of 1970, the Right to Self-determination can be exercised by a people, who had reached a certain level of awareness and as such, the people of Manipur lacked the primary awareness—qualification to exercise their right to Self-determination in 1947-1949, at the time when Indian colonial power laid the trappings for military siege, occupation and annexation of Manipur in 1949. The signing of the Instrument of Accession by the king of Manipur and subsequent treacherous trappings had deprived the people of Manipur to exercise the right to self-determination in 1947-1949. But for the geographical and geo-political isolation, Manipur should not miss the opportunity of seeking UN membership in 1947. This basic right cannot be extinguished either as it had not been exercised in the past.

3.04. The independence and sovereignty of Manipur had been strengthened, when Manipur adopted her own political constitution, namely, the 'Manipur State Constitution Act, 1947' (Annexure No. V). And an elected popular and responsible Government had been installed in the form of Manipur Legislative Assembly (read as Parliament), constituted by 53 members, duly elected by universal adult-franchise and a council of Ministers to aid and advise the Maharajah as the constitutional head had also been installed. As per the basic parameters of the Montevido Convention, 1933 that qualifies a state, Manipur constituted an independent State in 1947 till 1949.

3.05. The illegal annexation of Manipur by India on 15 October 1949 has been a carefully drawn-out plan, measured by stages.

Chronology of Illegal Annexation

Annexation of Manipur

1947	
1. 19 April	Nehru ultimatum to States - Threats with hostility.
2. 15 May	Manipur Draft Constitution ready.
3. 20 May	British Cabinet resolution-State to be fully independent.
3.a. 2 June	Nehru-Mountbatten's Secret Revised Plan.
4. 3 June	Mountbatten's Negative attitude to the States.
5. 15 June	AICC stand: State's sovereignty lies with State people.
6. 17 June	Jinnah categorical: States to be independent, sovereign.
7. 25 June	Interim Cabinet accepts state department creation.
8. 1 July	Manipur King (Maharajah) becomes nominal figurehead.
9. 2 July	Assam-Manipur agreement: Indian agent to stay in Imphal.
10. 2 July	Secretary of State Listowell: States not subject to British Parliamentary legislation.
11. 5 July	Patel on Blood theory, all knit by bond of blood possibly Aryan-Dravidian blood theory (?) of State.
12. 5 July	Gandhi to Mountbatten: States should not be independent. Gandhi possibly wants Indian empire (not British).
13. 10 July	Indian Independence Act, 1947: British suzerainty over States in Indian continent lapses.

14. 25 July	Mountbatten officially declares States' independence.
15. 26 July	MANIPUR CONSTITUTION ADOPTED.
16. 28 July	Mountbatten reception to Rulers (Lunch on August 1): diplomatically pressurizes for Indian Dominion (His ambition to be India's Governor General).
17. 31 July	States Negotiating Committee approves 2 agreement drafts.
18. 8 August	Mountbatten reports to Listowell: States remain independent save three subjects - States not committed to Indian Constitution or, Govt. of India Act, 1935 etc.
19. 9 August	Listowell approves Mountbatten's 25 July proclamation.
20. 10 August	Manipur King directly takes over hill administration.
21. 11 August	King signs Standstill Agreement and Instrument of Accession: Under clause 7 & 8, Manipur's independence retained in the escape clause (cf. 5 April 1946 meeting of Nikhil Manipur Mahasabha & MPM., Reso. 6 part II, Manipur to be independent - R.K. Bhubon in Chair).
22. 14 August	King swears in the Interim Council: Manipur, proclaimed independent.
23. 15 August	King hoists PAKHANGBA FLAG in Council hall, Paramountcy, cleared in Manipur.
24. 28 August	King reiterates - Manipur is sovereign.
25. 6 Nov.	Indian Congress agent Debeshwar Sharma admits that Manipur is Sovereign: Sovereignty lies with Manipur people (categorical).
	1948
26. 1st Jan.	Deputy P.M. of India Sardar Patel visits Shillong for 3 days.
27. 2nd Jan.	Manipur King attends Rulers' meeting at Shillong, attended by Sardar Patel and States Ministry. - Later announced that Manipur becomes independent.
28. 28th Feb.	Hijam Irabot attends Calcutta Communist Conference with Asian revolutionaries - Adopts militant Chinese revolutionary line (later on practised too).
29. 18th April	Rawal Amar Singh takes Dewan's charge.
30. 25th May	Congress Election Manifesto: To abide by Manipur

	Constitution (Congress members - majority in the Constitution drafting Committee).
31. 26th May	Assam Prime Minister Gopinath Bordoloi pleads Autonomy for Manipur State.
32. 11th June-27rd July	Manipur Assembly Election - popular Government.
33. 23rd June-3rd July	Akbar Hydari's reconnaissance to annex Manipur.
34. 2nd Aug.	Akbar Hydari's letter to the King: Dewan simply watches TREATY RELATIONS' between two countries - Manipur and India. He is very categorical about the word Treaty like Kaju.
35. 22nd Aug.	Akbar Hydari abolishes Dominion agency.
36. 22nd Aug.	P.C. Ghosh preaches Purbanchal theory meeting organised by Tompok Congress.
37. 18th Sept.	Manipur Hills and Plains meeting opposes Ghosh proposal.
38. 20th Sept.	Tomal Congress writes to Indian Constituent Assembly: Manipur independent unit of India (probably in the sense of continent).
39. 21st Sept.	Manipur State Council declares Krishak Sabha and Praja Sangha unlawful organisations.
40. 21st Sept.	Hijam Irabot goes underground.
41. 18th Oct.	Manipur Legislative Assembly opened: popular sovereign government operates.
42. 26th Nov.	Prajashanti led - government (non-Congress) sworn in; Insignificant Congress minority propagates for Indian annexation of Manipur: Annexation would nullify unlawfully the Manipur Constitution, they themselves drafted in the committee.
43. 29th Nov.	Priyobarta holds C.M. post plus Dewanship.
	1949
44. 10th Mar.	Assembly Question Number 21 by L. Achou about Government's knowledge of the information about Manipur's Merger with India.
45. 22nd Mar.	Assam Governor Shri Prakasa discusses with King about Manipur Communist insurgency: Rustomji Chatterjee at Imphal.
46. 14th April	Indian Government asks King to transfer all power to Dewan (an unconstitutional, parallel centre in power).

47. 16th April	King appoints Major General Amar Singh as Dewan.
48. 5th June	Manipur Socialist Party Meeting urges for referendum on Manipur-India relation.
49. 25th June	Prakasa secret Memo. to King - India does not recognise Manipur State Council and the elected assembly (popular sovereign).
50. 26th July	Congress bulletin 4: Indian Congress backs Manipur Congress-slogan to dethrone the Constitutional figurehead - King.
51. 27th July	Hill M.L.As oppose annexation of Manipur by India.
52. 29th July	Hill M.L.As Against annexation of Manipur by India.
53. 3rd Aug.	Public meeting resolution to India's Prime Minister, Manipur cannot be merged with India.
54. 15th Aug.	4,000 Congressmen celebrate Independence day and Student's Federation hoists black flag. Ex. Minister Dr. Leiren Hoists black flag.
55. 25th Aug.	Ruling Manipur M.L.As against annexation of Manipur, Meeting resolution to Deputy Prime Minister, India not to annex Manipur to his country.
56. 7th Sept.	Shri Prakasa Telegrammes King to discuss 'affairs of State' at Shillong.
57. 8th Sept.	Young Socialist League Meeting opposes annexation.
58. 13th Sept.	Bhagyabati Patrica hints annexation.
59. 14th Sept.	Speaker T. S. Tiang Kham on issue of annexation.
60. 15th Sept.	Maharaja leaves Imphal for Shillong.
61. 17th Sept.	King reaches Shillong.
62. 18th-19th Sept.	King communicates to Indian agent at Shillong that he lacks capacity to enter into treaty, as all political powers have been lawfully transferred to people.
63. 18th Sept.	Shri Prakasa telegrammes to Patel and V.P. Menon: Manipur Maharajah detained under regulation III & 'ANY OTHER MEANS' (code language of house arrest of King under military siege) - King as captive, mental torture and coercion by Indian forces.
64. 18th Sept.	P.S. to King writes to Shillong S.P. to withdraw forces encircling Manipur King - siege continues - Maharajah's all communication lines, snapped.

	Literally, he was a captive and prisoner.
65. 20th Sept.	Psychic oppression and siege continues on the King.
66. 21st Sept.	King, coerced under duress to sign annexation treaty.
67. 21st Sept.	Bhagyabati Patrica - Manipur public opinion: Manipur cannot be subjugated and made subservient to a foreign nation (India).
68. 25th Sept.	Maharajah leaves Shillong.
69. 15th Oct.	Mr. Velody, State Ministry of India occupies Manipur; Congress celebrates the loss of their motherland. Major General Amar Singh takes over Manipur against peoples' will.
70. 15th Oct.	Gazette of India, Ministry of State, Notification No. 219 dated 15th October 1949 order to dissolve popular Ministry and the elected Manipur Legislative Assembly. (suspended sovereignty).

3.06. The Manipur king Maharajah Bodhachandra Singh had been kept under Regulation III and "any other means" which empowered military siege, arrest and captivity of Manipur King by the Indian army at Shillong from the 17th to the 21st September, 1949. Sri Prakasa, Governor of Assam sent the following Telegram to Sardar Patel, Deputy Prime Minister of India describing the abduction and captivity of Manipur king for coercing him to sign the Manipur Annexation agreement, 1949:

"... HH (sic. Manipur king) must not under any circumstances be allowed to return to Manipur with his advisors and I have accordingly instructed police to detain here his party if they attempt to return before signing of agreement (sic. 1949 Merger Agreement).

Please telegraph immediately repeat immediately authority for detention of HH and advisors under Regulation III (sic. abduction and kidnapping of the king by foreign Indian security forces) or by whatever other means you consider might be appropriate.

Have already warned sub-area to be prepared for any eventuality (sic. covert military aggression and coup) in Manipur. Grateful for further instructions. Ends."

The further instructions as cited above are undoubtedly mandate for invasion in Manipur and coup of the power-centre of the sovereign state of Manipur. Orders of invasion and aggression are not yet made public. The appropriate committee of the UN should seek all the comprehensive documents of the invasion of Manipur by the Indian invading army. The Defence Ministry and the External Affairs Ministry of India classify the aggression as top secret.

3.07. The Manipur Maharajah in captivity of the enemy was physically and mentally forced to sign the Manipur Merger Agreement on 21.9.1949 under duress and coercion (Annexure No. VII). The Manipur Maharajah had formally communicated to the representative of the Government of India at Shillong that he was no longer functioning as a plenipotentiary of Manipur, since the political power had been totally transferred to the people of Manipur. The Maharajah being a constitutional monarch did not have any power under the Cabinet system of government to sign any effective and valid agreement or treaty with the foreign Government of India. In the past, the Government of India had interfered in the Manipur Administration by forcing the Manipur Maharajah to appoint one Major General Rawal Amar of the colonial Indian army as a Dewan of the State, which post had been manifestly extraneous and unconstitutional, as per the provisions of the Manipur State Constitution Act, 1947. These interventions are precursor to the Indian aggression in Manipur in 1949.

3.08. The Government of India had incited and instigated the so-called Manipur Congressmen the Aryan fifth columnists in Manipur, to persuade and press the Manipur Administration to merge the State of Manipur with India. However, the majority of the people's representatives of the 53 members Member Assembly (read Parliament) had opposed Indian annexation of Manipur, while only 13 Congress Deputies (members) who had been in the microscopic minority welcomed it. Besides, the people of Manipur in general had opposed the annexation by holding public meetings on 3.8.1949, 25.8.1949, 8.9.1949, 14.10.1996 and on several occasions till date. The forcible annexation of the sovereign State of Manipur by the foreign Indian administration has been null and void under both the customary International Law and the Vienna Convention of Treaties, 1969 vide its article nos. 49, 51 and 52 which render treaty reached by fraud and coercion as void. The Indian annexation of Manipur in 1949 is a blatant violation of article 2(4) of the UN Charter, the UN GA Resolution 2625 of 1970 and other norms of state practices of that period.

3.09. The popular resistance to India's annexation of Manipur State had been rendered by the militant guerillas even before Manipur was subsequently annexed. The Communist Party of Manipur in that period had maintained ties with the Communist Parties of Burma (now Myanmar) and also with her Indian counterpart. It had the militant upsurge against the Indian colonialism since 1949 onwards till 1950-51; however, the colossal Indian occupation army suppressed the movement by repressive means for half a century. Notwithstanding the gagging of the Indian media and ignorance of the world Christian media, Manipur National Liberation Movements had been pro-active in 1950-51, 1963, 1964, 1969, 1978 onwards unremittingly decades before Western Sahara, East Timor, Northern Ireland, Kosovo sparked off.

IV. National Liberation Movement–Genesis

4.01. Subsequently after the Manipuri armed struggle in 1949 and 1950 against Indian colonialism and occupation, the Manipur Nationalist Party in the 1950s had demanded in public the revocation of the Manipur Merger Agreement with India. Several representatives of various parties including Shri Yangmaso Saiza, a Manipuri Tangkhul from Ukhrul district of Manipur, who later became Chief Minister of Manipur, resisted the annexation of Manipur. Even after the Indian annexation of Manipur, popular movements have ceaselessly continued. Although the methods of protests had been partly democratic and partly militant, in the later 1960s, national liberation movement had turned out pro-active in Manipur to free Manipur from Indian subjugation and colonisation. The Manipur National Liberation Movement in 1960s had been a precursor of the world-wide de-colonisation movements that liberated a hundred independent States of the world. The UN took notice of European colonisation and ignored Indian colonisation.

4.02. In late 1960s, National Liberation Movement of Manipur and militant resistance had been started by the Meetei State Committee that militarily resisted the Indian forces. It was closely followed by the Revolutionary Government of Manipur (RGM). The nucleus of a sister liberation struggle had been seeded in 1964. After the dismantling and disbandment of the RGM, the Revolutionary People's Front (RPF, the political wing of the People's Liberation Army of Manipur) was formed on 25 February 1979 and the PLA started operating for the liberation of Manipur from the Indian occupation army and Indian colonialism along with several sister organisations. In 1978, there had been PLA's full scale armed resistance all over the State against the Indian occupation army after sending publicity materials - 'DAWN' to all embassies of the world. Since then, the Manipur freedom fighters unremittingly opposed militarily the Indian occupation army. Several hundreds of PLA freedom - fighters have laid down their lives to liberate their motherland.

4.03. Professor Emeritus V.V. Rao of the University of Gauhati in his books on the North-Eastern India, has recorded that the PLA has the broad vision encompassing the interest of all the colonised, subjugated people elsewhere, beyond the contours of Manipur. Inspite of the PLA's best efforts to render the Manipur national question and national liberation, an international agenda of the world community by enlightening all the embassies of the countries, which received series of volumes of - "DAWN" publication, the members of the UN have failed to raise the issue of Manipur National Liberation on the floor of the General Assembly or, the Security Council of the United Nations. Eradication of colonialism by the UN. by 2000 AD shall not be completed, therefore, without listing the colonialism of Manipur in the UN agenda, which has been due since the UN members individually took note of the issue from the "DAWN" in 1978. The UN should have listed East Timor and Manipur in the same slot of colonised states or, people before two decades. Several national daily papers of Indian colonialism, however, flashed the international attention, as sought by PLA through all the embassies. The national liberation movement of Manipur has been consistently opposing the colonial Government of India on political terms and had been struggling against the occupation army of India on military terms since the time of the Indian annexation of Manipur in 1949 till today. The PLA's armed resistance against the Indian occupation was contemporaries with FRETLIN's resistance in East Timor and POLISARIO's resistance in Western Sahara. The UN selectively took up similar cases by shelving de-colonisation of Manipur in the cold freeze. Ironically, the UN discriminates Indian colonialism against European colonialism.

4.04. Very few liberation movements in the world have been left outside the closest attention of the UN and her members except the half-century old National Liberation Movement of Manipur. The UN objective of eradicating colonialism by 2000 AD would remain a futility without de-colonising Manipur and her neighbourhood colonies of India like Assam, Nagaland and Tripura. The colonial government of India had permanently perpetuated colonialism of Manipur by proclaiming the national liberation movements including the armed struggle triggered off by the PLA (RPF) since 1978 as unlawful organisation under the Prevention of Unlawful Activities Act, 1967 and suppressing the human rights since 1958 by invoking the draconian, black Law the Armed Forces (Special) Powers Act, 1958 (amended in 1972), the Punjab Security of State Act, 1953, the Terrorists and Disruptive Activities Prevention Act, 1985 and the National Security Act, among other equally repressive laws. Absolutely in self-defence and self-preservation, the occupation army is resisted by the movement.

4.05. The colonial government of India has extrajudicially liquidated, tortured, molested, raped, maimed, injured thousands of Manipuris on the hills (Manipuri Tangkhuls, Mao, Kukis etc.) and Manipuri in the valley (Meiteis etc.) and destroyed properties worth crores annually. For adult population of 9 lakh Manipuris (in 19 lakh population), Indian security forces numbering about 90, 000 are put into repressive service for colonial occupation. 30,000 Manipuri youths are drug/AIDS infected as a result of counter-insurgency approach of the colonialism.

V. Socio-Economic and Political Colonisation

5.01. The people of Manipur have been deprived of their inalienable birth-right to determine their political and socio-economic status on their own due to Indian colonial process, subjugation, alien and racist national oppression. They have been deprived of their inalienable right to exploit their natural resources as per their self-determination and this right has to be restored to them. Following the ICJ verdict, 1995 on Timor Gap Treaty, it is a criminal wrong for India to usurp the natural resources of Manipur. They have to exercise their inalienable right to self-determination for their permanent sovereignty over their natural resources, biomass, water-bodies, fauna and flora, among others.

5.02. The pre-dominantly Mongolian population of Manipur has been subjugated by the Indian racist and colonial regime which represents only the blue blood of the Aryan and Dravidian races (Annex No. VIII, Indian Party Representatives and Manipur Peoples, Photo). The administering power, i.e., the Indian colonial regime has never appointed any indigenous people of Manipur who are of Mongolian origin to any important position whatsoever in the Indian colonial regime. The people of Mongolian origin are treated as subjects and subjugated race only to be ruled by the occupation army. Since 1949 onwards till today, not a single day has ever passed in Manipur without the repressive measures taken by the Indian colonial army by torturing, insulting or extra-judicially murdering the indigenous people of Manipur. As cited above, a number of repressive laws or laws of legitimizing State Terrorism including the Armed Forces (Special) Powers Act, 1958, the Terrorist and Disruptive Activities (Prevention) Act, 1987 and several other draconian laws have been systematically introduced and enforced in the State of Manipur in order to subjugate the people of Manipur and incapacitate them from determining their own political destiny (Annexure No. IX). The UN Human Rights Committee and global NGOs have denounced them as incompatible with the International Bill of Rights, 1966 to which the colonial government of India has been a party. The government of India is accountable for enacting laws incompatible with the Covenants, ratified by her.

5.03. Under Section 4 of the Armed Forces (Special) Powers Act, 1958, the Armed Forces of the Union of India have been empowered to kill anybody on suspicion or out of hatred without any judicial process. Besides, this has enormously encouraged the Indian Armed Forces to precipitate and heighten their extra-judicial torture and execution of the Mongolian people bordering on genocide of the Mongolian races in Manipur. Even the Supreme Court of India, upheld the black law by its judgement given on 27 November, 1997. Not a single Manipuri has been appointed to the Supreme Court in the last half a century of annexation. These judges are racists and chauvinists like their political mentors.

5.04. It may be added that the Aryan and Dravidian racists in the Indian colonial regime have been guided by sacred religious scriptures like the 'Manusmrity'. In all its chapters, it authorised Aryan and Dravidian racists, specially persons from high castes, to execute or torture women, infants and the races who are not of Dravidian or Aryan origin. The people of Manipur are not Hindu Sudras but Mongolians. From their in-built mental perspective, they cannot help but to conceive every people of Manipur as sub-Sudra, who is to be physically tortured and slaughtered. Hence, from the perspective of the Indian Colonial Army, whenever they physically execute any Mongolian people, they conscientiously assume that they have performed a sacred religious duty and rite to fulfil the scriptural mandate of their racist ancestors. It may be recalled that the 'Arthasastra' of Kautilya the equivalent of a military manual of colonial Blue books, gives religious sanctity to the suppression and wiping out of smaller nations and countries in order to establish Indian imperialism and colonialism. Therefore, the Indian Colonial Army and the Indian colonial political rulers have no alternative than cherishing a heritage of conquering smaller nations and physically executing people who are not of Aryan or Dravidian origin. The British Colonial Power, however, did not have such a transmitted mandate from their Bible. Indian Colonial regime and the Indian Colonial Army operated in such sophisticated and orchestrated way that the International community cannot easily understand or recognise the entire consequences of the overt and covert Indian colonialism, unless the UN despatches visiting missions to Manipur. The UN has not been successful to appoint a Special Human Rights Rapporteur for India, although one has been appointed for Myanmar.

5.05. The colonial development process and the colonial economy had not been helpful to the people of Manipur. Not a single major industry, much less an important establishment has ever been established in Manipur. Whereas several hundreds of crores of Rupees have been spent apparently on paper maintained for the record in order to refuel and recycle their colonial apparatus, quite a few families in Manipur are also used as colonial subsidiaries, the economic condition of the average people of Manipur specially those in the hill areas has not improved even up to the level of subsistence. People survive on grassroots in the Manipur hill areas because of colonial economic process. The Manipuri hillsmen and plainsmen are divided by the Presidential approval to a divisive law - the Manipur Land and Revenue Act, 1960 which debar plainsmen to seek access to Manipur hills. The apartheid has been created.

5.06. The colonial economy of Manipur has pushed down 68% of Manipur people below the Poverty line. Centre for Monitoring Indian Economy in 1992-93 indicated that whereas Indian state of Punjab has reached index of 205, Manipur's index is 71. As per the Asian Development Bank Report, 11 May, 1997, Manipur rice production in kg/hectare is 1400 (against Indian average of 1740), Road in 100 sq. km. in Manipur is 32.64 km (against Indian average of 62.82 km), Banking credit in Manipur is Rs. 44/- (Indian is Rs. 1722.11), p.c.i. of Manipur is Rs. 5,326/- (against Indian average of Rs. 6,929/-), Annual budget of Rs. 400+ crore is literally for the maintenance of 90,000 colonial Indian army, innumerable mercenaries, police, espionage, supporting pro-colonial families and half the budget allocation is not available due to colonial fiscal policy.

5.07. We have living testimony of the socio-cultural colonisation of the indigenous people of Manipur by the casteist and racist socio-cultural apparatus of India. Firstly, the captive market is at the hands of Hindustanis; Secondly, no industry has been set-up for attaining industrial growth; Thirdly, all the natural resources have been exploited by the colonial regime; Fourthly, Manipur survives on subsistence economy. Details will be presented to the UN Visiting Mission. Not a single watch, electronic industry has been set up in Manipur, let alone major and heavy industries.

5.08. In sum, the national liberation movements in Manipur have strongly endorsed the view that Manipur has socio-economically and politically been exploited by the Indian colonial regime beside the political and military subjugation of the people of Manipur since 1949 till today. Majority of the colonised Manipuris have to learn Hindi and baptised in colonial religion.

5.09. Proxy elections are conducted by spending crores of Indian Rupees in order to perpetuate colonialism through quislings, puppet regimes and fifth columnists under the proxy election process by way of misleading the illiterate electorate. The Indian colonial regime can in no way justify the electoral process whatsoever, since the people of Manipur cannot exercise their "independent political will" and resolve their destiny at the gunpoint of the massive, racist Indian colonial army and several thousands of mercenaries, subversives and spies. The colonial elections held in the mighty presence of occupation army, mercenaries and pouring crores of rupees for bribery have debarred the people to exercise their free will and no plebiscite on de-colonisation had ever been held. Alcoholics, drugs, heroin, brown sugar and narcotics are freely distributed to the voters in the colonial elections.

VI. On Continuation of the Sovereign State of Manipur

6.01. The sovereign State of Manipur continues to exist since the Christian era, despite unlawful, political and military occupation by a foreign colonial power-India. Therefore, India and her intervention in Manipur is a political process. The nature of the sovereign State of Manipur is represented as follows:

6.02. Firstly, the sovereign status of Manipur state had been recognised bilaterally, when Manipur entered the Anglo-Manipuri Friendship Treaty in 1762 AD (Annexure No. II). The international recognition is vital, as Montevido Convention, 1933 defined independent state as one capable of entering treaty relations.

6.03. Secondly, the political sovereign independence of Manipur had been officially recognised by both the Burmese Government and the British Government as per the provisions of the Yandaboo treaty, 1826 (Annexure No. X). The independent political status of Manipur has once again been re-affirmed in the 19th century.

6.04. Thirdly, after the military defeat of Manipur by the British army in 1891, the British Government did not annex Manipur to its empire (Annexure No. III); that itself gives testimony to the unremitting independence of Manipur. The debate on the independent political status of Manipur in the British Parliament for nearly one month in 1891 has been recorded in the Hansards. In 1891, Churachand was Manipur King and British official Maxwell ruled the country. The British transferred the charge of administration to Manipur King on 17 May 1907. In 1916, the British official became the President of Manipur Darbar under the supervision of the King. In 1931, Manipur opened direct external relations with British India. In 1941, Maharajah Bodhachandra had succeeded Maharajah Churachand. Since 1942, Manipur unlike India has been the theatre of the Second World War. On 26 July, 1946, Manipur established her constitutional government thereby reducing the Maharajah to a titular head. These constitutional developments re-established the sovereign, independent status of Manipur and the official independence was declared on 14-15, August, 1947.

6.05. Fourthly, despite the British and Indian interference in Manipur affairs, Manipur became fully independent and sovereign on 15.8.1947 vide Indian Independence Act, 1947 (Annexure No. IV, and Annexure No. VI Indian Supreme Court rulings, 1954 to 1993). Manipur has fully regained her full sovereignty, which had been intervened by the British Paramountcy that retained the former as international protectorate.

6.06. Fifthly, although Manipur had entered into the treaty known as the Instrument of Accession on 11.8.1947, Manipur did not transfer more than 3 subjects to the Dominion of India. The Instrument of Accession was signed on 11.8.1947 (Annexure No. XI) in between Manipur and Dominion of India. It had clearly given prerogative right to Manipur to retain her sovereignty and independence and terminate the Accession treaty unilaterally, as the treaty did not incorporate a termination clause, as required by customary International Law, that has been codified by the Vienna Convention in 1969 and the subsequent convention.

6.07. Sixth, Manipur State Constitution Act, 1947 (Annexure No. V) was in operation at the time of signing the Merger Agreement between the Manipur Maharajah (King) who lacked the capacity and authority to enter into any treaty with any power or, the representative of the Government of India on 21.9.1949, since he was not the plenipotentiary of the independent and sovereign state of Manipur of which he was only the constitutional head. The cabinet government that Manipur installed in 1948 after holding elections to the Manipur Assembly (read Parliament) had neither authorised the king to sign the 1949 treaty nor ratified the same after 21.9.1949. It may be noted that a valid agreement or, treaty could be signed or, acceded by the plenipotentiary of Manipur as a High contracting party with the Indian government after fulfilling the following conditions:

1. Empowerment by the Manipur Cabinet;
2. Signature by the Chief Minister (read Prime Minister);
3. Constitutional endorsement;
4. Ratification by the National Assembly (read Parliament);
5. Enactment of a municipal law on the accession of the treaty, as it is being done in Republic of India by now or, British Parliament;
6. Final endorsement by a popular referendum or, plebiscite in the event of altering the political status of the state.
7. The Merger Agreement of 1949 had been reached in blatant violation of these basic rules and therefore, it had been void *ab initio*.

6.08. Seventh, the people of Manipur had not deputed a genuine representative, duly elected by the people of Manipur to the then Constituent Assembly of India. Although from the Indian colonial perspective, a foreign national was considered as representative to the Constituent Assembly of India, who helped the illegal annexation. Any representation of Manipur people by a person of the colonial country professing to represent the people of Manipur is absolutely inconceivable, preposterous and accordingly null and void, as the foreign national lacked the capacity and jurisdiction. Hence, Manipur cannot be brought within the colonial constitutional framework of India, since it was not part of it. There has been no lawful representation of genuine representative of Manipuri people in the colonial Constitutional Assembly of India. Manipur people have not been a party to the Indian constitutional making process.

6.09. Eighth, no referendum or plebiscite of the people of Manipur had ever been held concerning the annexation or merger of Manipur to a foreign country the republic of India, whereas the annexation of Junagadh by imperial India in 1948-49 had been justified by three plebiscites held on the annexation of the former to the latter. Colonial rulers of India knew that Manipur people as a whole reject the merger with India.

6.10. Ninth, the installation of a colonial government on 15.10.1949 in the soil of Manipur did not repeal the Manipur State Constitution Act, 1947, although the colonial government without having any jurisdiction whatsoever had passed a colonial order under Notification no. 219-p. Gazette of India, Ministry of State, dated 15.10.1949. It illegally and unconstitutionally dissolved the popular Ministry as well as the popular Assembly (read Parliament) of Manipur, on the basis of an illegal Manipur Merger Agreement, 1949. Indian proximity - colonialism has gobbled up independent Manipur and the UN helplessly remained silent by giving a free-hand to Indian occupation army till today.

6.11. Tenth, there is widespread popular awareness among the people of Manipur that the Manipur Merger Agreement, 1949, as stated above is null and void and unconstitutional from the point of view of the Manipur State Constitution Act, 1947. Moreover, it is in the backdrop of contemporary norms of the International Law that the National Convention on the Manipur Merger Issue was convened from the 28th to the 29th October, 1993 in the capital city, Imphal. The Convention has unanimously resolved in plenum that the impugned Merger Agreement with India on 1949 is illegal and unconstitutional, considering the entire process and circumstances that led to the Manipur Merger Agreement (Annexure No. XII).

6.12. Eleventh, the UN Security Council in similar circumstances had proclaimed similar annexations illegal, void, and untenable. The Security Council declared annexation of Goa by India as illegal (vide S/5033, SCOR, 988th meeting, 18 December 1961). But no liberation movement ensued in Goa. It acted against Iraq under Security Council Resolution No. 660-678 for annexation of Kuwait in 1991. The UN declared annexation of East Timor and Western Sahara illegal. The UN precedents, contemporary International Law, *Jus Cogens* and Vienna Convention of Law of Treaty would clearly regard annexation of Manipur by India in 1949 after two years of the independence of Indian independence unjustified and illegal. The official stance of the colonial government of India that the illegal annexation has assumed finality is not only absurd, null and void but also unacceptable to the people of Manipur, who are yet to exercise their right to self-determination. The colonial Government has failed to justify her annexation of Manipur, under International Law.

6.13. Twelfth, considering the historical materials and the records, documents and treaties which are enclosed herewith, the sovereign and independent political status of Manipur, which had been continuing for at least 2,000 years has been dislocated by the Indian colonial Administration, and by the physical occupation of the Indian colonial army. The unlawful colonial occupation of Manipur shall have to be terminated by the Indian government at the earliest moment in adherence of the UN eradication of colonialism by 2000 AD. The UN is yet to oversee this process.

VII. Right to Self-Determination

7.01. It is significant to reiterate the absolute commitment of the United Nations to eradicate colonialism in all its forms and manifestations by 2000 AD and to put in record the emergence of 135 independent states in conformity with the global de-colonisation process that sparked off since 1960s and 1970s. The official deadline for eradication of colonialism remaining unaltered, colonialism will be sustained in proximity-colonies of India like Manipur, Nagaland, Assam, Tripura and Kashmir and nearly fifty other territories, many of which are incorporated in the list of 48 unrepresented peoples of the UNPO - the Hague based Unrepresented Nations and Peoples Organisation. These colonies will survive the 2000 AD UN deadline, unless the UN and its main organs initiate pro-active de-colonisation, as much as it did in 1960s and 1970s. The UN would not fulfil its objectives of total de-colonisation, in the event of sustaining the above colonies or, peoples who are yet to exercise their right to self-determination. India being a member of the UN De-colonisation Committee has to initiate de-colonisation of Manipur.

7.02. The Government of India has the treaty obligations to allow alien, dependent, subjugated and oppressed people like the Manipur people to exercise their inalienable right to self-determination, as the Government has rectified the ICCPR, 1966 and ICESCR, 1966, besides its being a regional power which facilitated national liberation and de-colonisation of several colonised peoples in the Third World. The UN Human Rights Committee in 1997, July has urged upon the Government of India to withdraw her reservation in respect of common article 1 of the ICCPR, 1966 and ICESCR, 1966. The government has to comply with this recommendation and report compliance by 2000 AD at the time of submitting the 4th periodic report to the UNHRC vide article 40 of the ICCPR, 1966.

7.03. Government of India's declaration in respect of her ratification of the ICCPR, 1966 on 10 April, 1979, is as follows:

ICCPR, Article 1

para 10. It has been the position of India ever since its independence that adherence to self-determination is co-existent with the principle of sovereign equality. The principle of domestic jurisdiction of state as enshrined in the United Nations Charter is to be equally respected.

para 11. In conformity with this position of principle on self-determination, India made the following declaration in 1979 at the time of its accession to the International Covenant on Civil and Political Rights:

> "With reference to article 1 of the International Covenant on Civil and Political Rights, the Government of the Republic of India declares that the words 'the right to self-determination' appearing (in this article) apply to people under foreign domination ...".

7.04. The Manipuri people, who had never constituted a part of Hindustan or India or, British India had been placed under Indian foreign domination in the event of the illegal annexation of Manipur in 1949. The caveat to the declaration makes room for according the right to self-determination to the people of Manipur. The Vienna World Conference on Human Rights, 1993 and the UN Human Rights Committee in July, 1997 have mandated the government of India to remove even this narrow caveat and accord the right to deserving people including the Manipuri people who had been sovereign for two millennia before Indian annexation. India's present stance[18] prevents the world wide de-colonisation process and hence, she owes an explanation for her defence of colonialism of Manipur.

7.05. India's Declaration[19] stipulated that "Declaration contains enunciation of certain basic principles". Paragraph 1 declares, "The subjection of peoples to alien subjugation, domination and exploitation constitutes a denial of fundamental human rights ...". The people of Manipur obviously falls into the Indian enunciation of alien subjugation and domination. The colonial government of India has to prove that Manipuris are not alien to Indians.

7.06. The people of Manipur, who are colonised by alien Indian administering power are people of non-self-governing territories as much as the East Timorese after Indonesian annexation in 1975 constitute people of non-self-governing territories. Indonesian elections had been held in East Timor since 1977, yet East Timor is recognised as non-self-governing territory by the United Nations. Similarly, colonial elections have been held in occupied Manipur by the Indian administering power without any prejudice to the sovereign political status of Manipur.

7.07. The ICJ in Portugal vs. Australia, 1995 has decided that East-Timorese have their *right to self-determination* erga omnes (against the whole community). Similarly, the people of Manipur have their *right to self-determination* erga omnes, notwithstanding India's preposterous prevarication against the colonised Manipuris.

VIII. Territorial Integrity

8.01. The colonial government of India defines in her 1950 Constitution, the territorial integrity of India in two places. Firstly, in the first schedule serial No.19, Manipur is defined as "The territory which immediately before the commencement of this constitution was being administered as if it were a Chief Commissioner's province under the name of Manipur".

8.02. The first schedule itself clearly and categorically records that the territorial State of Manipur preceded the Constitution of India. No other constitutional provision has more clearly given testimony to the illegal annexation of Manipur than this provision. Before Indian Commissioner had occupied Manipur, she remained independent till 1949.

8.03. Article 1 of the Constitution of India defines the territory of India as follows: (1) India, that is Bharat, shall be a union of states. (2) [The states and the territories thereof shall be as specified in the first Schedule]. (3) The territory of India shall comprise - (a) the territories of states; (b) the union territories specified in the First Schedule; and (c) such other territories as may be acquired.

8.04. The Constitution of India, being a colonial and imperial instrument imposed upon the occupied people of Manipur after the illegal annexation, lacks legal and constitutional validity in regard to the annexed, occupied state of Manipur. East Timor has also been annexed as the 27th province of Indonesia and Kuwait in 1990 as the 9th province of Iraq. The United Nations has denounced these illegal annexations, let alone the validity of the colonial Constitution. The territorial integrity of India cannot lawfully incorporate colonial, occupied territory of Manipur. Nor can it impair the territorial integrity of Manipur as it existed in 1947 under the uti Possidetis Juris rule of International Law.

8.05. The state sovereignty doctrine has been enunciated in articles 2(4) and 2(7) of the UN Charter as well as by the UN GA Resolution 2625, Declaration on Friendly Relations, 1970. The union government of India pleads that her territorial integrity would be impaired if Manipur would be allowed to secede from the Indian Union. The argument may be further strengthened by citing the prevention of disruption of the "national unity and the territorial integrity" of India, as it is understood after the adoption of the 1950 Constitution (see para.6 of the UN GA Resolution 1514(XV) of 14 December, 1960). This argument is fallacious and ridiculous. State practices have denounced similar claims made by Indian colonial administration.

8.06. The unity and territorial integrity as well as sovereignty of independent Manipur state has been impaired and terminated by the illegal Indian annexation of Manipur on 15 October, 1949. The government of India can never plead the illegally annexed territory of Manipur as her territorial integrity in the same way as the British failed to defend her 50 colonies as her territorial integrity. The para. 6 of the UN GA Resolution 1514(XV) of 14 December, 1960 should be understood in the genuine historical context of Manipur. The UN and the government of India are under obligation to accept Manipur as

> "Non-self-governing territory" in the same way as East Timor has been accepted. The union government of India should transmit information about Manipur to the UN under article 73(e) of the Charter. No judicious member of the UN should discriminate Manipur against East Timor.

IX. Aggression

9.01. The captivity of Manipur Maharajah at Shillong on 18 September, 1949 by the Security forces of India and the Indian military intrusion in the soil of Manipur state with the active connivance of the fifth communists and covert subversives, planted by the government of India deep in the Manipur administration constitute Indian aggression in Manipur. At present, nearly every hill-top in the hilly state of Manipur has been occupied by battle-ready Indian army.

9.02. All the available documents and records give eloquent testimony to the parameters of Indian aggression in Manipur. On 19 April, 1947, Nehru sent threatening ultimatum to states. By an agreement reached on 2 July, 1947, Indian agency had been allowed to stay in Manipur. On 5 July, 1947, Hindu dictator M.K. Gandhi allegedly a pacifist communicated to Lord Mountbatten that state should not be given independence. Indian agent Akbar Hydari had abolished dominion agency in Manipur on 22 August, 1948. On 14 April, 1949, the colonial government of India asked the Manipur king to transfer all powers to an Indian Dewan under immense pressure and coercion; and the king was forced to appoint on 16 April, 1949 one Indian colonial Major General Amar Singh as Dewan of Manipur. Assam Governor Shri Prakasa sent a memo. on 25 June, 1949 that India de-recognised the Manipur State Council and elected Manipur Assembly (read Parliament of Manipur). All the political institutions and municipal administration had been subverted by India's Assam Governor Shri Prakasa who also initiated the covert Indian aggression in Manipur.

9.03. After the covert aggression had been triggered off by the colonial Governor of Assam, Shri Prakasa in Manipur, the second stage of his aggression is use of Indian security forces to keep Manipur king in captivity at Shillong by inviting him for professedly harmless negotiation. The Indians in their 2 millennia history had perfected the state-of-art treachery of inviting kings and annexing their territory and even their most respected theocratic leader M.K. Gandhi stood for conquest of states. (Read Arthasastra of Kautilya for these tactics). On 18 September, 1949, Indian administration used force to keep Manipur king as captive. The private Secretary of the king wrote on the same day to withdraw the aggressive Indian forces, but they refused. The colonial government classifies the military details.

9.04. The United Nations should invite all the Government of India's records concerning Indian aggression in Manipur for the period 1947-1949 and can easily determine the facts in no time. 9.05. Manipur in 1949 had no obligations under the UN Charter, but the Indian Dominion, being a member of the UN since 1945 has Charter obligations not to use force against Manipur and also to honour the territorial integrity of independent Manipur. Article 2(4) of the Charter determines this responsibility:

> "All Members shall refrain in their international relations from the threat or use of force against the territorial integrity or political independence of any state, or in any manner inconsistent with the purposes of the United Nations".

9.06. The colonial government of India has further violated article 1 of the UN Charter by committing aggression and breach of peace. The national liberation movement is exercising its right to self-defence and self-preservation, without any prejudice to the genuine integrity of India.

9.07. The UN General Assembly in its Resolution 3314(1974) defines aggression in article 1: "Aggression is the use of armed force by a state (read India here) against the sovereignty, territorial integrity or political independence of another state, or in any other manner inconsistent with the Charter of the United Nations,...". Further, Indian military occupation and annexation of Manipur by use of Indian forces constitutes aggression under article 3 of the Resolution 3314(1974), regardless of declaration of war.

9.08. The UN GA Resolutions 2625(XXV), 1970 and 2734(1970) provide that no territorial acquisition resulting from the threat or use of force shall be recognised as legal. Hence, India's military occupation of Manipur since 1949 till date is illegal and creates no legitimate claims of India over the sovereignty of Manipur.

X. Illegal Annexation

10.01. As stated above in the context of aggression, Indian annexation of Manipur is illegal, null and void and unenforceable, notwithstanding the ongoing colonial occupation. (Please see para. 5.07 supra). The ICJ evolved the principle of non-annexation in South-West Africa case (1950, ICJ Reports, p. 132).

10.02. In the event of integrating Manipur to India, the freely expressed wishes of the people of Manipur should have been ascertained either by holding a referendum or plebiscite at the time of annexation. That did not happen at all in 1949 and the right of the Manipur people to self-determination had not been exercised in 1949 or, thereafter. This right has not been extinguished.

10.03. The principle IX of the UN GA Resolution 1514(XV) of 1960 provides that:

(a) The integrating territory should have an advanced stage of self-government with free political institutions, so that its peoples would have the capacity to make a responsible choice through informed and democratic processes.
(b) The integration should be the result of the freely expressed wishes of the Territory's peoples acting with full knowledge of the change in their status, their wishes having been expressed through informed and democratic processes impartially conducted and based on universal adult suffrage. The United Nations could, when it deems it necessary, supervise these processes.

10.04. Manipur did not have an advanced stage of self-government and the "freely expressed wishes" of the people of Manipur had not been ascertained by the colonial government of India at the time of annexation. Therefore, Indian annexation lacked legality. (Annexure No. XIII).

10.05. The colonial government of India and their advocates would occasionally trace historical argument by advancing a fallacious statement that Manipur while remaining under British paramountcy till 1947 had certain historical nexus with British India, which was under British imperialism. They might even argue that Manipur and Dominion of India became independent under a common Indian Independence Act, 1947. The absurdity of "historical ties" statement has been rejected by the International Court of Justice in its advisory opinion on Western Sahara. It may be noted very carefully that Indonesia's argument in favour of her annexation of East Timor has been rejected by the ICJ judgement in Portugal vs. Australia in 1995 and innumerable the UN General Assembly resolutions and resolutions of the Security Council since 1975. The UN and De-colonisation Committee have to apply the same standard to East Timor and Manipur on equal terms.

10.06. In 1976-77, the General Assembly of the United Nations by its Resolutions 31/53 and 32/34 rejected the Indonesian annexation of East Timor. The UN Security Council by Resolutions 384 (1975) and 389 (1976) while demanding the respect for the territorial integrity of East Timor categorically affirmed the right of the East Timorese to self-determination. Of late, the Special Committee on De-colonisation at its 1474th to 1477th meetings on 16 and 17 June, 1997 re-affirmed the earlier UN positions. The same principle is applicable in the case of Indian annexation of independent Manipur. The Security Council by its Resolutions 660-678 (1991) had rendered Iraqi annexation of Kuwait null and void. The same norms is applicable to Manipur.

Post-Occupationxi. Gross Human Rights Violations & Humanitarian Law

11.01. During India's repressive, colonial regime in Manipur, human rights violations have been massive, colossal, brutally de-humanizing and absolutely barbarian. Indian military occupation, compounded by the invocation of the world's most barbaric laws including the Armed Forces (Special) Powers Act, 1958 for half a century in both the hills and plains of Manipur and shielding the entire genocidal progroms from the glaze of independent international media by prohibiting any foreigner to step into Manipur under the *Restrictive Areas Permit Act* without the closest scrutiny of the Home Ministry of India, resulted to unprecedented state terrorism, repression and barbaric human rights violations. Ironically, execution of five Catholics in Northern Ireland is a news - even in the headlines of the global media, but daily execution by the state of India, of several dozens of civilians or freedom fighters in Manipur has not been accepted as newsworthy. Manipur had been shielded like Gulag

Archipelago from the outside world for half a century and therefore, the United Nations took action in favour of 8 lakh Christian East Timorese since 1975 but closed its eyes to 20 lakh non-Christian Manipuris' cause since 1949 till today. Even the super-powers had maintained double standards.

11.02. The government of India and her defence forces which are under obligations after government of India's accession to the Four Geneva Conventions, 1949 and subsequent enactment of the Geneva Conventions Act, 1961 by the Indian Parliament, to fully comply with the humanitarian laws, had consistently breached the humanitarian laws by way of committing relentless state repression on the unarmed civilians of Manipur and captured combatants or horse de combat of the Manipur National Liberation Movement. Even the ICRC has not been allowed to visit Manipur, since the Home Ministry refused to lid off the Auschwitz iron curtain of Manipur. No force-commander nor even a single military General has ever been punished for the breach of the Geneva Conventions, 1949 or, the Geneva Conventions Act, 1961 passed by the Indian Parliament. No other testimony could be more appropriate than citing the Government of India's refusal to sign, accede and ratify the two "Protocols Additional to the Geneva Conventions of 12 August 1947", 1977 and the Rome International Criminal Court (ICC) treaty, July 17, 1998. The leaders and cabinet of the Gandhian state of India, who led the Non-Aligned Movement and the global de-colonisation Movement had been deliberately committing "war crimes", "crimes against Humanity", "Genocide", and "Aggression" in Manipur for half a century, while the international community chose to remain a silent spectator for half a century.

11.03. From the year 1978, the People's Liberation Army had relentlessly fought and resisted against the occupation Indian army without any rest in order to defend the Manipur People against Indian colonialism and Indian military occupation. Several hundreds of PLA freedom fighters sacrificed their lives for the sake of their motherland. Nearly every top, middle-ranking PLA leader died or killed while fighting the occupation army in quick succession, thereby pushing forward the national liberation movement, which is more extensive and mass-based after more than two decades of unremitting armed resistance to the occupation forces and regime.

11.04. Article 1(4) of the First Additional Protocol, 1977 provides legal protection to peoples, who are "fighting against colonial Domination and alien occupation and against racist regimes in the exercise of their right to self-determination", but the occupation army of India has been ceaselessly torturing by using 3rd degree methods, arrested POW guerillas of the National Liberation Movement. The RPF - Revolutionary People's Front of Manipur and its military wing PLA - People's Liberation Army has signed common article 3 of the Four Geneva Conventions in 1997 and has been strictly complying with the International Humanitarian Laws, but the Indian occupation forces, their mercenaries who love to wear civilian dresses while committing heinous crimes against mankind in the midst of the civilian populace have routinely committed grave breach of the Geneva Conventions. These common criminals are awarded and rewarded profusely and ostentatiously by the President of India (read Union Cabinet) in public annually for committing heinous crimes against mankind in Manipur. The 10 channels of the official television - DD, 3000 Indian racialist dailies, 300 Radio stations daily project Manipuri freedom fighters as criminals and terrorists. This hatred campaign helps the genocide with impunity.

11.05. The anti-National Liberation Movement networks of the colonial government has degraded the lives of 30,000 Manipuri youths and students into drug-addicts and HIV/AIDS patients in order to distract them from joining the National Liberation Movements. It is noted by the government that a Cabinet Minister late Mr. Ngurdingleng has been leading the Heroin—HIV/AIDS trade some years back, till he was executed in a church in southern part of Manipur. Dailies publish news of several army personnel, and police-men, who have been caught red-handed with narcotic drugs while transporting them for trade. Nearly all of them have been released scot-free, if not rewarded with national medals and honours. No massive Heroin trade could have been possible in the thick of army, mercenaries and spies without the connivance of the colonial government.

11.06. The United Nations and its appropriate agencies, the ICRC, NAM, ASEAN, SAARC, among others, refrained from making a close watch on monitoring and deterring the de-humanizing human rights violations, committed by the Indian state terrorism and the occupation Indian army. Consequently, peace and stability in this part of the world have been a permanent casualty and would remain so until the colonial army is withdrawn as it has been done in Kosovo.

XII. Petition

12.01. The Revolutionary People's Front (RPF) wholeheartedly acclaims the UN action in the de-colonisation process and the UN's efforts to eradicate colonialism by 2000 AD. The Revolutionary People's Front (RPF) therefore, draws your kind immediate attention to the above-mentioned facts and the evidence of colonialism, thrust upon the people of Manipur by the Indian colonial power and its occupation forces by despatching a

"VISITING MISSION" to Manipur on a war-footing and for hearing the National Liberation Movement in the appropriate forums of the UN De-colonisation Committee and the Fourth Committee, among others, of the UN General Assembly.

12.02. The Revolutionary People's Front (RPF) holds the opinion that the UN's endeavour to eradicate colonialism shall be materially achieved only after de-colonising proximity or, neighbourhood colonialism in Asia-Pacific, beyond the scope of the classical European Salt-water colonialism. In this sacred UN Mission, the UN cannot leave the world half-decolonised and half-recolonised. Indonesia and India, which are considered to be world-leaders in neutrality movement or, in some contexts, had non-self-governing territories or, colonies like East Timor in Indonesia and Manipur in post-1949 India.

12.03. The Revolutionary People's Front (RPF) strongly urges upon the UN Secretary-General, UN agencies, Fourth Committee of the UN GA and the "open-ended Bureau" of the UN Special Committee on De-colonisation to kindly enlist "Manipur" in the list of NON-SELF-GOVERNING TERRITORIES of the UN and initiate all necessary action towards eradicating Indian colonialism and hostile military occupation of Manipur.

12.04. The Revolutionary People's Front (RPF) beseechs and petitions all the appropriate UN authorities to allow the indigenous Manipur people to exercise their inalienable right to self-determination, independence and sovereignty.

SIGNATORIES

sd/-
IRENGBAM CHAOREN
PRESIDENT

sd/-
MANOHAR MAYUM NGOUBA
VICE-PRESIDENT

sd/-
SANASAM GUNEN
SECRETARY-GENERAL

sd/-
YANGAMBAM GUNI
SECRETARY, EXTERNAL AFFAIRS

sd/-

WANGKHEM IBOHAL
SECRETARY, FINANCE

sd/-
GURUMAYUM JAME
EXECUTIVE COMMITTEE MEMBER

sd/-
AHANTHEM MEMA
EXECUTIVE COMMITTEE MEMBER

Dated
21st Day of September 1999

ANNUAL STATEMENT OF THE CENTRAL COMMITTEE, UNITED LIBERATION FRONT, MANIPUR

43rd Foundation Anniversary
24 November 2007

Dear Compatriots,

Today, 24 November 2007, on the occasion of the 43rd Foundation Anniversary of the United National Liberation Front: Manipur (UNLF), the UNLF Central Committee extends heartiest revolutionary greetings to all our compatriots and take this opportunity to present the Annual Statement of the Central Committee 2007 highlighting the following major issues:

1) The Core Issue of Manipur
2) The Present Critical Situation
3) Accelerating the Pace of National Liberation Struggle
4) National Liberation Struggle and Manipur's Economy
5) Human Resource Development
6) Negative Cultural Influence from India
7) Contract/Supply and People's Life
8) National Liberation Struggle and Factionalism
9) India's Trap—the 'Peace Talk'
10) Co-existence of the Region's Ethnic Groups

At the outset we ask for our people's forgiveness for any mistake and wrong doings that the UNLF may have committed during the year.

1. The Core Issue: The gravest of dangers confronting 'Manipur' today is the colonial rule of India that began with the forcible annexation of Manipur in 1949. Therefore, the core issue of today is the satisfactory resolution of the Manipur-India Conflict to restore Manipur's sovereignty and independence. The logical step in this direction is to ascertain the democratic opinion of the people so as to resolve the conflict satisfactorily, which will determine the fate of Manipur's people themselves. In this regard the UNLF issued a declaration on 31 January 2005 outlining a four-point proposal stating that the best democratic means to resolve the Manipur-India Conflict is to hold a plebiscite under the aegis of the United Nations, to deploy a UN Peace Keeping Force in Manipur to ensure a free and fair plebiscite, the UNLF to deposit arms and ammunition to the UN authority ahead of the plebiscite and India to withdraw all her military and para military forces from Manipur back to India, and the UN to handover political power in accordance with the result of the plebiscite. That the verdict of the people in such a plebiscite would be honoured by the UNLF has also been declared.

However, we would reiterate the firm stand of the UNLF to continue the armed struggle for regaining the sovereignty and independence of Manipur, even more vigorously, so long as the issue of plebiscite remains unsettled. Because, to the patriotic people of Manipur, as it is to the UNLF, no other issue is more important than the restoration of sovereignty and independence. Protection of our distinct national identity, ensuring the basic human rights of our people, attaining happiness and pride of being essentially self-reliant in clothing and food, especially the fraternal coexistence and co-development of all the ethnic groups of Manipur that would evolve a collective life, are all the essential elements for existence as a nation. But then it is not possible to attain these essential elements of our national life without sovereignty and independence. Therefore, it is imperative for our people to be aware of the grim prospects of failure to regain sovereignty and independence of Manipur, that is, the tragedy that will engulf our nation remaining under Indian colonial occupation. Our population of just about 1.8 million people, excluding about 7 lakh illegal migrants, is not even a small drop in the vast ocean of 100 crore above population of India. We should be aware of the fate of our small population being drowned in this vast population of India. Therefore, despite all the negative factors that may have affected the image of our National Liberation Struggle, its legitimate justification and historical necessity for existence can never be negated.

Ever since the 1949 annexation, India has adopted several constitutional measures to dilute our National Identity within the so-called Indian mainstream. The process of intensive 'Indianisation', creation of social divisions in the name of democracy such as 'scheduled tribe', 'scheduled caste', and 'other backward classes' has only widened the social divide in Manipur rather than consolidating social harmony. This is deliberately done to weaken our social fabric by pitching these artificially created social groups against one another in grabbing more 'quotas'. We call upon our people to deliberate on the disintegrating effects of this 'divide and rule' policy of the Indian Government. However, the most perceptible aspect of Indian colonial rule directly felt by the people is the inhuman atrocities of the Indian Occupation Forces (IOF), such as enforced disappearance, random arrest and killing of innocent peoples and the rape of our women folk at will. Our pride against all these racist repression of Indian colonial rule is that they have not been able to subdue our national character. Rather, their repression has become the factor that has awakened our hitherto dormant national character. It is precisely because of this factor that being unable to suppress the popular resistance against Indian colonial rule, the form of Indian colonial rule had to change from one after another, from the rule of a 'Chief Commissioner' to that of the present 'statehood', so as to appease our people.

Today, the Indian colonial rule has reached its final stage of development, the next and the last being that of 'full autonomy'. Hereafter, Manipur becoming a sovereign independent State by severing the colonial relation with India is an inevitable historical process in time. After installing the administration of an Indian Chief Commissioner in Manipur, directly controlled by New Delhi immediately after the annexation of 1949, India began to undertake a series of administrative reforms to pacify the surging democratic movement of our people. First, direct colonial rule through a Chief Commissioner, then Advisory Council to Territorial Council, then to an 'elected' 30-member Territorial Assembly, giving a semblance of democracy, but without any legislative power. This also could not satisfy the aspirations of our people and by 1970-71 the democratic movement intensified in which a number of agitators were killed by Police firing. It was also about this time that the existence of underground national liberation movement became public in Manipur. This new factor compelled the Indian government to raise the status of Manipur to 'full-fledged Statehood' within Indian Union on 21 January 1972. The new status provided for a 60-member 'State Assembly' having some legislative powers listed in the Indian constitution. However, this did not alter the colonial status of Manipur as her sovereign independence was still under Indian domination. In fact, India has been using the so called democratic facade to hide the inhuman atrocities being perpetrated by the IOF against the people of Manipur. As such Manipur still remains a colony of India. Therefore, the UNLF reiterate that the core issue of Manipur today is the restoration of her sovereignty and independence by a satisfactory resolution of the Manipur-India Conflict.

2. The Grave Situation: However, a paradox exists today as to resolving the core issue of Manipur-India Conflict. The increasing isolation of the revolutionary organisations from the masses of the people over the years is paradoxical to the challenges of the struggle, and this is not reassuring. This paradoxical situation is giving India the opportunity to drive a wedge between the revolutionary organisations and the people. Grabbing this advantage the IOF is making good use of their unaccounted money to enlist the service of financially unstable elements in the society, including women as informer against our national struggle. The factors helping them are – the use of intimidation and force, as felt by the contributors, by revolutionary parties in money collection; dismal performance of the Parties as generally perceived compared to the huge amount of money they have collected; the confusion among the people about the direction and thrust of the struggle resulting from the lack of concrete and action oriented unity among the parties.

However, the most important reason for the increasing isolation of the struggle from the people is the inability of the Parties to identify the national liberation struggle with the struggle for existence of the masses of the people. This should be construed as an ideological shortcoming of the parties while the practical weakness is the inability of the parties to build a united leadership so as to give a correct direction to the national struggle. If this weakness is not addressed soon, there is danger awaiting our national liberation struggle. Because any revolutionary struggle isolated from the people cannot win victory.

Another dangerous aspect of the situation in Manipur is the political game of some ethnic 'politicians' abusing their ethnic armed groups for narrow political interests, particularly in rigging 'elections'. The number of such armed groups and politicians is highest among the Kuki community. It is now an open secret that the frequent clashes among Kuki armed groups are mostly instigated by such politicians. Such unscrupulous instigations by some Kuki politicians have claimed the life of many innocent Kuki youth. It is time now for our Kuki community, particularly Kuki youth, to take stock of the situation. Otherwise, the Kuki community will be the ultimate loser if the fratricidal killings pushed by petty interests of their so-called politicians do not stop. It is high time for the Kuki community to take a stand on the issue.

3. Acceleration of the National Struggle: The UNLF stand on the matter is that the first step in accelerating the national struggle is to bring about sincere unity among the Parties having similar views on fundamental national issues and fight together against Indian colonial rule. This is the voice of the people as well. This is simple, because without sincerity having similar views and stand on basic issues is not enough to work together. Therefore, Parties having similar views should take a sincere and firm stand to fight together against India and maintain reasonable flexibility on Party interests in the larger interest of the national struggle. This ideal led to the formation of the MPLF, a united front of PREPAK-RPF-UNLF. Unfortunately, however, the MPLF remains an incomplete experience. This has dampened the new-found hope and trust of the people in the MPLF, rather the national struggle. Naturally, the general public wants to know the reason why the Parties have failed to closely work together. Our Parties owe an answer to the people. Now, though PREPAK-KYKL-UNLF have begun to work together in some areas, there is still the need to take strong collective steps in fighting against Indian colonial rule, and on major social issues as well. Another matter which is no less important is the sincere appreciation of the necessity to take collective measures for resolving internal contradictions of a fraternal Party which have the propensity to become fratricidal conflicts.

4. Liberation Struggle and Manipur's Economy: We have highlighted above the bounden collective duty of our Parties to remove the impediments holding back the acceleration of our national liberation struggle. As to the identification of our national struggle with the struggle for existence of the people, the UNLF line is to take concrete steps to practically expose the tightening noose of the Indian colonial rule on the day-to-day existence of our people. The UNLF firmly believes that this should be created by a Socio-Economic Campaign to build an Essential Self-Reliant Economy on basic items for survival. In fact, this is a part of the overall revolutionary strategy of the UNLF.

It needs to recall here the ideological line of the UNLF that the ultimate goal of the national liberation struggle is not just restoration of sovereignty and independence, but to attain the logical and inseparable goal of socialism wherein a wholesome national life of all the ethnic groups of Manipur would become a reality. The basic precondition for the victory of this revolutionary struggle is people's faith in the said goal and their participation in the struggle. In the first stage of the revolution, that is the present National People's Democratic Revolution, all our ethnic groups will be liberated not only from colonial bondage but also from the outdated remnants of feudal relations along with the liberation of Manipur from Indian colonial occupation and will bring all the ethnic groups of Manipur together to build a new, united, democratic country having autonomy at all levels and respecting one another's distinct identities under the guiding slogan Coexistence and Co development. This is the basic political line of the UNLF. It is common knowledge that the first and foremost task of a sovereign and independent country is to build an essential self-reliant economy. But in our present situation the question arises as to whether we should wait for independence to be restored, or, is it not possible to start building our economy, according to our own program, even during the national struggle. The UNLF believes that it is possible, and should be possible. This is a policy line determined by the dialectical relation between our national struggle and Indian colonial rule. However, in view of the existing repressive colonial situation, the building of Manipur's self-reliant economy should of necessity pass through two main stages. First, measures to be taken during the process of the national struggle – main objective to lay the foundation for a self-reliant economy taking maximum advantage from India and also utilise own resources prudently. Second, measures to be taken after restoration of sovereignty and independence – take up comprehensive economic development programme. This apparently paradoxical, but inherently linked together, approach of laying the foundation of our self reliant economy during the process of the liberation struggle itself needs to be propagated as the very struggle for existence of our people. In this regard, we present herein below an outline of the salient features of the National Economic Policy of the UNLF:

i) Agriculture: Our 'Manipur', being an agricultural country, decides that the logical basis of our economic development should also be agriculture. Though the budget allocation for agriculture under the colonial dispensation may be handsome, there has been no planned development of this sector because of the lack of direction and massive corruption, in short because of the systemic failure. Under the circumstances in a captive market economy the masses of our peasants are losing the day-to-day struggle for existence. As such, development of agriculture, according to our own programme, shall have to be the thrust of laying the foundation of our self reliant economy during the liberation struggle. The first and foremost objective of this programme shall be Self-Sufficiency in Food. To attain this objective the UNLF shall embark on a widespread campaign to increase agricultural production by motivating our peasants. In this campaign the UNLF shall endeavour to modernise the Agricultural Sector with the latest knowledge of Science & Technology adapted to the specific needs of our socio-economic situation. However, the process of modernisation shall in no case displace wage-earner peasants from their livelihood. That means the use of new technology and machineries shall maintain a balance with the available human resources. This measure besides attaining self sufficiency in food grains in a few years time will have some surplus as well which can be shared with neighbouring States like Mizoram and Nagaland where there is food deficit because of natural constraints in agricultural productions. This will also strengthen the interdependent coexistence among the States in the Region. Above all, Self-Sufficiency in food shall liberate the mind of our people from the prevailing Indian-injected dependent psychology of 'Can we survive when separated from India?' That is, when the condition of imposed dependency of food grains on India is removed our people will find their own bearing for the future. This will be a big step forward in the liberation struggle. Therefore, the responsibility of our peasants in the movement for Self Sufficiency in Food is obviously the biggest of all. This is in fact the responsibility of liberating our society, our country from colonial bondage. In short, our peasants are the main force in liberating our Motherland from Indian colonial occupation. Therefore, urged by this national and social necessity, the UNLF earnestly appeal to our peasants to launch a new patriotic movement to increase food production to the maximum possible.

Horticulture: Our fruits, flowers (particularly Orchids), valuable medicinal and scented plants are a potential source of major income. As such, horticulture could be developed as a major industry by utilising the latest knowledge of Biotechnology. This industry can earn huge foreign exchange much needed in our economic development.

However, despite the necessity to be Self-Sufficient in Food, the UNLF would discourage the extensive use of Chemical Fertilisers in view of its long term harmful effects on the soil and human health besides being expensive. Therefore, our agricultural revolution should give emphasis on organic farming by encouraging massive production of compost and biofertilisers.

Thus, the role to be played by Agriculture and Horticulture in building an Essential Self-Reliant Economy of Manipur is fundamental. From this perspective we heartily congratulate our Agricultural scientists for their outstanding achievement and continuing effort in developing high-yielding varieties of paddy with local taste producing more than 30 Phoupot in a quarter hectare. We also highly appreciate the patriotic efforts of our Biotech scientists and entrepreneurs for discovering the immense possibilities in the field of horticulture. The UNLF would appeal to all concerned that from now on all these activities be coordinated and play their due role in the movement to attain the goal of Essential Self-Reliant Economy.

ii) Small & Medium Enterprise (SME): As explained above, it is a basic element of the UNLF's National Economic Policy that Agriculture should be the basis of our economic development. Particularly, "Self-Sufficiency in Food" shall be the basis of our people's existence. But then it is also common knowledge that industry is the leading factor of economic development. In our specific conditions, the leading factor of economic development shall have to be the Small & Medium Enterprise, now popularly known as SME. Therefore, along with the extensive campaign in the Agricultural Sector, the UNLF would embark on a programme to encourage establishment of suitable SMEs by patriotic entrepreneurs. In the First Phase of this programme, Food Processing Industry based on own raw materials of Agriculture and Horticulture, and other essential items which could compete Indian (foreign) products in quality, shall be given priority. The UNLF highly appreciate the labourious efforts of successful entrepreneurs in this field. Taking these enterprises as good examples, we appeal to our cash rich patriotic individuals to invest in such

SMEs and become responsible citizens in building a new Manipur instead of squandering their money.

iii) Incentives: The UNLF will extend full support to the above mentioned Agro-Horticulture based projects and SMEs invested by ethnic Manipuris, residing in foreign countries as well. The UNLF will also support foreign companies willing to establish industries in Manipur as a component of our economic development. As incentives to the projects and industries stated above, the UNLF will NOT levy any kind of 'tax' from them for fifteen years counted from the date of commissioning. The justification for keeping the ceiling of fifteen years is that the enterprise will have earned profit if it could survive for fifteen years and that a small portion of their profit should be contributed to social welfare projects.

iv) Power Projects: One of the basic infrastructures of economic development is power. So, wherefrom we get the necessary power in view of the zero-power situation in Manipur today? The Indian government sponsored Loktak Hydro Electric Project in the valley of Manipur has completely destroyed one of the rare eco-system in the region. This project, once boasted to light-up a new era of economic development has actually blacked-out Manipur. And now, another colonial project of India, the Tipaimukh Dam over the Barak River for a Hydro Electric Project in the Churachandpur District of Manipur, is going to submerge Manipur under water. The UNLF will NOT support such colonial projects primarily intended to exploit Manipur's natural resources for India's benefit and which will also destroy the eco-system. The devastating effect of Tipaimukh Dam will be felt as far as Bangladesh. Therefore, the UNLF strongly support the public movement against this project. Should it become necessary, the UNLF will use all the means at its disposal to stop the project. For Manipur, the immediate step that is needed to be taken is to generate electricity for meeting the domestic requirement first. This could be done easily by taking up Mini and Micro Hydel Projects in the Hill Districts.

v) Kitchen Economy: An important social factor which cannot be ignored in the economic development of Manipur is the traditional role of the Manipuri women in running the kitchen economy. This is our grassroots economy. The distinctive status and role of our women in national and social life is the embodiment of the responsibility they take in the kitchen economy. Today also, this responsibility of our women remains an important element of our social economy. Except for some families in the urban areas 80% of our household kitchen economies are shouldered by women. Therefore, the UNLF will introduce a micro credit system to support such women in their struggle for day-to-day existence.

The UNLF will endeavour to build the united strength of such micro credit network as the torchbearer of the new economic movement throughout Manipur. The guiding slogan of this campaign shall be One Home One Profession.

vi) Interdependent Economy: One important aspect to be taken care of in the campaign for Essential Self Reliant Economy as described above is the different but inseparably linked geographical reality of the Hills and the Valley. As such, integration of the two geographical entities by utilising their available products from agriculture, horticulture, etc. into an interdependent economy shall be a fundamental aspect of the economic campaign. The activities of this integrated economy shall give rise to a new qualitatively different integrated life bound together by a shared bond of struggle for existence. From this integrated life will emerge a collective cultural identity which in turn will build a wholesome national life. This is the reality when the present antagonistic contradiction between the Hills and the Valley shall transform into that of a bond of fraternal interdependence.

vii) Responsibilities: When we achieve self sufficiency in food, when every kitchen can feed the family two square meals a day, when our own products can replace Indian (foreign) products in some essential items, then our economy will have become essentially self reliant. This could be achieved only by the collective effort of the entire people. Particularly, the local 'MLAs and Ministers' in the Indian dispensation should realise their responsibility in the campaign for Essential Self Reliance, even though within the bounds of the Indian constitution. They should take up all possible economic development projects in earnest. Here the UNLF would emphasise the imperative necessity for the revolutionary Parties to work together. As such, it is the firm stand of the UNLF to work together to the maximum possible.

viii) Our Economy and Globalisation: The campaign for building our self reliant economy shall be, in a sense, a measure to face the challenges of globalisation being deliberately pushed through by India's 'Look East Policy'. If our economic foundation is laid to some extent along with the development of essential human resources which can absorb the impact of globalisation to some extent, the intended objective of undercutting our liberation struggle by the impact of globalisation sweeping away our society will not be possible to achieve. However, the physical threat to our national identity is the proposed railroad connecting India with Myanmar through Manipur. If specific measures to control the huge influx of Indians through this railroad are not taken, our distinctive identities will be simply erased in 30 years time. This is actually a strategic component of India's 'Look East Policy'. Therefore, our people should not make the suicidal mistake of ignoring the fact that the 'globalisation' through India's 'Look East Policy' is the life and death question of our nation.

5. Development of Human Resource: One of the essential requirements of economic development is the availability of human resource. As such development of appropriate human resource according to the strategy of building our self reliant economy shall have to be an essential component of our longer term economic development. However, the present state of education system in Manipur under the highly corrupt Indian colonial rule is simply chaotic being mainly used as a medium for Indianisation of our younger generations. All the government High and Higher Secondary Schools have been deserted by students for chaotic administration, poor teaching quality and lack of teaching staff. Government colleges also leave much to be desired. Thus tens of thousands of students have migrated to private schools and colleges in various cities of India thereby draining out a huge amount of money every month. On the contrary, private mission schools are performing well despite their commercialization of education. Even the 700 odd 'government aided' Junior Schools are doing well except for a few in the urban areas. However, the plight of these schools is that teachers do not get salaries regularly because of non release of fund by the State government for months together. Under the circumstances, development of the required human resources is not possible. The chaotic situation, therefore, demands a thorough analysis to trace the root cause in order to restore the semblance of normal education. Unless and until the root cause is traced and appropriate rectification measures taken, ensuring quality education in Manipur will remain a far cry. To the best of UNLF's knowledge, modern education spread in Manipur when enlightened individuals began the 'private school movement' in the late 40s. It is a matter of pride for our people that all the junior schools, high and higher secondary schools (except one) and colleges began their mission as private institutions. The private schools were managed by competent managing committees while colleges were run by committed governing bodies. Though the salaries of teachers under private management were pittance and irregular as compared to today's government teachers, teaching quality and administration were far better than today's. Students were also more serious in their studies. This quality did not suffer much even when the private institutions became 'government aided' financially while administrative control was still private. However, once the private institutions were taken over completely by the State government, overall quality of education began to suffer because of the corrupt State administration. More important, education began to be used by India as the medium of Indianisation. This means the root cause for the destruction of normal education, let alone quality education, in Manipur is the Indian colonial system. Corruption inherent in the Indian system soon began to spread its tentacles in Manipur's educational institutions. Appointment and transfer of teachers, transformation of textbook writing and production into contract/supply system became convenient nests of corruption. This new phenomenon of corruption completely destroyed the original ideals of our education system. Ultimately the education system was transformed into a medium for Indianisation by replacing from the syllabus anything and everything related to Manipur by everything Indian. Therefore, it is distinctly clear that normal education, let alone quality education, in Manipur will remain illusive so long as our schools/colleges remain under the clutches of the corrupt administration of the State government. In view of the existing colonial situation, a stop-gap arrangement to arrest the nose-dive in education is to handover the administration/management of government schools/colleges to autonomous governing bodies while the State government continues to take care of the financial aspect. This arrangement seems to be the only way out as of now. The issue demands close scrutiny of the general public. Revolutionary Parties should also respond to the situation collectively.

6. India's Cultural Influence: In the campaign for building a self reliant economy a closely related aspect which cannot be ignored is the negative cultural influence from India. The generally perceived influence is from religion, Hindi films and their dance and songs, Indian dress and clothing inimical to our cultural values. In this regard, the banning of Hindi films in Manipur and the imposition of Phanek (Manipuri skirt for women) as the uniform in schools/colleges are commendable measures. As a result, production of digital Manipuri film has proliferated which in turn has given a new lease of life to cinema halls closed long ago with the banning of Hindi films. However, there still are traces of Indian cultural symbols, such as 'Manggal Sutra' around the neck and 'sindur' on forehead adorned by married Indian women copied by Manipuri artistes in local digital films. As far as dress goes, use of Saari and Salwar-kamiz by women and kurta-pajama by men in an out of place manner in traditional social functions continues. In this regard, there is a strong need for production of local digital films which can spread the visual message of rediscovering our distinctive cultural identity more or less on the basis of the guideline given by Film Forum Manipur. Though the consciousness for wearing Phanek in schools/colleges has spread, it is yet to give any impetus to the local handloom industry as the Phaneks used by school/

college girls these days are all modified from cloths produced by Indian textile mills. Specific measures need to be taken to address the situation. Even so, that a step in the right direction has been taken is commendable.

However, the most dangerous negative cultural invasion which is engulfing our society like cancer is the system of contract/supply under the Indian colonial rule. This system, instead of serving the people, has transformed swindling of public money into a fine-tuned cultural practice. Today there is hardly any aspect of our social life that has not been affected by the big corrupting money of contract/supply, beginning from sending their wards to India for studies and providing them with rented flats, motor bikes and hi-fi gadgets to giving cars and what not as Awunpot to daughters (traditionally not, but becoming, 'dowry') are reflections of the changes in our culture impacted by the big money of contract/supply. The important aspects that are undermining the inner strength of our society by the big money of contract/supply are:

(i) The urge to get easy money without labour;
(ii) Proliferation of giving/taking bribes in soliciting for work;
(iii) Squandering of the easy money in womanising and booze parties leading to degeneration of character and breaking up of families creating social problems;
(iv) Creation of a class of social upstarts, becoming VIPs in the society, then becoming 'MLA/Minister' using money power, transformation of politics as their big business where the people, whom they are supposed to serve, become political commodities;
(v) Deterioration of the situation further by the unscrupulous participation of the revolutionary organisations in contract/supply work, erosion in their revolutionary character and unity, petty frictions among revolutionary parties in vying for projects, thus distracting them from the basic task of the liberation struggle; and
(vi) The hitherto invincible revolutionary organisations by India's military might being gradually swallowed by the contract/supply system.

Thus, the present corrupting system of contract/supply and the valueless big money derived from it has been eating into the very fabric of our social life. If allowed to continue uncontrolled, it will have become a dangerous disease to fight even after our independence is regained. Because this disease has become a state of the mind. This is a negative phenomenon inimical to our goal of socialism and the new culture that will emerge therefrom. The influence of Hindi films can be checked by producing our own original songs along with the banning of Hindi films. Also culturally undesirable dresses can be discarded overnight. However, the contract/ supply system and the big easy money being drained through it has become the dangerous fountainhead of corruption which has gripped all aspects of our social life. The problem is, there is no alternative to changing the system itself which is not possible to tackle separately from the larger colonial system. But, as of now, some specific measures to arrest the downtrend, should be possible. Judging from this perspective, the UNLF cannot find any justification in encouraging, directly or indirectly, the contract/supply system which is becoming the graveyard of the revolutionary Parties. The situation demands a serious rethinking and collective understanding on the part of the revolutionary Parties.

7. Contract/Supply and People's Life: It is the declared stand of the UNLF to work together with other like-minded revolutionary Parties in the economic campaign described above. In this regard, any work or projects having direct link with the life and health of the people and education related works or projects will henceforth, in coordination with other parties, come under close scrutiny of the UNLF. For example, construction/repair/maintenance of hospitals, supply/purchase of medical equipments, drugs and medicines under Medical head; water supply schemes, purchase of water purification chemicals, etc. under PHED; and construction/repair of buildings for educational institutions, text book production including writing, supply/purchase of laboratory equipments and research facilities, etc. within the purview of education should strictly comply with quality specifications. Therefore, anybody found directly involved in swindling money through 'akash bill', not keeping quality in contract and supply works shall be given severe punishment. Because the UNLF has always maintained that any dirty work with the motif of earning easy money by exposing people's life to extreme danger is a serious crime against human life and scuttling of human resource development by siphoning off allocated funds is as serious a crime against the society. Therefore, the UNLF appeal to all concerned to stop henceforth all these anti people and anti social activities. We appeal to other revolutionary Parties also to check such activities in their own capacity and extend fraternal hands for working together in protecting people's life.

Relevant here, is the battle for overall control of contract/supply works by some Parties as being 'their projects'. The UNLF would propose that any work up to 20 lakh be released to 'Open Tender'. If such small works are awarded properly by the collective intervention or influence of our Parties, a small step could be taken to introduce a new work culture of our own in the contract/supply system. This will be a new culture to stop swindling public fund and work sincerely for the welfare of the people. All our parties could work out together a system to oversee socio-economic projects. The UNLF further propose NOT to levy any percentage from any contract/supply work up to 20 lakh. For the UNLF no such percentage will be levied beginning 01 January 2008.

The UNLF sincerely believe that the proposed arrangements will be a small step towards liberating our society from the clutches of the corrupt system of contract/supply.

8. Liberation Struggle and Factionalism: Besides the corrupting impact of the contract/supply system on the society, another unhealthy phenomenon visits the scene from time to time. That is, the phenomenon of factionalism becoming fratricidal conflicts. In the history of Manipur's liberation struggle, factional fights have been a factor for weakness. Causes of the factional fights range from differences in ideological principles and without any such principles. In 1968-69 a faction led by Oinam Sudhir Kumar broke away from the UNLF and formed CONSOCOM-RGM; in 1978-79 the RGM split into two groups, one led by N. Biseshwar formed the PLA Unit, Eastern Region and the other led by Sudhir Kumar formed the Poirei Liberation Front (POLIF). Sudhir Kumar later became counter revolutionary and the two groups had a spell of bloodshed in which Sudhir Kumar was killed. In 1980-81 two factions of PREPAK had long spell of bloodshed. At about the same time the UNLF also suffered a second split, though without bloodshed, which was patched up in 1987. However, the UNLF split again in 1991, this time followed by heavy bloodshed for nine long years. Meanwhile, in 1985-86 internal feuds within two groups of the RPF/PLA resulted in some loss of life. And now again, the recent killings between two groups of PREPAK is the unfortunate manifestation of factionalism within our struggle.

Actually, splits and factionalism are contradictions that developed at a certain stage in human society. In our society also this has been existent for a long time. However, unprincipled splits and factionalism encouraged by intrigues appeared in our society with the advent Hinduism in Manipur. It is quite natural for such social phenomenon to spread into revolutionary parties as well. What the revolutionary Parties ought to do is to find ways to resolve the contradiction on the basis of the objectives of the liberation struggle and ideological standpoint. Contradictions without differences on such basic principles should be able to be resolved within the party; otherwise any faction not subscribing to the basic principles should be treated as unprincipled. What is unfortunate is, reconcilable contradictions which should be resolved within the Party often lead to factional fights even today. Under the circumstances, the principled stand that the Parties are morally bound to take together is that any contradiction, if there is no difference in the objective of liberation, within a party and among Parties, should be resolved through dialogue and peaceful means without resorting to violent methods. Our people who have rather become wary of the armed organisations would applaud the revolutionary Parties if they could collectively take this principled stand.

9. India's Trap – 'Peace Talk': In the effort to suppress the liberation struggles of the Region, one of the means India has been using craftily is the trap for 'peace-talk' besides using massive military force. That such 'peace-talk' can never resolve the existing conflicts of the Region with India has often been reiterated by the UNLF. The Mizo struggle ended in capitulation when the Mizo National Front signed the 'Mizo Accord' in 1986. The Tripura National Volunteer also followed suit soon after. However the most glaring example of the success of India's 'peace-talk' is the India-NSCN (IM) 'peace-talk' that began in 1997 and still continuing. In this protracted exercise of 'peace-talk' India has gained everything, while the NSCN (IM) has lost everything. Today the NSCN (IM) has become wary and exhausted and ready for a compromise. At one time the NSCN (IM) shouted that 'Naga sovereignty and independence are non negotiable', but today they are ready to give up the position on sovereignty and independence for a 'special federal relationship' within Indian constitution. Ten years ago, a leader of the NSCN (IM) boasted that "This ceasefire is different. India is sincere this time. Other Parties in the region should try to understand India." It is high time for the NSCN (IM) to realise their own naivety in reading the Indian mind. They still do not analyse why the Indian government is dragging the 'peace-talk' process. The Indian objective is – to demolish the personality of the two senior leaders of the NSCN (IM) which commanded the trust and confidence of the Naga people in general, to destroy the faith and confidence of the Naga people in the two leaders, to lure away the immediate leaders of the NSCN (IM) to the comforts of an extravagant settled life, to destroy the fighting morale of the lower level cadres by making them enjoy an easy life. Above all, what is disturbing is the trend Naga freedom fighters frequently visiting Indian Occupation Forces camp to take Indian military issue of XXX RUM and also the widespread use of SP tablets. The Naga struggle which Indian military prowess could not suppress for over 40 years has now been rendered ineffective by the 'peace-talk' trap. The question now is – Even if the NSCN (IM) decides to withdraw from the 'peace-talk' process, can they persuade the Naga people, who have enjoyed a non-conflict situation for over ten years now, to resume the armed struggle against India?

The overall degeneration which has affected the NSCN (IM) as a result of the 'peace-talk' is a warning to other struggles in the region. On the other hand, the UNLF congratulates those revolutionary parties in the region taking a firm stand against 'peace-talk' with India. The UNLF appeal to those parties now in 'ceasefire' with India, but have not entered the 'peace-talk' process, to realise the danger of 'peace-talk' and return to the fold of struggle against the common enemy – India. The UNLF particularly appeal to the entire peoples of the region to understand together that the future of the region lies in coexisting together in independence after overthrowing Indian colonial rule. To this end, we should build up our unity by resolving all the contradictions among us as between fraternal peoples and fight together against India.

10. Interdependence of the Region: One of the basic lines of approach of the UNLF is that the Region (the so-called north eastern region) is a composite whole made up of inseparable and interdependent parts having a common historical, social and cultural background. The UNLF firmly believes that the liberation of the Region from Indian colonial rule is historically inevitable. And the interdependent existence of the Region shall take the form of building together an economy of Collective Self Reliance. Therefore, Manipur's economy will have to be developed keeping in perspective the regional reality.

11. Message to Ethnic Groups: On the occasion of the UNLF's 43rd Foundation Anniversary, our message to all the ethnic groups of Manipur is—Let us overcome the grave situation confronting all of us today by the collective strength and wisdom of all the ethnic groups and build an independent and united national life. In such a national life, each and every ethnic group, particularly the small ones, shall enjoy the right to protect, preserve and develop their distinct cultural identities and that the bigger ones should not forcibly assimilate smaller ones. This is a prerequisite condition for coexistence and co development. Therefore, the UNLF reiterate its firm stand to support all the ethnic groups, particularly the smaller ones, in protecting their respective cultural identities.

12. Other Matters: A social problem which is disturbing all of us today is the widespread abuse of drugs, particularly by our younger generation having lost bearing in life. This is indeed a very painful. What is consoling, however, is the public awareness and the social movement against drugs. This has given us the confidence that our society will not be swept away by drugs. The UNLF, therefore, will extend unreserved support to the ongoing social movement against drugs and related crimes.

Another matter no less important is the use of Urea to quicken the process of Ngaari (fermented dry fish) production so as to turn over quickly by unscrupulous producers. The UNLF consider this practice to be a serious offence. Considering the dangerous effect of the practice to the health of millions of people, the UNLF has started investigation into the matter. We caution all those concerned to stop the practice immediately. The UNLF hereby declare that anyone found indulging in the said practice will be punished not only with forfeiture of related properties but may also be given severe punishment.

13. A Few Words on the UNLF: So far we have concentrated on the ideological and political line, policy and programme of the UNLF. Now a very brief report about the UNLF itself, its progress and problems, and preparedness:

With the support of our people, the UNLF and its armed wing MPA has successfully carried out many works in various places of the Hills and the Valley. In the Hills the UNLF/MPA has progressively expanded the base areas of our liberation struggle. In these base areas, the UNLF/MPA is providing free medical service to the local people, distributing rice freely in lean seasons, laid several kilometers of pipes for supplying drinking water and provided water pumps and pipes to irrigate paddy fields to enhance agricultural production. The UNLF/MPA is not only engaged in agricultural production but has also taken up large scale plantation of orange, pineapple, banana, etc. and fishery, poultry in the base areas. In the four districts of the Valley, including Jiribam, more than 25,000 hectares of marshy lands have been reclaimed for agricultural production. Besides, projects for construction of earthen Dam and dredging of several existing canals were implemented. Potato, Mustard, Sugarcane, Peas, etc. were also grown widely.

While the above mentioned socio-economic programme was being carried out the UNLF/MPA was also engaged continuously against the Indian Occupation Forces (IOF). In the current year 7 engagements took place of which 5 were major. The IOF suffered several casualties. The MPA also suffered some casualties.

Thus, maintaining close touch with the masses of the people the UNLF have been building its strength continuously so as to intensify the confrontation with the IOF. Basic Military Training to new recruits is being imparted batch after batch throughout the year. Procurement of arms and ammunition, including heavy weapons, is also continuing. All these have been made possible by the support of our people. Thus, the strength of the UNLF have become the strength of the people. The UNLF call upon the entire people and all the revolutionary Parties to for a united struggle to overthrow Indian colonial rule.

14. People's Stand: In view of the changing situation of our liberation struggle, it is time for our people to take a clear-cut stand on related issues. Our people are called upon to distinguish between right and wrong, and good and bad aspects of the policy and programme of the revolutionary Parties. Particularly, it is time to specifically point out and rectify only the 'erring' Party and stop the practice of heaving the blame on all. Otherwise the mistakes will repeat. Therefore, when mistakes occur it should to be pointed out and rectified, while good works needs to be commended and strengthened.

We have stated above the UNLF line on national, social and economic issues and the stand of the UNLF thereof. We urge our people to deliberate on the issues raised by the UNLF. If inconsistencies are found, we would welcome corrections. These may be discussed on the columns of newspapers, or, sent by email to unlfmanipur@yahoo.com The UNLF Central Committee appeals to our people to extend full support to the UNLF if the issues raised by the UNLF are considered to be relevant in the context of our existing reality. Our people should play a big role in steering the liberation struggle towards the correct direction.

15. Revolutionary Greetings:

(i) On this occasion of the 43rd Foundation Anniversary of the UNLF, the UNLF Central Committee offers hearty revolutionary greetings to Party Cadres and Local Members, Officers, NCOs and Privates of the Army, family members of the martyrs, those rendered handicapped by IOF tortures, those in enemy jails, those performing their respective duties in various places outside Manipur and to all our compatriots taking part in today's functions;

(ii) On this day, the UNLF Central Committee extends fraternal revolutionary greetings to all the revolutionary parties of Manipur fighting for sovereignty and independence of Manipur and also reiterate the stand for a united struggle;

(iii) Also, the UNLF Central Committee extends revolutionary greetings to the leaders and fighters of fraternal Parties of the Region—KLO, NSCN (K), TPDF and ULFA. We are proud of the firm stand being taken by these fraternal Parties not to enter into 'ceasefire' and 'peace-talk' with the Indian government;

(iv) As before, the UNLF Central Committee also extends fraternal greetings to the Kashmiri people and wish speedy victory to their struggle;

(v) Especially, on this occasion, the UNLF Central Committee offers sincere greetings and gratitude to the foreign countries, CSOs and NGOs giving moral support to the cause of the Manipur people's 'Right to national self determination' and also to the international media for their stories on the Manipur-India Conflict.

16. Revolutionary Salute: On this sacred day of the UNLF, the UNLF Central Committee offers revered homage and revolutionary salute to the departed founder-leaders and Party Cadres, martyred fighters of the Army, and all the compatriots killed by the IOF. The UNLF will fight on relentlessly following their ideals of struggle and sacrifice until final victory is won. We will follow their path steadily and surely.

Before we conclude here the 'Annual Statement of the Central Committee 2007' the UNLF Central Committee once again offers revolutionary salute to the entire people of Manipur.

"Long Live, UNLF!"
"Victory to MPA!"
"Victory to our people!"

Central Committee, UNLF

Kangla,
24 November 2007

Bibliography

PRIMARY SOURCES

Archival

Manipur Administration Report

1907–08; 1908–09; 1918–19; 1919–20; 1927–28; 1931–32; 1938–39; 2005–06

Manipur Durbar Resolution

No. 12 of 13-7-1908; 1 January 1928; No. 3 of 20 February 1935; No. 11 of 9 February 1938; 27 June 1938; No. 1 of 21 December 38; 15 March 1939; No. 12 of 12 July 1939; No. 28 of 7 and 8 March 1945; No 1 of 20 July 46; No. 17 of 21 August 1946; No 10 of 20 November 1946; No. 14 of 23 December 1946; No. 25 of 30 April 1947; No. 22 of 18 May 1947; No 29 of 4 June 1947.

Documents

- Manipur King's Memo No. 1001- P.1.1, 11 April 1939, submitted to the Manipur Durbar.
- Fortnightly confidential 31st Reports 1964–66, Imphal, Government of Manipur, MSA.
- His Highness the Maharajah Memo No. 715 I-I, MSD Proceeding, 1928.
- Kuki Rising, 1917–19; File, L/PS/10/724, Oriental and India Office Collections (OIOC).
- Letter from C. Gimson to Mills, Imphal, 19 February 1940, MSA.
- Letter from LO Clarke, PA in Manipur, to Commandant, 23 September 1920; File, Bazaar Boycott of 1920, MSA.

- Letter of King Churachand sent to Gimson, 19 February 1940; File No. 18 C/40, Confidential Programme B, December 1940, R-a/S-C/144, MSA.
- Memorandum No. 124 submitted by H. Irabot, President, Nikhil Manipuri Mahasabha to the Maharajah of Manipur on 2 November 1939; Governor's Secretariat Program for December 1940, R-1/S-C/170, MSA.
- Disturbance in Manipur 1904 (Women Agitation) 1904, R-1/S-A, MSA.
- Rani Gaidinliu case file 1930–35, R-1/3-B, 35.

Acts, Bills, Orders

- Armed Forces (Special Powers) Act 1958, Act No. 28 of 1958, 11 September 1958.
- Criminal Law Amendment Act, 1961, Act No. 23 of 196, 17 May 1961.
- Environment Protection Act (EPA), 1986.
- Foreigners (Protected Areas) Order, 1958.
- Indian Constitution (Scheduled Tribes), (Part C States) Order, 1951.
- Indian Union Territories Act, 1963.
- Land Acquisition Act 1894.
- Manipur (Hill Areas) District Councils Act 1971; Act No. 76 of 1971, 26 December 1971.
- Manipur (Village Authorities in Hill Areas) Act, 1956, No. 80 of 1956, 22 December, 1956.
- Manipur Administration Order, 15 October, 1949.
- Manipur Constitution Act of 1947.
- Manipur Land Revenue and Land Reforms Act, 1960.
- Manipur Merger Agreement or Shillong Accord of 1949.
- Manipur Naturalisation Act, 1947.
- Manipur Official Language (Amendment) Bill, 2003.
- Manipur Official Language Act, 1979.
- Manipur State Constitution Act, 1947.
- Manipur State Hill Peoples (Administration) Regulation, 1947.
- Naga Hills-Tuensang Areas Act, 1957, No. 42 of 1957, 29 November, 1957.
- North Eastern Council (NEC) Act, 1971.
- North-eastern Areas (Reorganization) Act, 1971, Act No. 81 of 1971, 30 December 1971.
- Right to Information Act, 2005; Act No. 22 of 2005, 15 June 2005.
- State of Nagaland Act, 1962, No. 27 of 1962, 4 September 1962.

Parliamentary and State Assemblies Sources

- Address by His Excellency, the Governor of Manipur, Shri B.K. Nehru to the Manipur Legislative Assembly, 30 March 1972.
- Agricultural Policy of the Manipur State, Questions orally answered in Manipur Legislative Assembly Secretariat, Tuesday, 8 May 2007.
- Calling attention to discrimination and racial profiling faced by the students from the North-eastern states in some part of the country, Parliament Debate, 4 May 2012.
- Calling Attention, Manipur Legislative Assembly session, Imphal; 6 July 2005 and 13 July 2005.
- Constituent Assembly Debates, Volumes I, II, IV, VI, VII, IX and XI.
- Further discussion on the Motion of Thanks on the President's Address initiated by Dr Vijay Kumar Malhotra and seconded by Dr S. Venugopal, 7 March, 2001; Lok Sabha, 8 March 2001.
- Inaugural speech of the First Chief Commissioner of Manipur at the First Session of the State Advisory Council; Manipur State Gazette, Extraordinary, No. 84-E-44 10/10/50. 26.
- Lok Sabha Stared Question No. 25 to be answered on 24 July 2001, No. 31 to be answered on 24 July 2001, No. 31 to be answered on 24 July 2001, No. 155 to be answered on 30 July 2003.
- Lok Sabha Unstarred Question: No. 972 to be answered on 01 March 2000, No. 6610 to be answered on 9 May 2000, No. 840 to be answered on 23 November 2000, No. 3490 to be answered on 20 March 2001, No. 275 to be answered on 24 July 2001, No. 1422 to be answered on 31 July 2001, No. 4297 to be answered on 21 August 2001, No. 1680 to be answered on 28 November 2001, No. 4637 to be answered on 19 December 2001, No. 4579 to be answered on 18 December 2002, No 275 to be answered on 22 July 2003, No. 3252 to be answered on 21 December 2004, No. 1076 to be answered on 29 November 2005.
- Manipur Assembly Resolution on Territorial Integrity of Manipur 24 June 2005.
- Manipur State Assembly Resolution, 15 April 1977, 23 March 1983, 29 February 1984.
- Rajya Sabha Unstarred Question No 371 to be answered on 25 July 2001, No. 3249 to be answered on 24 April 2002.
- Report of the Frontier Areas Committee of Enquiry, Camp Maymyo, dated 21 April 1947.

- Law and Order Situation in Manipur, Lok Sabha, Tuesday, 17 August 2004.
- The Minister of External Affairs' Statement on Reported statement made by the Ambassador of China on Arunachal Pradesh, submission by Members; Lok Sabha Synopsis of Debates, (Proceedings other than Questions & Answers), Friday, 24 November 2006.
- Compensation for the Loktak Affected Areas, Questions orally answered in Manipur Legislative Assembly Secretariat, Tuesday, 8 May, 2007.

Memorandum

- A draft policy to protect and uphold the unique historical features, existing historical boundary and also for bringing emotional integration of the people of Manipur to achieve faster economic development of the state (henceforth UCM draft policy), Imphal, United Committee Manipur (UCM), 2002.
- KNO's Memorandum to the Prime Minister of India 2006, Ref. ZG/GEN 02-671/06, 9 August 2006.
- KSO Memorandum to the Prime Minister of India, Imphal, 6 March 2007.
- Memorandum of Citizens' Concern for Dam and Development submitted to the Prime Minister of India, Dr Manmohan Singh to desist from laying the foundation stone of Tipaimukh High Dam in his proposed visit on 2 December 2006, 28 November 2006.
- Memorandum of the Forum of Chief Ministers of the North Eastern States Submitted to the Prime Minister, June 21, 2000.
- Memorandum of the JAC Lei-Ingkhol to the Chief Minister, Manipur, 28 December 2010.
- Memorandum of the JAC Lei-Ingkhol to the Chief Minister, Manipur, Manipur, 26 April 2005.
- Memorandum of the JAC Lei-Ingkhol to the Governor of Manipur, 21 February 2005.
- Memorandum on the protection of the Territorial Integrity of Manipur submitted to the Prime Minister of India, by All Political Party Delegation from Manipur, 20 January 2003.
- Memorandum submitted by Naga Civil Societies to the President of India, 24 April 2001.
- Memorandum Submitted by the Manipur People's Party to the Prime Minister of India, 4 October 1978.

- Memorandum submitted to Dr Kofi Anan, Secretary-General, United Nations Organization, Geneva, by the Kuki National Organization, May 2005.
- Memorandum submitted to His Majesty's Government, Government of India and its Constituent Assembly through the Advisory Sub-Committee by the Mizo Union, 1947.
- Memorandum Submitted to Prime Minister Rajiv Gandhi by the Manipur Kuki Tribes Recognition Demand Committee, 28 April 1987.
- Memorandum Submitted to the Prime Minister of India by the Mizo National Front General Headquarters, Aizawl, Mizoram, 30 October 1965.
- Memorandum submitted to the Prime Minister of India by the Zomi Re-Unification Organization (ZRO), 6 September 1993.
- Memorandum submitted to the Prime Minister of India by All Political Party Delegation from Manipur on the protection of the Territorial Integrity of Manipur, 20 January 2003.
- Memorandum submitted to the Prime Minister of India, Submitted by the Kuki Students' Organization Delhi demanding Withdrawal of Centre-NSCN(IM) Ceasefire Extension beyond Nagaland, 27 June 2001.
- Memorandum submitted to the Prime Minister of India, submitted by the Manipur Land Revenue and Land Reform Act Extension Demand Committee, Ref No. Fax 3029545, 7 May 2002.
- Memorandum submitted to the Secretary-General United Nations and the Chairman of the Decolonization Committee (committee of 24) for de-colonization of Manipur from Indian colonialism and alien racist regime, enlisting Manipur in the list of the non-self-governing-territories of the United Nations and, restoration of independence and sovereignty of Manipur, Revolutionary People's Front (RPF), Manipur, 2nd ed., 1999.
- Memorandum submitted to the Secretary-General, United Nations by the Zo Reunification Organization (ZORO) on 20 May 1993.
- Memorandum to the Chief Minister of Manipur, submitted by the United Committee Manipur, File, UCM, Ref. No. 3/1/Memo/2002, 24 April 2002.
- Memorandum to the Member Secretary, Manipur Pollution Control Board, expressing Objection regarding the Public Hearing to be held at Sibapukhrikhal Community Hall, Churachandpur district on 21 November 2012, submitted by the Secretary-General of the Zomi Human Rights Foundation, 19 November 2012

- Naga Memorandum to Simon Commission, 10 January 1929. Signed by representatives of Angami, Kacha Naga, Kuki, Sema, Lotha, and Rengma tribes.
- Office Memorandum under the subject 'Advisory on the discrimination and racial profiling faced by Indian citizens North Eastern States in some parts of the country – Measures needed to curb regarding. F. No. 15011/34/2012–SC/ST–W, Government of India/Bharat Sarkar Ministry of Home Affairs/Grih Mantralaya, North Block Delhi/CS Division, New Delhi, 10 May 2012.
- Petition of the women society of the east 'submitted to the Chief Minister of Manipur by the Manipur Nupi Khunnai', Imphal East, 16 May 1980.
- Submission of Committee on Human Rights (COHR), Manipur on Human Rights Situation in Manipur (India) to OHCHR Concerning the Universal Periodic Review of the Government of India at UN Human Rights Council, April 2008.

Administrative, Police and Legal Sources

- All India Reporter, 1998, Supreme Court of India, 463-464.
- Confidential letter to the Chief Justice, Guwahati High Court, from Registrar General, 25 May 2005, in the Guwahati High Court (In the Court of Assam, Nagaland, Meghalaya, Manipur, Tripura, Mizoram & Arunachal Pradesh): File No. HC, III-83/2004/1801/G dated 26 May 2005, from the Registrar General, Guwahati High Court, Guwahati, to the Chief Secretary, Government of Manipur, Imphal.
- Deputy Commissioner Imphal East District, Notification No. DC (IE)/59/2006 (Pt), 6 May 2011.
- Industrial Policy of Manipur, 1996.
- Judgment, Guwahati High Court, Bench BNJC, Sagolsem Indramani Singh And Ors. vs State Of Manipur, 26 May, 1954: Equivalent citations, 1955 CriLJ 184.
- Manipur Culture Policy: A Draft, Department of Arts and Culture, Government of Manipur, November 2002.
- Notice for provisional enrolment of refugees in the electoral roll of the house of people, Notified by P.C. Deb, Reform Officer, Imphal, 25 August 1949; document in possession of (late) Padmashree Ningthoukhongjam Khelchandra, Uripok, Imphal.
- Notification by District Collector, Imphal East District, No. DC (IE)/12/52/2004, 20 January 2005.

- Notification by District Collector, Imphal West, No. DC (II)/6/186/LA/MLAs/2004, 11 January 2005.
- Notification, Office of the Chief Commissioner, Manipur, No. 0001/CC. of 15 October 1949 (12 Noon), the Manipur Gazette, extraordinary published by the authority, No. 1E1, Imphal, Saturday, 15 October, 1949, Government of Manipur, Orders by the Chief Commissioner, Personal collection of (late) Padmashree Ningthoukhongjam Khelchandra, Uripok, Imphal.
- Order, Guwahati High Court, Bench BNC in Ram Manohar Lohia and Ors. vs V.S. Sundaram on 26 April, 1955: Equivalent citations: 1955 CriLJ 1603.
- Secretariat, Revenue Department, Government of Manipur, Notification No. 4/42/LA/2010-Com (Rev), 24 March, 2011.
- Manipur Gazette, Wednesday, 26 October 1949, No. 219.
- Notification No. 8597-601 H.D., dated, 18 November 1950; Manipur Gazette, 29 November 1950.
- Manipur Gazette, Monday, 9 December 1996.
- Legal Notice, dated 1/8/2003, claimed to be submitted to: the Secretary of Home Affairs, Government of India, New Delhi, and the Secretary of Home Affairs, Government of United Kingdom, London by one Sanasam Sarat Singh, an advocate based in UK on behalf of the Universal Friendship Organization based in Manipur.
- Arrest Memo issued by the 17 Assam Rifles, 11 July 2004, 3.30 p.m., Annexure to Home Department, Government of Manipur Office, Memorandum Number 2/8 [86] 96-H-dated 5 June 1997.
- Judgment, 31 December 2010, Civil Original Jurisdiction Suit No. 10 of 2005/20/09, Civil Judge (Sr) Division No. II, Manipur East.

Sources from CSO

- 'Request for financial assistance ...for XIX cultural Meet on 28 and 29 August 2002'; Application submitted to the United Committee Manipur by the Sandang Shenba Maring Youth Club, Imphal.
- Application by Rameshkumar to the UCM; File UCM, 15 June 2002.
- Application by Sitlhou Council India, Head Office, Motbung, Sadar Hills, Manipur, Ref. No. 1/3/S.C.1-2002, 18 July 2002.
- Application by the Demand Committee on Restoration of Gaan-Ngai Holiday (A Joint Action Committee of ZU, ZYF, ZSUM, ZUCAMV, ZWS, AZACO, ZCC and ZRCP) addressed to the President UCM/AMUCO/AMSU/MSF/KIM/LFWPK, November, 2002.

- Application submitted to the AMESCO by S. Dangsa Maring, President, Maring Students' Union, February 2004.
- Application submitted to the AMESCO by the Nupi Khunai Chaokhat Lamjinglup (Soceity of Women Towards Development), Moreh, Chandel District, 8 February 2004.
- Application submitted to UCM by Alen Thanga, Secretary General, Kangchup Chiru Youth Club; Ref. No. 41, 31 August 2003.
- Application submitted to UCM by All Manipur Muslim institute, HO Haoreibi Turel Ahanbi, BPO, Ningei; Ref. No. 11(c)/AMMI/ 2002, 29 August 2002.
- Application submitted to UCM by D.T. Merung Maring, Chairperson, Seven Village Development Committee, Heinoukhong, Chandel District, Manipur, 6 February 2004.
- Application submitted to UCM by the Komrem Students' Union, Manipur, HQ: Zone III, C/3 National Game Village, Imphal, 3 November 2002.
- Application to the Superintendent, Department of Archaeology, Government of Manipur; Ref. No. L/1/UCM/AC, 13 March 2002.
- Petition with a prayer for assistance of Rs 30,000/- for purchasing a second hand motorbike had been, Petition to the United Committee Manipur by a member from Kuki Inpi Manipur; Imphal, 22 January 2004.

Pamphlets, Leaflets, Invitations

- Calendar Programme for 2004, AMESCO; File, Ref. No. AMESCO/ CP/04.
- Copies of the protest pamphlets circulated by the JAC Lei-Ingkhol, May 2005.
- Eikhoigee wakat (Our complaint), Communication group Manipur Nupee Kanglup Kangleipak (Manipur) Imphal, 27 May 1980.
- Expedition Tousem; Invitation letter circulated by All Manipur Ethnical Socio-cultural Organization, 1999.
- Gan-Ngai Festival Invitation; State Level Celebration, Kuki Inn, 8 January 2001.
- International Women's Day invitation circulated by All Manipur Women's Volunteer Association, 1 March 2000.
- Invitation Mera Houchongba-2002; Ethno Heritage Council (HERICOUN), October 2002.
- Invitation to attend Manipur Defense Rally on 28 September 2008; Apunba Manipur Kanba Ima Lup (AMKIL) and National Identity

Protection Committee (NIPCO), 18 September 2000.

- Invitation to Inter Community Cultural Festival 2003, organized by RPDF, REACH-M, ATWO & PAACWA (Pallel mixed community organization).
- Invitation to take part in Kangla Marathon 1999 circulated by Manipur Pari Apunba Lup (MAPALUP) and United Club Organization (UCO).
- 'Kangla Question', 5 August 2000, Delhi, Eramdam Manipur Mothers' Association.
- 'Let us protect Unity and Integrity of Manipur', pamphlet circulated by AMUCO, July and August 1997.
- Manipur Dark Day invitation card, 17 April 1999, circulated by Chanura Lamjinglen Kangleipak.
- Mera Houchongba Invitation, Imphal, United People's Council Thongju, Ref. No. 06/UPC/02/346, October 2002.
- Pamphlet circulated by AMUCO, 30 May 2002.
- Pamphlet entitled 'The Marginalised Indigenous Hill People in Manipur' jointly circulated by the Sinlung Indigenous Peoples Human Rights Organization and Zomi Human Rights Foundation, December 2006.
- Pamphlet released by AMKIL and NIPCO, 18 September 2009.
- Invitation circulated by the United Peoples' Front Manipur (UPF) for the celebration of the spirit of peaceful co-existence at the 2nd Chingmee Tammee Ningol Chakkouba Thouram (Grand Feast for the women of Hill and Valley) on Wednesday, 10 November, 1999 at 8 a.m. at the Lainingthou Puthiba Sanglen, Khurai'.
- 'Root Cause of Kuki-Zomi Conflict', A pamphlet published by the Zomi National Volunteers, 1997.
- 'War cry of the bloodstained Manipuri women', Coordinating Committee, Manipur Nupi Kanglup, 17 June 1980

Reports

- *5th Report of the Second Administrative Reforms Commission*, Government of India, June 2007.
- *A Study in National Security Tyranny Armed Forces Special Powers Act*, South Asia Human Rights Documentation Centre, Delhi.
- *Census of India 1991, Series-15, Manipur, Primary Census Abstract, Part II-B*, Directorate of Census Operations, Manipur, 1995.
- *Census of India 1991, Series-15, Manipur, Part II-A, General Population Tables*, Directorate of Census Operation, Manipur, 1995.

- *Census of India 2001, Administrative Atlas*; Delhi, Registrar General of India, 2005.
- *Country Reports on Human Rights Practices-2007*, Bureau of Democracy, Human Rights, and Labour, USA, 11 March 2008.
- *Criticism and constructive submission regarding the study on treaties, agreements and other constructive arrangements between states and indigenous populations*; Report submitted by Centre for Organization and Research Education, Manipur to the Sub-Commission on the Prevention of Discrimination and Protection of Minorities, Commission on Human Rights, UN, March 1999.
- *Economic Survey Manipur 2005-2006*, Directorate of Economics & Statistics, Government of Manipur, 2006.
- *Manipur Department of Information Technology Times*, Vol. 1, Issue 1, May 2011.
- *Manipur State Development Report, July 2006*, Report of a project sponsored by Planning Commission of India, Institute for Human Development, New Delhi
- *Official Sanction for Killings in Manipur, Amnesty International*; AI INDEX: ASA 20/014/1997, 1 April 1997, India.
- *Report of the Committee to Review, the Armed Forces (Special Powers) Act, 1958*, 2005 also known as Jeevan Reddy Committee Report.
- *Report of the Sub-Committee on Northeast Frontier (Assam) Tribal and Excluded Areas*, Annexure IV, Appendix C, No. OA/24/Cons/47, Constituent Assembly of India, Council House, New Delhi, 4 March 1948.
- *State of Environment Report, Manipur* in http://www.manenvis.nic.in/stateprofile1.pdf as accessed on 22 May 2009.
- *Statistical Handbook of Manipur 2002*, Imphal, Directorate of Economics and Statistic, Government of Manipur, 2002.
- *Tenth Five-Year Plan*, Planning Commission of India, New Delhi.
- *Transforming the Northeast, Tackling Backlogs in Basic Minimum Services and Infrastructural Needs*, High Level Commission Report to the Prime Minister, Government of India, submitted by the Planning Commission, New Delhi, 7 March 1997.
- *Where peacekeepers have declared war, report on violations of democratic rights by security forces and the impact of the Armed Forces Special Powers Act on civilian life in the seven states of the northeast*, Delhi, National Campaign Committee Against Militarization and Repeal of Armed Forces Special Powers Act, 1997.

Dossier, Booklet, Manifesto

- *A Critical Analysis of the Capital Project, Manipur;* Imphal: Citizens' Concern for Dams and Development, 2005.
- *A Nation and Her People Under Siege*; Delhi: The Other Media and Mizzima, August 2004.
- Brief History of Kuki, Kuki Students' Democratic Front (n.d.).
- Manifesto of the Kuki National Organization.
- *Manipur Fact File 2001,* Imphal: All Manipur College Teachers' Association, 2001.
- *On Naga Hoho's Naga Integration*, Naga Socialist Council of Nagaland, (Khaplang Faction), 2002.
- *People of Manipur Rise to Save Unity and Territorial Integrity*, Imphal: United Committee Manipur (UCM), 2002.
- *Polititcal History of Manipur* (15 July 1947 to 02 March 2000), Delhi: Manipur Information Centre, 2002.
- *Unity, development and peace in Manipur: Findings and proposition of the first phase of public dialogue on Unity Development and Peace in Manipur*, Imphal, AMUCO, 2001.
- *Why Manipuris Fight for Right to National Self-Determination,* Manipur: United National Liberation Front, 3rd ed., 2001
- *Why not South Nagaland by the forgotten Nagas*, Naga Integration Committee Manipur, 1969.

Statement, Declaration, Observation

- An introductory statement concerning the Kukis on the occasion of the United Old Kuki Army joining the Kuki National Organization; Ref. No. ZG/IS 02-06/07, 4 December 2007.
- Chapter II, clauses 138.35, 138.44, and 138.45 in United Nations A/HRC/WG.6/13/L.8, 29 May 2012
- Concluding Observations of the UN Human Rights Committee 1991, India; UN Ref. CCPR/C/37/Add.13.
- Joint statement of United National Liberation Front (UNLF), Manipur, Revolutionary People's Front (RPF) Manipur, People's Revolutionary Party of Kangleipak (PREPAK), National Socialist Council of Nagaland (NSCN), United Liberation Front of Asom (ULFA) and Tripura People's Democratic Front (TPDF) (henceforth Joint Statement of the NE Undergrounds 1999), 6 August 1999.
- Kohima Declaration adopted by the civil society groups 'from Nagalim and the Indian Subcontinent', 19 March 2001.

- Naga Peoples Convention, Senapati Declaration, 28 June 2001.
- Nonibala's statement on the occasion of a discussion of publication on democracy, 21 March 2003 at State Guest House, Imphal, organized by Human Rights Alert, Imphal and American Centre, Calcutta.
- Noticed issued in the name of Azang Longmei, General Secretary, United Naga Council, Senapati, 19 October 2003.
- People's declaration to defend the territorial integrity of Manipur, 26 June 2001.
- Solemn Declaration of the Existence of the National Socialist Council of Nagaland (NSCN), 31 January 1980.
- Solidarity statement of Northeast underground organizations, that is, Arunachal Dragon Federation, Achik National Volunteers Council, Dima Halam Daoga, Hynniewtrep National Liberation Council, Kamatapur Liberation Organization, Manipur People's Liberation Front (composed of Revolutionary People's Party of Kangleipak, Revolutionary People's Front & United Liberation Front), National Democratic Front of Boroland, National Socialist Council of Nagaland (Khaplang Faction), National Liberation Front of Twipra, Tripura People's Democratic Front, United people's Democratic Solidarity (Karbi Anglong), United Liberation Front of Asom, 10 January 2001.
- Statement by Dhanabir Laishram Centre for Progress of Manipur Peoples at the UN Working Group on Indigenous Populations 17th Session 26 to 30 July 1999.
- Statement issued on the occasion of the leaders' meet organized by United Committee Manipur at GM Hall, Imphal, 20 May 2002.
- Statement of Khagen Das, an MP from Tripura, in the Rajya Sabha, 28 November 2001, Session 194.
- Statement of Support by Gloria Kim, President and Mughali Achumi, General-Secretary, Naga People's Friends Network Korea, 18 August 2006.
- Statement of the Collective Leadership of the NSCN (IM), 12 April 2001.
- Statement of the Collective Leadership, Statement issued by the NSCN-IM Leadership, 7 March 2001.
- Statement of the NSCN (IM) to the UN Working Group on Indigenous Populations, 12th Session at Geneva, 27 1994.
- Statement of the UCM on the terrorist activities of the NSCN (IM)

against the people of Manipur; Imphal, UCM, 28 March 2002.
- Statement of Yumnam Jiten, Citizen's Concern for Dam & Development, April 2005.
- The Dhaka Declaration on Tipaimukh Dam; Dhaka, Bangladesh, International Tipaimukh Dam Conference, 30 & 31 December 2005, Bangladesh.
- Proclamation of King Bodhachandra, 18 October 1948.

International Instruments and Observations

- Charter of the United Nations 1945.
- Concluding Observations of the UN Human Rights Committee 1991, India; UN Ref. CCPR/C/37/Add.13.
- Concluding Observations of the UN Human Rights Committee 1997, India in UN Ref. CCPR/C/79/Add.81, 4 August 1997.
- Convention against Torture and Other Cruel, Inhuman or Degrading Treatment or Punishment, 1984.
- Convention on the Non-applicability of Statutory Limitations to War Crimes and Crimes against Humanity, 1968.
- Convention on the Prevention and Punishment of the Crime of Genocide, 1948.
- Declaration on the Rights of Persons Belonging to National or Ethnic, Religious and Linguistic Minorities, 1992.
- Geneva Convention relative to the Treatment of Prisoners of War, 1949.
- International Convention on the Elimination of all forms of Racial Discrimination, 1966.
- International Covenant on Civil and Political Rights, 1966.
- International Covenant on Economic, Social and Cultural Rights, 1966.
- UN Declaration on the Granting of Independence to Colonial Countries and Peoples, 1960.
- United Nations General Assembly resolution 49/214, 17 February 1995; International Decade of the World's Indigenous People.
- United Nations General Assembly, Resolution 1514 (XV), 14 December 1960; Declaration on the Granting of Independence to Colonial Countries and Peoples.
- Universal Declaration of Human Rights, 1948.
- Vienna Declaration and Programme of Action Adopted by the World Conference on Human Rights in Vienna, 25 June 1993.

Accords, Treaties and Agreements

- Mizoram Accord of 1986.
- Naga-Akbar Hydari Accord, 1947.
- Mizoram Accord of 1986.
- Sixteen Point Agreement between the Naga People's Convention and the Government of India, 1960.
- Text of Final Peace Accord between Zomis and Kukis for Restoration of Peace and Normalcy, on behalf of Kukis and Zomis respectively by the representatives belonging to Zomi, Kuki, Meetei, Thadou communities, and Government of Manipur, 1 October, 1998.
- Treaty of Yandaboo, 24 February 1826.
- Standstill Agreement of Manipur, 2 July 1947.
- Instrument of Accession, 11 August 1947.
- Merger Agreement of Manipur, 21 September 1949.
- Shillong Accord of 11 November 1975 between the Government of India and the Naga National Council.

Minutes, Resolution, Decisions and Orders

- Decision of the Lei-ingkhol Youth Development Organization and Lei-Ingkhol Khunsem Leimarol Apunba, 15 April 2005.
- Declaration of Manipur People's Solidarity with the United Nations on the occasion of the UN Day Rally at Imphal, 24 October 1999.
- Human Rights Resolutions of the National Seminar on Human Rights, held at Gandhi Memorial Hall, Imphal in Manipur State, 8-9 December 1994.
- Joint resolution of Lei-Ingkhol Youth Development Organization and individuals belonging to Tharon, Tarung and Tangmeiband localities, 21 Febrary 2005.
- Joint Resolutions of the JAC Lei-Ingkhol and Civil Societies, 22 April 2005 and 29 April 2005.
- Manipur Congress Party resolution in favour of the integration of Manipur into India, 29 April 1949.
- Meeyamgi Warep; Imphal, Convention at GM Hall, 23 January 2003.
- Minutes of a Joint Border Meeting held between the representatives of the Burma Government and the Manipur State, 17 December 1947.
- Minutes of the proceeding and resolutions of Manipur State Constitution Making Committee Resolution of 14, 25, 27, and 29 March 1947.

- Minutes of the proceeding of meeting organized by Lei-Ingkhol Youth Development Organization, 12 April 2005.
- Motion for a Resolution on Nagaland Pursuant to Article 47 Part I of the Rules of Procedure tabled by Olivier Dupuis and Gain Franco Dell' Alba on behalf of ARE Group, 2007, http://www.radicalparty.org/humanrights/nag_res.htm; accessed on 25 June 2009.
- Proceeding of the Convention of Ethnic Reconsolidation (Before forming HERICOUN), Imphal, Thursday, 16 May, 2002.
- Proceedings of the understanding made between Shri R.K. Dorendro Singh, Hon'ble Chief Minister, Shri M. Kumar Singh, Hon'nle State Minister (Physical Education & Sports) Manipur, representing Manipur Governmnt and the Students Representatives of All Manipur Students Union (AMSU) and All Manipur Students' Coordination Committee (AMSCOC) at the Chief Minister's Office, 22 July 1980 and 5 August 1980.
- Resolution adopted on the occasion of the Seminar on Kuki National Reconcialation, held at Moreh, organized by Kuki Students Democratic Front (KSDF), Kuki People's Congress (KPC) and Kuki Women Human Rights Organization (KWHRO), 30 November-2 December 2006.
- Resolution No. 6 passed in a joint sitting of the Nikhil Manipuri Mahasabha and the Manipur Praja Mandal, 5 April 1947.
- Resolution of the 1st World Zomi Convention, Aizawl, Mizoram, 19–21 May 1988.
- Resolution of the joint conference of the Nikhil Manipur Mahasabha and Manipur Praja Mandal, 5 April 1946.
- Resolution of the Joint Meeting of the Lei-ingkhol Youth Development Organization & Lei-Ingkhol Khunsem Leimarol Apunba, 13 April 2005.
- Resolution of the Meeting organized under the aegis of the JAC Lei-Ingkhol, 21 April 2005.
- Resolution of the National Convention on Manipur Merger Issue, 28 and 29 October 1993, G.M. Hall, Imphal, Manipur.
- Resolution of the Public Discussion organized by the Committee on the Protection of Natural Resources in Manipur at Jiribam, 29 July 2012; Concerning the Manipur Pollution Control Board's Public Hearings for Oil Exploration in Manipur at Jribam, Parbung and Nungba, 30 July, 8 and 17 August 2012.
- Resolution on the occasion of the International Human Rights Day on 10 December, 1992.

- Resolutions adopted by the Executive Committee of the League Against Imperialism and for National Independence, Berlin, 2 June 1931
- Rules for the Management of the Manipur State; File, Confidential, Government of Eastern Bengal & Assam, Political Department, Political Affairs, September 1907, MSA.
- Supplementary Agreement to the Shillong Accord on 5 January 1976, regarding implementation of Clause II of the Shillong Accord, 11 November 1975.
- Text of Final Peace Accord between Zomis and Kukis for Restoration of Peace and Normalcy, 1 October 1998.
- Text of the agreement signed in the presence of Lt. Gen. V.K. Nayar PVSM, SM (Retd.) Governor of Manipur at the Banquet Hall, Raj Bhavan, Imphal on the 9 November 1994 at 3 p.m. between the All Manipur Students' Union represented by its president Shri Naorem Mohilal and the Government of Manipur represente by Shri K.K. Sethi, IAS, Chief Secretary, Government of Manipur.
- The Dhaka Declaration on Tipaimukh Dam; Dhaka, Bangladesh, International Tipaimukh Dam Conference, 30 & 31 December 2005.
- The Kohima Declaration by the civil society groups from Nagalim and the Indian Subcontinent, adopted on 19 March 2001.

Speeches, Lectures

- Romanes Lecture on the subject of Frontier by Lord Curzon of Kedleston, Viceroy of India (1898–1905) and British Foreign Secretary (1919-24).
- Speech Delivered by Isak Chishi Swu, President, Government of the People's Republic of Nagalim, 21 March 1998.
- Speech delivered by L.K. Advani, on the occasion of Manipur Patriots Day, organized by the Manipur Diaspora Community, Delhi, 13 August 2008.
- Tryst with Destiny; Nehru's speech, 15 August 1947.

Letters

- A facsimile of a signed letter by Wolfgang Heinz, Asia Research Department, Amnesty International, 10 Southampton Street, London WC2E 7HF, England, addressed to Yambem Laba, 24 September 1980.
- KNO Greeting from Zale'n-gam to Mizo National Front; Ref. ZG/LT No. 01-66/06, 10 April 2006.

- KNO letter to Senior Gen Than Shwe, Chairman, State Peace and Development Council, Burma; Ref. ZG/GEN 02-672 Camp Geneva, 9 August 2006.
- Letter from Minister of State for Labour & Employment (Independent Charge), Government of India, Oscar Fernandes to the Secretary, Joint Action Committee against the Eviction of Lei-Ingkhol, 7 November 2006.
- Letter from JE Webster, Chief Secretary to the Chief Commissioner of Assam. To the Secretary to the Government of India, Foreign and Political Department, Shillong, 27 June 1919.
- Letter No. 10/PM/1373-6 of 22 June 1968 of Manipur Territorial Congress Committee.
- Letter to H.E. Mr. Gopinathan Achamulangare, Permanent Representative, Permanent Mission of India, Rue du Valais 9 sent by Anwar Kemal, Chairperson of the Committee on the Elimination of Racial Discrimination, 2 September 2011, Reference GH/ST, United Nations High Commissioner for Human Rights.
- Letter to UCM submitted on 21 August 2002, by K. Bhogendrajit, Lairikyengbam Leikai, Imphal, Phone number 222 848.
- Political Department, Political Branch No. 6310 P from Mr. JE Webster, Chief Secretary to the Chief Commissioner of Assam. To the Secretary to the Government of India, Foreign and Political Department, Shillong, 27 June 1919.
- Sardar Patel's letter to Jawaharlal Nehru, 7 November, 1950

Visual and Oral Sources

- Green banners imprinted with the slogan *Punna Hingminnabagi Leepulna Manipurgi Ngamkhei Ngakli* (The bond of co-existence has been defending the boundary of Manipur) raised by the AMUCO for the few years after 2001.
- Interaction with Hareshwar Goswami, May 2005.
- Interaction with N. Ranjan, a clerk in the Guwahati High Court, Imphal bench, April 2005.
- Interaction with Nilachandra, September 2006.
- Interaction with Rocky, April 2005.
- Interaction with Tum Tum, April 2005.
- Photographs of casualty of the 6 June 2005 police repression on the JAC Lei-Ingkhol.
- Photographs of the 10 May 2005 from Lei-Ingkhol Village to Capitol Project Foundation Stone site at Thangmeiband.

- Photographs of the 30 April 2005 protest in front of the gate of CM's Bungalow by the residents of Lei-Ingkhol.
- Photographs of the 4 May 2005 half road blocked on National Highway 39 carried out by JAC Lei-Ingkhol.
- Photographs of the May 2005 cycle rally from Lei-Ingkhol to Athokpam in Thoubal district.
- Song sung by (late) Khundrakpam Joukumar, entitled 'Malemda saknaribaa Meetei Nupeegi Nupi-Lal' (World famous women's war of Meetei women), 1992.
- Song title 'Loktak Project' in Abok 2; Tapta Volume 9, Imphal, MK. Productions, 2002.
- Statement of Giridhon (70), a leper who belong to the first generation of immigrants, April 2005.
- The foundation stone of the Great June Uprising Memorial Complex installed by the UCM.
- Video recording of 18 June ritual organized by the UCM and the AMUCO, 18 June 2005.
- Video recording of relief package donated by the All Manipur United Clubs Organization to the Lei-Ingkhol Residents, 24 May 2005.
- Video recording of July Protest against AFSPA in Manipur, 2004.
- Video recording of the visit of the Union Minister of State for Labour Oscar Fernandes to the Lei-Ingkhol Village, Imphal, 12 September 2006.

SECONDARY SOURCES

News

Sangai Express

- 2000: 8 October and 21 December
- 2002: 6 May; 14, 18 and 19 June
- 2003: 6 July; 5 August; 7, 8, 9, 10, 13, 14, 15, 16, 17, 21, 23, 24, 25, 29 and 30 October
- 2005: 5 and 21 April; 24 May; 2, 3, 5, 6, 8, 9, 12, 15, 16, 17, 18, 19, 21, 23, 25, 26, 28 and 29 June; 4 and 16 July
- 2006: 11, 15, 22, 25, 26 and 27 July; 1, 8, 9, 17, 22, 23, 24 and 27 August; 7, 9, 10, 27 and 29 September; 2 October; 4 and 5 November
- 2007: 1 January; 25 May; 10, 11, 12, 13, 14, 20, 21 and 26 June; 5, 10, 29 and 22 July; 15, 16, 20 September; 17 October
- 2008; 19, 20 and 28 March; 10 July; 2 and 12 December
- 2009: 21 and 28 January; 5 and 12 April; 14 May; 29 August

Hueiyen News Service, Imphal: 2001, 8 February; 2009, 4 and 9 March, 18 August; 2012, 20 November

Manipur Mail: 2003; 10, 14, 18, 24, 25, 25, 27 October and 4 November

Imphal Free Press: 2000, 19 and 20 December; 2005, 29 April, 11 May; 2006, 17 February; 2008, 25 August

The Telegraph, Calcutta: 2007, 4 February, Sunday

Amrita Bazaar Patrika, Calcutta: 1970, 6 and 18 August

Press Statements

- Annual Statement of the Central Committee United National Liberation Front Manipur, 40TH Anniversary, 24 November 2004.
- Appeal issued by the Publicity Wing, Zomi Reunification Organization (ZRO), 9 August, 1993.
- Bomb blast in front of the Tasar Gate; Press statement of the JAC, 25 June 2005.
- Boycott India's Independence Day in our region; a joint appeal circulated by the Manipur People's Liberation Front, 6 August 1999.
- Freedom Fighter Rani Gaidinliu (1915–1993); Press statement by the Haipei Rani Gaidinliu Birth Anniversary Celebration Committee, 2007.
- Government not to hinder 14 June, 18 observations; www.e-pao.net, news archive, 14 June 2002.
- Govt's secret dealing with ONGC exposed; Oil Exploration in Manipur, Hueiyen News Service, Imphal, 15 December 2012.
- Greetings from Zale'n-gam, the Kuki nation! 10 April 2006.
- Holiday appeal; www.e-pao.net, news archive, 15 May 2005.
- Joint press release of Zeliangrong Union, Action Committee against TIpaimukh Dam, Citizens' Concern for Dams and Development, Committee against Tipaimukh Dam circulated, 13 December 2006.
- KNO Rebukes UNLF's Duplicitous Statement; Kuki National Organization, Ref. No. ZG/PR 04-06/07, 11 June 2007.
- Lam Amukkasu Lousin-gadouri in Poknapham Daily, Sunday, 19 December 2010.
- Letter to Our Meetei Brothers and Sisters; NSCN (IM), 8 March 2001.
- Message of Gratitude; NSCN-IM, 1 July 1999. http://nscn.livejournal.com.
- NSCN-(IM) threatens to end ceasefire; 4 September 2000.
- Policy Yaodaba Leingaklonna Khutsemgi Ethnic Crisis thokhan-gadouribra (Is the politics that lacks policy going to instigate ethnic crisis?); press statement released by AMESCO; File, AMESCO/

CCP- 01/02, 30 October 2001.

- Press Release by the Ministry of Home Affairs on the Extension of ceasefire with the NSCN-IM, 14 June 2001.
- Press Release circulated by the Manipur Information Centre, New Delhi, 27 July 2001.
- Press statement of AMUCO; File, No. 3/2/SP(AMUCO)/PR/2003-28.
- Press statement of AMUCO; File, PR 3/1/2003; No. 3/1/SP (AMUCO)/PR/2003.
- Press statement of Naga People's Movement for Human Rights, 17 September 1993.
- Press Statement of NSCN-IM Stand on Extension of ceasefire, 21 June 2000.
- Press statement of Tharon Village Authority sent to the ISTV Network, Imphal, 12 November 2004.
- Press statement of the Naga People's Movement for Human Rights, Imphal, 17 September 1993.
- Proclamation by the President of the People's Republic of Nagaland, 2 March 1999.
- RPF imposed a complete ban on Hindi Movies in Manipur.
- SIPHRO's stand on Tipaimukh Dam, 29 March 2008.
- UCM wants June 18 declared state holiday; www.e-pao.net, news archive, 6 May 2002.
- UCM, UNC explain stand on June 18; www.e-pao.net, news archive, 12 June 2005.
- Who is the author of division among the Nagas and their territory?; NSCN-IM, September 2006.
- ZUCAM bandh; August 24, 2002.
- ZUCAM ultimatum; 10 August 2002.

Articles

'A nutshell on Kuki Occupied Territories,' Kukiforum.

'Army Rule' in *Economic and Political Weekly*, Vol. 22, No. 40, 3 October 1987.

'Army vs Civil Administration' in *Economic and Political Weekly*, Vol. 24, No. 6, 11 February 1989.

'Damaged in Body and Mind Source' in *Economic and Political Weekly*, Vol. 25, No. 37, 15 September 1990.

'Different Norms' in *Economic and Political Weekly*, Vol. 23, No. 34, 20 August 1988.

'Guarding the Guards' in *Economic and Political Weekly*, Vol. 25, No. 23, 9 June 1990.

'Meenei Naithanggi Punshi' (An enslaved life) in Lamyanba; *Pan Manipur Youth League*, Imphal, October 1974.

'Murder in Plain Sight', *Tehelka,* Vol. 6 Issue 31, Delhi, August 2009.

'Naga Nation', 16 April 1994.

'Revolutionary nationalist party and Sagolsem Indramani', Imphal, *Sangai Express*, 24 April 2007.

'The Evolution of Nehru's Policy on Tibet: 1947-1954'; *Tibetan Bulletin*, Official Journal of the Tibetan Administration, May-June 2000.

'The Nagas Struggle for Freedom & Justice' in *Justice & Peace*; Boston, MA 02127-1093, 28 May 1994.

Amer, Moamenla, 'Identity and Autonomy Issues in Nagaland' in Singh, L. Muhindro, ed., Conflict Transformation, Peace and Ethnic Divide in *India's Northeast: The Context of Recent Trends,* Guwahati, Kamakhya Publishing House, 2013.

Borgohain, Homen, 'Manipur: Anatomy of Despair,' *Economic and Political Weekly*, Vol. 17, No. 46/47, 13-20 November, 1982.

Bose, Tapan, 'Obstructing Justice' in *Economic and Political Weekly*, Vol. 24, No. 5, 4 February 1989.

Dipankar Dasgupta, Pradip Maiti, Robin Mukherjee, Subrata Sarkar, Subhendu Chakrabarti, 'Growth and Interstate Disparities in India', *Economic and Political Weekly*, Vol. 35, No. 27, 1-7 July, 2000.

Dena, Lal, 'The unresolved issues of the Hmar' (n.d.)

Dewan, Deepak, 'Breach of Trust; an exclusive interview with Thuingaleng Muivah', Delhi: *Northeast Sun*, 1 July 1998.

Dutt, Srikant, 'Migration and Development: The Nepalese in Northeast' in *Economic and Political Weekly*, Vol. 16, No. 24, 13 June 1981.

Dyakov, M, 'The National Question in the Indian Union and Pakistan' in *Revolutionary Democracy*; Vol. IX, No. 2, New Delhi, September 2003.

Gogoi, Nitin, 'Government rejects NSCN demand for extension of ceasefire to other Northeastern states', NSCN-IM, 3 August 2000.

Greenfield, Liah, 'Nationalism in Western and Eastern Europe Compared' in Stephen E. Hanson and Willfried Spohn, eds., *Can Europe Work? Germany & the Reconstruction of Postcommunist Societies*, London: University of Washington Press, 1995.

Guha, Amalendu, 'The Indian National Question: A Conceptual Frame,' in *Economic and Political Weekly*, Vol. 17, No. 31, 31 July 1982).

Guha, Amalendu, 'Little Nationalism Turned Chauvinist: Assam's Anti-Foreigner Upsurge, 1979-80' in *Economic and Political Weekly*, Vol. 15, No. 41/43, Special Number, October 1980.

Haokip, P.S., 'Ideological Aspects of Zale'n-gam', Kuki International Forum, 2008.

Haokip, P.S., 'The Zale'n-gam and Kangleipak Equation' in *Zale'n-gam: The Kuki Nation*, 1998.

Haokip, P.S., *Zale'n-gam: The Kuki Nation*, Kuki National Organization, private circulation, 1998.

Kamei, Gangumei, 'Origin of the Nagas' in *Nagas at Work*, Delhi: Naga Students' Union, 1996.

Dena, Lal, ed., *History of Modern Manipur (1826-1949)*, Delhi: Orbit Publishers, 1991.

Laba, Yambem, 'Human Rights: Issues at Stake in Manipur' paper presented at the National Seminar on Human Rights, 8-9 December 1994 at the Gandhi Memorial Hall, Imphal, Manipur.

Leach, E.R., 'The Frontiers of Burma' in *Comparative Studies in Society and History,* Vol. 3, No. 1, October 1960, Cambridge University Press.

Luntinsat, 'Kuki-Meiteis: Not Border Fencing but Farewell', KSDF, 2007.

Macha Leima, Nupigi Numit, Special Issue, Imphal, 12 December 1999.

Mao, A. Kholi, 'Communal Harmony', paper presented at a 'Seminar on Communal Harmony', A three-day seminar on impact of administration on mutual relationship of Manipuris, Organized by Integrated Peoples Progressive Union (IPPU), Imphal, 2001.

Mathur, Kuldeep, 'The State and the Use of Coercive Power in India' in *Asian Survey,* Vol. 32, No. 4, April 1992, University of California Press.

Maxwell, Neville, 'Forty Years of Folly: what caused the Sino-Indian boundary conflict and why the dispute is unresolved' in *Mainstream*, Vol. Xli, No. 18, Delhi, 19 April 2003.

Meister, Irene W., 'The Bandung conference: an appraisal' in Harry Hazard, W. and Hupe, Robert Strausz, eds., *The Idea of Colonialism*, New York, Frederick A. Praeger, 1958.

Misra, Tilottoma, 'Assam: A Colonial Hinterland' in *Economic and Political Weekly*, Vol. 15, No. 32, 9 August 1980.

Mohendro, N., 'Development experience in Manipur (1891-1969) and the lost article of self-reliance,' 2002.

Morris, Glenn T., 'Race Wars in Nagaland, Brahmanic Kautilyan Policies of Divide and Rule, Nagaland: Still Fighting After All These Years'; *Fourth World Bulletin*, April 1994, Reproduced by the NSCN-IM on 14 April 1994.

Nabakumar, W., 'The inter-ethnic relationship of the different communities of Manipur, a critical appraisal', Paper presented at a three-day seminar on impact of administration on mutual relationship of

Manipuris, organized by Integrated Peoples Progressive Union (IPPU) Imphal, 2001.

Nath, Lpita, 'Migrants in flight; Conflict-induced internal displacement of Nepalis in Northeast India' in *Peace and Democracy in South Asia*, Vol. 1, No. 1, January 2005.

Navlakha, Gautam, 'Growing Indo-US Military' in *Economic and Political Weekly*, Vol. 30, No. 36, 9 September 1995.

Nilbir, Sairem, 'The relation between the hill and plain peoples since time immemorial' in *Meeyamgi Khollao,* Imphal: Khurai Pana Apunba Singlup, 2002.

Nilbir, Sairem, 'The revivalist movement of Sanamahism' in Naorem Sanajaoba, ed., *Manipur: Past and Present*, Vol. II, Delhi: Mittal Publications, 1991.

Oinam, G.S., 'The Kukis', Kuki International Forum, 2006.

Pamei, Aram, 'Havoc of Tipaimukh High Dam Project' in *Economic and Political Weekly*, Vol. 36, No. 13, 31 March-6 April 2001.

Patel, Vibha J., 'Naga and Kuki: Who is to Blame?' in *Economic and Political Weekly*, Vol. 29, No. 22, 28 May 1994.

Purcell, Mark 'A place for the copts: imagined territory and spatial conflict in Egypt' in *Cultural Geographies*, DOI: 10.1177/096746089800500403, 1998.

Rajen, Thokchom., 'Lamdamsida meira paibeegi eehou' in Macha Leima, *Nupigi Numit*, Special Issue, 12 December 1999.

Rajesh, Salam, 'Kangla Impass', *Manipur Update*, Vol. I, Issue IV, Imphal: Human Right Alert, 2000.

Ramsan, Achan, 'The basis of territorial integrity and history: a quest for justice in retrospection'.

Ratner, Steven R., 'Drawing a Better Line: Uti Possidetis and the Borders of New States' in *American Journal of International Law*, Vol. 90, Issue 4, 1996.

Robb, Peter, 'The Colonial State and Constructions of Indian Identity: An Example on the Northeast Frontier in the 1880s' in *Modern Asian Studies*; Vol. 31, No. 2, May 1997, Cambridge: Cambridge University Press.

Roychowdhury, Amitabha, 'Resolve core issue of integration, IM tells GoI', New Delhi, 17 June 2005.

Sanajaoba, Naorem, 'Manipur's Aborted 1950 Revolution, On Afoji Hari alias Jogeshwar alias Irabot', private circulation, 2008.

Sanajaoba, Naorem, 'Why India cannot disturb Manipur boundary of 1947? uti possidetis juris', 2001.

Sandeep, 'Institutionallisation of insurgency in Manipur', news@ashanet.org, 1999.

Scelle, Georges, 'Obsession du Territoire' in *Symbolae Verzijl* (1958) in Steven R. Ratner, 'Drawing a Better Line: Uti Possidetis and the Borders of New States' in *American Journal of International Law*, Vol. 90, Issue 4, 1996.

Shimray, U.A., 'Naga Integration Movement: A Historical Perspective'.

Singh, A.K. and Sunder Kumar, 'Distribution pattern of population in Manipur; A geographical analysis' in *Journal of the Geographical Society of Manipur*, Vol. 1, No. 1, Imphal, July-December 1997.

Singh, Bhogendro, 'Manipur the right of self-determination, a summary' (n.d.).

Singh, P. Lalitkumar, 'The People of Manipur,' 2001.

Stankiewicz, W.J., 'Nationalism' in *World Encyclopaedia of Peace*, Second Edition, Vol. III.

Talukdar, Sushanta, 'Siege within', Delhi: *Frontline*, Vol. 22, Issue 16, 30 July-12 August 2005.

Zernatto, Guido, 'Nation: the history of a word' in Hutchinson, John, and Smith, Anthony D., eds., *Nationalism: Critical Concepts in Political Science*, Vol. I, London: Routledge, 2002.

Books

.... *Annexation of Manipur 1949*, Manipur: Peoples' Democratic Movement, 1995.

..........*Bharatki Loilam Manipur* (Manipur, the colony of India), Imphal: Pan Manipuri Youth League, 1993.

.........*Naga Resistance and the Peace Process*, Delhi: The Other Media, 2001.

.........*Youths' Mental Unrest in Manipur*, Imphal: National Research Centre Manipur, 1996.

.........*Meira Paibee*, Manipur: Imphal National Research Centre, 1999.

Adhikari, G., ed., *Marxist Miscellany*, Vol. 8, Bombay: People's Publishing House, 1946.

Agamben, Giorgio, ed., *State of Exception*, Chicago: University of Chicago Press, 2004.

Anderson, Benedict, *Imagined Communities: Reflections on the origin and Spread of Nationalism*; London: Verso, revised ed., 1995.

Barnard, Calvin James, *The China-India Border War*, Marine Corps Command and Staff College, 1984.

Barsamian, David and Noam Chomsky, *Propaganda and the Public Mind*, Delhi: Madhyam Books, 2001.

Bayly, Susan, *Caste, Society and Politics in India from the Eighteenth Century to the Modern Age*, Delhi: Cambridge University Press, 2002.

Billig, Michael, *Banal Nationalism*, London: Sage Publications, 1995.

Bisheswar, Nameirakpam, *Manipur gi neta anouba santidas gosaini* (new politician of Manipur is a Santidas Gosai), Imphal, 1988.

Chatterjee, Partha, ed., *Wages of Freedom*, New Delhi: Oxford University Press, 1999.

Chaube, S.K., *Hill Politics in Northeast India*, Patna: Orient Longman, second ed., 1999.

Constantine, R., *Manipur, Maid of the Mountains*, Delhi: Lancers Publications, 1981.

Das, Durga, ed., *Sardar Patel's Correspondence 1949-50*, Vol. 8, 1973.

Ibid., Vol. 10.

Devi, Kh. Sarojini, ed., *Manipur Who is Who 1891*, Imphal: Manipur State Archives, 1990.

Dhar, Maloy Krishna, *Open Secrets: India's Intelligence Unveiled*, Delhi: Manas Publications, 2006.

Evans, Sir Geoffery, and Antony Brett James, *Imphal: A Flower on Lofty Heights,* London: Macmillan & Co, 1964.

Ghosh, Suniti Kumar, *The Himalayan Adventure: India-China War of 1962-Causes and Consequences*, Mumbai: Research Unit for Political Economy, 2002

Ghosh, Suniti Kumar, *India's Nationality Problem and Ruling Classes,* Calcutta, January 1996.

Guha, Ramchandra, *India After Gandhi*, Delhi: Picador 2008.

Gupta, Karunakar, *Spotlight on Sino-Indian Frontiers*, Calcutta: Friendship Publications, 1983.

Haokip, P.S., *Zale'n-gam: The Kuki Nation*, Kuki National Organization, private circulation, 1998.

Hobsbawm, E.J., *Nations and Nationalism Since 1780, Programme, Myth, Reality*, Cambridge: Cambridge University Press, Second Edition, 1997.

Hobsbawm, Eric, and Terence Ranger, eds., *The Invention of Tradition*, Cambridge: Cambridge University Press (reprinted), 1996.

Jadumani, Sapamcha, *Kangleipakta Inner Line Permit System Amasung Masigi Eehou,* Imphal: 2011.

Jamir, S.C., *Bedrock of Naga Society*, Nagaland Pradesh Congress Committee (I), 2000.

Johnstone, Sir James, *Manipur and The Naga Hills*, Delhi: Manas Publications, reprint, 1990.

Kahin, G.M., *The Asian-African Conference*, New York: Cornell University Press, 1956.

Khanna, V.N., *Foreign Policy of India*, 4th edn., New Delhi: Vikas Publishing House, 2001.

Kshetri, Rajendra, *The Emergence of Meetei Nationalism,* New Delhi: Mittal Publications, 2006.

Laishram, Dhanabir, *Chaokhatpa Khunnai amasung Meeyam* (Developed Society and the People), Imphal: Centre for Progress of Manipuri People, 1998.

M.R.T., *Nationalism in Conflict in India*; Delhi: Discovery Publishing House, 1986.

Mangang, Paonam Labanggo, *Kangleipakta Revolution* (Revolution in Manipur), Imphal: 1997.

Maxwell, Neville, *India's China War*; Bombay: Jaico Publishing House, 1970.

Menon, V.P., *Integration of Indian States*, Madras: Orient Longman, 1985.

Nandy, Ashis, *The Intimate Enemy: Loss and Recovery of Self under Colonialism*, New Delhi: Oxford University Press, 2004.

Panikkar, K.M., *The Future of India and South East Asia*, Bombay: Allied Publishers, 1945.

Pemberton, R.B., *The Eastern Frontier of India*, (first published in 1835), Delhi: Mittal Publications, 2000.

Reinhart, Tanya, *Israel/Palestine: How to End the War of 1948*, Delhi: Left World Books, 2003.

Rustomji, Nari, *Enchanted Frontier*, Bombay: Oxford University Press, 1971.

Rustomji, Nari, *Imperilled Frontiers*; Delhi: Oxford University Press, 1983.

Said, Edward W., *Covering Islam: How the Media and the Experts Determined, How We See the* Rest *of the World*, New York: Vintage Books, 1997.

Said, Edward W., *The End of the Peace Process*, New Delhi: Penguin, 2002.

Sanajaoba, Naorem, ed., *Manipur Treaties and Documents (1110-1971)*, Vol. 1, Delhi: Mittal Publications, 1993.

Sanaton, S.K., ed., *Manipur's Integrity and Manipur Peoples' Party*; Imphal: Organizing Committee 35th MPP Foundation Anniversary Celebration, 2002.

Selected Works of Jawaharlal Nehru, Vols. 2 and 23, Delhi: Nehru Memorial Fund.

Sharma, Aribam Brajakumar, ed., *Influx of immigrants into Manipur; A threat to the Indigenous Ethnic People,* Imphal: United Committee Manipur, 2005.

Singh, Karam Manimohan, *Hijam Irabot and Political Movement in Manipur*, Delhi: B.R. Publishing Coorporation, 1989.

Singh, Lairenmayum Ibungohal and Ningthoukhongjam Khelchandra Singh, ed., *Cheitharol Kumbaba*, Imphal: Manipur Sahitya Parishad, 2nd ed., 1989.

Singh, Mayengbam Anandamohan, *Shillong 1949*, Imphal: M. Akshayakumar Singh, 2005.

Singh, N. Lokendra, *The Unquiet Valley,* Delhi: Mittal Publications, 1998.

Smith, Anthony D., *Theories of Nationalism*, London: Duckworth, Second Edition, 1983.

Stalin, Joseph, *Marxism and the National and Colonial Question*; Delhi: Kanishka Publishing House, 1991.

Sundar, Nandini, *Subaltern and Sovereigns: An Anthropological History of Bastar 1854-1996*, Delhi: Oxford University Press, 1999.

Tarapot, Phanjaobam, *Bleeding Manipur*, Delhi: Har Anand Publications, 2003.

Toynbee, Arnold, *Between Oxus and Jumna*, London: Oxford University Press, 1996.

Vashum, R., *Nagas' Right to Self-determination*, Delhi: Mittal Publications, 2000.

Verghese, G., *India's Northeast Resurgent: Ethnicity, Insurgency, Governance, Development*, Delhi: Konark Publishers, 1996.

Volkogonov, D., *The Psychological War*, Moscow: Progress Publishers, 1986.

Yoshino, Kosaku, ed. *Consuming Ethnicity and Nationalism*, Hawaii: University of Hawaii, 1999.

Unpublished Research Works

Devi, Mayanglambam Kunjeshwari, *The Women Movements in Manipur*, M. Phil. Dissertation, Imphal: Manipur University, 1992.

Devi, Oinam Momon, *A Study of the Students Organization in Manipur as a Pressure Group (1980-1990)*, M. Phil. Dissertation (Unpublished), Imphal: Manipur University, 1993.

Devi, Wahengbam Memcha, *Administration of Justice 1947 to 1972*, M. Phil Dissertation, Imphal: Manipur University, 1991.

Tamphasana, R.K., *Zelianrong Naga Movement (1927-1980): A Study in Some Aspects of Ethnic Process in Northeast India*, Ph.D. Thesis, Imphal: Manipur University, 1998.

Tarunkumar, Ngashekpam, *A Study of the Meiteis of Manipur*, MA Dissertation, Political Science Division of Jawaharlal Nehru University, Imphal: 1980.

Internet Sources

- http://mdoner.gov.in, accessed in May 2009.
- http://nscn.livejournal.com.

- http://six.pairlist.net/pipermail/burmanet/20070612/001220.html, accessed on 15 June 2007.
- http://www.angelfire.com/mo/Nagaland/, accessed in April 2002 (dead link now).
- http://www.assamrifles.net, accessed in June 2009.
- http://www.daga.org/daga/readingroom/justpeace/nagaland/nagalim.htm, accessed on 25 July 2009.
- http://www.dipr.mizoram.gov.in, accessed in April 2009.
- http://www.e-pao.net.
- http://www.geocities.com, accessed in January 2009.
- http://www.globalsecurity.org, on 9 September 2009.
- http://www.hindu.com, accessed on 25 June 2009.
- http://www.hrdc.net, accessed in November 2008
- http://www.indianexpress.com.
- http://www.iwgia.org.
- http://www.kanglaonline.com.
- http://www.ksdf.org, accessed on 24 December 2006 (dead link now).
- http://www.manenvis.nic.
- http://www.manipuronline.com.
- http://www.manipurpolice.org, accessed in December 2008.
- http://www.manipurtoday.com.
- http://www.nscnonline.org.
- http://www.radicalparty.org.
- http://www.satp.org.
- http://www.sialkal.com/home_doc_PNC.htm, accessed on 25 June 2009.
- http://www.telegraphindia.com.
- http://www.zalengam.org.
- http://www.zogam.org.

Index